D1437174

HUMAN RIGHTS AND SCOTS LAW

Human Rights and Scots Law

Edited by
ALAN BOYLE
CHRIS HIMSWORTH
ANDREA LOUX
HECTOR MacQUEEN

•HART•
PUBLISHING
OXFORD – PORTLAND OREGON
2002

Hart Publishing
Oxford and Portland, Oregon

Published in North America (US and Canada) by
Hart Publishing c/o
International Specialized Book Services
5804 NE Hassalo Street
Portland, Oregon
97213-3644
USA

Distributed in the Netherlands, Belgium and Luxembourg by
Intersentia, Churchillaan 108
B2900 Schoten
Antwerpen
Belgium

Hart Publishing is a specialist legal publisher based in Oxford, England.
To order further copies of this book or to request a list of other
publications please write to:

Hart Publishing, Salter's Boatyard, Folly Bridge,
Abingdon Road, Oxford OX1 4LB
Telephone: +44 (0)1865 245533 or Fax: +44 (0)1865 794882
e-mail: mail@hartpub.co.uk
WEBSITE: http//www.hartpub.co.uk

British Library Cataloguing in Publication Data
Data Available
ISBN 1–84113–044–3 (hardback)

Typeset by Hope Services (Abingdon) Ltd.
Printed and bound in Great Britain by
Biddles Ltd *www.biddles.co.uk*

Foreword

The period since the entry into force of the Scotland Act 1998 and the Human Rights Act 1998 has been one of the unusually rapid change in Scottish legal and constitutional culture. The courts have had to cope with a large volume of litigation concerning the unfamiliar law of the European Convention on Human Rights. They have had to assess the compatibility with the Convention of common law principles which had long been taken for granted, and of statutory provisions which could not previously have been questioned. They have grown accustomed to the citation of case law from around the world, and have become conscious of their own decisions being the object of reciprocal interest in other jurisdictions. They have had to assume a more prominent constitutional role under the devolution settlement than they had formerly played, and to accept that the new dispensation has given the legal system and its participants a higher public profile than in the recent past. The legal profession and the university law faculties have equally had to cope with a demanding period of transition. Amongst the general public, there has been increased interest in the Scottish legal system and those who are active in it, with such issues as the appointment of the judiciary and the regulation of the legal profession, receiving increased attention.

The period of transition has not yet ended. The courts are still in the process of determining the meaning and scope of some of the basic concepts employed in the statutory provisions: what, for example, constitutes an 'act'; what precisely is meant by 'incompatibility'; and what is the consequence of requiring to courts not to 'act' in a manner which is 'incompatible' with the Convention. As successive cases pose new problems, and from time to time place in issue the appropriateness of the solutions proposed in earlier cases, the courts slowly feel their way towards a position which can be taken as more or less settled. That stage has not been reached.

In this situation, it is more than usually difficult for writers on the law to produce a commentary: new cases continue to flood out of the courts, some of them raising issues of fundamental importance. At the same time, and for the same reason, it is more than usually important that commentaries should be offered by those who can stand back from the fray, discerning any patterns that are emerging, assessing their implications and offering a view on their appropriateness.

The present volume has its origins in a conference held at the University of Edinburgh in 1998, at which an attempt was made to predict the potential implications of the legislation which was then emerging from Parliament. The contributions to that conference have been revised and supplemented in the light of experience, and assess that experience from a wide variety of perspectives. Not the least interesting and useful aspect of the collection is the diversity of opinions expressed.

The present collection of essays will naturally be of interest to those working in universities who take a critical interest in the development of Scots law. For those of us grappling with problems on a daily basis as practitioners or as judges, a work such as the present is equally useful, reporting on our progress from a clearer vantage point, and enabling us better to steer a safe course.

Court of Session   ROBERT REED
Parliament House
Edinburgh
1 April 2002

Preface

This short book had its genesis in a conference organised by the Faculty of Law at Edinburgh University in 1998. The intention at that time was to educate ourselves in the changes in Scots law likely to ensue from the entry into force of the Human Rights Act. In doing so, we sought to encourage Scots lawyers to think about their specialisations from a human rights perspective. We also saw a need to learn from other legal systems that had undergone similar recent transformation, most notably Canada and Sweden. And of course, we had to grapple with the constitutional changes that the Act and its incorporation in the devolution legislation would bring about. Although much has been added or altered since then, these remain the objectives of this book.

Much of what could be said in 1998 was necessarily speculative. Four years on, it has been possible to begin to address the reality of what the Act has so far achieved, at least in Scotland, although many topics remain to be further explored in future litigation, or indeed in future books. All those who participated in the 1998 conference found it illuminating to look afresh at old law from a new perspective. We hope that these essays will achieve a similar impact on a wider audience.

Our thanks are due to Myra Reid, Peggy Dwyer and Felicity Stewart for their help in preparing the final manuscript for publication, to Richard Hart and Hannah Young at Hart Publishing for their patience and support, and to our contributors, for remaining with us to the end.

THE EDITORS
June 2002

Contents

Abbreviations

AD	Case of the Labour Court of Sweden (Arbetsdomstolens domar)
ALR	Alberta Law Review
Appln No.	Application Number
BBC	British Broadcasting Corporation
BSC	Broadcasting Standards Code
BverfG	Federal Constitutional Court of Germany (Bundesverfassungsgericht)
CFLQ	Canadian Family Law Quarterly
CJFL	Canadian Journal of Family Law
CJWL	Canadian Journal of Women and the Law
CLJ	Cambridge Law Journal
CLP	Current Legal Problems
CLR	Criminal Law Review
CSA	Campaign for a Scottish Assembly
DLJ	Dalhousie Law Journal
DPP	Director of Public Prosecutions
EC Law	European Community Law
ECHR	European Convention for the Protection of Human Rights and Fundamental Freedoms
ECtHR	European Court of Human Rights
ECJ	European Court of Justice
Edin LR	Edinburgh Law Review
EHRLR	European Human Rights Law Review
EHRR	European Human Rights Reports
EJIL	European Journal of International Law
EU Law	European Union law
European LR	European Law Review
Fam Law	Family Law
Fam LB	Family Law Bulletin
GYbIL	German Yearbook of International Law
HC Deb	House of Commons Debate (Hansard)
HL	House of Lords
HL Deb	House of Lords Debate (Hansard)
HWLJ	Harvard Womens' Law Journal
ICCPR	International Covenant on Civil and Political Rights
ICLQ	International and Comparative Law Quarterly

IJLF	International Journal of Law and the Family
ILM	International Legal Materials
ISPs	Internet service providers
JCPC	Judicial Committee of the Privy Council
JLSS	Journal of the Law Society of Scotland
JR	Juridical Review
JT	Juridisk Tidskrift vid Stockholms Universitet (Law Journal of Stockholm University, Stockholm)
KU	Report of Sweden's Parliamentary Committee on the Constitution
LEAF	Women's Legal Education and Action Fund (Canada)
LCP	Law and Contemporary Problems
LQR	Law Quarterly Review
Med L Rev	Medical Law Review
MLI	Medical Law International
MLR	Modern Law Review
MP	Member of Parliament
MSP	Member of Scottish Parliament
NILQ	Northern Ireland Legal Quarterly
NJA	Cases of the Supreme Court of Sweden (Nytt juridisk arkiv)
NLJ	New Law Journal
OHLJ	Osgoode Hall Law Journal
OSAG	Office of the Solicitor to the Advocate General
PCC	Press Complaints Commission
PL	Public Law
PLI	Perspectives on Labour and Income
RÅ	Cases of the Supreme Administrative Court of Sweden (Regeringsrättens årsbok)
RCS	Review of Constitutional Studies (Canada)
RF	Swedish constitutional document, the Instrument of Government (Regeringsformen)
RH	Cases of the Court of Appeal of Sweden (Rättsfall från hovrätterna)
RSC	Rules of the Supreme Court
SCC	Scottish Constitutional Convention
SCLR	Supreme Court Law Review (Canada)
Scot Law Com	Scottish Law Commission
SFS	Swedish statute book (Svensk författningssamling)
SHR	Scottish Historical Review
SLPQ	Scottish Law & Practice Quarterly
SLR	Statute Law Review
SLT (News)	Scots Law Times (News)
SNP	Scottish National Party

SOU	Swedish Commission Report (Statens offentliga utredningar)
SvJT	Svensk Juristtidning (Swedish Law Journal, Stockholm)
UN	Decision of the Swedish Aliens Board (Utlänningsnämnden)
YbEL	Yearbook of European Law

Table of Cases

England and Wales

OTHER NATIONAL COURTS

Germany

Ireland

Jersey

South Africa

Sweden

INTERNATIONAL TRIBUNALS

European Court of Human Rights

European Commission on Human Rights

European Court of Justice (ECJ)

UN Human Rights Committee (ICCPR)

Table of National Legislation

UNITED KINGDOM – NORTHERN IRELAND

SCOTLAND

CANADA

UNITED STATES

Table of Treaties and Other Instruments

1

Human Rights and Scots Law: Introduction

ALAN BOYLE*

WITH THE ENTRY into force of the Human Rights Act 1998, the protection of human rights in the United Kingdom has clearly entered a new phase.[1] It is the purpose of this volume to explore some of the implications of this change, and in particular to examine its impact on Scots law. The history of human rights in Scotland is different from the story an English lawyer would have to tell, and as several of the following chapters indicate, its future may be different too. In seventeenth century Scotland, Stair founded the whole of his *Institutions of the Law of Scotland* on the concept of rights, observing that these are 'the formal and proper object of law.'[2] But Scotland had no habeas corpus act, no case law outlawing general warrants, and few of the *causes célèbres* which defined the English law of civil liberties.[3] In Dicey's vision of English law, civil liberties were defined by remedies, not by rights, and he decried the attempts of civil lawyers to accord systematic pre-eminence to bills of rights.[4] Famously, Jeremy Bentham described the idea of natural and inalienable rights as 'nonsense upon stilts.'[5]

Bentham and Dicey notwithstanding, it is rarely appreciated that the United Kingdom played a leading role in the elaboration of the European Convention for the Protection of Human Rights and Fundamental Freedoms (ECHR), adopted by the Council of Europe in 1950. It is of course this Convention on which the UK legislation is now based. Just how important the British

---

* Professor of Public International Law, University of Edinburgh.

[1] The literature is extensive, but see generally S Grosz, J Beatson, P Duffy, *Human Rights: The 1998 Act and the European Convention* (Sweet & Maxwell, London, 2000), and D McGoldrick, 'The United Kingdom's Human Rights Act 1998 in Theory and Practice' (2001) 50 *ICLQ* 901.

[2] Stair, *Institutions of the Law of Scotland*, I.1.22, 6th edn (D M Walker, Edinburgh, 1981). See MacQueen and Brodie, below, ch 8.

[3] See generally K Ewing and W Finnie, *Civil Liberties in Scotland: Cases and Materials* 2nd edn (W Green, Edinburgh, 1988). But Scots courts did uphold the right of former slaves to liberty in Scotland: see *Knight v Wedderburn*, Mor.14545 (1778).

[4] A V Dicey, *An Introduction to the Study of the Law of the Constitution* 10th edn (Macmillan, London, 1967). His scepticism finds unwitting echoes in contemporary calls by some politicians for suspension of the Human Rights Act 1998 in response to terrorist attacks on New York.

[5] H L A Hart, *Essays on Bentham* (Clarendon Press, Oxford, 1982), 79.

contribution to the development of the ECHR proved to be is made clear in an illuminating article by Anthony Lester which appeared in *Public Law* in 1984.[6] As he points out, the British delegation promoting the convention in the Council of Europe's Consultative Assembly included Winston Churchill, Harold MacMillan and Sir John Foster, strongly supported by the Foreign Office.[7] Sir David Maxwell-Fyffe (later Lord Kilmuir) chaired the Assembly's Legal Committee, while the principal draftsman of the Convention was a former Home Office Legal Adviser. This may help to explain why the rights created and the exceptions to them are in many cases spelt out with greater precision than usually typifies most human rights treaties or national bills of rights.[8] There remained strong opposition in cabinet to the ECHR,[9] however, which had to be overcome before ratification could proceed. Securing this approval entailed substituting an optional right of individual petition for a compulsory one in the final text of the Convention, relegating certain rights, such as protection of property, to optional protocols and doing nothing to incorporate the Convention into domestic law. Not until 1965 did the UK finally declare its acceptance of the right of individuals to refer complaints against the United Kingdom to the European Commission on Human Rights. Not until the election of a new Labour government in 1997 was political opposition to incorporation of the Convention rights into law overcome.

By then, the United Kingdom had been respondent in more cases before the Strasbourg institutions than any other Western European member state of the Council of Europe.[10] This was not because human rights were less respected in the UK than elsewhere. In part it reflected a greater litigiousness in common law countries, but mostly the reality that almost every other party had given domestic effect to the ECHR, or already had a comparable bill of rights of its own. Even Sweden had by now followed suit.[11] It was thus Strasbourg litigation, rather than proceedings in UK courts, which had led to significant reforms in the law relating to prisons, mental health, freedom of expression, corporal punishment and terrorism in Northern Ireland, inter alia. But even in its unenacted state, the Convention was increasingly relied on by English courts when interpreting legislation and determining the common law, the high water mark being reached by the House of Lords in *Brind*.[12] Scottish courts eventually followed suit in the important case of *T Petitioner*.[13] Thus the immediate impact of the Human

---

[6] Anthony Lester, 'Fundamental Rights: The United Kingdom isolated' [1984] *PL* 46.

[7] But not by the Colonial Office.

[8] Compare for example the 1966 United Nations Covenant on Civil and Political Rights and the US Bill of Rights.

[9] Especially from the Lord Chancellor, Lord Jowitt.

[10] The most important Scottish case is probably *Campbell and Cosans v UK* (1982) 4 EHRR 293.

[11] See Cameron, below, ch 7.

[12] *R v Secretary of State for the Home Department, ex parte Brind* [1991] 1 AC 696, and see other cases cited by McGoldrick, above n 1, 903–5.

[13] *T Petitioner* 1997 SLT 724. See MacQueen and Brodie, below, ch 8.

Rights Act 1998 on existing law was less radical than it might otherwise have been. Government Departments and judges had already become familiar with its provisions, even if the implications for law reform were sometimes still resisted.

Nevertheless, as Lord Clarke argues in the next chapter of this book, the change brought about by the new Act may amount to more than mere evolution in the law of human rights in Scotland. For him, the legal system is at the threshold of a potentially revolutionary change. No longer is compatibility with the ECHR secured only as a matter of interpretative presumption; instead, all legislation must, so far as possible, be read in a way that gives effect to the Convention rights. The impact this may have on judicial review of public authorities will, in his view, be profound, with judges tending henceforth to focus on the substance of decisions as much as on the process.

It is important for the non-Scots reader to appreciate that the rights created by the ECHR affect Scots law at two levels. Firstly, while public authorities and courts in Scotland have the same duty to give effect to these rights under the Human Rights Act 1998 as public authorities and courts elsewhere in the United Kingdom, the United Kingdom Parliament's legislative powers with respect to Scotland remain formally unconstrained by the Act, apart from the possibility of a court issuing a declaration of incompatibility insofar as Convention rights are denied. Secondly, however, the devolution of certain legislative powers to a Scottish Parliament is limited by the Convention rights: unlike Westminster Acts, Scottish legislation inconsistent with these rights is to that extent unconstitutional. This interlinkage between the Human Rights Act 1998 and the devolution settlement is explored by Himsworth in chapter 3. He also notes that legislation on human rights is not as such outside the competence of the Scottish Parliament, but while it may add to the corpus of protected rights, it cannot amend or repeal the Human Rights Act 1998 or the relevant provisions of the Scotland Act 1998. Unlike their English counterparts, Scottish judges and the Privy Council will therefore have to exercise *Marbury v Madison* powers of judicial review over Scottish legislation which until now have existed within the United Kingdom only in respect of acts of the former Northern Ireland Parliament and its successors.

How that control over the legislative competence of the Scottish Parliament can be set in motion is addressed by Lynda Clark, the first Advocate-General for Scotland. Her chapter explains how the Advocate-General is responsible to the United Kingdom Government for advice on questions of Scots law. In that capacity it is her task to advise, inter alia, on the compatibility of Scottish legislation with Convention rights, and to initiate or intervene in such cases before the Privy Council whenever necessary. Of course the existence of this special power does not preclude other litigants from challenging the validity of Scottish legislation in ordinary judicial proceedings, but it does enable her to have such questions determined at a much earlier stage. While her role is not limited to human rights issues, the Advocate-General is in a uniquely powerful position as a guardian of human rights in Scotland.

However, it is the role of judges in interpreting and applying the new rights which is perhaps the most interesting institutional dimension of these constitutional changes, and which generates the greatest degree of debate and divergence among the contributors to this book. Stephen Tierney shares Lord Clarke's vision of a new constitutionalism giving judges a more central role in the management of constitutional change. He poses as the main question how judges should approach their task of balancing the competing interests of the individual and the state, of Westminster and Holyrood. To the inescapable dilemma of choosing between judicial activism or judicial restraint the new legislation has thus added an inherent tension between devolution and protection of human rights. Quite what conception of either human rights or devolution will emerge is far from clear. For Tierney, unlike Clarke, this is a problem, because the question whether judicial processes are either a legitimate or appropriate way of deciding these issues remains unanswered.

In her chapter on administrative law, Jane Convery takes a more restrained position than Clarke or Tierney. She is sceptical of claims that the scope of judicial review may be significantly expanded by the new law. While reliance on standards of proportionality and margin of appreciation may sharpen the jurisprudence, in her view they will not fundamentally alter the role of courts vis-à-vis the executive. Moreover, the floodgates of litigation under the Human Rights Act 1998 are limited by the need for litigants to show that they are 'victims of a violation' of their Convention rights. In this respect the Act is perhaps closer to the Scots law requiring those seeking judicial review to show title and interest, a narrower test than the English formula of 'sufficient interest'. She acknowledges that there may be a case for giving public interest groups greater standing to seek declarations of legislative incompatibility, but otherwise sees the courts' receptiveness to third party intervention as providing adequate representation for broader public interest in human rights cases. Convery's answer to the problem of the democratic illegitimacy of judges is thus the one traditionally given by orthodox British constitutional lawyers: judicial restraint combined with procedural control.

These opening chapters are mainly concerned with the impact of the new legislation on Scots public law and institutions. Of course, we should remember that while the UK may have led the way in promoting the ECHR, in Western Europe it has come last in the race to implement it through domestic law. Even when compared to other common law countries of the Commonwealth, we have been slow. Of the old dominions, Canada, South Africa and India have all adopted their own bills of rights, and their courts are now a rich source of human rights jurisprudence. The ECHR has also been exported to most of the former British colonies that became independent in the 1960s and 70s; this explains why, for example, law students in Mauritius study the Convention jurisprudence and why it is heavily relied on in Mauritian courts. Thus it should not be assumed that persuasive precedents applying Convention rights can be found only in Europe.

A number of chapters in the book are devoted to exploring what comparative lessons can be learnt from the experience of other jurisdictions. Perhaps the most apposite is Sweden, if only because their incorporation of the Convention into national law only briefly preceded the UK legislation. From this perspective, Iain Cameron shares some of Jane Convery's scepticism. Based on the Swedish example, he argues that we should not overestimate the significance of incorporation. Construing legislation consistently with the Convention is not in his view really constitutional review. He accepts however that there have been relatively few cases in Sweden so far, and only a small range of issues have been raised.

However, in their chapter on Scots private law, MacQueen and Brodie share Lord Clarke's more expansive view of the Act's potential effect. Although the human rights legislation applies only to public authorities, they argue that it will nevertheless transform Scots private law just as much as public law or criminal law. Because the state, and the courts, now have a positive obligation to secure convention rights to everyone, the authors conclude that it will have a 'horizontal effect' on both the statute and common law affecting relations between private parties. How strong or weak this effect may be is difficult to predict, but they explore its possible impact on the law of negligence, contract, privacy and civil procedure, as well as the potential for filling in 'gaps' in the common law.

The implications of this 'horizontal effect' on private law are further explored by Susan Boyd in her chapter looking at the impact of Canada's Charter of Fundamental Rights on family law. Boyd notes the difficulty of applying a rights paradigm to family law, but identifies three different effects: firstly, it may induce or structure legislative reform; second, equality and right to life or private life provisions often afford a basis for challenging the validity of family or social legislation; and thirdly, there is the potential horizontal effect on otherwise private relations. Lillian Edwards pursues some of these issues in a Scottish setting. She notes how the 1989 UN Convention on the Rights of the Child already provides an internationally agreed framework of childrens' rights, based on the paramountcy of the best interests of the child. In contrast, the ECHR does not confer rights specifically on children and ECHR jurisprudence lacks, in her view, an awareness of the potential conflict between childrens' rights and parents' rights. In this respect the Canadian experience outlined by Boyd stands as something of a warning of the possible dangers of prejudicing existing child-centred law by giving parents stronger rights.

In his chapter on sexual identity Martin Hogg explores the implications of Articles 8 and 12 of the Convention for sexual identity, marriage and other forms of partnership, sex discrimination and adoption and custody. In some of these cases the ECHR has already exercised a reforming influence, while in others it remains to be seen what effect it may have. Graham Laurie also considers Article 8, but in the context of medical law, where a rights culture is beginning to emerge. For the present it is only possible to speculate on how the Act might change the law. It clearly raises questions, in his view, about rights for the unborn, the advancement of the 'best interests' of children, the refusal of care and the right to die, and openness and non-disclosure of medical information. His conclusion is that the 'margin of appreciation' afforded to national governments on all these matters means that judges are unlikely to be significantly more activist in this area than hitherto.

Turning to a rather different set of private law issues, George Gretton focuses on Protocol No 1, Article 1 of which protects the right to possessions and property. He draws attention to the difficulty of interpreting this article, especially in its English text. There is, he believes, no clear conception of what is meant by property in this provision, whose meaning can only be determined by reference the jurisprudence of the Strasbourg court. The court's attempts to distinguish between an outright taking of property and an exercise of control over property have not been particularly consistent, however. The implications of this become apparent in his discussion of the reform of Scots land law, involving the abolition of certain feudal tenures and other rights and posing the obvious question how far compensation is required when such reforms are instituted.

Chapters 14 and 15 look at criminal law and procedure. This is where the legislation has had the greatest impact on Scottish courts so far. Conor Gearty provides an overview of the early cases, taking a comparative look at England as well. The case of *Brown v Stott* became the first case to reach the Privy Council under the Scotland Act, where the High Court of Justiciary's decision was unanimously overruled on the ground that the privilege against self-incrimination was not absolute but had to be balanced against the public interest. This Scottish ruling has been followed by English courts. Other important cases on burden of proof suggest to Gearty that the Courts have begun to use the Human Rights Act to 'reshape' legislation in ways that Parliament never intended, but that it would be a mistake to regard this as evidence of significant judicially inspired law reform. In general, he suggests instead that the courts have shown themselves anxious to get away from the notion that Convention rights, including the right to a fair trial or the privilege against self-incrimination, are absolute. In this respect, far from being revolutionary, the impact of the Convention may in some cases be profoundly conservative, enabling judges to reassert dormant common law values overturned by legislation. However, in chapter 15, Ferguson and Mackarel come to a somewhat different conclusion about the effect on Scots criminal law and procedure. Relying particularly on *Brown v Stott* and *Starrs v Ruxton*, in which the appointment of temporary sheriffs to try criminals was found to violate Article 6, they conclude that 'testing Scots criminal law against the standards of the Convention can only serve to further the long term fairness and integrity of the proud tradition of criminal law in Scotland.'

Finally, Andrea Loux explores the possibilities for third party intervention in human rights cases, a development already foreshadowed by the House of Lords in the *Pinochet* case, where both Amnesty International and the Government of Chile were represented in the extradition proceedings.

In concluding this introduction we should remember that although the focus of this book is on the incorporation into Scots law of rights enshrined in the European Convention on Human Rights, this by no means exhausts the human rights content of Scots law. The evolution of individual rights in European Community law continues, and the new European Union Charter of Fundamental Rights may in time become an important statement of existing and evolving rights enforceable in domestic courts. As we saw earlier, the possibility also exists that a Scottish Parliament may choose to create its own bill of rights to supplement the 1998 Act. It might also create new institutions to enforce the Act, such as a Human Rights Commission. Moreover, courts applying the Human Rights Act 1998 are not bound to follow Strasbourg precedents. While they must take them into account, and ensure that Convention rights are not denied, they may in appropriate cases develop the law beyond what Strasbourg requires. In doing so, national courts have often been additionally guided by international human rights law in general. International law is part of the law of Scotland,[14] and international human rights law is an important branch of general international law, although it remains true that most of it is treaty law, and without further enactment, still governed by the decision of the House of Lords in *Brind*. Nor should we forget that human rights and civil liberties are sometimes just as effectively, or better, protected by ordinary legislation on matters such as discrimination in employment, or by judicial review of administrative action. The Human Rights Act 1998 does expand and improve the protection of human rights, but it neither renders pre-existing rights and remedies redundant nor does it operate in splendid isolation from the rest of Scots, or English, law.

---

[14] *Lord Advocate's Reference No 1 of 2001.*

2

Human Rights, Devolution and Public Law

THE HON LORD CLARKE*

W HEN I JOINED the Scots Bar in 1978 the number of public law cases which came before the courts were few and far between. Since then, of course, with the advent of the procedures for judicial review, public law cases have become a very significant part of the business of the Court of Session. Having been Junior Counsel in the case of *Brown v Hamilton District Council*,[1] which can be seen as the foundation stone of the modern law of judicial review in Scotland, and having been Senior Counsel in the case of *West v Secretary of State for Scotland*,[2] which to a large extent gave us guidance as to how and when these procedures were to be operated, I am proud to say that the effect of those cases taken together, along with the judicial review rules, have meant that access to the court by litigants seeking to have the acts and decisions of public authorities scrutinised has been greatly increased. But the reforms were, to a large extent, concerned with procedural matters in two senses. First, the relevant Rule of Court made the processing of complaints against public authorities in the exercise of their powers and discretions subject to a quick and efficient procedure. Secondly, the law which is applied in these cases has been law which, on the whole, is largely concerned not with establishing and enforcing rights as such, but ensuring that the decision-maker has followed the rules up to the point when the decision itself was taken. The much uttered words of the judicial review judge (sometimes tinged with an audible sigh of relief) that, of course, his or her role was not to substitute their view of the merits of the matter for that of the decision-maker, but rather simply to ensure that things have not gone off the rails, is a reflection of that fact. As a result, public law litigation has remained more adjectival rather than substantive in character. I often think of the analogy of the hospital matron who parades the wards to ensure that the beds have been properly made, that there is no dust under them and that the medicines are being

---

* The text of this chapter is taken directly from that of a talk given by Lord Clarke (as MG Clarke QC) in 1998, with updating only where essential to the meaning.

[1] *Brown v Hamilton District Council* 1983 SC (HL) 1.
[2] *West v Secretary of State for Scotland* 1992 SC 385.

properly dispensed to the patient, but who has no concern as to whether diagnosis of the patient's condition is good or bad.

From that being the position, the courts and practitioners in Scotland have been hit by a dramatic change brought about by the combined effect of the Scotland Act 1998 and the Human Rights act 1998. They have had to readjust their approach to the scrutiny of the acts and decisions of government and public authorities to accord with a rights-based system. Notwithstanding the fact that a particular piece of legislation or decision is *intra vires,* in the sense that it falls within the competence of the legislature or the body in question, notwithstanding that it does not suffer from any procedural impropriety, notwithstanding that it may not have been considered to be irrational in the '*Wednesbury*'[3] sense, the Courts now have to satisfy themselves that it does not involve any illegitimate inroad into rights of the individual under the European Convention for the Protection of Human Rights and Fundamental Freedoms (ECHR). Overnight there has been a huge gear change in the way in which judges and practitioners address questions which may have a public law aspect. We have to apply a new way of thinking and become familiar with a corpus of jurisprudence, delivered over the years from Strasbourg, against which to test the substantive validity of acts and decisions of public authorities. In Scotland, we have not had the advantage of many of our continental cousins who have had written constitutions for decades which set out very often the rights which are embraced in the ECHR and which also have constitutional and administrative tribunals which are used to dealing with issues of the kind that the ECHR raises. As Sir Stephen Sedley said in his magisterial Paul Sieghart Memorial lecture entitled 'Human Rights: A Twenty-First Century Agenda':[4]

> If, as is almost inevitable, this voyage is going increasingly to take us into the deep water of fundamental rights, this is a culture which English lawyers are going to have to acquire and absorb. To rest, as our courts sometimes do, on the laurels of having been the first to articulate a number of the freedoms the world now takes for granted, is not really enough, not least because the content of these rights has at present to be subordinated to the Diceyan monolith, giving the courts the currently watertight defence for illiberal decisions. But where, in John Mortimer's metaphor, we have so far survived by clinging to the wreckage, rights adjudication under a fundamental law of some description is going to mean that we have to learn to swim. This much is uncontentious. But what may be more contentious is the proposition that the waters in which we shall be swimming are shark-infested and that our human rights armoury at present gives us little protection against the predators.[5]

I posed a question as the foreword to the synopsis of my contribution—Evolution or Revolution? I tend to the view that what has happened will, in due course, be regarded as amounting to a revolution in public law. Nevertheless

---

[3] *Associated Provincial Picture Houses Ltd v Wednesbury Corp* [1948] KB 223.
[4] [1995] PL 386.
[5] *Ibid,* 398–9.

that is not to say that there have not been some harbingers of what will come, some seeds of what we will develop, already planted in the existing law in the recent past.

At the highest level, at least in the courts in England, there have been pronouncements in recent years that, notwithstanding the non-incorporation of the ECHR into UK law, government and public authority acts require to be tested against a presumption that they were not intended to encroach on what should be regarded as values shared by modern liberal democracies which are translated into basic human rights. So, in *Bugdaycay v Secretary of State for the Home Department*,[6] we had Lord Bridge say:

> The most fundamental of human rights is the individual's right to life and when an administrative decision under challenge is said to be one which may put the applicant's life at risk, the basis of the decision must surely call for the most anxious scrutiny.

The right of freedom of speech, not to be found set out in writing in any constitutional document in this country has, however, been proclaimed in the House of Lords. So in *Derbyshire County Council v Times Newspapers Ltd*,[7] Lord Keith pronounced:

> It is of the highest public importance that a democratically elected government body, or indeed any government body, should be open to uninhibited public criticism. The threat of a civil action for defamation must inevitably have an inhibiting effect on freedom of speech.

Accordingly his Lordship, with whom all the other members of the judicial committee agreed, held that as a matter of principle, neither central nor local government should be allowed to maintain a cause of action in libel because as he put it:

> It is contrary to the public interest that they should have it. It is contrary to the public interest because to admit such actions would place an undesirable fetter on freedom of speech.

Those pronouncements extolling the importance of freedom of speech had been pre-echoed in previous speeches of Lord Keith in *Lord Advocate v The Scotsman Publications Ltd*[8] and *Attorney General v Guardian Newspapers (No 2)*.[9] Again in *R v Secretary of State for the Home Department, ex parte Leech*,[10] the Court of Appeal declared that a prison rule which allowed correspondence to be stopped by the governor was *ultra vires* because it was inconsistent with the fundamental right of unimpeded access to the courts. They considered that the more fundamental the right interfered with by a rule the more difficult it is

---

[6] *Bugdaycay v Secretary of State for the Home Department* [1987] AC 514.
[7] *Derbyshire County Council v Times Newspapers Ltd* [1998] QB 770 (CA), [1993] AC 534.
[8] *Lord Advocate v The Scotsman Publications Ltd* 1989 SLT 705.
[9] *Attorney General v Guardian Newspapers (No 2)* [1988] 3 WLR 776, [1990] 1 AC 109.
[10] *R v Secretary of State for the Home Department, ex parte Leech (No 2)* [1994] QB 198.

to imply authority for any power to make such a rule. But note the way in which the decision was arrived at, that is, by concluding that there was no place for implying authority to make the rule. The position might have been quite different if the rule itself had found its place in clear, unequivocal terms in primary legislation. Increasingly, however, the ECHR has been regarded as a very significant backdrop against which it is presumed that government and public authorities would wish to have their actions judged. So in *R v Canon Park Medical Health Review Tribunal*,[11] Sedley, J was able to say:

> The principles and standards set out in the Convention can certainly be said to be a matter of which this country now takes notice in setting its own standards. Once it is accepted that the standards articulated in the European Convention march with the common law and inform the jurisprudence of the European Union, it becomes unrealistic and potentially unjust to continue to develop English public law without reference to them.

This is a dictum which survived scrutiny in the Court of Appeal. In Scotland, of course, a very significant development in this respect came about by virtue of the Lord President's decision in the case of *T, Petitioner*,[12] where as you will recall Lord President Hope stated:

> In my opinion, the Courts in Scotland should apply the same presumption as that described by Lord Bridge, namely that, when legislation is found to be ambiguous in the sense that it is capable of a meaning which either conforms to or conflicts with the Convention, Parliament is to be presumed to have legislated in conformity with the Convention, not in conflict with it.

There is no doubt that this movement has to a large extent, been influenced by the fact (as Sedley, J, observed in the dictum just quoted) that European Community law includes as part of its jurisprudence the requirement of observation of the ECHR's rights. A recent graphic example of this in Scotland is to be found in the decision in the case of *Booker Aquaculture Ltd v Secretary of State for Scotland*[13] involving a challenge to the British Government's failure to grant compensation to fish farmers who were ordered to destroy their stocks of turbot which had been infected by disease. The order to destroy stocks was made under Regulations which had as their source European Community law. Lord Cameron of Lochbroom held that the Government had acted illegally in failing to uphold the right of property under the ECHR. The matter was, however, appealed to the First Division. While the Court held that the right to property was recognised as a fundamental right under EC law and that the availability of compensation was relevant to any consideration of whether the right had been respected when Community rules were implemented, it went on to say that the fundamental issue was whether the matter of compensation was

---

[11] *R v Canon Park Medical Health Review Tribunal* [1993] 1 All ER 481.
[12] *T, Petitioner* 1997 SLT 724 at 733–4.
[13] *Booker Aquaculture v Scottish Ministers* [1999] 1 CMLR 35.

governed by EC law or by national law. It referred that fundamental question to the ECJ.[14]

But important as all of these decisions have been, there still is no doubt, to my mind, that the incorporation of the ECHR into the law of the UK will accelerate these developments and requires these issues to be approached in quite a different way than heretofore. No longer will the position to be adopted be one of a presumption that legislation, acts and decisions were intended to have been arrived at in accordance with the ECHR's provisions. Now all legislation and acts and decisions of public authorities will require to be tested against the fact that there are vested rights which prima facie must not be invaded, whatever the motive or wishes of the authority might have been. The focus will be on the rights, and any apparent infraction of these rights will have to be justified by the authorities establishing valid exceptions thereto. Moreover, the courts will now be obliged to interpret all legislation, past, present and future, in a way that is compatible with the ECHR.[15]

All this means that in the field of public law and, in particular, judicial review, there may very well be, in due course, in my view, a very marked shift away from approaching matters from the point of view of ensuring that questions of form have been observed, to considering the very substance of the matter. The court will have the Convention rights, figuratively, if not literally, on the bench with it acting, as it were, as the ten commandments which the public authority must not break unless in certain prescribed exceptional circumstances. Section 6 of the Human Rights Act 1998 could not be clearer when it states: 'It is unlawful for a public authority to act in a way which is incompatible with a Convention right.' Section 57(2) of the Scotland Act 1998 is equally forthright when it says:

> A member of the Scottish Executive has no power to make any subordinate legislation, or to do any other act, so far as the legislation or act is incompatible with any of the Convention rights. . . .

By sections 7 and 8 of the Human Rights Act 1998 the teeth are provided in the remedies that are set out in those provisions. All of this involves rules of substance. To a large extent, as I have already indicated, our public law to date had focused on seeing whether non-substantive rules have been broken or not and provided these were observed the act or decision in question would generally be upheld, whatever the moral or policy merits of the act, or decision, may have been. So, provided the right facts were taken into account, no irrelevant factors were taken into account, there was no misdirection of law and no out-and-out irrationality, the act or decision would be upheld, irrespective of the overall objective merit of the decision or policy in question. In the new world, in fields where the Convention applies, the judges will not only be required to be deeply concerned as to whether there has been any failure in the sense I have just

---

[14] 2000 SC 9 (1st Div); and see now the opinion of the Advocate-General of 20 Sept. 2001 in Joined Cases C–20/00 and C–64/00.

[15] See s 3 of the Human Rights Act 1998.

referred to, but will also need, in some cases, to inquire more closely into the merits of the decision to see, for example, that the necessary justification for the limitation of any positive right has been established and that it was no more of a limitation than was needed. This is a major shift which potentially, at least, can be called revolutionary. What is more, one has to bear in mind that it is in the nature of the way in which the rights are stated in the ECHR's provisions that they present generalities that, as often as not, raise more questions than provide answers. That allows for them to be seen as modelling clay by inventive advocates to support cases in new situations. It means also that they have a flexibility and a dynamic which, as a study of the jurisprudence of Strasbourg over the years will show, means that they can be adjusted to reflect new social and moral values. For example, the right to life and the right to protection of family life are rights, the meaning of which, and scope of which, will vary from time to time, if not from place to place. This brings with it new techniques and new demands. Anyone who still thinks that the changes which will be brought about might not be all that significant has not, I would suggest, read carefully the case law of the ECHR and the Commission.

I will provide a small selection of examples where the incorporation of the Convention may provide opportunities for challenging public authorities under the law which heretofore would have been unthinkable or, at least, hardly stateable. They are a totally random selection. My first example refers to environmental cases under reference to Article 8 of the ECHR. Just let us remind ourselves of what Article 8 of the Convention says: 'Everyone has the right to respect for his private and family life, his home and his correspondence'. For those of you who might be saying '*what on earth does that have to do with environmental law cases*'—well, if you are thinking such thoughts, I'm afraid that that betrays a lack of the imagination and lateral thinking which will be required in the new world. As Sir Stephen Sedley pointed out in the lecture to which I previously referred, the right to an unpolluted environment has recently been held by the Indian High Court to be extracted from the constitutional right to life in that jurisdiction.[16] In the jurisprudence of the European Court of Human Rights (ECtHR) it is, as yet, not Article 2 which has been seen to have the potential in this area, but Article 8. In the case of *Rayner v UK*,[17] the applicant complained that the intensity and persistence of aircraft noise interfered with his rights to respect for his private life and home and he brought his claim under Article 8. The Government maintained that the claim fell outwith Article 8 altogether but the Commission took the view that Article 8 covered 'indirect intrusions which are unavoidable consequences of measures not directed against private individuals' (the measures here being the operating of major airports), and, it went on: 'considerable noise nuisance can undoubtedly affect the physical wellbeing of a person and thus interfere with his private life.' That

---

[16] [1995] *PL* 386 at 400.
[17] *Rayner v UK* (1990) 12 EHRR 355.

clearly opened up the prospects for environmental claims being brought within Article 8(1) and, indeed, in the later case of *Lopez-Ostra v Spain*[18] the applicant succeeded in establishing that the failure by the State to act to prevent or protect her from serious pollution damage, namely fumes from a waste disposal plant dealing with waste from a tannery, did constitute a failure to respect her home and her private and family life.

One of the things the courts are going to have to get used to dealing with is the competition between rights that can arise from the ECHR. In this respect the problems of reconciling the Article 8 right to have respect for private life and the Article 10 right to freedom of expression is undoubtedly, in my view, going to be productive of some very interesting developments in relation to press freedom. The question as to whether it will mean a duty on the courts to develop a law of privacy is something that exercised the Press Council and the Lord Chancellor. Article 10 states that the right to freedom of expression shall include freedom to hold opinions and to receive and import information and ideas without interference by public authorities and regardless of frontiers. It might put the fear of death into Mr Rupert Murdoch to learn that in the case of *De Geillustreede Pers NV v Netherlands*,[19] the Commission observed that the existence of that right might impose on States the duty to take steps to guard against 'excessive press concentration'.

The importance of education for the Scots could also result in the ECHR clay being moulded for cases involving the right to education under the First Protocol Article 2. The *Belgian Linguistics*[20] case has established that the rights protected thereby are: (1) a right to access to educational institutions existing at a given time; (2) a right to an effective education; and (3) a right to official recognition of the studies a student has successfully completed. Taken together with the Article 14 obligation to protect against discrimination, might it be that this could be a basis upon which to challenge government legislation distinguishing between English and Scots students with regard to fees!

I trust these few examples have given a flavour of how potentially wide-reaching the effects of the new regime will be.

The new situation will also, in my view, inject new life into existing tools for attacking acts and decisions of public authorities. The notions of 'proportionality' and 'legitimate expectations' certainly will get a new lease of life as these are concepts, which have been borrowed from Europe, and are part of the armoury of the jurisprudence of Strasbourg. Related to them are the principles of legal certainty and the margin of appreciation. Extremely interesting and difficult questions arise as to how that latter important concept, the margin of appreciation, will fall to be used and applied by the courts in the United Kingdom in a way that is different from the way it has been applied by the

---

[18] *Lopez Ostra v Spain* (1995) 20 EHRR 277.
[19] *De Geillustreede Pers NV v Netherlands* [1979] FSR 173.
[20] *Belgian Linguistics* (1968) 1 EHRR 252.

Strasbourg institutions, since when they are using it they are doing so with the respect that an international body considers is due to a sovereign government. That will not be the position of the domestic courts, but nevertheless it seems to me that this concept which already has emerged in cases within the UK will have a role to play, although one would, perhaps, like to think that its role will not be driven too far, in the domestic context, to the extent of emasculating the effects of the Act.

There are important limitations in the Human Rights Act 1998 itself. Sections 3 and 4 are designed to maintain, to some extent, a recognition of the sovereignty of Parliament. When a court, *having* attempted to construe legislation in a way which is compatible with the ECHR, fails to achieve that result, it can declare the legislation to be incompatible with those rights but that declaration is said by section 4(6)(b) not to be binding on the parties to the proceedings in which it is made. That means that the successful pursuer or petitioner will not have obtained from the court a remedy which will provide him with, for example, damages for having his rights breached as a result of legislation which is incompatible with the ECHR.

Furthermore, there would appear, perhaps at first sight, to be a real problem with regard to the future development of class or representative actions in this field because of the provisions of section 7 of the Human Rights Act 1998 which provide that only persons who are victims of unlawful breaches of the ECHR may bring proceedings under the Act. Section 7(4) expressly provides that in judicial review only such a person shall have title and interest to bring the proceedings. That may be regarded as possibly placing unnecessary and unjustifiable inhibitions on public law proceedings where the development of class and representative actions should be actively promoted, for this is an area where, as individuals, we are defined very often by our relationships with others and where which social cadre is to be the context of an individual's rights is itself a function of the rights debate.

However, one should bear in mind that the concept of the 'victim', in itself, is one that comes from Article 34 of the ECHR, which requires that the applicant to a claim must be a victim of a violation of one of their rights in the Convention. This has been held by the ECtHR to mean that he or she must be in a position to establish that they are directly affected in some way by the matter complained of. The court in Strasbourg has applied this concept, however, in a flexible and broad way in certain cases. So, for example, in the case of *Open Door Counselling Ltd and Dublin Well Woman Centre Ltd v Ireland*,[21] the court, in effect, recognised a representative or class action in a case which concerned the Irish Supreme Court granting an injunction against the provision of information by the applicant companies concerning abortion facilities outside Ireland, on the footing that all women of childbearing age could claim to be victims since they

---

[21] *Open Door Counselling Ltd and Dublin Well Woman Centre Ltd v Ireland* (1992) 15 EHRR 244.

belonged to a class of women which may be adversely affected by the restriction. The domestic courts and tribunals are directed by the Human Rights Act 1998 (s 7(7)), to apply the Strasbourg jurisprudence in relation to the concept of '*victim*' and, therefore, the apparent limitation on developments in relation to class and representative actions may not be so severe as appears at first sight.

I have up until this point been concentrating on the provisions of the Human Rights Act 1998 itself. We in Scotland, however, have had to deal with human rights issues immediately in the context of the Scotland Act 1998. Here, the starting point is to appreciate that the new institution of the Scottish Parliament itself, its executive and officials are all constrained from doing anything which would be in breach of a ECHR right and the question as to whether they have or have not so acted is justiciable before the courts. The historical coincidence of the Human Rights Act 1998 being enacted at or about the time the Scotland Act 1998 was being passed, has resulted in the Scottish Parliament's competence being circumscribed by reference to the ECHR. So the fundamental provision in the Scotland Act 1998 which deals with the legislative competence of the Scottish Parliament, that is section 29, having stated in subsection (1) that 'An Act of the Scottish Parliament is not law so far as any provision of the Act is outside the legislative competence of the Parliament', then goes on to provide, inter alia, in subsection (2), that a provision is outside that competence so far as it is incompatible with any of the Convention rights.[22] This is in stark contrast to the provisions in the Human Rights Act 1998 regarding Westminster legislation. That legislation remains law even if it is incompatible with the ECHR, until the relevant Minister of the Crown brings forward the amending legislation.

With regard to subordinate legislation of the Scottish Parliament, the relevant section is section 57(2) of the Scotland Act 1998 which provides that:

> A member of the Scottish Executive has no power to make any subordinate legislation, or to do any other act, so far as the legislation is incompatible with any of the Convention rights.

Accordingly, a challenge to the validity of the Scottish Parliament's primary and secondary legislation on the basis that it contravenes a ECHR right, if successful, can result in the court immediately striking down that legislation and the power of the court in that respect is extended, very significantly, such that the legislation in question can be declared to be, to use the language of section 29, 'not law'. In section 102 the court or tribunal can make an order removing or limiting any retrospective effect of a decision and suspending the effect of a decision for any particular period. This then involves a substantial difference of approach from what is found in the Human Rights Act 1998 vis-à-vis the validity of legislation. In other respects, however, the two Acts march in step. Section 100(1) provides that the Scotland Act 1998 does not enable a person (a) to bring any proceedings in a court or tribunal on the ground that an Act is

---

[22] See Scotland Act 1998, s 29(2)(d).

incompatible with the Convention rights or (b) to rely on any of the Convention rights in any such proceedings unless he would be a victim for the purposes of Article 34 of the Convention. The approach to damages is also the same in both Acts. Section 101 takes an approach, similar to, but not identical with, that of section 3 of the Human Rights Act 1998 in relation to the construction of legislation over the whole range of questions of interpretation. But then again we see some divergences. Proceedings brought under section 7 of the Human Rights Act 1998, by section 7(5) must be brought within one year of the act complained of, or such longer period as may be allowed within the discretion of the court. There is no such limitation period put in place in the Scotland Act 1998.

These last mentioned divergences may lead one to consider one of the most difficult questions that occurs, regarding the existence of the two Acts and their apparent overlap to some extent. The question is, which Act and, therefore, what procedures will one be employing in a human rights case involving the Scottish Parliament? That is a topic, however, which deserves at least a paper to itself and I must confine myself simply to drawing attention to the problem.

Lastly, I would like to mention the impact that all of this might have on the procedure of judicial review in Scotland. Section 7(11) of the Human Rights Act 1998 provides for the relevant Minister to make orders regarding remedies which might be available in tribunals in respect of acts which are regarded as unlawful in terms of section 6. That subsection, taken together with the general provisions in section 7(1) with their references to 'an appropriate court or tribunal' and 'any legal proceedings' have the potential, in my view, to introduce a significant erosion of, or modification to, the exclusive review jurisdiction of the Court of Session as an aspect of its supervisory jurisdiction, all as set out and discussed in the *locus classicus* of the opinion of Lord President Inglis in *Forbes v Underwood*,[23] as subsequently affirmed in *Brown v Hamilton District Council*,[24] and re-emphasised in *West v Secretary of State for Scotland*,[25] where the act or decision of the body or person in question involves simply a question of a breach of human rights. Neither the Human Rights Act 1998, nor the Scotland Act 1998, expressly limits the law as set out in *Forbes v Underwood*, far less do they expressly abolish it, so it may be that quite difficult questions of classification of issues will arise when a human rights question emerges, before it can be determined whether judicial review in the Court of Session is the only way in which the issue can be aired or otherwise.

All in all, we have embarked on a voyage of discovery for which those engaged in public law in Scotland are going to require energy, enthusiasm, clear thinking and ingenuity.

---

[23] *Forbes v Underwood* (1886) 13 R 465.
[24] *Brown v Hamilton District Council* 1983 SC (HL) 1.
[25] *West v Secretary of State for Scotland* 1992 SC 385.

3

The Hamebringing: Devolving Rights Seriously

A. INTRODUCTION

D URING THE REPORT stage of the Human Rights Bill in the House of Lords, one of the amendments proposed by the Opposition peer and former Lord Advocate, Lord Mackay of Drumadoon, would have introduced into the Bill a cross-reference to a provision in the Bill which was to become the Scotland Act 1998.[1] In response, the Lord Chancellor expressed some sympathy with the substance of the proposal (to permit a Scottish Minister to intervene in proceedings on an issue of 'incompatibility'),[2] but said that it raised questions of how to 'interlink' the two Bills.[3] He explained this to mean the interesting points of procedure which inevitably arose when two parallel Bills were moving through Parliament in the same session. There must be cross-referencing between the two measures but neither could make final and unconditional reference to the other because neither existed in its finally agreed form. They were matters of timing and co-ordination and were largely technical.

But[4] there is more to 'interlinkage' than that. There are many other more important issues which arise from the coupling of the two great constitutional projects of New Labour—to 'bring home' human rights and to establish devolved governments in Scotland, Wales and Northern Ireland[5]—and these provide the subject-matter of this chapter. The project to protect human rights at an international level makes assumptions about the desirability of uniformity of definition of rights and the quality of the mechanisms for their protection.

---

* Professor of Administrative Law, University of Edinburgh.

[1] HL Deb Vol 584, col 1317 (19 Jan 1998).
[2] Later included in the Human Rights Act 1998 as s 5(2)(b).
[3] HL Deb Vol 584, col 1318 (19 Jan 1998).
[4] One right reaffirmed by the Human Rights Act 1998 is the right to begin a sentence with 'But'—see s 8(2).
[5] This paper focuses almost exclusively on the position in Scotland but very similar provision has been made to 'interlink' the Human Rights Act 1998 and the Northern Ireland Act 1998. Because of the absence of legislative devolution to Wales, comparison with the Government of Wales Act 1998 is much less close.

A United Nations covenant demands world-wide respect. The European Convention for the Protection of Human Rights and Fundamental Freedoms (ECHR) makes similar claims to prescribe uniform standards across the territories of the 44 member states of the Council of Europe. Its own preamble refers to the aim of achieving greater unity between members and the need for a common understanding and observance of human rights.

As international agreements between states, human rights treaties make the states themselves responsible, within the limits of their own jurisdictions, for ensuring that the treaty obligations are upheld. It may be that individual human beings (or other persons) are seen as the primary beneficiaries of the rights and freedoms guaranteed and, in the case of the ECHR, individuals are provided with the uniquely helpful facility of the direct right of access to the European Court of Human Rights (ECtHR) at Strasbourg. The states themselves, however, are the respondents to proceedings. They themselves are required, if necessary, to give effect to the ECtHR's findings. It is true that the picture of the universal application of standards is complicated by the possibility of state derogations under Article 15 and, more widely, by the opportunities for states to vary their degree of adherence to the ECHR by their decisions to opt into or out of the additional obligations in the Protocols. These, however, are also mechanisms which leave member states fully in control of a system which seeks to guarantee a uniformity of standard of protection between, and also within states—whether by Spain in Madrid and the Canaries, by Russia in Moscow and Vladivostok or by the United Kingdom in London and Derry, Cardiff, Edinburgh and Rockall.

Mention of the further-flung communities *within* the territories and jurisdictions of the member states of the Council of Europe brings to mind those other forces of political organisation which pull not in the direction of rules of universal application made and enforced by states, but in the direction of the diversity and subsidiarity represented by the decentralised governments of nations, regions and local communities. There *may be* a compelling attraction in the project which seeks to treat all citizens of the states of the Council of Europe equally. No one should lack the guarantees of protection in their dealings with their governments, police forces or prison services. No state should escape its obligations under the ECHR across its entire territory. There should be no people to whom the writ of the ECtHR does not run. On the other hand, the forces of decentralisation, devolution and subsidiarity pull in the other direction. For reasons of both principle and pragmatism, they assert that the opportunity to be different is good rather than bad; that social, cultural and legal conditions are already different and must be respected; that governmental decision-making is better done—more democratically, more justly and more efficiently—at levels lower than the internationally recognised states; and that rights protection should be sensitive to difference where difference demands. This may go to differences in the articulation of rights themselves and the standards required. Perhaps more significantly, differences in modes of implementation and enforcement should be permitted and will, in any event, inevitably arise. Courts are different, one from another. Access to courts is different. The availability of legal aid or other assistance is different. And attitudes to judicial rather than political remedies differ. Notwithstanding the formal rules of the ECHR, some would prefer, to differing degrees, to entrust the protection of rights not to judges, but to the political process.

There is, therefore, an evident tension between, on the one hand, the state-enforced universalism of the theory of human rights protection and, on the other, the celebration of diversity upon which devolution insists, along with its denial of exclusive authority to the state and its denial of a single state-imposed solution to the problem of ensuring human liberty, dignity and welfare. It is to some indications of this tension, already revealed in the legislative provisions to give 'further effect' to the ECHR and to establish the Scottish Parliament and Administration, to which we turn in section E (Devolving Rights) and the concluding section F (Rights and Wrongs of Devolving a Rights Culture). First, however, a brief account of the relevant provisions of the Acts themselves. Some provisions of the Human Rights Act 1998 and the Scotland Act 1998 are treated separately in sections B and C respectively although the degree of overlap between the two Acts compels some combined treatment. In section D (The Acts in Tandem) these overlapping aspects are developed further.[6]

B. THE HUMAN RIGHTS ACT

One of the most fascinating aspects of the proceedings on the Human Rights Bill was the revelation by the Lord Chancellor to a surprised peerage that it was by no means the purpose of the Bill to incorporate the ECHR into UK law. This was initially puzzling because the White Paper *Rights Brought Home: The Human Rights Bill,*[7] published on the same day as the Bill itself, referred to the Government's own manifesto commitment to introduce legislation to 'incorporate' the ECHR[8] and restated the 'case for incorporation'.[9] The language of incorporation has continued to be used by the Government but the Lord Chancellor adopted the position that this was a strictly inaccurate description of what was intended. It was true that the Bill did itself define 'the Convention rights' as the rights and fundamental freedoms set out in the relevant Articles of the ECHR and its Protocols.[10] Subject to any designated derogation or

---

[6] The content of sections B, C, D draws heavily upon C Himsworth 'Rights versus Devolution' in T Campbell, K Ewing, and A Tomkins (eds), *Sceptical Essays on Human Rights* (Oxford University Press, Oxford, 2001).

[7] Cm 3782, 1997.

[8] *Ibid*, 'Introduction and Summary' at 2.

[9] *Ibid*, para 1.14. And see Lord Lester of Herne Hill at HL Deb Vol 584, cols. 1257–58 (19 Jan 1998).

[10] See now s 1(1) of the Human Rights Act 1998.

reservation, those Articles were stated 'to have effect for the purposes of the Act'[11] and they were set out in Schedule 1. Courts and tribunals were required, when 'determining a question which has arisen under this Act in connection with a Convention right', to take into account judgments of the ECtHR[12] and it was stated that:

> '[s]o far as it is possible to do so, primary legislation and subordinate legislation must be read and given effect in a way which is compatible with the Convention rights'.[13]

Perhaps most importantly, it becomes unlawful for a public authority to 'act in a way which is incompatible with a Convention right'.[14] But still this did not mean that the Convention rights were part of the law of the United Kingdom. The Lord Chancellor agreed that this might have the appearance of a 'theological dispute'[15] over a rather meaningless distinction.

That distinction, however, remains an important part of the strategic design of the legislation which relies for its operation upon drawing a clear line between the treatment to be afforded, on the one hand, to 'primary legislation' held to be incompatible with the Convention and, on the other, subordinate legislation and other acts of public authorities. It is a distinction which has important consequences for the future treatment of the legislation of the Scottish Parliament. Because the Human Rights Act 1998 does not, in a strong sense, incorporate the ECHR and make it part of UK law, it leaves earlier Acts of the Westminster Parliament unaffected by any implied repeal by the ECHR's terms and instead makes provisions of both earlier and later Acts subject to the procedure in section 4 of the Human Rights Act 1998, according to which their compatibility with the Convention rights may be adjudicated upon and, if appropriate, remedial action may be taken under section 10 and Schedule 2. Under the scheme adopted by the Human Rights Act 1998, however, all legislation which is not defined by the Act as 'primary legislation' is treated as 'subordinate legislation' which may, like other acts of a public authority, be held by a court to be unlawful if incompatible with a ECHR right and subject to the procedures laid down in sections 6 to 9 of the Human Rights Act 1998.

It is, on the face of it, clear that Acts of the Scottish Parliament are not to be treated as 'primary legislation' under the Human Rights Act 1998 and are, therefore, vulnerable not to the incompatibility and remedial procedures of sections 4 and 10 and Schedule 2 but to the more immediate procedures under sections 6 to 9 which apply to subordinate legislation. That this was an accurate reading of the position and that it was quite right in principle that Acts of the Scottish

---

[11]   Human Rights Act 1998, s 1(2).

[12]   *Ibid*, s 2(1).

[13]   *Ibid*, s 3(1). See F Bennion 'What Interpretation is "Possible" under Section 3(1) of the Human Rights Act 1998?' [2000] *PL* 77.

[14]   *Ibid*, s 6(1).

[15]   HL Deb Vol 585, col 422 (5 Feb 1998).

Parliament should be treated as 'subordinate legislation' was reaffirmed in debate on the Bill.[16]

This is not a position which went entirely uncontested. It may be argued that, although it is possible to draw a sharp line between Acts of the Westminster Parliament and all other types of legislation, whether local authority byelaws or Acts of the Scottish Parliament, that is a categorisation which produces too little differentiation on the 'subordinate' side of the line. On this view, a distinction *should* be drawn between the legislative product of a local authority or a minister and the legislative product of a Parliament.[17] The Scottish Parliament should be treated in a manner similar to that adopted for the Westminster Parliament.

Such arguments have, however, been rejected in the general scheme of the Human Rights Act 1998 and, as we shall see, the Scotland Act 1998. On the other hand, it seems possible that the primary/subordinate classification may yet be a cause of difficulty and discrimination in the operation of the Human Rights Act's own provisions. An existing Westminster Act may be amended by a later Act of Parliament and, also, if within its legislative competence, by the Scottish Parliament. Such amendments could be made in identical terms and could, therefore, raise identical questions of compatibility with Convention rights but with different consequences for their resolution under the Human Rights Act 1998.[18] The procedures for resolution (at Westminster or at Holyrood) of an incompatibility arising from the terms of the Westminster Act are considered below.

C. THE SCOTLAND ACT

Turning to the Scotland Act 1998 itself, we find the human rights restrictions on the Scottish Parliament and Executive represented in a different way. They appear as limitations on the legislative competence of the Parliament and then, by extension, on the competence of the Executive. The Parliament may make laws to be known as Acts of the Scottish Parliament.[19] However, an Act is not

---

[16] See, for example, the Lord Chancellor at HL Deb Vol 583, col 539 (18 Nov 1997); Lord Lester at HL Deb Vol 583, col 543 (18 Nov 1997). See also A Bradley, 'Constitutional Reform, the Sovereignty of Parliament and Devolution' in The University of Cambridge Centre for Public Law (ed), *Constitutional Reform in the United Kingdom: Practice and Principles* (Hart Publishing, Oxford, 1998), 35.

[17] See Robert Reed QC (now Lord Reed), 'Devolution and the Judiciary' in *ibid*, 28. See also Lord Henley at HL Deb Vol 582, col 1304 (3 Nov 1997).

[18] This takes at face value the Human Rights Act's categorisation of the Acts of the Scottish Parliament as being always 'subordinate legislation' in s 21(1). Presumably this means that they could never be another 'instrument' which amends primary legislation and thus primary legislation themselves? The definition of 'primary legislation', which seems not to correlate precisely to that of subordinate legislation, includes instruments amending primary legislation with the specific exception of instruments made by a member of the Scottish Executive, but not, in terms, Acts of the Scottish Parliament.

[19] Scotland Act 1998, s 28(1).

law 'so far as any provision of the Act is outside the legislative competence of the Parliament'.[20] In turn, a provision is outside that competence so far as any of a list of conditions apply. Of greatest general importance is the stipulation that a provision will be outside the competence of the Parliament if it relates to 'reserved matters' as defined by Schedule 5 to the Scotland Act 1998. A provision will, however, also be outside the competence if 'it is incompatible with any of the [ECHR] Convention rights', as defined in the Human Rights Act 1998[21] or if it is incompatible with Community law.

Of most direct relevance to this account is clearly the restriction on legislative competence which derives from incompatibility with Convention rights, but it is important first to take note of the restrictions contained in the 'reserved matters'. There is no general reservation of matters relating to human rights. Part I of Schedule 5 reserves some aspects of 'The Constitution'[22] but these have no direct bearing on human rights. Also reserved by Part I of the Schedule, however, are international relations but that reservation is expressly stated not to include observing and implementing international obligations, obligations under the Human Rights Convention (or under Community law) or assisting Ministers of the Crown in matters of international relations.[23] It would not be within the competence of the Scottish Parliament or Executive to negotiate a new international convention. Observing and implementing existing obligations is, however, competent.

Probably the only other reservation which has direct consequences for human rights is that contained in Section L2 of Part II of Schedule 5 of the Scotland Act 1995. This reserves 'equal opportunities' by reference to the subject-matter of the four anti-discrimination Acts[24] and represents a significant restriction on the Parliament's competence. It was a restriction strongly opposed in debate on the Bill.[25]

In addition to the specific reservation of 'equal opportunities', other provisions in Schedule 5 may be interpreted as restricting legislative competence in the general field of human rights, eg the reservations on data protection, most aspects of elections, firearms, entertainment (video and film), immigration, official secrecy, consumer protection and employment law. The reservation of these matters might well constrain the competence of the Scottish Parliament to modify existing rights and freedoms.

Then, as already noted, the Scotland Act 1998 deliberately reinforces the provision made in the Human Rights Act 1998 by providing directly that the Parliament must not legislate in a way which is incompatible with any of the

---

[20] Scotland Act 1998, s 29(1).
[21] *Ibid*, s 126(1).
[22] *Ibid*, Sch 5, para 1.
[23] *Ibid*, Sch 5, para 7.
[24] The Equal Pay Act 1970, the Sex Discrimination Act 1975, the Race Relations Act 1976 and the Disability Discrimination Act 1995.
[25] See, for example, HC Deb Vol 309, cols 1114–32 (31 Mar 1998).

Convention rights. The consequences of this overlapping of provisions are considered in section D below, as are the effects of Schedule 4 to the Scotland Act 1998 which protects the Human Rights Act 1998 itself from modification.

As far as members of the Scottish Executive are concerned, they derive their general powers from sections 52 and 53 of the Scotland Act 1998 and their 'devolved competence' is defined by reference to the Parliament's legislative competence including, therefore, compatibility with Convention rights. It is, in addition, specifically provided that

> [a] member of the Scottish Executive has no power to make any subordinate legislation, or to do any other act, so far as the legislation or act is incompatible with any of the Convention rights or with Community law.[26]

In addition to imposing these restrictions on the competence of the Scottish Parliament and Executive, the Scotland Act 1998 lays down special procedural provisions for securing compliance and for the resolution of disputes which may arise. As a precautionary device similar to that required by section 19[27] of the Human Rights Act 1998, a member of the Scottish Executive in charge of a Bill must make a statement that, in his or her view, the provisions of the Bill would be within the legislative competence of the Parliament, a formula which embraces compatibility with Convention rights.[28] Under section 33 a Bill which has been passed by the Scottish Parliament may be referred to the Judicial Committee of the Privy Council by the Advocate General, the Lord Advocate or the Attorney General for consideration of whether the Bill (or any provision in it) would be within the Parliament's legislative competence. Any such reference must be made within four weeks of the passing of the Bill and submission of the Bill for Royal Assent has to be deferred for the purpose.[29] A Bill which is held to be outwith competence cannot be submitted for Assent in its unamended form. In addition to this pre-Assent challenge by a law officer, there is scope for post-enactment challenge to the competence of an Act of the Scottish Parliament (or something done by member of the Scottish Executive) which may be taken up in ordinary proceedings thereafter. There is no direct provision for the regulation of such proceedings in the Scotland Act 1998 and it may be assumed that judicial review will often be appropriate. This option is, however, strongly supplemented by Schedule 6 to the Scotland Act 1998 which defines and makes special provision for the handling of 'devolution issues'. Thus a question whether an Act of the Scottish Parliament or any provision of an Act of the Scottish Parliament is within the legislative competence of the Parliament is a devolution

---

[26] Scotland Act 1998, s 57(2). That provision extends the obligation to act compatibly with the ECHR to powers transferred under s 63 of the Scotland Act 1998. For valuable discussion, see I Jamieson, 'Relationship between the Scotland Act and the Human Rights Act' 2001 *SLT (News)* 43, cited in *Mills v HMA (No 2)* 2001 *SLT* 1359 at 1364.

[27] Brought into force on 24 Nov 1998 by SI 1998 No 2882.

[28] Scotland Act 1998, s 29. There is not, of course, the option of *not* making such a statement, as is permitted by s 19 of the Human Rights Act.

[29] *Ibid*, s 32.

issue and this is joined by questions of whether the exercise (or proposed exercise) of functions by members of the Scottish Executive is within devolved competence; or incompatible with any of the Convention rights. A question whether a *failure* to act by a member of the Scottish Executive is similarly incompatible can also be a devolution issue.[30] The procedures laid down for the handling of devolution issues (arising in England and Wales and Northern Ireland as well as in Scotland) include special provision for the involvement of law officers and the reference of devolution issues, whether directly or on appeal, to the Judicial Committee of the Privy Council.[31]

The provision made by the Scotland Act 1998 for the imposition of human rights limitations on legislative and executive competence and then for their classification as devolution issues raises certain boundary questions. One concerns the line drawn between, on the one hand, the bodies whose activities may raise human rights questions and which may on that account give rise to devolution issues and those, on the other hand, which are incapable of giving rise to devolution issues as defined. Thus, the Scottish Parliament apart, only the legislative and other activities of the Scottish Executive can give rise to devolution issues and not, for instance, the activities of bodies beyond the Executive itself. Local authorities, health bodies and quangos are not included and, although the practical consequences of the distinction may turn out to be not very great, it is, at the very least, a curiosity that whilst the low-level act of a civil servant in a Scottish department may give rise to a devolution issue (perhaps being referred for its resolution to the Judicial Committee), a decision by a health authority or by Scottish Environment Protection Agency (SEPA) will not. So long as Scottish Homes remained a quango, its activities did not raise devolution issues. Since its relocation as a (next steps) agency within the Scottish Administration,[32] they may do so.

D. THE ACTS IN TANDEM

There must be added to this account of the two Acts some further consideration of the ways in which they may be expected to operate in combination:–

1. There is first the transitional point that, in its earliest months of operation, the Scotland Act 1998 stood alone. That Act was almost entirely in force by 1 July 1999[33] but the Human Rights Act 1998 was not generally in force until 2 October 2000. This was an eventuality anticipated in the Scotland Act 1998

---

[30] Scotland Act 1998, s 29, Sch 6, Part I.
[31] *Ibid*, Sch 6, Parts II–V.
[32] See Housing (Scotland) Act 2001, Pt 4. And see SI 2001 No 397.
[33] The Scotland Act 1998 (Commencement) Order 1998, SI 1998 No 3178. Importantly, the activities of the Scottish law officers became subject to the Act with effect from 20 May 1999.

itself[34] and the result was a substantial quantity of litigation dependant upon the treatment of human rights questions as 'devolution issues'.[35]

2. An additional comment is, however, required on the impact of the Scotland Act 1998 on the remedial procedures in section 10 and Schedule 2 of the Human Rights Act 1998.[36] Section 5(2) of the Human Rights Act 1998 itself already anticipates the involvement of the Scottish Ministers by enabling a member of the Scottish Executive to become a party to any proceedings in which a court is considering whether to make a declaration of incompatibility in relation to a provision of an Act of Parliament. This is because, in areas where competence is devolved, the Scottish Ministers may have an interest in the outcome and it would fall to a member of the Scottish Executive to take any remedial action under section 10. The general provisions of the Scotland Act 1998 ensure that, within areas of 'devolved competence', executive authority is transferred from Ministers of the Crown to the Scottish Ministers[37] and that procedures in relation to subordinate legislation in the Westminster Parliament are translated into procedures in the Scottish Parliament.[38] Within the devolved field, incompatibilities are to be remedied by the Scottish Ministers, with recourse to the Scottish Parliament. In contrast with a remedial amendment made at Westminster, however, but in line with the general distinction between primary and subordinate legislation already mentioned, any remedial order made by a member of the Scottish Executive is, in terms of section 21 of the Human Rights Act 1998, subordinate rather than primary legislation.

3. The shared reliance of both Acts upon the concept of 'the Convention rights' has already been mentioned. Interlinkage between the Acts assumes a common interpretation of those rights but, whilst this is not the place to develop general questions about the difficulties that this process of interpretation will pose for courts in general, two specific points should be mentioned. One is that, in so far as Convention rights questions are taken as 'devolution issues', they may be finally resolved by the Judicial Committee whereas the same question, whether from Scotland or elsewhere but not taken as a devolution issue, is (in civil matters) determined by the House of Lords.[39] The other is that a Convention rights issue taken as a matter of the competence of the Scottish Parliament or, in relation to subordinate legislation (but not the other acts) of a member of the Scottish Executive, is to be interpreted with

---

[34] See Scotland Act 1998, s 129(2).

[35] Thus in *Starrs v Ruxton* 2000 JC 208 (challenge to temporary sheriffs) the case depended upon the involvement of the Lord Advocate. See also *Millar v Dickson* 2002 SC (PC) 30. And, separately, *Hoekstra v Lord Advocate (No 3)* 2001 SC (PC) 37.

[36] Schedule 2 was amended to clarify the adaptation of Westminster parliamentary procedure to apply to Holyrood by the Scotland Act 1998 (Consequential Modifications) Order 2000, SI 2000 No 2040, Art 2 and Sch, para 21.

[37] Scotland Act 1998, ss 53, 54 and 117.

[38] *Ibid*, s 118.

[39] Section 103(1) of the Scotland Act 1998 declares decisions of the JCPC to be 'binding in all legal proceedings (other than proceedings before the Committee)'.

reference to section 101 of the Scotland Act 1998. That section requires that, if a provision *could* be read in such a way as to be outside competence, it shall be read 'as narrowly as is required for it to be within competence, if such a reading is possible, and is to have effect accordingly'. The meaning to be attributed to this section may not be wholly clear but the point has been taken that its interpretation may produce a result which is different from that which might be produced when section 3(1) of the Human Rights Act 1998 is applied.[40] That subsection provides simply:

> So far as it is possible to do so, primary legislation and subordinate legislation must be read and given effect in a way which is compatible with the Convention rights.[41]

Whether these features will, in practice, produce different results is not easy to predict but the use of a different court and reference to a different interpretative aid may quite reasonably result in different outcomes.[42]

4. Some further steps have, however, been quite deliberately taken to try to assure a parallel application of the law by specific provision in the Scotland Act 1998. Section 100(1) restricts general access to courts on ECHR grounds to 'victims', in line with section 7 of the Human Rights Act 1998. That restriction is expressly not applied to law officers and would not, therefore, curb their right of pre-assent challenge to a Bill in the Scottish Parliament. Section 100(3) restricts the award of damages for breach of a ECHR right, in line with section 8(3) and (4) of the Human Rights Act 1998. By section 57(3), a similar protection is extended to the Lord Advocate, in relation to criminal prosecutions and investigation of deaths, as is given by section 6(2) of the Human Rights Act 1998 to authorities required to enforce provisions which are themselves incompatible with a ECHR Right.[43]

5. Another interesting form of interlinkage between the two statutes developed and indeed changed very significantly as the Scotland Bill moved through the House of Commons. One question which the initial version of the Bill left unclear was whether the Human Rights Act 1998 itself would be amendable or indeed subject to repeal by the Scottish Parliament.[44] The obligation not

---

[40] See Lord Mackay of Drumadoon at HL Deb Vol 593, cols 1954–56 (28 Oct 1998).

[41] That the application of this interpretative aid may not always produce a result favourable to a 'generous' application of the ECHR has already been commented on. See G Marshall, 'Interpreting Interpretation in the Human Rights Bill', [1998] *PL* 167 at 170.

[42] For further speculation about the possible consequences of setting up the two different procedural routes, see Lord Hope of Craighead, 'Devolution and Human Rights', [1998] EHRLR 367, and A O'Neill, 'The Scotland Act and the Government of Judges', 1999 *SLT (News)* 61. Mr O'Neill refers to the particular difference that might emerge from the availability to courts of section 102 of the Scotland Act 1998 under which the effects of retrospective decisions on matters of legislative competence may be varied. See also A O'Neill, 'Judicial Politics and the Judicial Committee: The Devolution Jurisprudence of the Privy Council', (2001) 64 *MLR* 603.

[43] On the differences of practice between Scotland and England in the review of prosecutorial decisions see Lord Hope, *ibid*, at 377 and see also HL Deb Vol 583, col 805 (24 Nov 1997). The Court rejected arguments based on s 57(3) in *Starrs v Ruxton*, above n 35, 2000 SLT 42 at 58 and 73. See also *Millar v Dickson*, above n 35.

[44] See C M G Himsworth, 'Devolving Rights', (1998) *Scotland Forum*, Issue 3, 3.

to legislate in a manner incompatible with the ECHR did not seem to protect the actual terms of the Human Rights Act 1998. There was no reason why its subject matter should be treated as a reserved matter as part of 'The Constitution'. If, however, this was a loop-hole in the original scheme, it was one which was closed at Report Stage in the Commons.[45] The structure of legislative competence was redesigned with a new role given to Schedule 4 to the Act. Instead of merely providing a list of exceptions to the general exclusion of amendment of the Scotland Act 1998 itself, it now serves also to 'entrench' some other statutory provisions against amendment by the Scottish Parliament. Among these 'constitutional Acts'[46] is the Human Rights Act 1998. That Act may not be modified by amendment or repeal. The same applies to the provisions of the Scotland Act 1998 mentioned in paragraph 4 above.

An interesting position has, therefore, been created in which 'human rights' are not, as such, a reserved matter, although some aspects of human rights—notably equal opportunities—*are* reserved. On the other hand, the Human Rights Act 1998 itself cannot be modified by the Scottish Parliament. The full consequences of this conjunction of rules on legislative competence will no doubt be worked out in practice. Whether difficulties arise will depend as much as anything on the enthusiasm of the Scottish Parliament for legislating in this area. Issues may be raised if, for instance, the Parliament chooses to enact legislation which is parallel to but different from the Human Rights Act 1998 itself. Such legislation must not expressly amend the Human Rights Act 1998 or the Scotland Act 1998 but presumably, for instance, legislation to establish an advisory Human Rights Commission in Scotland but which made no reference to the Human Rights Act 1998 would cause no difficulty?[47]

What would be the result, however, if the Scottish Parliament without reference to the Human Rights Act 1998, enacted a comprehensive new code of rights protection—perhaps more 'generous', perhaps more restrictive than the ECHR, perhaps some of each but, at all events, different? Would a court be empowered to strike down something which appeared to be an implied amendment of the Human Rights Act 1998 as legislatively incompetent? If not, which of two sets of provisions would it uphold? Would any additional problem be caused if the new code purported to provide access wider than that offered to ECHR 'victims' or to provide a wider range of remedies than is currently permitted?

---

[45] HC Deb Vol 312, col 261 (12 May 1998).

[46] Others include Arts 4 and 6 of the Acts of Union so far as they relate to freedom of trade, and section 1 and some other provisions of the European Communities Act 1972.

[47] The Scottish Executive issued a consultation document in March 2001—Protecting our Rights: A Human Rights Commission for Scotland. The decision to establish a Commission was announced on 10 Dec 2001

E.   DEVOLVING RIGHTS

The interlinkages between the two Acts do not merely produce conundrums—some hypothetical, some more practical—for resolution in the early years of devolved government in Scotland. They also prompt the questions mentioned earlier about what freedom of manoeuvre the Scottish Parliament *ought* to have and how it might reasonably use its freedom. Some such questions accept the contingencies of the present statutory dispensation in both its more certain and more ambivalent aspects. Others, however, question the lines of demarcation of authority drawn up under that dispensation.

It may be convenient to proceed by referring to some of the arguments which have been presented, sometimes explicitly but in other areas more implicitly, as impediments to a devolved—and, therefore, differentiated—approach to human rights protection and then by offering rejoinders to them. Some of those arguments have a greater potential importance than others. Some of them over-lap with each other. Taken separately, however, they may be presented as follows:

(1) Convention Rights must, like Community law, apply uniformly

Convention rights and Community law are given a sort of equivalence of treat-ment by the Scotland Act 1998. As we have seen, neither the Scottish Parliament nor the Scottish Executive may perform its functions in a way which is 'incom-patible with any of the Convention rights or with Community law'.[48] A provi-sion in a Scottish Bill or Act or the exercise of an executive function has to clear both hurdles. Placing the two in parallel in the Act, however, gives the impres-sion that the legal justification for each is the same and that, because the demands for uniformity of application of Community law are high—in order to maintain the Community's objective of a level playing field, the same must be true of Convention rights. If not only substantive Community obligations but also rules relating to 'remedies and procedures from time to time provided for by or under the Community Treaties'[49] must be sustained across the European Union, then an equivalent position must be maintained across the ECHR states of the Council of Europe. If this were all true, then it might indeed be a short step to the conclusion that procedural and remedial rights assured by the Human Rights Act 1998 should continue to be uniformly applied not only across Europe but also across the United Kingdom. There is, however, no need

---

[48] Scotland Act 1998, ss 29(2)(d), 54 and 57. 'Community law' means '(a) all those rights, pow-ers, liabilities, obligations and restrictions from time to time created or arising by or under the Community Treaties, and (b) all those remedies and procedures from time to time provided for by or under the Community Treaties' (*ibid*, s 126(9)).

[49] *Ibid*, s 126(9).

to draw this conclusion. The regimes are quite different. Community law *does* require to be applied directly by all domestic courts. The ECHR does not itself make this demand. Even Community law places less of a premium on procedural and remedial equality of protection than might be expected.[50] The ECHR does not itself require incorporation of either its substantive rights or the means of their enforcement. The UK record of non-incorporation—maintained even beyond the passing of the Human Rights Act 1998—reconfirms this. The case for the uniform application of Community law is not applicable to Convention rights.

(2) The United Kingdom's obligations under the ECHR itself lead to the need to maintain uniform mechanisms for its observance across the whole of its territories

It may be argued, however, that, because it is the United Kingdom itself which is the signatory to the Rome Treaty and upon which the ECHR's obligations bear, the state must have the right to impose on all parts of the United Kingdom the mechanisms it deems necessary to ensure compliance with the ECHR. The United Kingdom is the member state and the Westminster Parliament must, therefore, be entitled to make appropriate provision, including, ultimately, the provision deemed necessary to ensure that the United Kingdom is not held liable for breach of the ECHR or vulnerable to any consequential sanctions.

This was an issue which was interestingly raised in the report stage debate on the Human Rights Bill in the House of Lords, though not in the first instance in relation to devolution to Scotland, Wales or Northern Ireland. It arose instead in relation to the Isle of Man and the Channel Islands and in the form of a question as to how those territories might best be accommodated alongside the provision to be made for the United Kingdom. It was recognised that human rights issues arising in the island territories had produced difficulties for the United Kingdom in the past—in particular the *Tyrer*[51] case from the Isle of Man and *Gillow*[52] from Guernsey.

Lord Lester sought to extend the Bill to the Channel Islands and the Isle of Man,[53] treating the incorporation of human rights as an 'exceptional circumstance'[54] which justified legislation from Westminster without the consent of the Islands themselves. For the Government, Lord Williams of Mostyn referred to the 'great reservoir of ignorance about the true constitutional arrangements

---

[50] See, for example, C M G Himsworth, 'Things Fall Apart: The Harmonisation of EC Judicial Procedural Protection Revisited', (1997) 22 *European LR* 291–311.

[51] *Tyrer v UK* (1978) 2 EHRR 1.

[52] *Gillow v United Kingdom* (1986) 11 EHRR 335.

[53] HL Deb Vol 584, col 1303 (19 Jan 1998).

[54] The language of the *Report of the Royal Commission on the Constitution* (Cmnd 5460) para 1473.

between the Channel Islands, the Isle of Man and the United Kingdom'.[55] Westminster could, if it wished, legislate for all the territories, even against their will, but it would be contrary to convention. In the case of the Human Rights Bill, all had been consulted and had rejected the extension to them of the Bill's provisions, although the Isle of Man authorities had communicated an intention to introduce similar legislation on their own behalf.[56]

The comparison, in this respect, between the islands and the territories within the United Kingdom itself was not lost on some of Lord Williams' fellow peers and indeed Lady Blatch took up the point about consultation. If the Isle of Man and the Channel Islands could be consulted on the extension to them of the Bill and could be allowed to reject extension if they wished, the same right to consultation should extend to Scotland: 'Surely the arguments are exactly the same.'[57] For Lord Williams the arguments were 'not remotely' the same[58] and the constitutional circumstances are indeed different. But the exchange does illustrate one aspect of the case for diversity rather nicely. Despite Lord Williams' dismissive approach to the comparison made between the different categories of territory for which the UK Government and Parliament *do* have an ultimate responsibility to ensure ECHR compliance, the nature of that responsibility and the choices available in the discharge of it are revealed. It is at least made clear that the UK Government does not assert the need to maintain complete uniformity of provision for implementation and enforcement of the ECHR across all the territories for which it has responsibilities in international law.

(3) Even if this is not formally demanded of the United Kingdom as a party to the Convention, there is general imperative for its 'even application'

In the debate at the Committee stage of the Human Rights Bill in the House of Lords, Lord Lester stated that '[o]ne effect of the Bill will be to ensure an even application of the Convention domestically throughout the whole kingdom'.[59] At one level, this seems an unremarkable ambition and one which should be achievable by the means adopted into the Act. It is a uniform set of Convention rights which are scheduled to the Act and, as already discussed, it is a uniform set of provisions to be applied, by courts in particular, to give effect to those rights.

It is not, however, obvious that a high degree of uniformity in the interpretation and application of the ECHR is achievable or, in the end, desirable. The tendency to diversity, as Lord Lester also pointed out in debate, is evident right at the core of the system in the ECtHR itself. Deploying the argument, which he

---

[55] HL Deb Vol 584, col 1307 (19 Jan 1998).
[56] *Ibid*, col 1308.
[57] *Ibid*.
[58] *Ibid*, col 1309.
[59] HL Deb Vol 583, col 538 (18 Nov 1997).

hoped was not unduly chauvinistic, that there was an opportunity for British judges to give a lead to Strasbourg, he said that there was 'the danger of variable geometry developing in the human rights area'.[60] There would be a ECtHR of:

> up to 40 judges who come from very diverse backgrounds and from countries in eastern, central and western Europe. Therefore this enormous Court will find itself having great difficulty in developing consistent principles of law.[61]

Assuming that any 'lead' from the United Kingdom courts will have no, or only a very slight, impact in practice, and the development of consistent principles remains elusive, how much greater will be the difficulties in achieving an 'even application' of human rights law across all the territories of the Council of Europe?[62] And, if that goal is elusive, why insist on 'even application' across the territories of the United Kingdom? Not only are the necessary substantive principles of law of doubtful consistency but other rules and conditions will tend to undermine even application. The 'victim' test has been incorporated but there has been no general provision to iron out present differences or to prohibit future discrepancies in the general rules of representative *locus standi*, third party participation in proceedings or access to legal aid. All are important to human rights protection and all would need to be taken seriously if even application were a consistent aim.

(4) A mandatory uniformity of protection is the best response to past failures

Associated with the aim to produce a general uniformity of provision by means of the Human Rights Act 1998 has been the knowledge that, in one sense at least, Scotland would be starting from a lower base and that the effect of the Act would be to eliminate the effect of that historically different position. The difference in starting point relates to the degree of recognition already given by courts to the ECHR in the years prior to 'incorporation'. It is well known that, whilst the English courts had, over many years and with a developing pace, permitted themselves to take Convention rights and Strasbourg jurisprudence into account in appropriate circumstances, the Scottish courts had taken a much more restrictive view.[63] In England, it had come to be assumed that the resolution of ambiguity in the construction of a statute might be assisted by reference to the ECHR.[64] Rights protection had, in particular, acquired a special

---

[60] HL Deb Vol 584, col 1269 (19 Jan 1998).

[61] *Ibid*. See also the article by Lord Lester, 'Universality versus Subsidiarity: A Reply', [1998] EHRLR 73.

[62] See H Petzold, 'The Convention and the Principle of Subsidiarity' in R St J Macdonald *et al* (eds), *The European System for the Protection of Human Rights* (Martinus Nijhoff, London, 1993).

[63] For a good account, see J Murdoch, 'Scotland and the European Convention' in B Dickson (ed), *Human Rights and the European Convention: The Effects of the Convention on the United Kingdom and Ireland* (Sweet & Maxwell, London, 1997).

[64] *R v Secretary of State for the Home Department, ex parte Brind* [1991] 1 AC 696.

importance in relation to judicial review,[65] although not derived solely from the ECHR. Some recognition had been given to the use of the ECHR in resolving uncertainties in the common law.[66] However, '[o]ne looks in vain in Scottish jurisprudence for as strong an interpretation of the convention as has been given by the English courts'.[67] Scotland had suffered the lingering impact of the unhelpfully dismissive dicta of Lord Ross in *Surjit Kaur*[68] where he had declared that in Scotland a court was not entitled to have regard to the ECHR either as an aid to construction or otherwise.[69] An attempt to revisit and revise that approach had been made in 1996 by Lord President Hope, shortly before his translation into the House of Lords, in the case of *T, Petitioner*.[70] But his remarks were obiter and came too late in the day to bring great change to the system before the Human Rights Act 1998 brought even greater change.[71]

It is a short step from this inter-jurisdictional comparison which certainly placed the performance of the Scottish judiciary in a generally poor light, to an assumption that, looking ahead, if devolution were to transfer freedom in human rights matters, it would be a freedom used to reduce the impact of the ECHR on the Scottish system. This is a conclusion bolstered, in some respects, by the strongly held doubts of judges, other than Lord Ross, who have expressed views publicly on the subject.[72] But it is also a conclusion born of the same sort of distrust often felt by those at the centre of a devolving structure—'if left to themselves, they will choose not to do it; they will lower standards; they will take the easier or cheaper way out.'

It is, however, also a position which ignores the potential use of a power to amend or repeal the Human Rights Act 1998, if that were permitted, not only to produce rules arguably better integrated into the Scottish system but also to strengthen rights protection. The rules on standing, kept down to a 'victim' level by Westminster could perhaps be made more generous. A human rights commission, also rejected at Westminster, could be added to the scheme.[73] New rules on judicial appointments, seen by some as an essential pre-condition of

---

[65] *Bugdaycay v Secretary of State for the Home Department* [1987] AC 514; *R v Ministry of Defence, ex parte Smith* [1996] QB 517, [1996] 1 All ER 257, [1996] 2 WLR 305.

[66] See, for example, the Court of Appeal in *Derbyshire County Council v Times Newspapers Ltd* [1993] QB 770 (CA), [1993] AC 534.

[67] Lord Lester at HL Deb Vol 583, col 538 (18 Nov 1997).

[68] *Surjit Kaur v Lord Advocate* 1980 SC 319.

[69] *Ibid*, at 329.

[70] *T, Petitioner* 1997 SLT 724. For a revealing account of his campaign leading to *T, Petitioner*, see Lord Hope, above n 42, at 370.

[71] But see also *McLeod v HM Advocate (No 2)* 1998 SLT 233; *Kriba v Home Secretary* 1998 SLT 1113; *Singh v Home Secretary* 1998 SLT 1370.

[72] See especially Lord McCluskey, *Law, Justice and Democracy* (BBC Reith Lectures delivered in 1986)—recalled by him in his second reading speech on the Human Rights Bill at HL Deb Vol 582, cols. 1265–1269 (3 Nov 1997). It was a speech in which he declared his continuing hostility. For the further consequences of Lord McCluskey's publicly aired views, see *Hoekstra and others v HM Advocate (No 1), (No 2)* 2000 JC 387, 391.

[73] See n 47, above.

greater judicial power, could be instituted.[74] Nor would pressure in the direction of such strengthening be totally improbable. Evidence of a wish to take stronger control of rights protection in Scotland was seen in the resistance to the 'reservation' to Westminster by the Scotland Act 1998 of matters relating to equal opportunities.[75]

To assert the potential for a stronger human rights protection in Scotland is to reflect the experience of Northern Ireland over a long period. *Of course* Northern Ireland is different. *Of course* Northern Ireland has been the victim of human rights abuses unknown in Scotland. *Of course*, therefore, the human rights debate has been conducted in a different way. But Northern Ireland has at least demonstrated the capacity for regional initiatives within a UK context to establish different anti-discrimination codes[76] with their own supporting institutions and a general human rights commission in the shape of the Standing Advisory Commission on Human Rights in Northern Ireland and the successor Northern Ireland Human Rights Commission established under the Northern Ireland Act 1998.[77] There may also be a Bill of Rights for Northern Ireland in supplementation of the ECHR.[78] Much of this diversity of experience in Northern Ireland has been imposed from London rather than being home-grown. It does, however, provide evidence of a working asymmetry in human rights protection as much as in other aspects of government.[79]

(5) The assumption of a uniformity of floor, with variable ceilings

Speaking during the Report stage of the Human Rights Bill in the House of Lords, Lord Lester said that 'the European Convention contains a floor of minimum rights guaranteed under international law, but does not create a ceiling'.[80] The metaphor of floors and ceilings is not unfamiliar in this context. It has a ring of common sense to it. The ECHR can be seen as providing a minimum guaranteed level—a level below which no member state should be permitted to fall. The assumption is, however, that, at the option of the state concerned, it can pitch its own guarantees at a 'higher' level. Such a conception of floors and

---

[74] This has begun to happen. A Scottish Executive consultation document was published in April 2000. Since then a new system of appointments including public advertisement and a Judicial Appointments Board has been established on a provisional basis and, on 5 July 2001, it was announced that the first two judges had been appointed under the new system. Revised procedures, involving public advertisement, for shrieval appointments have also been introduced, with first appointments announced on 15 June 2001. The first substantive chair of the Judicial Appointments Board, Sir Neil McIntosh, was appointed on 8 Apr 2002.

[75] See, for example, HC Deb Vol 309, cols. 1114–32 (31 March 1998).

[76] See especially the Fair Employment (Northern Ireland) Acts 1976, 1989.

[77] Northern Ireland Act 1998, s 68. See also the Equality Commission (s 73).

[78] Belfast Agreement, Cm 3883, 1998.

[79] But see also the proposal for a single human rights commission, albeit with devolved characteristics, in S Spencer and I Bynoe, *A Human Rights Commission: The Options for Britain and Northern Ireland,* (IPPR, London, 1998).

[80] HL Deb Vol 585, col 411 (29 Jan 1998).

ceilings readily accommodates and seeks to prevent the risk of a fall below the floor to the sort of unacceptably low level of protection discussed in the last section but also the potential use of rights guaranteed not by the ECHR but by domestic law to rise above the floor without imposition of a ceiling. This is seen to fit in a devolutionary situation where it seems unobjectionable for the state itself to ensure that the floor is maintained across the entire territory but with the option open to a devolved Parliament to make provision to a higher level for its own area. Although floors and ceilings may be imagery principally associated with substantive protection, it is extendable into the realm of procedural protection as well. So, for instance, the 'victim' test is the floor level of standing for protection at Strasbourg but the grant of broader access is simply a permissible rise above that floor. In this way, the case can be made for Westminster reserving to itself the right to guarantee not only the floor of substantive rights but also the floor of procedural rights—achieved in the case of Scotland by the provisions in the Scotland Act 1998 already discussed. Thus both sets of provisions should be seen as correctly 'reserved'.

Some of the arguments against such an entrenchment of the Human Rights Act 1998 have already been considered. They should also be seen as contestable, however, as part of a challenge to the general architecture of floors and ceilings. That imagery, despite its evident attractions, is fatally misleading in its portrayal of human rights protection as a one-dimensional process. Protection starts at the floor and gets 'better'. Rights start weak but can be 'strengthened'. They start few but the list can be extended. There may be different criteria but they all point towards a ranking of protection. It is either better or it is worse. The 'floor' is constructed at the minimum level thought acceptable for the time being.

An alternative approach requires the rejection of this one-dimensional measurement of rights protection. This is an approach which concentrates on the essential tensions between rights. Rights as a whole are not better or worse protected. Rather the function of a system of rights protection is to maintain a relationship between the rights laid down or at least to provide the machinery whereby that relationship may be established over time.[81] Freedom of expression provides a good illustration and cannot be unique. That freedom cannot simply be 'increased' by raising the level of protection above a notional floor. To expand the rights of some (eg the press) is to reduce the rights of others (eg those whose privacy is invaded). The balance can be changed but that change does not produce movement in a one-dimensional direction measured by reference to a floor. On this view, the prescription of a national floor with the opportunity for regional variation above the floor produces a meaningless model of human rights protection and further undermines the case for entrenchment.

---

[81] A process nicely described by Lord Williams of Mostyn in the House of Lords as a balancing of rights that pull in different directions. See HL Deb Vol 584, col 1296 (19 Jan 1998).

F. RIGHTS AND WRONGS OF DEVOLVING A RIGHTS CULTURE

It may be already apparent from the arguments so far presented in this chapter that, underlying the support given for local choice in the extent and means of human rights protection, there is an implied agenda of scepticism about the value of the contemporary human rights project. That scepticism should now be made more explicit because it has a direct bearing upon the case for choice. It is a scepticism which derives from all the well-known doubts about the recasting of social and political issues and programmes by reference to rights; the removal of the formulation, implementation and enforcement of rights from parliaments to courts; in particular, conferring on courts final powers of adjudication and review; and the imposition, in the name of a rights culture, of a juridification of political discussion and decision-making.[82]

Such scepticism in no way denies the fact of the oppression of people by other people, historically and today; both in distant societies and in our own. Nor does it necessarily cast doubt upon the symbolic and more instrumental impact of declarations of internationally accepted lists of rights. What it does contest is the assumed advantage of enforcement by courts of broadly-cast declarations of rights cutting inelegantly, unhelpfully and potentially unjustly across the web of rules of a sophisticated legal system. Many have argued that the ECHR was simply not intended or designed for this purpose and it would be curious indeed if the ECHR began to make a serious impact on the legal systems of the United Kingdom just at the time when the idea of the judicially-enforced rights culture is being seen to have had its day.

This is, in part, an argument to be conducted at a relatively abstract level with a principal focus upon the question of what institutions and procedures best create and preserve freedom in democracies. How far should the response to the perceived failings of democratic institutions be the strengthening of the powers of external monitors such as courts? How far instead should the institutions themselves be strengthened?

At the more practical level of current issues which are undoubtedly difficult but also undoubtedly in need of resolution in one way or another, one has to ask whether the prospect of the ECHR domestically enforced is helpful or unhelpful. Such issues include the proposed reform of the law of the tenement and of land tenure in general;[83] 'aggressive begging' on the streets; wheel-clamping; the regulation of 'raves' and child-safety curfews; paedophile registers and the

---

[82] For a very important recent critique, see K D Ewing, 'The Human Rights Act and Parliamentary Democracy', (1999) 62 *MLR* 79–99. See also T Campbell, K Ewing, A Tomkins (eds), *Sceptical Essays on Human Rights*, (Oxford University Press, Oxford, 2001).

[83] See the two relevant Reports of the Scottish Law Commission: (1997–98) HC 583; (1998–99) HC 185. Scot Law Com nos 163 and 168. The Abolition of Feudal Tenure etc (Scotland) Act 2000 has been passed.

detention of psychopaths;[84] and 'anti-social' tenants and neighbours. No one doubts that 'rights' are in some measure at stake in all these circumstances. Nor is it doubted that imaginative legal minds could restate some aspects of all of these issues in terms of ECHR protected rights. But in what respects is it helpful to have them passed to courts rather than Parliaments for their resolution? It was pointed out by the Judicial Committee of the Privy Council (JCPC) as it dealt with the aftermath of *Starrs v Ruxton*[85] that the lack of independence enjoyed by temporary sheriffs had attracted adverse criticism as early as 1993[86] but was it sensible to have change—however desirable—inflicted on the system overnight and the position of temporary sheriff abolished immediately?

For many, the answer is that the expansion of human rights protection is a deliberate response to the failure of democracy at Westminster. But seen in that light, it becomes particularly ironic that it is just at the time when one limb of the current constitutional project seeks to expand democratic decision-making by the devolution of legislative power to a Parliament made newly accountable to the Scottish people and which may, because of proportional representation and a fixed term, never become an 'elective dictatorship', that another limb of the project seeks to adhere to the old agenda of democratic failure by the super-imposition of a uniform and rigid human rights regime.[87] The principal threats to the liberty of the people of Scotland do not come from the Scottish Parliament and Executive but from those whom it is the democratic mission of the Parliament to regulate and control. The Parliament should be in a strong position to determine for itself how far judicially enforced rights should be a part of its strategy.

---

[84] See the Mental Health (Public Safety and Appeals)(Scotland) Act 1999 and the (unsuccessful) challenge in *A (A Mental Patient) v Scottish Ministers* 2002 SC (PC) 63.

[85] Above n 35.

[86] *Millar v Dickson*, above, n 35, at para 36, citing I D Willock, 'Temporary Sheriffs', 1993 *SLT (News)* 352.

[87] See also C A Gearty in this collection and his article, 'Here Come The Judges', *London Review of Books*, 4 June 1998.

4

The Role of the Advocate General for Scotland in the New Constitutional Settlement

DR LYNDA CLARK QC MP*

THE HISTORY OF lawyers in government is as old as the history of government itself. It is not surprising that lawyers, who deal daily with laws enacted by Parliament, should have sought from the outset to influence the framing of these laws. Governments have always recognised the need to have authoritative legal advice and the Law Officers supply this.

In England, the exact origin of the Attorney General is imprecise, but there are records of lawyers being appointed as 'King's Attorney' from the mid-13th century. The first recorded appointment as Attorney General, so called, was that of John Herbert in 1461. The establishment in Scotland of the office of Lord Advocate is also obscure but in the 1470s John Ross of Montgrennan appeared in court designed as 'Advocate for the King' and the line of Lord Advocates can be traced back to 1483.[1] The importance of the Lord Advocate grew, becoming a significant constitutional position in Scotland's governance, and an ex officio member of the pre-Union Scots Parliament. From 1707 to 1999 the Lord Advocate was always a member of the UK Government in his role of chief legal adviser on Scots law. That changed as a result of devolution introduced by the Scotland Act 1998.

A. THE OFFICE OF ADVOCATE GENERAL FOR SCOTLAND

While the establishment of other Law Officers is vague, I can be precise about my own. The devolution White Paper, *Scotland's Parliament*,[2] contained the first reference to the then unnamed position, stating somewhat baldly:

---

* Dr Clark is Advocate General for Scotland.

[1] See further J Finlay, 'James Henryson and the Origins of the Office of King's Advocate in Scotland' (2000) 79 *SHR* 17.

[2] Cm 3658, July 1997.

The UK Government will continue to need advice on Scots law (whether reserved or devolved). Accordingly a new post of Scottish Law Officer to the UK Government will be created.[3]

As a Law Officer, the Advocate General is appointed by Letters Patent by the Queen under Her Majesty's prerogative powers. The office came into being just before midnight on 19 May 1999.[4] The Advocate General is a new UK Law Officer created as a result of devolution.[5] Since devolution I have inherited the role as adviser on Scots law to the UK Government which was previously carried out by the Lord Advocate and the Solicitor General for Scotland who ceased to be UK Law Officers and became the Law Officers to the devolved Scottish Executive. As Advocate General I was also given a new constitutional role which is explained later.

The role of the Advocate General and of the Lord Advocate and Solicitor General for Scotland, post-devolution, was debated during the passage of the Scotland Act 1998. The Conservatives were opposed, in principle, to the devolution of the Lord Advocate. They proposed that the Solicitor General become the Scottish Executive's Law Officer with the Lord Advocate remaining as a UK Law Officer. This would have 'the added advantage of eliminating the so-called 'Harry Lime' position, whereby a third man [the Advocate General] is suddenly introduced'.[6] Michael Ancram contended that 'no one is quite certain what the Advocate General for Scotland will do.'[7] The Minister of State for Devolution, Henry McLeish, replied that:

> The Government believe that both the Lord Advocate and the Solicitor General should be the Law Officers to the Scottish Executive, and that the two offices should continue to have the sort of relationship that has existed for more than three centuries.[8]

For the Liberal Democrats, Jim Wallace stated that the Advocate General,

> will be an important post, because large areas of responsibility affecting Scotland will remain with the House of Commons, and we hope that the advice on Scottish law that the Government of the day are given will be of the best quality.[9]

---

[3] Cm 3658, July 1997, para 4.9.

[4] At a ceremony in the Court of Session I took the oaths of office, and when appearing in the Court of Session and High Court of Justiciary I am entitled to sit at the table within the Bar, immediately below the Bench at the left hand side of the Chair.

[5] S 87 of the Scotland Act 1998 inserts entries for the Advocate General in Part III of Sch 1 to the Ministerial and other Salaries Act 1975 (salaries of the Law Officers) and in Sch 2 to the House of Commons Disqualification Act 1975 (Ministerial offices). Section 48(6) removes the existing entries in these Schedules for the Lord Advocate and the Solicitor General for Scotland.

[6] Michael Ancram alluding to the eponymous character in Graham Greene's *The Third Man*: HC Deb 10 Feb 1998, col 164.

[7] *Ibid.*

[8] HC Deb 10 Feb 1998, col 175.

[9] HC Deb 10 Feb 1998, col 180.

He proposed[10] that all three Law Officers should require to be either members of the Faculty of Advocates or solicitors under the Solicitors (Scotland) Act 1980. Henry McLeish replied that it had

> not been felt necessary in the past to prescribe the qualifications for office of the Scottish Law Officers, and it is not clear why this should be necessary now. To do so would be inconsistent with the Government's intention to legislate for a responsible Parliament and Executive, which can be expected to ensure that holders of these vital offices of state are qualified for them.'[11]

Henry McLeish stated that

> the UK Government would wish to appoint [as Advocate General] only an eminent Scottish lawyer to a ministerial office of that nature, but there is no need to specify those qualifications in legislation.[12]

The House of Lords also debated qualifications and the proposal that the Advocate General must be an advocate or Scottish solicitor was supported by Lords Mackay of Drumadoon, Hope of Craighead, Fraser of Carmyllie and Rodger of Earlsferry.[13] The Lord Advocate, Lord Hardie of Blackford agreed 'about the principle that whoever is appointed to this post should have appropriate standing and qualification in Scots law'.[14] However he resisted the proposed amendment, arguing that it was unnecessary and that the formulation suggested would exclude, for example, 'a professor of law who is not a member of either profession.'[15]

The Advocate General is necessary because the UK Government needs advice on Scots Law which should have the same authority as that of the Attorney General and Solicitor General for England and Wales in respect of English law. This advice should also have the same authority as that received by the Scottish Executive from their Law Officers. Only a Law Officer trained in Scots Law can provide such advice. The UK Government could not rely on advice from the Law Officers to the Scottish Executive because there would be a potential conflict of interest. Indeed section 99(1) of the Scotland Act 1998 provides for litigation between

> the Crown in right of Her Majesty's Government in the UK and the Crown in right of the Scottish Administration by virtue of a contract, by operation of law or by virtue of an enactment as they may arise between subjects.

The Government and the Scottish Executive have their own respective interest and agenda and require their own independent legal advice.

---

[10] HC Deb 10 Feb 1998, col 167.
[11] HC Deb 10 Feb 1998, col 173.
[12] HC Deb 10 Feb 1998, col 174.
[13] HL Deb 6 Oct 1998, cols 371–378.
[14] HL Deb 6 Oct 1998, col 375.
[15] HL Deb 6 Oct 1998, col 376.

As was noted during the Scotland Bill debates, the UK Government needs advice on Scots law because many areas of law are reserved, such as tax, defence, foreign affairs, consumer protection, energy, equal opportunities, immigration, social security, employment, company law, and road traffic law. Government Departments, when acting in Scotland, are subject to Scots law and the Office of my Solicitor provides them with legal services.[16] The Government also requires advice concerning what is devolved and what is reserved under the devolution settlement. In relation to European law and the European Convention for the Protection of Human Rights and Fundamental Freedoms (ECHR) advice is required which is valid for Scotland because even in devolved areas, the UK Government are ultimately responsible for ensuring compliance with European law and the ECHR.

It is therefore important, post-devolution, that the UK continues to have a Scots law adviser at Ministerial level. I ensure that Scots law is always fully considered and that Scots lawyers continue to influence UK decision-making. As the first Advocate General I have tried to ensure the influence of the post in the governmental machinery of Whitehall[17] and also to shape the development of Scots law. In addition to the advisory duties which the Advocate General inherited from the Lord Advocate, I was also given a range of new powers and functions under the Scotland Act 1998. These include the power to intervene in 'devolution issues' cases and, under section 33, to refer Bills of the Scottish Parliament to the Judicial Committee of the Privy Council. Developing this new constitutional role of the Law Officers has been both interesting and challenging.

B. LEGAL ADVISER ROLE

My principal role is as the adviser on Scots law to the UK Government. The Ministerial Code describes the principles governing the duty of Ministers and their Departments to refer questions to the Law Officers (myself together with

---

[16] The Office of the Solicitor to the Advocate General (OSAG) consists of 17 lawyers based in Edinburgh and they also prepare Westminster legislation and subordinate legislation which extends to Scotland and support me in my statutory functions under the Scotland Act 1998. There are also three lawyers in my Legal Secretariat, based in Edinburgh and London, who assist me in giving formal legal advice to the Government and prepare briefings for Cabinet Committees and Parliamentary business.

[17] My Office is within the Scotland Office which serves, separately, two Ministers, the Secretary of State for Scotland and her Ministerial team and the Advocate General. We each have entirely distinct functions and our own teams of advisers. The Advocate General has a role in giving the Secretary of State legal advice concerning her functions. The Secretary of State's role is to: represent Scottish interests within the UK Government in reserved matters; promote the devolution settlement by encouraging co-operation between Edinburgh and London and act as an honest broker as appropriate in disputes, or otherwise intervening as required by the Scotland Act 1998; pay a grant to the Scottish Consolidated Fund and manage other financial transactions; and exercise certain residual functions in reserved matters (eg conduct and funding of elections; making of private legislation at Westminster).

the Attorney General and Solicitor General for England and Wales[18]) as follows, but the description is not exhaustive:[19]

> The Law Officers must be consulted in good time before the Government is committed to critical decisions involving legal considerations. It will normally be appropriate to consult the Law Officers in cases where:–
> (a) The legal consequences of action by the Government might have important repercussions in the foreign, European Union or domestic field
> (b) A Departmental Legal Adviser is in doubt concerning:-
>   (i) the legality or constitutional propriety of legislation which Government proposes to introduce or
>   (ii) the vires of proposed subordinate legislation or
>   (iii) the legality of proposed administrative action, particularly where that action might be subject to challenge in the courts by means of application for judicial review
> (c) Ministers, or their officials, wish to have the advice of the Law Officers on questions involving legal considerations, which are likely to come before the Cabinet or a Cabinet Committee
> (d) There is a particular legal difficulty which may raise political aspects of policy
> (e) Two or more Departments disagree on legal questions and wish to seek the view of the Law Officers.

A considerable diversity of topics may arise including, for example, questions concerning the devolution settlement, whether draft domestic regulations will correctly implement a European directive under the European Communities Act 1972 or whether legislative proposals are ECHR compatible.[20] In such cases the Advocate General will usually advise along with one or both of the Law Officers for England and Wales. In advising UK Ministers and Departments I am entitled to look after their interests, like any other legal adviser, subject to the professional rules applying to advocates.[21]

It is a long standing convention, adhered to by successive Governments and enshrined in the Ministerial Code, that neither the fact that the Law Officers have advised on a matter, nor the content of any advice which they may have given, is disclosed outside Government (even in Parliament) other than in

[18] The Attorney General for England and Wales holds the separate office of Attorney General for Northern Ireland (Northern Ireland Constitution Act 1973, s 10).

[19] *Ministerial Code: A Code of Conduct and Guidance on Procedures for Ministers* (Cabinet Office, London, 2001).

[20] Under s 19(1) of the Human Rights Act 1998 the Minister in charge of a Bill must, prior to the Second Reading, make a statement either that, in his view, the provisions of the Bill are compatible with the Convention rights or that although he is unable to make such a statement of compatibility the Government nevertheless wishes Parliament to proceed with the Bill.

[21] Former Lord Advocate, Lord Hardie, explained that 'the Law Officers . . . are . . . a convenient, not to say indispensable, method of resolving legal questions within Government. Since the Government must adopt a common position on legal issues some way must be found of settling legal differences over questions which cannot be litigated, just as some way must be found of settling policy differences between Departments and Ministers. The latter are resolved by collective ministerial decision; the former by referring matters to the Law Officers' (Scottish Grand Committee, Edinburgh, 8 March 1999).

exceptional circumstances. This is to protect the confidentiality of the legal advice given to the Government. Governments of different political persuasions have observed this convention. The Government, like everyone else, should be able to get the legal advice which it needs to perform its functions, without having to explain or justify this to outsiders, or indeed to reveal that it has concerns about the legal position. This ensures that the Government seeks, and gets, frank advice where appropriate, without having to worry about any political and presentational implications. Interestingly, Law Officers' Opinions, unlike other Ministerial papers, are generally made available to the Law Officers of succeeding Administrations.

Much of the Law Officers' role is not set down in statute and our work is done in private, advising the Government on a range of issues which rarely enter the public gaze. Law Officers occupy a unique position in Government as Ministers who are appointed for a combination of their political skills and legal expertise. The Government is entitled to receive objective legal advice and Law Officers, familiar with the political environment in which the Government operates, give this.

C. ROLE OF THE ADVOCATE GENERAL UNDER THE SCOTLAND ACT

The Advocate General has important new statutory functions under the Scotland Act 1998. Section 28 gives the Scottish Parliament general legislative competence subject to the limitations set out in section 29. Section 29(1) provides 'An Act . . . is not law so far as any provision of the Act is outside the legislative competence of the Parliament.' Under section 29(2) legislative competence is limited in several ways. In particular, an Act is not law so far as any provision of it: relates to matters reserved to the UK Parliament by Schedule 5; is incompatible with any Convention rights; or is incompatible with European Community law. Section 57(2) provides that a member of the Scottish Executive has no power to make any subordinate legislation, or to do any other act, which would be incompatible with 'Convention rights', which are defined as bearing the same meaning as in section 1 of the Human Rights Act 1998.

Whereas the Convention rights have been, from 2 October 2000, accessible in domestic law in the UK by means of the Human Rights Act 1998, the position in Scotland was different following devolution. The Scotland Act 1998 allowed human rights issues to be dealt with directly before Scottish courts in advance of the Human Rights Act 1998 coming fully into force if the matter related to the competence of the Scottish Ministers or Scottish Parliament legislation. Ultra vires acts of the Scottish Ministers and Scottish Parliament legislation are, subject to an order under section 102, suspending the court's decision or varying its retrospective effect, void *ab initio*. Therefore, from the moment of their inception, in May 1999, the Scottish Executive and Parliament were legally obliged to act in compliance with Convention rights. The legislation establishing the

National Assembly for Wales[22] and the Northern Ireland Assembly and Executive[23] similarly obliges these devolved institutions to comply with Convention standards.

D. 'DEVOLUTION ISSUES'

One of my important functions relates to 'devolution issues' raised in court and these are defined in Schedule 6 to the Scotland Act 1998:

1. a question whether any function which any person has purported, or is proposing, to exercise is a function of the Scottish Ministers, the First Minister or the Lord Advocate;
2. a question whether the purported or proposed exercise of a function by a member of the Scottish Executive is, or would be, within devolved competence;
3. any other question about whether a function is exercisable within devolved competence or in or as regards Scotland and any other question arising by virtue of the Act about reserved matters;
4. a question whether an Act of the Scottish Parliament, or any provisions within it, is within the legislative competence of the Scottish Parliament;
5. a question whether an exercise of a function (or a failure to act) by a member of the Scottish Executive is, or would be, incompatible with any of the Convention rights or with Community law.

Consequently court actions against the Scottish Executive or challenges to legislation of the Scottish Parliament alleging failure to comply with Convention rights are dealt with as 'devolution issues' and must be intimated to the Advocate General.[24] From May 1999 to April 2002 over 1400 devolution issues were raised, mostly in the lower criminal courts, and I intervened in 24 cases, all of which concerned ECHR points.

Since all devolution issues cases have to be intimated to me it was possible to keep track of the number and type of human rights points being raised. It is not as straightforward to collate detailed figures under the Human Rights Act 1998 as Convention points are intimated to the Crown only if the court is considering making a declaration of incompatibility.[25] It must be emphasised that, despite the entry into force of the Human Rights Act 1998, the human rights provisions of the Scotland Act 1998 have not been repealed. The *vires* check upon Scottish Parliament legislation and Scottish Executive acts remains in

---

[22] Government of Wales Act 1998.

[23] Northern Ireland Act 1998.

[24] See Act of Sederunt (Devolution Issues Rules) 1999, SI 1999/1345; Act of Adjournal (Devolution Issues Rules) 1999, SI 1999/1346; and Act of Sederunt (Proceedings for Determination of Devolution Issues Rules) 1999, SI 1999/1347.

[25] Human Rights Act 1998, s 5(1).

place. Acts which are beyond devolved competence are still *ultra vires,* and the procedural requirements of Schedule 6 to the Scotland Act 1998 continue to apply. Thus in every case where a challenge—other than one which is frivolous or vexatious—is made to the human rights compliance of Scottish Parliament legislation or an act of the Scottish Executive, a devolution issue arises and proper intimation must accordingly be made to me under Schedule 6.[26]

I consider all devolution issues intimated to me and my officials circulate notices to the appropriate UK Departments. In deciding whether to intervene I take account of any views submitted by the Departments. In the course of my work I have tried to ensure that problems arising from the application of the ECHR to the Scottish Parliament and Executive are understood by Whitehall Departments for their potential UK implications.

I intervene, as a UK Law Officer, where I consider there is good reason to do so. The reasons for intervention will vary according to the circumstances and the criteria I apply cannot be rigid. Intervention may occur, for example, when a provision of UK-wide legislation is at issue, and a judgment in the Scottish courts may have an influence in England and Wales, or when significant matters of principle arise. Most interventions have been at appeal or Privy Council level and very rarely at first instance and I consider that my submissions may be different from those of other parties. Most of my interventions have been at appeal or Privy Council level and not at first instance in the lower courts, because experience has shown that the vast majority of devolution issues involving human rights are disposed of successfully by the courts at first instance, without any need for intervention. If they have not been satisfactorily resolved by that stage, this may show that intervention is needed in the JCPC. I may, of course, intervene at first instance or appeal stage where the circumstances require it. There may be very good legal and policy reasons for non-intervention and my role as Advocate General is not to intervene in cases at any level, at significant public expense, merely because there is an interesting legal point being debated.

Devolution issues have largely concerned Convention rights and most primarily allege that in exercising his functions as head of the Prosecution Service, the Lord Advocate has breached Convention rights—mainly Article 6 of the ECHR, right to a fair trial.[27] Some devolution issues have related to compatibility with EC law, but there have been no 'pure' devolution issues—in the sense of disputes as to whether the Scottish Executive or Parliament has acted outwith devolved areas of competence. However in *Anderson, Doherty & Reid*[28] the first Act passed by the Scottish Parliament was challenged on the grounds of incompatibility with the ECHR. The Act concerned, the Mental Health (Public

---

[26] I made this submission in August 2001 to the Appeal Court, High Court of Justiciary in *Mills v HM Advocate* 1 Aug 2001 GWD 20–760. This case has been appealed to the Judicial Committee of the Privy Council.

[27] The question of what constitutes an act of the Lord Advocate, and therefore may give rise to a devolution issue, was discussed in *Montgomery and Coulter v HM Advocate* 2000 JC 111; 2001 PC 1.

[28] 2000 SLT 873.

Safety and Appeals) (Scotland) Act 1999, was enacted very quickly, completing all its parliamentary stages in one day. The legislation was challenged as being incompatible with Article 5(1)(e) and 5(4) of the ECHR concerning the right to liberty and security of persons. The First Division of the Court of Session accepted that the Act was not incompatible and this decision was upheld by the Judicial Committee of the Privy Council in October 2001.[29]

The other main broad categories of devolution issues are as follows:

Delay—claims that delays have prejudiced the accused's right to a fair trial 'within a reasonable time' under Article 6(1) of the ECHR. The point generally taken is that there has been an excessive delay between the offence coming to the attention of the authorities and proceedings being instigated, or between the accused being put on notice of the investigation and the start of proceedings. The decisions turn on their facts and circumstances.[30]

Road Traffic Act 1988, section 172—claims of a breach of the accused's right not to incriminate himself, implicit in Article 6(1), when he was questioned before being charged and was compelled to make a compulsory admission concerning who was driving the car at the time of the offence, under the penalty that failure to provide the information requested would be a criminal offence. In *Brown v Stott*[31] the Judicial Committee of the Privy Council held unanimously that section 172(2)(a) was compatible with Article 6(1) because the implicit rule against self-incrimination was not absolute.

Temporary Sheriffs—claims that since the Lord Advocate appointed temporary sheriffs for the short tenure period of one year usually and was responsible for the renewal of their commissions, these appointments could not be considered to constitute an 'independent and impartial tribunal' under Article 6(1) of the ECHR because the Lord Advocate is also head of the prosecution system. In *Starrs v Ruxton*[32] the High Court of Justiciary upheld the claim and the Scottish Parliament removed the offending legislative provisions and enacted legislation believed to be compatible.[33] In July 2001 the JCPC heard appeals concerning convictions by temporary sheriffs.[34]

Legal aid fixed fees—claims that an accused person's rights in Article 6(3) 'to have adequate time and facilities for the preparation of his defence' are prejudiced by fixed fees paid in criminal legal aid matters. It was argued that there did not exist equality of arms between the prosecutor and the accused but in May 2001 the JCPC held, in *Buchanan v McLean*,[35] that the fixed fee system as a whole is compatible.

[29] See decision of the JCPC in *A (A Mental Patient) v Scottish Ministers* 2000 SLT 873, 2001 SLT 1331 (PC).
[30] For discussion see Ferguson and Mackarel in this volume.
[31] *Brown v Stott* 2001 SC (PC) 43; [2001] 2 All ER 97.
[32] *Starrs v Ruxton* 2000 SLT 42.
[33] Bail, Judicial Appointments etc. (Scotland) Act 2000. This Act also sought to ensure that certain statutory procedures relating to bail and the district courts are ECHR compatible.
[34] See *Millar v Dickson* 2001 SLT 988.
[35] *Buchanan v McLean* 2000 SLT 928; 2001 SCCR 980.

Access to a solicitor—claims that the lack of access to a solicitor during police interviews is prejudicial to the accused's right to a fair trial. These cases have principally arisen from police powers to detain suspects and interview them without a solicitor being present.

Bail—claims that refusal of bail is incompatible with the accused's right under Article 5 of the ECHR to liberty and security.

District Courts—claims that the system of legally qualified Clerks in District Courts is not compatible with Article 6 of the ECHR because the Clerk is appointed by the local authority which collects all District Court fines. Hence the Clerk cannot be seen as independent and impartial as he has an interest in the outcome of cases.[36]

Privacy—claims that intrusive surveillance and covert police operations have breached the accused's rights under Articles 6 and 8 (respect for private life). It is argued that the actings of police officers amount to entrapment and the use of pseudonyms by officers creates an inequality of arms in preparation of the case and examination of witnesses.

Confiscation orders—claims that the assumptions which can be made by the courts in dealing with applications for confiscation orders under the Proceeds of Crime (Scotland) Act 1995 are incompatible with the Article 6(2) right that a person charged with a criminal offence is to be presumed innocent until proven guilty. In February 2001 the JCPC held in *McIntosh* that the statutory assumptions are ECHR-compliant.[37]

Pre-trial publicity—claims that prejudicial pre-trial publicity was incompatible with Article 6 of the ECHR.[38]

Planning cases—claims in *County Properties Ltd v Scottish Ministers*[39] and other cases that the determination of planning appeals by the Scottish Ministers did not satisfy Article 6 of the ECHR. In the English case of *Alconbury*[40] the House of Lords held that the planning system was Article 6 compliant.

The ability of courts to strike down, in full or in part, Acts of the Scottish Parliament, which are incompatible with the Convention, which would have been the result of a successful challenge in *Anderson, Doherty & Reid,* is in contrast to the position of the courts in relation to Acts of the UK Parliament. The White Paper, prior to the HRA, *Rights Brought Home,*[41] concluded:

> [C]ourts should not have the power to set aside primary legislation, past or future, on the ground of incompatibility with the Convention. This conclusion arises from the importance which the Government attaches to Parliamentary sovereignty. In this context, Parliamentary sovereignty means that Parliament is competent to make any law on any matter of its choosing and no court may question the validity of any Act that it passes.

[36] But see *Clark v Kelly* 2000 SCCR 821.
[37] *McIntosh v HM Advocate* 2000 SLT 1280; 2000 SCCR 1017.
[38] See *Montgomery and Coulter v HM Advocate* 2000 JC 111; 2001 PC 1.
[39] *County Properties Ltd v Scottish Ministers* 2000 SLT 965 but reversed at 2001 SLT 1125.
[40] *R v Secretary of State for ETR, ex parte Alconbury* [2001] 2 All ER 929.
[41] Cm 3782, October 1997.

Under section 4 of the Human Rights Act 1998 a court cannot strike down UK Acts but may make a declaration of incompatibility that it considers the Act, or a provision of it, to be in breach of Convention rights.[42] If a court rules that a provision of primary legislation is incompatible with the Convention, it remains in full force and effect until a remedial order is approved by Parliament and takes effect.

Some provisions of the Scotland Act 1998 ensure its broad congruence with the Human Rights Act 1998. Under section 100 of the Scotland Act 1998 a person cannot challenge legislation unless he can show that he would be a 'victim' for the purposes of Article 34 of the ECHR if proceedings in respect of the legislation which is challenged were to be brought in the Strasbourg Court. This provides the same test as section 7 of the Human Rights Act 1998. Similarly the Scotland Act 1998 [s 100(3)] does not enable a court to award any damages in respect of an act which is incompatible with Convention rights which it could not award if section 8 of the Human Rights Act 1998 applied.

Both Acts provide for 'reading down' legislation incompatible with the ECHR. Section 3(1) of the Human Rights Act 1998 states that 'so far as it is possible to do so' both primary and secondary legislation must be read and given effect in a way which is compatible with Convention rights. The Scotland Act 1998 [s 101(2)] requires that Scottish Parliament legislation 'is to be read as narrowly as is required for it to be within competence, if such a reading is possible.' This variance of wording does not mean that different results are intended. For both statutes the courts must search for a reading of the provision in the Act of the Scottish Parliament which is 'possible', having already examined the ECHR. Consequently, whichever Act the challenge is made under, the court will put a narrower construction on the provision than its terms would normally bear if the usual rules of interpretation were applied.

E. SECTION 33—BILLS OF THE SCOTTISH PARLIAMENT

Scotland's Parliament stated, in relation to possible disagreements between the Scottish Executive and UK Government:

> Prior to a Scottish Bill being passed forward from the Presiding Officer to receive Royal Assent, there will be a short delay period to ensure that the UK Government is content as to vires. In the event of a dispute . . . about vires remaining unresolved, there will be provision for it to be referred to the JCPC . . . The Judicial Committee will also be able to hear any subsequent disputes about devolution issues in relation to secondary legislation and Acts of the Scottish Parliament after Royal Assent.[43]

---

[42] Under s 4(5) the following courts may make a declaration of incompatibility: the House of Lords; the Judicial Committee of the Privy Council; the Courts-Martial Appeal Court; in Scotland, the High Court of Justiciary sitting otherwise than as a trial court or the Court of Session; and in England, Wales, or Northern Ireland, the High Court or Court of Appeal.

[43] *Scotland's Parliament*, above, n 2, para 4.17.

This policy intention was enacted by section 33, under which the Advocate General has the power to refer any Bill passed by the Scottish Parliament to the JCPC for a decision on whether it or any of its provisions is within legislative competency. This power, exercisable within four weeks of the Scottish Parliament passing the Bill but before it receives Royal Assent, is separately available to the Lord Advocate and the Attorney General. If all three Law Officers notify the Presiding Officer that a reference will not be made then the Bill can more rapidly proceed to Royal Assent.[44] A reference by the Lord Advocate in respect of Scottish Executive Bills may appear unlikely but one could be made, for instance, to clarify a legal uncertainty and deter future challenges to the Bill. References could also be in respect of Member's Bills which stand a greater chance of reaching the statute book than at Westminster because of the proportional representation voting system and the enhanced role played by Scottish Parliament Committees.[45] However, it seems more likely that a UK Law Officer would instigate a reference. Thus far no section 33 references have been made.

The Scotland Act 1998 also contains powers by which the UK Government could prevent the enactment of legislation by the Scottish Parliament. Under section 35 the Secretary of State may make an order prohibiting the Presiding Officer from submitting a Bill for Royal Assent if it contains provisions which:

(i)   would be incompatible with any international obligations or the interests of defence or national security; or

(ii) make modifications of the law as it applies to reserved matters and would have an adverse effect on the operation of the law as it applies to reserved matters.

Such an Order must identify the provisions, state the reasons for making it and be made during the four-week period beginning with the passing of the Bill or within four weeks following the disposal of any section 33 reference by the JCPC. An Order under section 35 will be subject to annulment by resolution of either the House of Commons or Lords. A parallel provision enabling the Secretary of State to intervene in the exercise of executive power by the Scottish Executive is contained in section 58. The Advocate General may advise the Secretary of State for Scotland on legal issues concerning her powers under the Scotland Act 1998.

It was intended that sections 33 and 35 would not be invoked regularly. The most effective way of ensuring this is by dialogue between the Government and the Scottish Executive. This was the intention of *Scotland's Parliament*, which referred[46] to giving UK Government Departments the opportunity to discuss any concerns they have about the vires of a Bill with the Scottish Executive at

---

[44]   Scotland Act 1998, s 33(3). This has occurred in relation to some Bills: eg the Bill which became the Mental Health (Public Safety and Appeals) (Scotland) Act 1999.

[45]   Several Member's Bills have been enacted: Sea Fisheries (Shellfish) Amendment (Scotland) Act 2000; Leasehold Casualties (Scotland) Act 2001; Abolition of Poindings and Warrant Sales Act 2001.

[46]   *Scotland's Parliament*, above, n 2, para 4.16.

any stage of its passage through the Scottish Parliament. There is regular contact at official level and, from time to time, at ministerial level. A central objective is to ensure 'no surprises' so that both administrations are kept fully informed about each other's legislative proposals.

Early dialogue and co-operation can eliminate the need for a section 33 reference or a section 35 Order in all but the most exceptional cases. If difficulties are identified before the Bill is passed the Scottish Executive can take action to avoid the use of section 33 or section 35. Consequently, Scottish Executive Bills are made available to Whitehall Departments at various stages of their legislative journey through the Scottish Parliament. With sensitivity, co-operation and openness there is no reason why the Law Officers' Judicial Committee reference power and the Secretary of State's Order power should cause tension between London and Edinburgh.

Under section 33 I will refer a Bill, or any provision of it, to the Judicial Committee when, as a UK Law Officer, I consider, in all the circumstances, that that is the appropriate course of action. I will consult the appropriate UK Departments and take their views into account in deciding whether to make a reference. I receive regular reports from my Solicitor about the progress of all Scottish Parliamentary legislation, highlighting potential competency problems, and the views of Whitehall Departments are regularly sought. Once a Bill is passed my Legal Secretary requests final comments from UK Departments before I decide whether or not to make a reference.

Section 33 is not intended to cause conflict with the Scottish Executive and its purpose is to provide a mechanism for the final settlement of disputes. Similarly, invoking section 35 may be viewed by the Government as a last resort, but it will be used if necessary. It must be emphasised that the primary duty to ensure that Bills are within legislative competence is placed, by the Scotland Act 1998, upon the Scottish Executive. It is the Scottish Ministers (and the Scottish Parliament's Presiding Officer) who are given the duty of certifying that the provisions of a Bill are within legislative competence.[47] No such duty is placed upon the UK Law Officers who in contrast have been given a discretionary power to refer a question concerning competence to the JCPC.

It is a tribute to the efficient liaison between the Scottish Executive and the Government, facilitated by the Scotland Office, that there has so far been no need to use section 33 or section 35. While I would not pretend that there have never been differences of opinion between Whitehall and Edinburgh, these have been resolved amicably in the course of a Bill's progress from policy to enactment. Although I have not used my powers under section 33 they serve a useful function nonetheless. My power to bring a particular provision before the JCPC is an incentive to the Scottish Executive to focus on keeping within the boundaries of devolved competence.

---

[47] Scotland Act 1998, s 31. Scottish Executive Bills must be certified by a member of the Executive and by the Presiding Officer. Members' Bills are certified by the Presiding Officer only.

The JCPC is the court of last resort for determining issues of competence regarding devolution. It has jurisdiction to hear questions relating to the competences and functions of the devolved legislative and executive authorities established in Scotland, Northern Ireland and Wales.[48] Cases can reach the JCPC through four routes:

1. Direct reference of a Bill of the Scottish Parliament or Northern Ireland Assembly, to be heard in the JCPC as a court of first instance.
2. Appeals from certain superior courts.
3. References from: Appellate courts, including the House of Lords; and any court, made on the application of the appropriate Law Officer.
4. References by the Law Officers of issues that are not the subject of current legislation or litigation.

By April 2002 nine devolution issues cases (all involving ECHR points) had been appealed to the JCPC from other courts and I intervened in five.[49] Under section 103 of the Scotland Act 1998 the JCPC is composed of Lords of Appeal in Ordinary (sitting or retired, and still under 75) and those who hold or have held 'high judicial office.'[50] This means, in respect of the latter category, judges of the Court of Session and of the English and Northern Irish High Court or Court of Appeal (who have been appointed to the Privy Council) and the Lord Chancellor. The quorum is three but benches of five, or (rarely) seven, may be convened. Thus far all the benches have been five-strong.

The role of the House of Lords, acting in its judicial capacity as the final court of appeal in civil cases arising from the Scottish courts,[51] is affected in two ways by the Scotland Act 1998. Firstly, paragraph 32 of Schedule 6 provides:

> Any devolution issue which arises in judicial proceedings in the House of Lords shall be referred to the Judicial Committee unless the House considers it more appropriate, having regard to all the circumstances, that it should determine the issue.

Secondly, section 103(1) provides: 'Any decision of the Judicial Committee in proceedings under this Act . . . shall be binding in all legal proceedings (other than proceedings before the Committee).' Consequently, for devolution issues the House of Lords has, in effect, ceased to be the final court of appeal in civil

---

[48] Jurisdiction provided by: Scotland Act 1998, ss 33, 103, Sch 6; Northern Ireland Act 1998, ss 11, 82, Sch 10; Government of Wales Act 1998, Sch 8; Judicial Committee (Devolution Issues) Rules 1999, SI 1999/665; and Judicial Committee (Powers in Devolution Cases) Order 1999, SI 1999/1320.

[49] I intervened and appeared personally before the JCPC in the following cases: *Brown v Stott*; *Montgomery and Coulter v HM Advocate; HM Advocate v McIntosh;* and *A (A Mental Patient) v Scottish Ministers.* I made written submissions to the JCPC in *Buchanan v McLean.*

[50] Defined by s 25 of the Appellate Jurisdiction Act 1876.

[51] The practice of taking civil appeals to the House of Lords at Westminster was established after the Union of 1707 and confirmed in the Appellate Jurisdiction Act 1876.

matters. This is perhaps not so significant a change since the House of Lords is already not supreme in relation to questions of European Union law.

G. ROLE OF THE ADVOCATE GENERAL IN COURT PROCEEDINGS

In cases where I litigate in court as Advocate General under the provisions of the Scotland Act 1998, I am ultimately responsible for giving instructions about the litigation although the practical and continuing conduct of litigation will be carried out by Counsel instructed on behalf of the Solicitor to the Advocate General. The situation is different in such cases where I choose to appear personally in court as Advocate General to conduct the case because then I am essentially acting as litigant in person.[52]

In other cases I may occasionally appear in Court in a representative capacity. In such cases I act as Senior Counsel to represent the Government position taking instruction from whichever department has been accepted as the lead department. The first case in which I appeared on this basis was *Re Lord Gray's Motion*.[53] In that case I appeared before the Committee of Privileges of the House of Lords. This was an unprecedented occasion in which a legal question was referred to the Committee during the passage of the House of Lords Bill.[54] As the preparation and Court time involved in such cases is very time consuming, my appearances on this basis will necessarily be rare.

In some cases also a litigant may raise proceedings against the Advocate General rather than the Minister in charge of a department.[55] In such cases the substantive policy responsibility for the Court proceedings lies with the relevant department.[56]

H. CABINET COMMITTEES

The Advocate General is a member of four Ministerial Cabinet Committees and Sub-Committees:[57]

---

[52] As in the cases cited in n 48 above.

[53] *Re Lord Gray's Motion* 2000 SLT 37; 2000 SC (HL) 46.

[54] As Cabinet Office Ministers were responsible for taking the House of Lords Bill through Parliament, the Cabinet Office acted as the instructing department.

[55] The Crown Suits (Scotland) Act 1857 and the Crown Proceedings Act 1947 as amended by paras 2 and 7 of Sch 8 to the Scotland Act 1998.

[56] Following devolution a number of minor statutory functions were transferred from the Lord Advocate to the Advocate General, largely by the Transfer of Functions (Lord Advocate and Advocate General for Scotland) Order 1999, SI 1999/679.

[57] The membership and terms of reference of Cabinet Committees are published but information relating to their proceedings or any briefing or correspondence relating to them, are classified and are not made public.

—Nations and Regions
   To consider policy and other issues arising from devolution to Scotland, Wales and Northern Ireland; and to develop policy on the English regions.
—Legislative Programme
   To prepare and submit to Cabinet drafts of the Queen's speeches to Parliament and proposals for the legislative programme; to monitor the progress of Bills in preparation and during their passage through Parliament; to review the programme as necessary; to examine all draft Bills; to consider the Parliamentary handling of Government Bills; European Community documents and Private Members' business, and such other related matters as may be necessary; and to keep under review the Government's policy in relation to issues of Parliamentary procedures.
—Incorporation of the ECHR
   To consider policy and other issues arising from the Government's decision to legislate for the incorporation of ECHR in UK law and to oversee implementation of the relevant legislation.
—Freedom of Information
   To consider policy and other issues arising from the Government's decision to legislate on freedom of information and from legislation on data protection; and to oversee implementation of the relevant legislation.

Cabinet Committees provide a framework for collective consideration of, and decisions on, major policy issues and matters of significant public interest. The Committees meet to resolve disputes and take decisions. Non-contentious issues can generally be agreed in correspondence. Committees relieve the pressure on Cabinet itself by settling business in a smaller forum or at a lower level, or at least by clarifying issues and defining points of disagreement. They enable decisions to be fully considered by those Ministers most closely involved in a way that ensures that Government as a whole can be expected to accept responsibility for them. Committees act by implied devolution of authority from the Cabinet and their decisions therefore have the same formal status as Cabinet decisions.

I. PARLIAMENTARY QUESTIONS (PQS)

Parliamentary Questions are important because they give Members of Parliament the opportunity to hold Ministers of the Crown accountable for our decisions and actions.[58] Such accountability is at the core of our system of parliamentary democracy. The two basic forms of parliamentary questions are questions for oral answer, on the floor of the House of Commons, and for written answer as a supplement to each day's Hansard. The purpose of a

---

[58] Other opportunities to hold Ministers to account include questioning Ministers before Select Committees. I have given evidence to a Select Committee on two occasions.

Parliamentary Question, as stated in its classical form by Erskine May,[59] is either to seek information or to press for action. It should engage the responsibilities of the government and it is not in order to seek to question one Minister on matters for which another is more properly responsible. Following devolution, the Speaker has ruled that it is not in order to question Ministers about matters which are the preserve of the devolved institutions.

I answer questions in the House of Commons on a monthly basis following questions to the Secretary of State for Scotland. From my appointment in May 1999 to the end of the last Parliament there were 14 sessions of Parliamentary Questions. I was asked 67 oral and written questions on a range of matters such as: the number and type of devolution issues cases; my appearances before the JCPC; the exercise of my section 33 powers; constituency cases on which my Office had given advice to UK Departments; and questions concerning the implementation and functioning of the Human Rights Act 1998. On several occasions I have been asked about possible advice on specific matters that I may have given to UK Departments. However, because of the long-standing convention that neither the fact that the Law Officers have advised on a matter, nor the content of any advice which they may have given, is disclosed outside Government (even in Parliament) I have been unable to give any specific information.

J. CONCLUSION

During debates on the Scotland Bill Lord Rodger of Earlsferry predicted the following future for the Advocate General:

> It is, however, a post of particular sensitivity. I suspect that the post will prove to be a bed of nails for the holder. He or she is unlikely to win many friends. It will be a difficult post.[60]

My role as Advocate General has been challenging, but rewarding, and I hope that more than a few friends have been won. In particular, I work closely with the two other UK Law Officers concerning: Law Officers' opinions; consultations about Scottish Parliament Bills and devolution issues; and regular meetings to discuss matters of common interest.

My main task is ensuring that, following devolution, the UK Government continues to receive authoritative advice on Scots law, including the impact on Scotland of European law and human rights. I have contributed to the stability of the devolution settlement by ensuring that the settlement is understood in Government and that legal issues are clearly identified and resolved. Apart from my participation in court actions, this involves a great deal of day to day work

---

[59] D W Limon and R W McKay, *Erskine May—Parliamentary Practice*, 22nd edn (Butterworths, London, 1997).
[60] HL Deb 6 Oct 1998, col 375.

behind the scenes—in the legal advice which I and my officials give to the Government, in scrutiny of Bills and consideration of devolution issues raised. Devolution, and the incorporation of human rights into domestic law, presents a significant challenge to Scots law and Scots lawyers and I am fortunate to play a part in these significant changes to the constitution of the United Kingdom.

5

Constitutionalising the Role of the Judge: Scotland and the New Order

STEPHEN TIERNEY*

'*To what quarter will you look to remedy an infringement of the constitution, if you will not look to the judiciary?*' John Marshall (1788)

A. INTRODUCTION

I N ROBERT BOLT'S play *A Man for All Seasons*, Sir Thomas More, who is subject to numerous conflicting loyalties, finds himself torn between his duty to the law and his own sense of morality. He resolves this difficulty by representing the latter as God's law with which he as Lord Chancellor is ill-equipped to engage: 'The currents and eddies of right and wrong . . . I can't navigate . . . I'm no voyager. But in the thickets of the law, oh, there I'm a forester.'[1] In sixteenth century England, about to embark on over a century of crude constitutional brinkmanship between King and Parliament, this rigid distinction was difficult enough to sustain, and indeed it came under severe trial during the constitutional upheavals of the next hundred years.[2] But in any mature democracy equipped with a modern constitution which vests judges with the tasks of defining the competence of each of the branches of government, and in those systems which are also federal, the balance of power between centre and region, judges to a far greater extent are inevitably embroiled in heavily politicised disputes which seem to require of them both forestry *and* navigational skills. Still there are those who hanker after an imaginary golden age of judicial self-abnegation contending that judges should establish clear points of demarcation between

---

* Lecturer in Law, University of Edinburgh. Earlier versions of this paper were presented in seminars at the University of Manchester, King's College, London and the European University Institute in Florence. I am grateful to delegates at these seminars and to an anonymous referee for helpful comments. The chapter updates an article which was originally published at (2001) 5 *Edinburgh Law Review* 49–72.

[1] *A Man for All Seasons*, Act One, in R Bolt , *Three Plays* (1963).
[2] *Dr Bonham's Case*, (1610) 8 Co Rep 114: *Case of Proclamations* (1611) 12 Co Rep 74; *Case of Ship Money* (*R v Hampden*) (1637) 3 St Tr 825.

constitutional law and its underlying value system.[3] For others, the complex inter-connections of the differing strands of political power in any modern constitutional system make hard and fast distinctions between law and morality and law and politics the stuff of fantasy. No such divisions are possible and instead judges should confront the task of constitutional adjudication conscious of both the intricacies of their job and of their own fallibility; they should be prepared to discuss transparently the process of dispute resolution in which they are engaged and the value judgements they bring to bear in defining the underlying norms of the state's political arrangements.

This is the task with which UK judges have now been vested as they face the challenge presented by an unprecedented period of constitutional change. In the past four years this process has been most keenly felt in Scotland with the establishment of devolved government under the Scotland Act 1998 which in turn gave effect to the Human Rights Act 1998 more than one year before it came into force throughout the UK. This chapter will address this interim period as a case study in the dynamics of British constitutional reform asking in particular what likely effects these change will have on the role of the judiciary.

The chapter will begin in Part B by arguing that the wide-ranging institutional reforms in the UK will in due course lead to a new constitutionalism and that the courts will be central to this development as judges are called upon to interpret and develop these changes. It will also contend that judges will, in addition, be required to reconsider their own role in this process and to assess the legitimacy of the courts as presently constituted to meet these new challenges. In this context the chapter will then address early cases involving devolution issues in Scotland which have already impacted on the judicial role in two main respects. The first involves the task of judicial self-definition, whereby judges evaluate the extent to which they themselves satisfy the requirements of due process in terms of two related matters: judicial impartiality and judicial independence.[4] The second element of the judicial role which has been called into question is concerned not so much with whether judges in an institutional sense satisfy the demands of procedural fairness but more with the substantive aspects of constitutional adjudication. In other words, with how judges confront the task of balancing the competing interests between individual and state and between centre and devolved unit which emerge from the new constitutional arrangements. Here, however, an element of self-examination will also arise as judges in undertaking these balancing exercises will be required to situate *themselves* within these power struggles and to adopt an approach which recognises not only the

---

[3] R Bork, *The Tempting of America: The Political Seduction of the Law* (Sinclair-Stevenson, London, 1990). Bork, at 354–55 cites Thomas More's wistful longing for a clear distinction between law and morality with considerable approval.

[4] Lord Irvine has described these concepts as two sides of the same coin. Lord Irvine, 'Activism and Restraint: Human Rights and the Interpretative Process' [1999] *EHRLR* 350, 356. Parallels are also drawn between impartiality and independence by Lord Bingham (at para 18) in the recent Privy Council decision *Millar v Dickson* 2001 SLT 988.

limited power of other political actors but also the appropriate restrictions placed upon their own role which oblige them to avoid both excessive activism and undue restraint in adjudication.

The chapter will therefore move first (in Part C) to a consideration of the 'self-definition' issue considering how both judicial impartiality and judicial independence have been challenged by early 'devolution issue' cases requiring the courts to question the very fairness of the legal system itself. In terms of judicial impartiality important decisions have recently been handed down in both Scotland and England which leave unclear the permissible limits of extra-judicial comment on controversial matters. This could become a significant problem as judges are increasingly required to adjudicate on matters of political sensitivity. Secondly, the question of judicial independence raised in the case of *Starrs v Ruxton*[5] will be addressed. This is now a case of some celebrity since it represents the first occasion on which a member of the Scottish Executive was found to have acted unlawfully under the Scotland Act 1998. The fact that both impartiality and independence have arisen as contested issues so early in the life of the new constitutional settlement and the impact these early decisions have had on the Scottish system of government perhaps illustrates that one dynamic of constitutional change is that judicial involvement in the process is essentially reactive or reflexive. In other words, judges play a role in the development of substantive constitutional principles only when they are called upon to adjudicate upon them, and it is also only at this time that they are required to re-evaluate their own role within the ongoing process and their readiness to meet the new tasks with which they are confronted.

Part D will address the second element of the judicial role which has also been called into question in the early stages of constitutional change. The appropriate balance between activism and restraint arguably raises the most difficult issues for judges, because it is in defining the appropriate limits of judicial deference to the other organs of government, both central and devolved, that the courts will reveal their understandings of the purposes which underpin both the devolution and civil liberties projects represented by the Scotland Act 1998 and Human Rights Act 1998 respectively. In this section extensive reference will be made to the processes, both extra-Parliamentary and subsequently Parliamentary, which led to the passage of the Scotland Act. It will also explore at some length the different visions of sovereignty which dominated debate on the Scotland Bill and this will lead on to an analysis of the important case of *Whaley v Lord Watson of Invergowrie*[6] in which the Court of Session began to articulate its overall conception of the devolution settlement. A second case, *A (A Mental Patient) v Scottish Ministers*[7] has also forced the courts to analyse how active a role they ought to play in balancing the differing types of

---

[5] *Starrs v Ruxton* 2000 SLT 42.
[6] *Whaley v Lord Watson of Invergowrie* 2000 SC 125.
[7] *A (A Mental Patient) v Scottish Ministers* 2000 SLT 873, 2001 SLT 1331 (PC).

counter-majoritarian interest represented respectively by the two Acts. The Scotland Act 1998 is designed to secure sectional agendas and, in so doing, delimit the competence of the institutions of central government; the Human Rights Act 1998 accords enhanced levels of legal protection to certain civil and political rights even when they conflict with the policy choices of the plurality of citizens. This can of course lead the Human Rights Act 1998 into conflict with devolved government as much as with central government, and the case of *A (A Mental Patient)* is an early example of the difficulties judges will face in attempting to achieve an appropriate balance between these differing, and at times contrasting, projects.

The chapter will conclude by questioning the extent to which changes in self-definitional or due process elements of the judicial role, in terms of impartiality and independence, connect to questions about the substantive role the courts ought to play in modelling and refining constitutional change itself. Judges will inevitably provide the detail of constitutional change and in doing so will play a significant part in refining these changes altogether. In other words, a more active judiciary in constitutional matters seems to be an inevitable by-product of constitutional change. It may be, however, that the courts will assume greater legitimacy for their expanding role in determining the substance of constitutional change first, by imposing greater stringencies upon themselves in terms of impartiality and secondly, by helping to formalise their own relationship with the other branches of government in terms of judicial independence.

B.   CONSTITUTIONAL REFORM: TOWARDS A NEW CONSTITUTIONALISM

Extensive constitutional reform can fundamentally alter the *modus operandi* of the political system which brings it about. This process manifests itself in two ways. First, there are the obvious changes to the institutional structure within which the body politic operates. But secondly and more subtly, constitutional changes themselves affect the way in which the system of government is thought about and talked about. For example, the Scotland Act 1998 and the Human Rights Act 1998 are formalising the boundaries of constitutionally acceptable behaviour, but in doing so they also demand a more sophisticated understanding of what those boundaries are, creating as it were a new language with which constitutional actors must now engage. Thomas Paine famously wrote, 'constitutions are to liberty, what grammar is to language: they define its parts of speech, and practically construct them into syntax.'[8] This remark reflects the social-contractarian belief in the power of institutions to shape human organisation which today, in qualified forms, remains an article of faith for the liberal project. No attempt will be made here to engage with the question of liberalism's inherent validity but it is still possible to adapt Paine's analogy to a more

---

[8] PS Foner (ed), *The Complete Writings of Thomas Paine* (Citadel Press, New York, NY, 1945).

value-neutral context by suggesting that constitutions are to *politics* what grammar is to language. Employing this parallel, it can be argued that when important constitutional changes take place, the very rhetoric of political discourse has to reform, shaped increasingly as it will be by new institutional realities and by the parameters these realities impose upon future political development. In short, the likely by-product of institutional reform will be the constitutionalisation of political language.

With the present wave of constitutional reform we might, therefore, anticipate the emergence of a new political idiom in the UK. The *ad hoc* political constitution with which British constitutional lawyers have so long had to work is undergoing a period of almost unprecedented formalisation. Before addressing the likely impact of recent constitutional changes, it is worth recalling that traditionally the British political system has been discussed more in 'political' than 'constitutional' terms. It is certainly the case that the language of the British constitution has for long been constrained by a very flexible institutional context which has largely disabled any meaningful assessment of the constitutionality of political behaviour. The weakness of the UK's constitutional infrastructure was exposed in recent decades by the dismantling of the so-called post-war political consensus,[9] a behavioural change which resulted in the increased preparedness of transient political elites to exploit informal constitutional norms for short-term political advantage.[10] The consequence of the flexible constitution has, therefore, been the ever closer elision of the political and the constitutional. Neither are discrete operatives in any case, but the willingness of successive governments in recent times to take political advantage of the license provided by lax constitutional structures, and the dearth of institutional safeguards to deter this promiscuity, have combined to render criticism of such opportunism on the grounds of its constitutionality virtually meaningless.[11]

This may now be changing as the UK moves, perhaps, from a political constitution to a new constitutional politics. As Parliament begins to articulate constitutional principles through legislation this process will elevate the role of judges at the expense of politicians to the position of pivotal constitutional actors, particularly as the courts are called upon to define the details of the institutional plate changes taking place below the political surface. To summarise, this process of constitutional development is likely to occur in three stages. First, a period of constitutional formalisation through legislation will, secondly, be consolidated as new constitutional principles are developed and refined through seminal judicial decisions. This is inevitable given both the enhanced role for

---

[9] D Marquand, *The Unprincipled Society: New Demands and Old Politics* (Cape, London, 1988).
[10] P Hennessy, *The Hidden Wiring: Unearthing the British Constitution* (Victor Gollancz, London, 1995) and *Muddling Through: Power, Politics and the Quality of Government in Post-war Britain* (Victor Gollancz, London, 1996).
[11] C Graham and T Prosser (eds), *Waiving the Rules: the Constitution under Thatcherism* (Open University Press, Milton Keynes, 1988).

judges which much of the legislation anticipates and the fact that both the Scotland Act 1998 and the Human Rights Act 1998 have considerable ambiguities at their core which will demand judicial clarification. Thirdly, in the longer term, we might envisage the emergence of a new constitutionalism which is adequate to accommodate the changing patterns of these institutional developments and which can also provide the syntax for their further refinement.

The Scotland Act: early judicial responses

If a new constitutionalism is to emerge in the UK then the application of the Scotland Act 1998 and its interaction with the Human Rights Act 1998 will influence much of this development. Already this inter-relationship has provided a series of tests for the Scottish judiciary. The remainder of this chapter will explore how judges have responded to these tests in terms of the related due process issues of judicial impartiality and judicial independence and of judicial restraint in the process of adjudication. Each of these will be addressed in turn in Parts II and III after an initial discussion of how the cases in which the Scotland Act 1998 and Human Rights Act 1998 have interacted have come about.

Typically, the early devolution cases in Scotland have taken the form of human rights claims arising from the obligations imposed by the Scotland Act 1998 upon the institutions of devolved Scottish government to behave compatibly with rights enshrined within the European Convention for the Protection of Human Rights and Fundamental Freedoms (ECHR). Both the Scottish Executive ('the Executive') and the Scottish Parliament are required to act and legislate respectively, in ways that are not incompatible with 'Convention rights.'[12] Convention rights is itself a term of art with the Scotland Act 1998 providing (section 126(1)) that it carries the same meaning in the Scotland Act 1998 as it does in section 1(1) of the Human Rights Act 1998.[13] Since cases seeking to challenge the Parliament for passing incompatible legislation have hitherto been rare[14] the following description of the procedure by which challenges may be brought as 'devolution issues' will focus on actions brought against members of the Executive.

Claims against members of the Executive that they are acting outwith their lawful competence as defined by the Scotland Act 1998 are termed 'devolution issues'. The procedure for raising a devolution issue is set out in Schedule 6 to the Scotland Act 1998[15] which also defines what types of incompatible behav-

---

[12] Duties imposed by Scotland Act 1998, s 57(2) in respect of the Executive and s 29(2)(d) in relation to the Parliament.

[13] Convention rights are defined by s 1(1) of the Human Rights Act 1998 as the rights and fundamental freedoms set out in Arts 2 to 12 and 14 of the ECHR, Arts 1 to 3 of the First Protocol, and Arts 1 and 2 of the Sixth Protocol, as read with Arts 16 to 18 of the ECHR.

[14] *A (A Mental Patient)*, above, n 7.

[15] Which is given effect by s 98.

iour may be subject to an action. The crucial provision which has been the focus of all devolution issues thus far raised in respect of the Executive is the question of 'whether a purported or proposed exercise of a function by a member of the Scottish Executive is, or would be, incompatible with any of the Convention rights',[16] a provision which reflects the obligation imposed upon the Executive by section 57(2).

The major provisions of the Scotland Act 1998 came into force on 1 July 1999 and since then most members of the Executive have been obliged to act compatibly with Convention rights. The one notable exception is the Lord Advocate who has been bound by these provisions since 20 May 1999.[17] Since every devolution issue so far raised in challenge to an act of a member of the Executive has involved the Lord Advocate, there was in effect a period of 18 months in which the prosecutorial authorities in Scotland were under a duty to act compatibly with Convention rights before their counterparts in the rest of the UK came under a similar obligation as public authorities per section 6(1) of the Human Rights Act 1998.[18] As a result, in the period between 20 May 1999 and 20 May 2000, 588 minutes were served on the Lord Advocate intimating that a devolution issue had been raised in court proceedings, of which 16 resulted in successful challenges.[19] This is a relatively small number, but of these, certain seminal decisions have sent ripples through the Scottish criminal justice system. These challenges have also required the judiciary to begin to articulate new constitutional principles with which to delineate the respective new relationships between Edinburgh and Westminster and between the devolution project set out in the Scotland Act 1998 and the UK-wide bill of rights represented by the Human Rights Act 1998. The first steps the courts have taken in performing this task have been in analysing the institutional framework of the legal system itself, evaluating its, and by implication their, adequacy for meeting the new adjudicatory demands placed upon judges.

---

[16] Scotland Act 1998, Sch 6(1)(d).

[17] Scotland Act 1998 (Commencement) Order 1998, SI 1998/3178. The Scottish Parliament has been subject to a similar limitation to its legislative competence per s 29(2)(d) since 1 July 1999.

[18] Effect was given inter alia to s 57(2) and to s 29(2)(d) by a transitional provision contained in s 129(2) Scotland Act 1998 which provided that s 57(2) would have the same effect until the time when the Human Rights Act 1998 was fully in force as it would have after that time. See also the Human Rights Act 1998 (Commencement No 2) Order 2000, SI 2000/ 1851. Attempts to argue that prosecuting authorities in England were under such a duty before 2 October 2000 failed: *R v Director of Public Prosecutions, ex p Kebiline and others* [1999] 3 WLR 972. See also *R v Hertfordshire County Council, ex p Green Environmental Industries Ltd* [2000] 1 All ER 773.

[19] *Crown Office and Procurator Fiscal Service* statistics.

C. DUE PROCESS AND THE TASK OF JUDICIAL SELF-DEFINITION

(1) Judicial impartiality

A major test for the judiciary within the UK's new constitutional arrangements is its capacity to act and to be seen to be acting impartially in this new and highly politicised environment.[20] This issue has already posed problems for one judge, Lord McCluskey.[21] He published a series of articles in a Sunday newspaper one of which criticised the ECHR and the impact it was having on Scots law in the post-devolution period. In this article Lord McCluskey was particularly critical of a decision of the High Court of Justiciary which had found part of the Road Traffic Act 1988 to be incompatible with Article 6(1) of the Convention.[22] Commenting on this decision he stated:

> I warned in the Reith Lectures (1986) that the Canadian Charter—copied from the ECHR—would provide 'a field day for crackpots, a pain in the neck for judges and legislators, and a goldmine for lawyers'. Prophetic or what?

And in direct reference to the Human Rights Act 1998:

> Somebody suggested to me that it was a bit like sailing in the Titanic toward a legal iceberg. My own fear is that the better simile (*sic*) is with an avalanche; all we can hear at the moment is a distant roar; but it is coming and we are going to have to struggle to avoid being buried in new claims of right.[23]

Lord McCluskey subsequently sat as part of a bench of three in a criminal appeal whereupon the appellants accused him of bias. This issue reverted to a separately constituted court which held that the appeal should be re-heard by three different judges. The Court found that the allegation of bias was well-founded. In his judgment for the Court Lord Rodger, the Lord Justice General, considered that Lord McCluskey's published comments would create in the mind of an informed observer an apprehension of bias against the Convention and against the rights deriving from it, even if in fact no bias existed in the way in which Lord McCluskey and the other judges had actually determined the scope of those rights in disposing of the issues in the case.

Lord McCluskey's wrongdoing seemed to derive from the tone of the newspaper article which, according to Lord Rodger, 'painted a picture of the Convention as something which threatened danger to the Scottish legal system'. Judges, said Lord Rodger, like other members of the public and other members of the legal profession, are entitled to criticise developments in the law in a measured way. Accordingly,

---

[20] *Stott v Minogue* 2001 SLT (Sh Ct) 25.
[21] *Hoekstra v Lord Advocate (No 3)* 2000 SCCR 367.
[22] *Brown v Stott* 2001 SC (PC) 43; [2001] 2 All ER 97.
[23] Cited by Lord Rodger in *Hoekstra v Lord Advocate (No 3)*, above, n 21, at 376, see also 380–81.

[t]he position would have been very different if all that Lord McCluskey had done was to publish, say, an article in a legal journal drawing attention, in moderate language, to what he perceived to be the drawbacks of incorporating the Convention into our law.[24]

However,

what judges cannot do with impunity is to publish either criticism or praise of such a nature or in such language as to give rise to a legitimate apprehension that, when called upon in the course of their judicial duties to apply that particular branch of the law, they will not be able to do so impartially.[25]

This case follows close on the heels of two English cases which also concerned the issue of judicial impartiality.[26] In the leading case of *Locabail*, the Court of Appeal actually dealt with five separate actions each of which involved allegations of bias. In categorising the types of situation in which judges should recuse themselves from sitting, the Court did not consider that extra-curricular utterances in general 'whether in textbooks, lectures, speeches, articles, interviews, reports or responses to consultation papers' were necessarily such a category.[27] However, such comments can still give rise to a real danger of bias and indeed in one of the five cases[28] the court upheld an appeal in respect of articles which appeared in legal journals. Here, as in *Hoekstra*, the tenor of the articles was central to the decision, with the Court of Appeal emphasising 'the tone of the recorder's opinions and the trenchancy with which they were expressed'.[29]

Cases like *Hoekstra* and *Locabail/Timmins* call into question the broader issue of extra-judicial utterances particularly since, in recent years, judges have become far more vocal in terms of speeches, academic articles and other public pronouncements than was traditionally the case.[30] In England this trend is

---

[24] *Hoekstra v Lord Advocate (No 3)*, above, n 21, at 381.

[25] *Ibid* at 382.

[26] *R v Bow Street Metropolitan Stipendiary Magistrates, ex p Pinochet Ugarte (No2)* [1999] 1 All ER 577 and *Locabail (UK) Ltd v Bayfield Properties* [2000] 1 All ER 65; [2000] 2 WLR 870. See K Malleson, 'Judicial Bias and Disqualification after *Pinochet (No2)*' (2000) 63 *MLR* 119; T H Jones, 'Judicial Bias and Disqualification in the Pinochet case' [1999] *PL* 391; A A Olowofoyeku, 'The *nemo judex* Rule: The Case Against Automatic Disqualification' [2000] *PL* 456 and D Williams, 'Bias; The Judges and the Separation of Powers' [2000] *PL* 45.

[27] *Locabail Ltd v Bayfield Properties*, above, n 26, at 77.

[28] *Timmins v Gormley* [2000] 1 All ER 65; [2000] 2 WLR 870.

[29] *Locabail Ltd v Bayfield Properties*, above, n 26, at 91. The Court (also at 91) stated: '[a]nyone writing in an area in which he sits judicially has to exercise considerable care not to express himself in terms which indicate that he has preconceived views which are so firmly held that it may not be possible for him to try a case with an open mind.'

[30] In the public law area see for example: Lord Browne-Wilkinson, 'The Infiltration of a Bill of Rights' [1992] *PL* 406; Sir Stephen Sedley, 'Human Rights: A 21st Century Agenda' [1995] *PL* 386; Sir John Laws, 'The Constitution: Morals and Rights' [1996] *PL* 622; Lord Woolf, 'Bringing Home the European Convention on Human Rights' (1997) *Denning Law Journal* 1; Lord Hope, 'Devolution and Human Rights' (1998) *EHRLR* 367; Sir John Laws, 'The Limitations of Human Rights' [1998] *PL* 254; Lord Hoffmann, 'Human Rights and the House of Lords' (1999) 62 *MLR* 159 and Lord Bingham, *The Business of Judging: Selected Essays and Speeches* (Oxford University Press, Oxford, 2000).

particularly noticeable since the revocation of the Kilmuir Rules in 1987 which
had required the Lord Chancellor's approval for public appearances by the judiciary. However, these recent decisions in both Scotland and England beg the
question how far judges may go in commenting on current legal issues. It is a
moot point whether allegations of bias will be entertained when they refer to
comments made by a judge either while sitting in judgment in an earlier case, or
in the course of Parliamentary debate.[31]

Much remains to be decided on this issue as judicial commentaries on controversial issues continue to be published. One interesting example which may
yet arise in the Scottish context concerns a speech made by Lord Hope at the
University of Glasgow[32] subsequently published in the *Juridical Review* in
which he discussed whether final appeal from the Court of Session to the House
of Lords is a reserved matter under the Scotland Act 1998. The relevant provision in the Scotland Act 1998 is Schedule 5, Para 1, Part 1[33] which classifies certain aspects of the Constitution as reserved matters.[34] This reservation was
controversial because it resulted from a Government amendment and in fact
narrowed a general reservation of the constitution which had appeared in the
Scotland Bill when it was first published.[35] The Conservative Party questioned
the purpose behind this amendment during debate on the Bill, querying in particular why the Government was seeking to replace a general provision with a
seemingly more narrow one in an area as crucial as the constitution.[36] Michael
Ancram for the Opposition admitted confusion over this amendment and
expressed concern about the role the courts would be required to play in determining what was now devolved and what reserved.[37] There was little clarification offered by the Government on this question and, accordingly, the vacuum
left for the courts to fill seems to be potentially quite wide.

---

[31] For example, Lord McCluskey in the House of Lords during debate on the Human Rights Bill
was no less outspoken than he was in the offending newspaper article. HL Deb 3 Nov 1997, col 1266.
On the question of fixed judicial views formed in an earlier case see *Greenwich LBC v Coleman*
[2001] 2 CL 330, although in this instance the two cases were very closely related.

[32] Lord Hope, The James Wood Lecture, 27 February 1998: published as 'Taking the Case to
London—is it all over?' 1998 *JR* 135.

[33] Scotland Act 1998, s 30(1) provides that Sch 5 shall have effect.

[34] Those aspects of the Constitution which are reserved are: the Crown, including succession to
the Crown and a regency; the Union of the Kingdoms of Scotland and England; the Parliament of
the United Kingdom; and the continued existence of the High Court of Justiciary and of the Court
of Session.

[35] The original paragraph read: 'The constitution, including the Crown, the succession to the
Crown and a regency and the Parliament of the United Kingdom, are reserved matters.' The amendment was tabled by Henry McLeish MP for the Government on the 3rd day of the Bill's report stage
on 19 May 1998.

[36] Henry McLeish replied that amendment was simply an attempt to clarify the meaning of para
1, HC Deb 19 May 1998, col 789.

[37] 'That which is left out is important, because a catch-all provision is being replaced by a specific provision that will weigh heavily in the minds of the courts, which may have to deal with the
question of what are devolved matters and what are reserved matters.' HC Deb 19 May 1998, col
788.

It was in this context that Lord Hope asked in his speech whether or not final appeal in civil matters from the Court of Session to the House of Lords is a reserved matter or whether it could potentially be abolished by the Scottish Parliament.[38] He came to the view that it was not reserved but also argued that the Scottish Parliament should not remove this right even though it was empowered to do so.[39] Lord Hope's view that this matter is devolved is unlikely to be universally shared and if the Scottish Parliament were to attempt to remove the right of final appeal to the House of Lords, such a move could well be challenged before the Judicial Committee of the Privy Council, in which event Lord Hope would possibly have to consider whether it would be appropriate for him to form part of the bench. This is of course all entirely hypothetical but even as a bizarre and improbable scenario it may serve to illustrate the difficulties which can potentially stem from extra-judicial activities in light of the decisions in *Locabail* and *Hoekstra*.

(2) Judicial Independence

A second aspect of the task of judicial self-definition which has arisen in the context of procedural fairness since devolved government was returned to Scotland is that of judicial independence.[40] The most prominent case to date in which a devolution issue has been raised was *Starrs v Ruxton* which called into question the independence of temporary sheriffs who had formed an important element in the administration of Scottish justice for nearly 30 years since the passage of the Sheriff Courts (Scotland) Act 1971. This case was a particular landmark because it was the first in which the Lord Advocate as a member of the Executive was found to have acted incompatibly with Convention rights and thereby *ultra vires* section 57(2) of the Scotland Act 1998.[41]

In this case Starrs and his co-accused raised a devolution issue in the course of their trial claiming that the temporary sheriff trying the case did not constitute an 'independent and impartial tribunal' within the meaning of Article 6(1) of the ECHR, and that the Lord Advocate, as a member of the Executive, by bringing a prosecution before a temporary sheriff through his representative the procurator fiscal, had acted incompatibly with the Convention rights of the accused contrary to section 57(2). The High Court of Justiciary on appeal from the Sheriff Court upheld this claim in a decision which took the Scottish Justice Department by surprise and emphasised that the courts were taking the issue of judicial independence very seriously. Since *Starrs*, however, there have been

[38] Lord Hope, above, n 32, 143.
[39] *Ibid*, at 148.
[40] A O'Neill, 'The European Convention and the Independence of the Judiciary—The Scottish Experience' (2000) 63 *MLR* 429.
[41] S Tierney, 'The Scotland Act and Temporary Sheriffs: *Starrs v Ruxton*' (2000) 4 *Edin LR* 223–28.

signs that the courts are becoming more cautious in their enforcement of the independence principle. The High Court of Justiciary on Appeal has subsequently modified the position taken in *Starrs* finding that the appointment of temporary sheriffs is not per se a violation of Article 6(1) and concluding that the relevant provision of the Sheriff Courts (Scotland) Act 1971[42] permits such appointments in certain circumstances and that these circumstances can be construed fairly widely and do not limit the appointment of temporary sheriffs to temporary emergencies.[43]

Similarly the courts have not extended the decision in *Starrs* to the case of temporary judges. The status of these judges was raised in *Clancy v Caird (No1)*[44] where, during a case before a temporary judge, one of the parties raised a devolution issue arguing that he was not an independent and impartial tribunal per Article 6(1). The case was reported to the Inner House of the Court of Session where two main arguments were presented. The first, which reflected the principal finding in *Starrs*, contended that the temporary judge lacked security of tenure and so did not meet the Article 6(1) test, and the second, that the judge in question, who continued to practice at the bar, might be subject to conflicts of interest. The Inner House found (in a way not dissimilar to the decision in *Gibbs v Ruxton*) that the appointment and use of temporary judges to hear cases, where the Crown was not involved in the claim, did not breach Convention rights. The Court adopted the approach of the European Court of Human Rights and applied both subjective and objective tests to assess impartiality and independence. What was crucial to its final decision was the issue of security of tenure which the Court found temporary judges did enjoy during the period of their appointment. Consequently, the absence of a guarantee of reappointment was not something which would affect their independence. Another feature which influenced this decision was the Lord President's control of the allocation of temporary judges to particular cases and the systems in place which would preclude the possibility of their sitting in potentially sensitive cases. Finally, the second argument was also not fatal to the independence of the temporary judge. Although he remained in practice, there were institutional safeguards in place such as the judicial oath and declinature which sufficiently guaranteed his independence.

---

[42] Sheriff Courts (Scotland) Act 1971, s 11(2)(c).

[43] *Gibbs v Ruxton* 2000 SLT 310. The Judicial Committee of the Privy Council has, however, recently held that persons convicted before temporary sheriffs in the period between the coming into force of s 57(2) Scotland Act 1998 and the decision in *Starrs v Ruxton* should be entitled to appeal against their convictions and should not be deemed, as was held by the High Court of Justiciary on Appeal, to have waived their Convention rights in this regard. *Millar v Dickson*, above, n 4.

[44] *Clancy v Caird* (No 1) 2000 SC 441; 2000 SLT 546.

D. THE JUDICIAL ROLE IN CONSTITUTIONAL CHANGE: ACTIVISM OR RESTRAINT

The assertive and speedy way in which the courts have reacted to the due process challenges to their own role might suggest that, in time, a judiciary better satisfied with the improvements made to its own institutional situation, and to the enhanced legitimacy such improvements give to judges, may be inclined to respond more vigorously to the second challenge posed to the courts by the ongoing process of constitutional change, namely, how to reach an appropriate balance between activism and restraint in the task of constitutional adjudication.[45]

Given that the Scotland Act 1998 and the Human Rights Act 1998 effectively re-write major areas of the UK's constitution and since both statutes contain a significant number of open-ended provisions which invite judicial elaboration, greater involvement by the judges in what have traditionally been seen as political aspects of the constitution is perhaps inevitable.[46] For many commentators a more prominent role for the courts in constitutional matters is, in any event, a welcome development. They argue that a more active judiciary will be beneficial if it serves to restrict the scope politicians enjoy to exploit the constitution for short-term political gain. The judicial guardianship of both devolution and the transposition of the ECHR into domestic law should, according to this view, mark new prioritisations within the British polity: of the principled over the strategic, and of the systematic in place of the opportunistic. This line of argument, however, seems to rest on an implicit acceptance of Dworkin's tentative suggestion that judges, when compared with other political actors, may provide a superior form of republican deliberation,[47] a proposition which is widely contested in the UK today by critics from (curiously) both the left and right wings of the political spectrum. The latter, in the shape of the Conservative Party, have been particularly opposed to the Human Rights Act 1998 which they sense will give judges very extensive powers which could be used ultimately to weaken Parliament's policy-making role. Similar concerns are to be found amongst members of the traditional left who have always distrusted the political inclinations of many judges. Critics such as John Griffith remain sceptical of an enhanced judicial role in areas which involve public policy and, like Conservative critics, his concerns are primarily with the Human Rights Act 1998 which he feels provides considerable scope for the application of specific ideological agendas.[48]

---

[45] Lord Steyn seems to hint at this in a recent Privy Council decision: 'it is a basic premise of the Convention system that only an entirely neutral, impartial, and independent judiciary can carry out the primary task of securing and enforcing Convention rights.' *Brown v Stott* 2001 SC (PC) 43 at 63G.

[46] C Harlow, 'Disposing of Dicey: From Legal Autonomy to Constitutional Discourse?' (2000) 48 *Political Studies* 356.

[47] R Dworkin, *Freedom's Law: The Moral Reading of the American Constitution* (Oxford University Press, Oxford, 1996), 31.

[48] J A G Griffith, 'The Brave New World of Sir John Laws' (2000) 63 *MLR* 159.

Despite these protests, a more active role for the judiciary seems inevitable in light of both the Human Rights Act 1998 and the Scotland Act 1998. Turning first to the Human Rights Act 1998, it contains provisions which first, invite a new and radical approach to statutory interpretation[49] and secondly, require judges to take account of the jurisprudence of the European Court of Human Rights (and that of the former Commission) in adjudicating on Convention rights.[50] This latter provision (s 2(1)) is particularly wide in its potential scope, leaving open to the courts the option of wholescale incorporation of Strasbourg precedents and perhaps also the adoption of the more purposive methods of adjudication which are applied by the European Court.[51] Similarly there are important sections in the Scotland Act 1998 which will require the courts to consider the very purpose of the devolution settlement as a whole.[52] For example, cases are likely to arise involving questions of *vires* and of the limits of devolved competence set out in section 28 (discussed below), and in the course of these disputes arguments will be presented which ask the courts to go beyond the literal meaning of the statute and to consider the fundamental constitutional parameters within which the Act as a whole operates and through which it interacts with other seminal pieces of legislation (most obviously the Human Rights Act 1998). At the heart of these disputes may emerge differing visions of what the entire devolution project seeks to achieve and this will consequently draw the courts into implicit, or indeed explicit, renderings of what they understand to be the guiding norms of the new relationship which the Scotland Act 1998 is carving out between Edinburgh and Westminster.

(1) Differing visions of the Scotland Act

Already the Court of Session has gone some way towards articulating its vision of the Scotland Act 1998 in the case of *Whaley v Lord Watson of Invergowrie*[53] where Lord Rodger, sitting this time as Lord President of the Court of Session, seemed to rebut any suggestion that the establishment of a Scottish Parliament

---

[49]   Human Rights Act 1998 s 3(1). See Lord Irvine, 'Activism and Restraint: Human Rights and the Interpretative Process' (1999) *EHRLR* 350; Lord Lester, 'Interpreting Statutes under the Human Rights Act' [1999] *SLR* 218; G Marshall, 'Two Kinds of Compatibility: More about Section 3 of the Human Rights Act 1998' [1999] *PL* 377; F Bennion, 'What Interpretation is "Possible" under Section 3(1) of the Human Rights Act 1998?' [2000] *PL* 77; S Grosz, J Beatson, and P Duffy , *Human Rights: The 1998 Act and the European Convention* (Sweet & Maxwell, London, 2000), ch 3, and S Tierney, 'Convention Rights and the Scotland Act: Redefining Judicial Roles' [2001] *PL* 38–49.

[50]   Human Rights Act 1998 s 2(1). See, S Grosz et al, above, n 49, ch 2; and Lord Lester and D Pannick (eds), *Human Rights Law and Practice* (Butterworths, London, 1999), at 21–3.

[51]   Bennion, above, n 49; and S Tierney, 'Devolution Issues and s 2(1) of the Human Rights Act' (2000) *EHRLR* 380–92.

[52]   At a more prosaic level there are also considerable ambiguities within the Act. Michael Ancram argued that the Scotland Bill was 'littered' with 'areas of potential conflict between Edinburgh and Westminster': HC Deb 12 Jan 1998, col 41.

[53]   *Whaley v Lord Watson of Invergowrie*, above, n 6.

promises to limit Westminster parliamentary sovereignty or that it marks the beginning of an inexorable process towards a federal system. Before addressing the Lord President's remarks in this case, it is instructive to consider how visions of the devolution settlement which differ widely from what appears to be Lord Rodger's approach have been constructed initially through the extra-Parliamentary, and subsequently by way of the Parliamentary, processes which led to the passage of the Scotland Act 1998.

For many political actors in Scotland (and not only those within the Scottish National Party (SNP)) devolution was expected to weaken Westminster's legislative supremacy at least insofar as it affects Scotland.[54] There are two linked arguments which together envisage a federal outcome to the devolution process begun by the Scotland Act 1998. The first is the contention that a distinctive constitutional tradition in Scotland survived the Union, a suggestion which has been hinted at from time to time by the Scottish courts.[55] The feeling in certain quarters was that the Scotland Act 1998 provided an opportunity to revitalise this tradition. Secondly, from the mid-1980s onwards, a popular movement for Scottish self-government gathered momentum which largely eschewed any search for an indigenous praxis stemming from Scotland's pre-1707 constitutional arrangements and which instead propagated an essentially political vision of sovereignty, arguing brusquely that the Scottish people were entitled to self-government by political right.

Turning first to the notion of a separate Scottish constitutional tradition, this thesis contests two of the assumptions which underpin the doctrine of parliamentary sovereignty: first, that the constitution is 'unwritten' and secondly, that all Acts of the Parliament are of equal value and are ultimately open to repeal by the UK Parliament. The constitution of the UK according to this line of argument is 'written' or is at least partially so, with particular reference being made to the modern foundation of the constitution through the Acts of Union of 1706 and 1707 which together are widely considered in Scotland to be a Treaty of Union.[56] From this process a new Parliament for Great Britain emerged which did not necessarily acquire all of the idiosyncratic trappings of its English predecessor among which most notably was the emerging notion of its own legislative supremacy. Instead, the argument continues, the Acts of Union are of higher constitutional value and certain aspects of them are not necessarily open to repeal by Parliament.

Certainly the Scottish courts have, on occasion, suggested that the Scottish legal system preserves a different constitutional tradition which accredits higher

[54] See also N Walker, 'Beyond the Unitary Conception of the British Constitution?' [2000] *PL* 383.

[55] *MacCormick v Lord Advocate* 1952 SC 396.

[56] JDB Mitchell, *Constitutional Law* 2nd edn (W Green, Edinburgh, 1968), 93–98 and C Munro, 'Scottish Devolution: Accommodating a Restless Nation', in S Tierney (ed), *Accommodating National Identity: New Approaches in International and Domestic Law* (Kluwer Law International, The Hague, 2000), 133–49 at 138.

status to the Acts of Union than to ordinary legislation and have thereby insinuated that Parliament itself may be bound by some of their more important terms. The dictum of Lord President Cooper in *MacCormick v Lord Advocate* is the most widely cited statement of this view:

> The principle of the unlimited sovereignty of Parliament is a distinctively English principle which has no counterpart in Scottish Constitutional Law. . . . Considering that the Union legislation extinguished the Parliaments of Scotland and England and replaced them by a new Parliament, I have difficulty in seeing why it should be supposed that the new Parliament of Great Britain must inherit all the peculiar characteristics of the English Parliament but none of the Scottish Parliament, as if all that happened was that Scottish representatives were admitted to the Parliament of England. This is not what was done.[57]

There have, however, been few such glimpses of a different and enduring Scottish tradition,[58] leading some to argue that the Acts of Union do not survive in any real legal sense as fundamental constitutional texts particularly given the numerous repeals and modifications to which they have been subjected[59] not the least of which is section 37 of the Scotland Act 1998 which provides that the two Acts of Union are to 'have effect subject to this Act'.

Turning to the more modern thesis of popular sovereignty, it is worth noting initially that Lord President Cooper's conclusion in *MacCormick* that the principle of the unlimited sovereignty of Parliament had no counterpart in Scottish constitutional law does not necessarily offer definitive guidance as to where, alternatively, sovereignty may be found within the Scottish constitution. It is perhaps partly on account of this vacuum that the political claims of popular sovereignty took on a quasi-legal dimension in both the extra-parliamentary campaign for devolution and in parliamentary debates on the Scotland Bill. The notion that sovereignty in Scotland is vested in the Scottish people who consequently have the right to determine their own political arrangements first emerged as a serious claim from the extra-parliamentary campaign for devolution in the 1980s and 1990s.

The impetus for constitutional reform in the modern era began in earnest with the Campaign for a Scottish Assembly (CSA) which was launched in 1985. In 1988 it issued the Claim of Right for Scotland which was drafted by a committee appointed by the CSA and which, in declaring the right of Scotland to self-government, had as its main thrust the claim that sovereignty in Scotland

---

[57] *MacCormick v Lord Advocate*, above, n 55, at 411.

[58] *Gibson v Lord Advocate* 1975 SLT 134. Attempts to raise this issue before the courts occur from time to time, see N Walker and C M G Himsworth, 'The Poll Tax and Fundamental Law' 1991 *JR* 45.

[59] *Pringle, Petitioner* 1991 SLT 330 and *Murray v Rogers* 1992 SLT 221. See also C Munro, *Studies in Constitutional Law* 2nd edn (Butterworths, London, 1999), 137–142. However, for the alternative view that the Acts of Union retain special legal significance see T B Smith, 'The Union of 1707 as Fundamental Law' [1957] *PL* 99; Mitchell, above, n 56, and N MacCormick, 'Does the United Kingdom have a Constitution?' (1978) 29 *NILQ* 1.

rests with the Scottish people. The Claim of Right called for a Scottish Constitutional Convention (the SCC) which was subsequently established (meeting for the first time in 1989) and vested with the task of drawing up proposals for home rule. Given the legitimacy it enjoyed amongst Scotland's political elite, involving inter alia the Labour and Liberal Democratic parties, local authorities, churches and the Scottish Trades Union Congress (STUC), the SCC acquired a high media profile which was reflected in the publicity attracted by its most important publication, 'Scotland's Claim, Scotland's Right',[60] which set out a detailed blueprint for devolution remarkably similar to the eventual model enacted through the Scotland Act 1998. What is particularly interesting about this document (bearing in mind the strong involvement of the Scottish Labour Party in the SCC) is that the Convention shared the earlier commitment of the CSA to the idea of popular sovereignty. As the SCC declared: 'we, gathered as the Scottish Constitutional Convention, do hereby acknowledge the sovereign right of the Scottish people to determine the form of Government best suited to their needs. . . .'[61]

The commitment of prominent politicians within the Scottish Labour Party, the SNP and the Liberal Democrats to the Scottish right of self-government whether stemming from constitutional history or from the notion of popular sovereignty was to be repeated frequently in the course of parliamentary debates on the Scotland Bill.[62] The crucial provision and the one which resulted in a heated dispute between these Scottish 'nationalists' and those who persistently reiterated the mantra of parliamentary sovereignty was clause 27 (now s 28). Section 28(1) empowers the Scottish Parliament to make laws, 'to be known as Acts of the Scottish Parliament.' The rest of the section is largely explanatory in nature until one comes to section 28(7) which reads: 'This section does not affect the power of the Parliament of the United Kingdom to make laws for Scotland'. This succinct provision at first sight seems a fairly straightforward reassertion of Parliament's self-ascribed supremacy but it does beg one very important question: whether Parliament retains the right to make laws for Scotland on devolved as well as reserved matters. By the traditional doctrine of Parliamentary sovereignty the answer to this is obvious but in Commons debate there was considerable confusion as to the intended effect of this subsection.

If section 28(7) is to be construed as a restatement of Parliament's legislative omnicompetence (and the frequent assertions made by Government ministers

---

[60] Published on 30 Nov 1995.

[61] This was signed by every Scottish Labour MP at the time with the exception of Tam Dalyell. Although advocating the modern notion of popular sovereignty, 'Scotland's Claim, Scotland's Right' also noted Scotland's differing constitutional tradition: 'This concept of sovereignty [the Westminster model] has always been unacceptable to the Scottish constitutional tradition of limited government or popular sovereignty.' See also N MacCormick, 'Is There a Constitutional Path to Scottish Independence?' (2000) 53 *Parliamentary Affairs* 721, 729–30.

[62] For example, Jim Wallace MP made reference to Lord President Cooper's dictum in *MacCormick*: HC Deb 28 Jan 1998, cols 358–59 (see also col 369).

during debate that sovereignty remains at Westminster[63] suggests it might), then it would appear to contrast with the SCC's understanding of Scottish devolution as 'a constitutional settlement in which the Scottish people, being sovereign, agree to the exercise of specified powers by Westminster but retain their sovereignty over all other matters.'[64] At a minimum the SCC's approach to the Scotland Act 1998 certainly appears to imply that the Westminster Parliament should not be in a position to legislate on devolved matters, a perspective which first, seems to be at odds with what the Government intended by section 28(7), and secondly, would subvert parliamentary sovereignty in a way not done since the passage of sections 2(1) and (4) of the European Communities Act 1972. The SCC, however, did seem to expect that, once created, the Scottish Parliament would assume an independent area of operation, leading in effect to a federal UK. Timothy Jones discusses the earlier assertion of popular sovereignty in the Claim of Right and concludes:

> it does not matter what view the UK Parliament takes of its own powers; as far as Scotland is concerned, the powers of Westminster would be limited to those agreed to by the Scottish Parliament . . . The ultimate logic of this approach is that actions of the Westminster Parliament could be declared *ultra vires* the constitutional settlement.[65]

Enabling the courts to declare legislation of the UK Parliament unlawful was certainly a step too far for the Government and no such provision appears in the Scotland Act 1998.[66]

Clause 27(7) drew criticism in Parliament both from those who would have preferred a more strident declaration that Parliament may not legislate in devolved areas and, on the other hand, from those who saw it as insufficient to preserve unequivocally the sovereignty of the Westminster Parliament. Those in the former camp included both the Liberal Democrats and the Scottish Nationalists who, in both the Commons and the Lords, proposed amendments to clause 27(7) which would have restricted Parliament's legislative power to reserved matters.[67] On the other side of the fence the Conservatives sought to re-

---

[63] See for example, the late Donald Dewar MP: 'We accept that sovereignty within a devolved system lies with the United Kingdom Parliament.' HC Deb 31 July 1997, col 457; and again, HC Deb 28 Jan 1998, cols 402–03; and Sam Galbraith MP, HC Deb 12 Jan 1998, col 115.

[64] 'Scotland's Claim, Scotland's Right', above, n 60. See T H Jones, 'Scottish Devolution and Demarcation Disputes' [1997] *PL* 283 at 293.

[65] Jones, *ibid*, at 293.

[66] One possible qualification to this, which highlights the confusion which prevailed as to the precise effect of cl. 27(7), was Brian Wilson's suggestion that Parliament would not be able to legislate on devolved matters by way of private members' bills: HC Deb 13 Jan 1998, col 152. He also somewhat cryptically stated (col 155): 'Within the areas of devolved responsibility, laws passed by the Scottish Parliament are not open to cancellation.' This was picked up by Alex Salmond MP at committee stage: HC Deb 28 Jan 1998, col 379 and was subsequently partially refuted by Donald Dewar at cols 402–03.

[67] For example, one such amendment tabled in the Lords by Lord (David) Steel and three fellow peers would have rephrased cl 27(7) to read: 'This section does not affect the power of the Parliament of the United Kingdom to make laws for Scotland *in relation to reserved matters*'. HL Marshalled Amendments, 19 June 1998 (emphasis added).

emphasise that parliamentary sovereignty would not be diminished by clause 27. Their first concern was with the location of clause 27(7), which was of course tagged on to the end of the clause.[68] They were, however, more concerned with the actual terms of the sub-clause which, for the Conservatives, were not sufficiently clear in either restating Westminster sovereignty or in restricting the jurisdiction of the Scottish Parliament to devolved matters.[69] Concern was voiced that the Scottish Parliament could develop its own independent sphere of jurisdiction which it could also expand through manoeuvring its competence into reserved matters.[70] Accordingly, the Conservatives sought to amend clause 27(7) to read:

> This section does not affect the power of the Parliament of the United Kingdom to make laws for Scotland *which may not be amended or repealed by the Scottish Parliament.*[71]

This and other Conservative attempts to amend the Bill failed however, leaving section 28(7) a seemingly less than whole-hearted consolidation of parliamentary sovereignty.

(2) The *Whaley* case and the status of the Scottish Parliament

It is in this context that the judgment given by Lord Rodger in *Whaley v Lord Watson of Invergowrie*[72] should be considered since in the course of this decision the Lord President discusses the status of the Scottish Parliament. In this case three petitioners who had various commercial or financial interests in the practice of hunting with hounds sought to interdict Mike Watson MSP from, inter alia, introducing the Protection of Wild Mammals Bill into the Scottish Parliament and from encouraging any other member from doing likewise. The petitioners argued that, by introducing the Bill, Watson would be in breach of

---

[68] As Liam Fox MP put it: 'We . . . would have liked it to be given greater prominence in the Bill, instead of being hidden in the undergrowth.' HC Deb 13 Jan 1998, col 167.

[69] Bernard Jenkin MP suggested that it represented only implicit and 'grudging' acceptance of the sovereignty of Parliament: HC Deb 13 Jan 1998, col 240, while Michael Ancram described it as only a 'half-hearted reassertion' of Parliament's pre-eminence: HC Deb 12 Jan 1998, col 42. At the Bill's committee stage he also emphasised the distinction between devolution and federalism. 'the concept of the Bill is not federalism, which by definition divides powers, but devolution, which delegates them': HC Deb 28 Jan 1998, col 360. See also Bernard Jenkin, col 373.

[70] Michael Ancram suggested that as things stood constitutional stalemate could result from cl 27(7) if both Parliaments were to assume the power to repeal one another's legislation: 'As it stands, the clause could be a cockpit for a struggle between the two legislatures. The power to legislate could be within the vires of this Parliament, because it is sovereign, while the power to repeal legislation, because it was not a reserved matter, would be open to the Scottish Parliament, and legislation could be batted back and forth, with the Judicial Committee of the Privy Council unable to make a decision, because both Parliaments would effectively be acting within their *vires*.' HC Deb 28 Jan 1998, col 361.

[71] Introduced at the committee stage of the Scotland Bill, HC Deb 28 Jan 1998, col 357 (emphasis added).

[72] *Whaley v Lord Watson of Invergowrie*, above, n 6.

Article 6 of the Scotland Act 1998 (Transitory and Transitional Provisions) (Members' Interests) Order 1999, SI 1999/1350 which prohibits an MSP from 'advocacy' whereby the 'member receives or expects to receive any remuneration'. The petitioners relied on the wide meaning given to remuneration which includes 'any salary, wage, share of profits, fee, expenses, other monetary benefit or benefit in kind.' The Lord Ordinary dismissed this petition, a decision which was appealed to the Inner House of the Court of Session. Here the Court concluded by majority (which included the Lord President) that any breach of members' interests rules in this case would be punished retrospectively by the criminal law and that the Order in question did not give a civil right of action to members of the public to secure compliance with it.

From a constitutional perspective the case is particularly significant not so much for the decision but for the way in which the Lord President found himself unable to endorse the Lord Ordinary's general observations about the relationship between the courts and the Scottish Parliament. At first instance Lord Johnston was strident in defence of the Scottish Parliament's prerogatives:

> The Scottish Parliament is entitled to make its own determination, in my opinion, upon its own rules and this Court should not even look at it on grounds of irrationality. It may be in due course that if there is a fundamental irrationality in its approach to the legislation it passes such could be challengeable by a number of reasons based on its legislative competence upon the view that an organisation that is acting beyond its powers is acting irrationally and therefore not within its competence . . . I offer no further view on that subject. What I am entirely satisfied about is that it is quite inappropriate for pressure groups, or individuals, however their interests may be affected, to have the right to tell, by way of legal action, a committee of this Parliament that its own view of its own rules is inappropriate or even wrong.[73]

The Lord President took the view that Lord Johnston had not accorded sufficient weight to the fact that the Parliament is a creature of Westminster statute.

> As such, it is a body which, like any other statutory body, must work within the scope of those powers. If it does not do so, then in an appropriate case the court may be asked to intervene and will require to do so, in a manner permitted by the legislation. In principle, therefore, the Parliament like any other body set up by law is subject to the law and to the courts which exist to uphold that law.[74]

Furthermore, MSPs are subject to the law and to the courts, and, except insofar as they enjoy immunity, the law applies to them in the usual way.

Although the Lord President referred to the Scottish Parliament as a creature of statute like any other statutory body, he went on to note that it was entirely normal for a legislature to be subject to the law of the land and to the jurisdiction of the courts.[75] He also observed that the relationship between Parliament

---

[73] *Whaley v Lord Watson of Invergowrie*, at 348, per Lord Johnston.
[74] *Ibid*.
[75] *Ibid*, Lord Prosser (at 358) also considers a limited parliament to be an obvious feature of the rule of law: 'a defined parliament is there to do not whatever it wants, but only what the law has

and the courts was somewhat peculiar and that Westminster sovereignty was under attack from a different direction.[76] There is no suggestion that the Scotland Act 1998 makes further inroads into that sovereignty but Lord Rodger does contextualise the Scottish Parliament in terms of Commonwealth legislatures which have done so:

> in many democracies throughout the Commonwealth, for example, even where the parliaments have been modelled in some respects on Westminster, they owe their existence and powers to statute and are in various ways subject to the law and to the courts which act to uphold the law. The Scottish Parliament has simply joined that wider family of parliaments.[77]

There is no hint in Lord Rodger's confirmation that the Scottish Parliament's competence is limited that it poses any challenge to Parliament's supremacy. Nonetheless, his reminder that EU membership has made inroads on Parliament's omnicompetence may serve to encourage those litigants who will increasingly seek to argue that Westminster's relationship with the courts in the new era of limited legislative power is becoming ever more anomalous. This is certainly an area which will test the courts further and which will demand further articulation of their vision of the devolution settlement as arguments continue to be advanced that Westminster's competence should be restricted to reserved matters.

(3) Devolution and human rights: balancing interests in *A (A Mental Patient) v Scottish Ministers*

Following the *Whaley* case the Court of Session was faced with another challenge involving the Scottish Parliament.[78] Here the issue was not one of the respective competencies of Edinburgh and Westminster but rather the competing counter-majoritarian principles represented by the Scotland Act 1998 and the Human Rights Act 1998. In *A (A Mental Patient)* the court was asked to decide if an Act of the Scottish Parliament was incompatible with Convention rights and hence outside the competence of the Parliament per section 29(2)(d). This calls into question how far the courts are prepared to allow the devolved legislature to go in pursuit of public policy objectives when individual rights are thereby put in potential jeopardy.

---

empowered it to do.' This is followed by what seems like a reference to the anachronistic nature of the UK's traditional arrangements as he contrasts such a limited legislature with 'the odd, and perhaps unsatisfactory, context of "sovereign" or undefined powers'.

[76] *Ibid,* '[T]he Westminster Parliament . . . is unusual in being respected as sovereign by the courts. And, now, of course, certain inroads have been made into even that sovereignty by the European Communities Act 1972' (Lord Rodger, at 349).

[77] *Ibid,* at 358.

[78] *A (A Mental Patient) v Scottish Ministers,* above, n 7.

Before analysing *A (A Mental Patient)* it is instructive to consider the recent judicial development throughout the UK of what has become known as the 'discretionary area of judgement', since this was central to the Court of Session's decision in *A (A Mental Patient)* and also seems likely to become a significant factor in Human Rights Act 1998 adjudication in general.[79] Even before the Human Rights Act 1998 came into force there were recent indications that the courts throughout the UK were becoming increasingly conscious of the need to balance human rights claims with public policy considerations. For example, in the leading case of *Kebiline* Lord Hope noted that the courts must recognise that:

> difficult choices may have to be made by the executive or the legislature between the rights of the individual and the needs of society. In some circumstances it will be appropriate for the courts to recognise that there is an area of judgement within which the judiciary will defer, on democratic grounds, to the considered opinion of the elected body or person whose act or decision is said to be incompatible with the Convention.[80]

This idea of a discretionary area of judgement available to the executive and legislature can also be expected to play a part in post-Human Rights Act 1998 case law because it is itself very similar to the definition of proportionality applied by the European Court of Human Rights as laid down, for example, in the classic *Soering* formulation:

> inherent in the whole of the Convention is a search for a fair balance between the demands of the general interest of the community and the requirements of the protection of the individual's fundamental rights.[81]

There are of course limits to this principle and the endorsement of the discretionary area of judgement was qualified in *Kebeline* by reference to human rights of fundamental political importance, particularly those considered to be 'constitutional rights'. Lord Hope in this context suggested that deference to the legislature would be more appropriate in areas where a balance is itself required by the ECHR or where questions of social or economic policy are at stake but would be 'much less' appropriate 'where the rights are of high constitutional importance.'[82]

In *A (A Mental Patient)*, Lord President Rodger considered the discretionary area of judgement in the context of Article 5 ECHR. In this case the Scottish Parliament had passed the Mental Health (Public Safety and Appeals)

---

[79] D Pannick, 'Principles of Interpretation of Convention Rights under the Human Rights Act and the Discretionary Area of Judgement' [1998] *PL* 545 and Lester and Pannick, above, n 50, 73–76.

[80] *R v Director of Public Prosecutions, ex p Kebiline and others* [1999] 3 WLR 972 at 994. Notably this dictum is cited by Lord Rodger in *A (A Mental Patient)*, above, n 7, para 48.

[81] *Soering v United Kingdom* (1989) 11 EHRR 439 at 468. A recent English case bears out the connection between the two principles. *R (on the application of Pearson) v Secretary of State for the Home Department* (2001) HRLR 39.

[82] *Kebiline*, above, n 80, at 994.

(Scotland) Act 1999 which introduced new rules on detention for mental health patients. The applicants who were detainees in a State hospital claimed that the Act violated their rights under Article 5(1)(e) and Article 5(4) of the Convention. The Lord President attempted to weigh up the conflicting interests at stake suggesting that the balance to be struck in considering Article 5 of the Convention was

> between the interest of the community in protecting the lives and health of members of the public and the protection of the individual rights of the restricted patients in question.

Lord Rodger was clearly conscious of Lord Hope's dictum in *Kebeline* as he continued,

> [t]he right to liberty which Art 5 enshrines is undoubtedly a high constitutional right. But it is not an absolute right and the exceptions which the Convention recognises arise in areas where social policy comes into play.[83]

Here liberty had to compete with another vital interest, namely 'the protection of the rest of the community from harm'.[84]

Lord Rodger ultimately deferred to the Scottish Parliament in this case allowing the legislature discretion to protect the community from harm even though the Mental Health (Public Safety and Appeals) Scotland Act potentially violated the 'high constitutional rights' of the applicants. Lord Rodger explicitly recognised that the Scottish Parliament was under a duty per the Scotland Act 1998 not to legislate in a manner incompatible with individual patients' rights under the Convention. Nonetheless, in this case the court should accord a measure of discretion to the democratically elected legislature to assess the policy issues involved[85] and, given the need to avoid danger to the safety of members of the public, the Act was held to be a proportionate means of protecting the public which, therefore, did not violate Article 5(4).[86]

This case perhaps hints at a general reluctance on the part of the courts to interfere with legislation passed by the Scottish Parliament.[87] Since this is the only case in which Scottish legislation has so far been challenged for its validity it is difficult to draw any general conclusions on judicial commitment to self-restraint. How the discretionary area of judgement is applied in future cases will nonetheless be a crucial factor in defining how the courts intend to develop the relationship between the Scotland Act 1998 and the Human Rights Act 1998 and

---

[83] *Ibid*, at para 51.
[84] *Ibid*.
[85] *Ibid*, at paras 52–53.
[86] *Ibid*, at para 101.
[87] It may well be that the argument for the existence of Scottish popular sovereignty will play a role in this type of dispute. As Lord Hope has written: 'There is a popular view that sovereignty is being returned to and will reside with the people of Scotland. So the will of the people as expressed through their elected representatives will, in the right context, have to be respected as a function of the principle of subsidiarity.' Lord Hope, 'The Human Rights Act 1998: The Task of the Judges' [1999] *SLR* 185 at 188.

indeed how they propose to balance the two models of counter-majoritarianism which now mark the boundaries of Scottish governmental power.[88]

E. CONCLUDING REMARKS

The ongoing programme of constitutional change in the UK will take time to bed down. In many respects it is too early to tell what the implications are likely to be for governmental institutions, processes of decision-making, inter-governmental relations, and the new contract between citizen and government(s). What is certain is that wide areas of public life are being constitutionalised and that judges will be left to define the detail of these developments in the course of often very contentious and high profile court actions. The experiences of the Scottish courts since the Scotland Act 1998 came into force offers observers an early window into the possible outcomes of this process.

What has been particularly noticeable is that among the first tasks which the courts have embarked upon as they address the appropriate balance between central and devolved government and between state and citizen is one of self-definition. As the arbiters of these great changes they are being called upon to assess how active a part they should play in the newly formalised power struggles which are beginning to emerge and which are drawing them into fundamental questions about Scottish government in terms of its relations with London and the extent to which its autonomy should be restricted in order better to protect individual rights. In beginning to address these issues the courts have, however, been confronted with the prima facie task of assessing whether they themselves, as presently constituted, represent appropriate fora for the resolution of these constitutional disputes.

In facing the challenge presented to them by a constitutional reform process which requires the courts to supply the details of a complex and contentious process of constitutional rearrangement, judges in Scotland have begun by asking whether the judicial process itself meets the fundamental requirements of procedural fairness. This has involved the courts in querying the adequacy of mechanisms already in place both to ensure impartiality and to secure judicial independence. In each respect they have sought with considerable vigour to bolster existing legitimising devices: in enforcing strict impartiality the courts are

---

[88] Lord Hope's dictum in *Kebeline* on the need to balance competing interests has now been cited by Lord Bingham in *HM Advocate v McIntosh* 2001 SLT 304; 2001 SCCR 191; [2001] 2 WLR 817; [2001] 2 All ER 638 at para 30. References to the principle are also to be found in recent English cases since the Human Rights Act 1998 came into force, eg *R v Secretary of State for the Home Department, ex parte Isiko*, [2001] HRLR 15 and *R v Bow County Court, ex p Pelling (No 2)* [2001] UKHRR 165. For a general preparedness on the part of the courts to defer to the legislature see (on the question of proportionality) *R (on the application of Pearson) v Secretary of State for the Home Department*, above, n 81, and (on the role of the Secretary of State in determining planning applications), *R (on the application of Holding & Barnes plc) v Secretary of State for the Environment, Transport and the Regions* [2001] 2 All ER 929.

attempting to make the adjudication process if not more accountable then certainly more transparent, and by imposing new strictures on judicial independence they are helping to formalise the relationship between the judiciary and the other branches of government, particularly the executive. The outcome of this process of self-appraisal may be a renewed assertiveness on the part of the courts stemming from a sense that they are now institutionally better equipped to respond more actively to the substantive questions with which they will be confronted.[89] A judiciary increasingly confident of its constitutional location and better satisfied with the processes in place for testing its own legitimacy may feel more inclined to expand its role in the development of ongoing constitutional change. Whether heightened levels of judicial activism will flow from the improved husbandry of judicial due process remains to be determined but what seems clear is that in any event a constitutional transformation is taking place which will lend radically different dimensions to the relationship between the judiciary and the other institutions of governance throughout the UK.

[89] See Lord Steyn's remarks in *Brown v Stott* 2001 SC (PC) 43 at 63G, above, n 45.

6

Judicial Review, Locus Standi *and Remedies: The Impact of the Human Rights Act 1998*

JANE MUNRO*

A DECADE AGO,[1] Lord Browne-Wilkinson argued that the common law was capable of offering, through judicial review, protection of fundamental rights equivalent to that furnished by what his Lordship described as a 'halfway Bill', meaning a Bill of Rights which declares the existence of certain fundamental rights, which renders it unlawful for the executive to infringe such rights and which enables the courts to presume, in the absence of clear and precise statutory words, that Parliament did not intend to infringe such rights; but which does not enable the courts to strike down Acts of Parliament on grounds of incompatibility with the Bill. This Lord Browne-Wilkinson distinguished from a 'full Bill', meaning a Bill of Rights conferring on individuals inviolable rights which cannot be overridden even by Act of Parliament.

The Human Rights Act 1998 might be described as a 'three-quarters Bill', in that while it empowers certain higher courts to declare an Act of Parliament incompatible with one or more of the Convention rights (of the European Convention for the Protection of Human Rights and Fundamental Freedoms (ECHR)), such declarations shall have no effect on the 'validity, continuing operation or enforcement' of the provision(s) in respect of which they are made. Their purpose, rather, is to alert Parliament, and the responsible ministers, to the existence of an incompatibility. It then falls to ministers and Parliament to rectify matters, should they see fit to do so.[2] Under section 7 of the Act, a person who claims that a public authority has acted, or proposes to act, in a manner incompatible with the Convention rights may bring proceedings against the authority in the appropriate court or tribunal. The appropriateness of judicial review as one mechanism for bringing such proceedings is self-evident.

---

* Assistant Director, Saltire Public Affairs, Shepherd & Wedderburn WS; Intrant, Faculty of Advocates.

[1] Lord Browne-Wilkinson, 'The Infiltration of a Bill of Rights', [1992] *PL* 397.

[2] To which end, s 10 and Sch 2 of the Human Rights Act 1998 confer a power to take 'remedial action' on a Minister of the Crown or Her Majesty in Council, as appropriate.

Resort to the supervisory jurisdiction to enforce Convention rights has carried consequences. The rules of *locus standi* applicable to proceedings brought under the Human Rights Act 1998 differ from those applicable in ordinary judicial review proceedings. The Act also confers on the courts new competence in relation to remedies. And interesting questions remain about the impact of the Act on the reach and intensity of judicial review. Well before 2 October 2000, purely domestic developments in administrative law (albeit developments influenced by the jurisprudence of the European Court of Human Rights (ECtHR)) had brought us to a point at which the courts on review were capable of offering a high level of protection to fundamental rights. This was particularly true of what is now the Administrative Court in England, but the trend found expression also in the Court of Session. In a number of important respects, however, judicial review fell short of providing a fully effective remedy for breaches of the Convention rights, more often than not because of traditional judicial sensitivities about the 'proper' scope of review. Even prior to the entry into force of the Human Rights Act 1998, the courts had begun to re-visit certain received limitations on the supervisory jurisdiction and the resultant developments are noted below. It will be suggested, however, that those developments have not greatly altered the essential nature of the supervisory jurisdiction. It will also be argued that the Human Rights Act 1998 will not bear the weight of some of the claims that have been made for it, in particular in relation to substantive review. The reception into domestic law of concepts such as proportionality and the margin of appreciation has sharpened our domestic human rights jurisprudence. But they do not alter the fact that in any legal order there must be a sensible division of labour between the judicial, executive and legislative authorities of the state.

A.   *LOCUS STANDI*: TITLE AND INTEREST

Under section 7(1) of the Human Rights Act 1998, a person who claims that a public authority has acted (or proposes to act) in breach of Convention rights may only bring proceedings against that authority if he is or would be a 'victim' of that breach. Section 7(7) then provides that a person is a victim . . . only if he would be a victim for the purposes of Article 34 of the Convention if proceedings were brought in the European Court of Human Rights in respect of that act. Article 34 states that the ECtHR may receive applications from any person, non-governmental organisation or group of individuals claiming to be the victim of a violation of one or more Convention rights. At the time of the enactment of the Human Rights Act 1998, a number of English commentators[3] criticised this test of *locus standi* as a substantial restriction on the normal test of standing in claims for judicial review, namely, whether the applicant has a sufficient inter-

---

[3] See for example J Marriott and D Nicol, 'The Human Rights Act, Representative Standing and the Victim Culture' [1998] *EHRLR* 731.

est in the matter to which the claim relates.[4] This condition was interpreted liberally so as to permit 'representative challenges' to the legality of administrative decisions by groups not directly affected by the decision in question.[5] What was less remarked upon was the fact that the adoption, for the purposes of the Human Rights Act 1998, of the 'sufficient interest' test as developed by the English courts would have fitted ill with Scots law on *locus standi*. The rules on title and interest in Scots law are less receptive to representative challenges.[6] The victim test, and its restriction upon the classes and categories of persons having title and interest to bring proceedings under the Human Rights Act 1998, was in that sense always of less moment to Scots lawyers than to their English counterparts.

Yet for a number of reasons, the concerns of those commentators who felt that the 'victim' test confined *locus standi* under the Human Rights Act 1998 within unduly narrow bounds appear misplaced. At a purely practical level, it makes sense for the Act to adopt the same test of *locus standi* as the Convention. It is true that the test as developed by the ECtHR is less generous than the 'sufficient interest' test applied in judicial review proceedings in England. Persons claiming to be victims must show a reasonable likelihood that the national measures complained of applied to, or will be applied to, them. Local authorities and other institutions connected with the state cannot initiate proceedings. But legal persons and other bodies—for example, companies, newspapers, churches, trade unions, political parties and pressure groups strictly so-called— may be able to rely directly on at least some Convention rights. If pressure groups are to be regarded as victims, they must show that they are in some way affected by the measure complained of and that they have authority to act on behalf of their members, who must be identified.[7] In short, the Convention's test

---

[4] Supreme Court Act 1981, s 31(3). This continues in force, although the corresponding provision in the old Order 53 of the Rules of the Supreme Court, rule 3(7), to the effect that the court shall not grant permission unless it considers that the applicant has a sufficient interest in the matter to which the application relates, does not appear in the new Part 54 of the Civil Procedure Rules 1998 (SI 1998 No 3132). Part 54 was inserted into the Civil Procedure Rules by The Civil Procedure (Amendment No 4) Rules 2000 (SI 2000 No 2092). Part 54 entered into force on, and thus applies to proceedings commenced on or after, 2 Oct 2000. Proceedings commenced between 26 April 1999 and 2 Oct 2000 were governed by Part 53 of the Civil Procedure Rules, which itself replaced the old RSC Order 53 and which is revoked by the new rules.

[5] See, for example, *R v Inland Revenue Commissioners, ex parte National Federation of Self-Employed and Small Businesses* [1982] AC 617; *R v Secretary of State for Social Services, ex parte Child Poverty Action Group* [1989] 1 All ER 1047; *R v Secretary of State for Foreign and Commonwealth Affairs, ex parte World Development Movement* [1995] 1 All ER 611.

[6] See, for example, *Scottish Old People's Welfare Council, Petrs* 1987 SLT 179; more recently, *Rape Crisis Centre v Secretary of State for the Home Department*, 2000 SC 527.

[7] Thus, for example, in *Norris v Ireland* (1985) 44 DR 132, the European Commission on Human Rights did not regard the National Gay Federation as a victim of the Irish law prohibiting homosexuality; but in *Open Door Counselling Ltd and Dublin Well Woman Centre Ltd v Ireland* (1992) 15 EHRR 244, which involved an injunction granted by the Irish Supreme Court to restrain the provision of information by the applicant organisations about abortion facilities outside Ireland, both the Commission and the Court found that all women of child-bearing age could claim to be victims since they belonged to a class of persons liable to be adversely affected by the injunction.

of *locus standi*—the concept of victimhood—is not absolutely coterminous with the concept of a directly affected individual. Indeed it has been said that the case law on Article 34 'demonstrates the elasticity of the notion of victim . . . as well as the uncertain and shifting boundaries between those directly affected by a particular measure and those remotely affected.'[8] On that score, it is worth recalling that one of the reasons why Scots law requires a petitioner to qualify a sufficient interest is that the job of the courts is not to pronounce on academic questions: 'no person is entitled to subject another to the trouble and expense of a litigation unless he has some real interest to enforce or protect.'[9] So to state is not to prefer the claims of administrative convenience over the public interest in administrative legality.

In any case, an active role for pressure groups in human rights litigation is by no means excluded by the Human Rights Act 1998. It remains open to them to fund, if not front, test cases in the human rights arena.[10] But more important than this are the changes that have been made to the rules of court north and south of the Border in order to facilitate third party interventions in judicial review proceedings (whether or not involving human rights).[11] In England, Rule 54.17 of the Civil Procedure Rules provides that any person may apply for permission to file evidence or to make representations at the hearing of the judicial review.[12] In Scotland, the relevant provision is made in the Act of Sederunt (Rules of the Court of Session Amendment No 5) (Public Interest Intervention in Judicial Review) 2000.[13] This inserts a new rule 58.8A into Chapter 58 of the Rules of the Court of Session.[14] Rule 58.8A provides that a person who is not directly affected by any issue raised in a petition for judicial review may nonetheless apply to the Court for leave to intervene in the petition or in an appeal in connection with the petition. The applicant must set out in his Minute of Intervention his name and description; the issue(s) in the proceedings which he wishes to address and his reasons for believing these to raise a matter of

---

[8] D J Harris, M O'Boyle and C Warbrick, *The Law of the European Convention on Human Rights* (Butterworths, London, 1995) 633.

[9] *Swanson v Manson*, 1907 SC 426 at 429, *per* Lord Ardwell.

[10] Following the decision in *Scottish Old People's Welfare Council*, above, n 6, a like solution to the restrictions on access to the supervisory jurisdiction in Scotland imposed by the rules on title and interest was proposed by A Bradley, 'Applications for Judicial Review—The Scottish Model' [1987] *PL* 313 at 319.

[11] The rules of the ECtHR were revised in January 1983 to facilitate third-party interventions. So, for example, in *McCann v United Kingdom* (1996) 21 EHRR 97 (the *Death on the Rock* case), leave was granted to Amnesty, Liberty, Inquest and the Committee on the Administration of Justice to submit written comments; as in the *Open Door Counselling and Dublin Well Woman* case, above, n 7, where leave was granted, on the one hand, to the Society for the Protection of the Unborn Child and, on the other, to the free speech campaign group, Article 19.

[12] Instances of this procedure being used include *R v Broadcasting Standards Commission, ex parte British Broadcasting Corporation* [2000] 3 WLR 1327, in which, with the consent of the parties, Liberty was granted permission to intervene on the appeal.

[13] Act of Sederunt (Rules of the Court of Session Amendment No 5) (Public Interest Intervention in Judicial Review) 2000 (SI 2000 No 317).

[14] Rules of the Court of Session (SI 1994 No 1443).

public interest; and the propositions he wishes to advance and his reasons for believing these to be relevant to the proceedings and likely to assist the Court. The Court may grant or refuse leave, with or without a hearing, but may only grant leave if satisfied that the proceedings raise, and the issue in the proceedings which the applicant wishes to address raises, a matter of public interest; that the propositions to be advanced by the applicant are relevant to the proceedings and are likely to assist the Court; and that the intervention will not unduly delay or otherwise prejudice the rights of the parties, including their potential liability for expenses. In granting leave, the Court may impose such terms and conditions as it considers desirable in the interests of justice, including making provision in respect of any additional expenses incurred by the parties as a result of the intervention. Where leave is granted, an intervention will normally take the form of a written submission, lodged with the Court and copied to the parties, not exceeding 5,000 words in length. The Court may exceptionally allow longer written submissions to be made, and may direct that it wishes to hear oral submissions.

This provision for third party intervention takes much of the heat out of the debate about *locus standi* under the Human Rights Act 1998. Only in one situation is it suggested that a strong case remains for permitting purely representative challenges. This is where the only remedy sought is a declaration of incompatibility under section 4. As Professor Gearty points out,[15] for an individual litigant, a declaration of incompatibility may well be little more than a Pyrrhic victory. Pressure groups, by contrast, may have no interest beyond securing a declaration that provisions of an Act of Parliament are incompatible with Convention rights. This would then provide powerful leverage in the political arena for obtaining changes in the law. If one of the main aims of the Human Rights Act 1998 is to create a culture of rights, and to the extent that pressure groups will be instrumental in furthering that project, the Act is deficient in altogether excluding such groups from direct participation.

B. THE GROUNDS FOR REVIEW

The grounds for judicial review, which are common north and south of the Border,[16] were encapsulated by Lord Diplock's classification in *Council for Civil Service Unions v Minister for the Civil Service*:[17] illegality, procedural impropriety and irrationality. Each of these headings is compendious and, in a sense, porous, being always open to adaptation and extension. When the Human Rights Act 1998 was enacted, it was suggested that incorporation would revivify domestic doctrine, in particular by displacing the test of *Wednesbury*

---

[15] See Gearty's contribution to this collection.
[16] See *West v Secretary of State for Scotland*, 1992 SC 385 at 405, *per* Lord President Hope.
[17] *Council of Civil Service Unions v Minister for the Civil Service* [1985] AC 374 at 410.

unreasonableness[18] for the more discriminating standards developed by the ECtHR: whether, for example, a restriction on a Convention right is in response to a 'pressing social need'; whether it is 'necessary in a democratic society' for the protection of certain specific public interests; whether it is proportionate to the legitimate aims of the state.

The *Wednesbury* test is, of course, the United Kingdom's concession to 'substantive review', and the threshold of judicial intervention is pitched at a high level in deference to traditional constitutional proprieties in the context of review. On this reckoning, review is concerned with the legality, not the merits, of administrative decisions. The job of the courts, in essence, is to identify and enforce the boundaries of conferred or delegated powers, in order to ensure that the donee of such powers does not stray outwith his jurisdiction and act where he was never intended to act. But where Parliament, in particular, has conferred decision-making power on an official or authority, it is not for the courts to usurp that power by substituting their judgment for that of the primary decision-maker.

The deficiencies of this traditional account of judicial review are well rehearsed.[19] But even before the enactment of the Human Rights Act 1998, it was misleading to represent judicial review as involving little more than statutory construction to locate the limits of the powers conferred, the enforcement of prescribed procedural requirements and the common law rules of natural justice, with *Wednesbury* as a long stop to catch those truly indefensible decisions which had somehow escaped censure on other grounds. Review at the level of illegality was and is concerned not only with the boundaries laid down by the enabling statute but with more open-textured matters, such as whether the public authority has misused its powers for some purpose extraneous to the statute or on the basis of considerations which are irrelevant in terms of the policy of the statute as a whole. This is not simply a dry and technical exercise in statutory interpretation, but one illuminated by considerations of judicial policy and, especially, by presumptions of the common law to which the courts have regard in interpreting statutes. The courts have for some time shown a readiness to construe primary and subordinate legislation subject to a robust presumption to the effect that fundamental rights are not to be overridden other

---

[18] *Associated Provincial Picture Houses Ltd v Wednesbury Corporation* [1948] 1 KB 223 (hereafter *Wednesbury*).

[19] It is, for one thing, Anglocentric: cf Lord Clyde, 'The Nature of the Supervisory Jurisdiction and the Public/Private Divide in Scots Administrative Law' in W Finnie, C M G Himsworth and N Walker (eds), *Edinburgh Essays in Public Law* (Edinburgh University Press, Edinburgh, 1991), 281–93; and see Lord Clyde and D J Edwards, *Judicial Review in Scotland* (Scottish Universities Institute, Edinburgh, 2000), ch 2. For other criticisms of traditional theory concerning the basis and nature of the supervisory jurisdiction, see, for example, D Oliver, 'Is the *ultra vires* Rule the Basis of Judicial Review?' [1987] *PL* 543; P P Craig, '*Ultra Vires* and the Foundations of Judicial Review' [1998] *CLJ* 63; M Elliott, 'The Demise of Parliamentary Sovereignty? The Implications for Justifying Judicial Review' [1999] 115 *LQR* 119.

than by clear and precise legislative words,[20] a technique not dissimilar to those imposed by Community law and, now, by section 3(1) of the Human Rights Act 1998.[21] Another technique was to treat fundamental rights as a relevant consideration, so that it required to be shown that a decision-maker had had regard to the impact of his decision on the right affected.[22] Review for procedural impropriety, meanwhile, is capable of catching a whole host of administrative sins: the most vigorous developments in judicial review as a whole have occurred in the context of the common law 'duty to act fairly'.[23] As for substantive review on *Wednesbury* grounds, it was by no means as impoverished as it was often depicted.[24] True it is that in *Brind*,[25] the House of Lords declined to adopt a principle of proportionality going beyond the traditional *Wednesbury* test. But their Lordships did not rule out the adoption of proportionality at some future date, and as Murray Hunt argued in 1997, the English courts at least had 'already in effect recognised proportionality' albeit 'without so far daring to speak its name.'[26] Indeed in a recent case involving European Community law, Lord Slynn remarked that in *Brind*:

> . . . the House treated *Wednesbury* reasonableness and proportionality as being different. So in some ways they are though the distinction between the two tests in practice is in any event much less than is sometimes suggested. The cautious way in which the European Court [of Justice] usually applies this test, recognising the importance of respecting the national authority's margin of appreciation, may mean that whichever test is adopted . . . the result is the same.[27]

[20] This, in essence, was the approach favoured by Lord Browne-Wilkinson in his 1992 article, above, n 1, and applied by his Lordship in *Wheeler v Leicester City Council* [1985] AC 1054 (although not followed in the House of Lords) and in *Marcel v Commissioner of Police for the Metropolis* [1992] Ch 225. See also, for example, *R v Secretary of State for the Home Department, ex parte Leech (No 2)* [1994] QB 198; *R v Secretary of State for Social Security, ex parte Joint Council for the Welfare of Immigrants* [1996] 4 All ER 385; *R v Lord Chancellor, ex parte Witham* [1997] 2 All ER 779; *R v Secretary of State for the Home Department, ex parte Pierson* [1998] AC 539.

[21] Although common law presumptions are less resistant to breaches of fundamental rights ordained by clear and precise legislative words than the interpretive obligation contained in s 3(1).

[22] See, for example, the unreported decision of Lady Cosgrove in *Mohammed Irfan Ul-Haq v Secretary of State for the Home Department*, Outer House, 3 December 1998. For the limitations of this technique, see below, n 43 and accompanying text.

[23] It is no accident, either, that complaints under Art 6 account for by far the majority of applications (successful and otherwise) to the ECtHR; nor that Art 6 has figured so prominently in human rights cases before the domestic courts to date, whether brought under the Human Rights Act 1998 or as 'devolution issues' pursuant to s 98 and Schedule 6 of the Scotland Act 1998. All eight devolution issues which, at the time of writing, had reached the Judicial Committee of the Privy Council involved alleged breaches of Art 6 in aspects of Scottish criminal procedure (all unsuccessful bar *Millar v Procurator Fiscal, Elgin* [2001] UKHRR 999, and HM *Advocate v JK*, 29 Jan 2002).

[24] See, for example, the criticisms of Lord Lester of Herne Hill QC and Professor Jowell in 'Beyond *Wednesbury*: Substantive Principles of Administrative Law' [1987] *PL* 368 and 'Proportionality: Neither Novel Nor Dangerous' in J Jowell and D Oliver (eds), *New Directions in Judicial Review* (Stevens & Sons, London, 1988), 51–73.

[25] *R v Secretary of State for the Home Department, ex parte Brind* [1991] 1 AC 696.

[26] M Hunt, *Using Human Rights Law in English Courts* (Hart Publishing, Oxford, 1997), 216.

[27] *R v Chief Constable of Sussex, ex parte International Traders Ferry Ltd* [1999] 2 AC 418. See, to like effect, Lord Slynn's speech in *Alconbury*, below, n 66, at para 51.

The fact is that, even prior to *Brind*, the courts would require more compelling justification for administrative decisions which impinged upon fundamental rights. In *Bugdaycay v Secretary of State for the Home Department*,[28] Lord Bridge held that:

> . . . the court must . . . be entitled to subject an administrative decision to the most rigorous examination, to ensure that it is in no way flawed, according to the gravity of the issue which the decision determines. The most fundamental of all human rights is the right to life and when an administrative decision under challenge is said to be one which may put the applicant's life at risk, the basis of the decision must call for the most anxious scrutiny.[29]

It is to be noted that in *Brind*, the majority of the House of Lords, at least,[30] did not dissent from the proposition that stricter scrutiny of administrative decisions is called for when the decisions interfere with human rights. In any event, *Brind* did not prevent the spread of the *Bugdaycay* approach. There is no shortage of cases in which the courts, alert to the human rights dimension involved, have responded by insisting that 'the more substantial the interference with human rights, the more the court will require by way of justification before it is satisfied that the decision is reasonable.'[31] Indeed, in the period immediately preceding the entry into force of the Human Rights Act 1998, the courts had effectively adopted the analytical approach and even the language of European jurisprudence 'as a matter of the common law.'[32] The converse of this 'high-intensity' review is adherence to orthodox *Wednesbury* standards in areas not impinging upon fundamental rights.[33] So established had the sliding scale of review become, indeed, that it attracted critical comment from the then Shadow Lord Chancellor, alive, perhaps, to the possibilities of strict judicial scrutiny as he looked forward to taking office.[34]

It will not have escaped the reader's attention that the cases so far mentioned are decisions of the English courts. Could the same be said of the Court of Session? To an extent, given the far greater volume of claims for judicial review in England, it is inevitable that English decisions should have driven developments in this field. Moreover, prior to the important judgment of Lord President Hope, as he then was, in *T, Petitioner*,[35] reference to the ECHR, even as an aid

[28] *Bugdaycay v Secretary of State for the Home Department* [1987] AC 514.
[29] *Ibid*, at 531.
[30] Lords Bridge, Roskill and Templeman.
[31] *R v Ministry of Defence, ex parte Smith* [1996] QB 517 at 554, per Lord Bingham MR (hereafter *Smith*).
[32] See, for example, *R v Secretary of State for the Home Department, ex parte Turgut* [2001] 1 All ER 719; *R (Mahmood) v Secretary of State for the Home Department* [2001] 1 WLR 840.
[33] See, for example, *R v Secretary of State for the Environment, ex parte Nottinghamshire County Council* [1986] 1 AC 240; *R v Secretary of State for the Environment, ex parte Hammersmith and Fulham London Borough Council* [1991] 1 AC 521; in Scotland, *East Kilbride District Council v Secretary of State for Scotland* 1995 SLT 1238.
[34] Lord Irvine, 'Judges and Decision-Makers: The Theory and Practice of *Wednesbury* review', [1996] *PL* 59.
[35] *T, Petitioner*, 1997 SLT 724.

to the construction of ambiguous statutory provisions, was impermissible before the Scottish courts. However, there were indications that the Court of Session too was prepared to take account of the human rights dimension in adjudicating on the rationality of administrative decisions. *Abdadou v Secretary of State for the Home Department* serves as an illustration.[36] The petitioner, an Algerian national, entered the United Kingdom illegally in 1992 and made his way to Glasgow, where he obtained employment. Early in 1996 he married a British national, which prompted him to seek to regularise his immigration status. An immigration official refused his application for leave to remain. The petitioner sought judicial review on the grounds that, in the circumstances of the case, the immigration official's decision was unreasonable and would result in a breach of Article 8 of the ECHR.

Lord Eassie held, following *Brind*, that:

> merely averring a breach of the Convention would [not] be relevant to invalidate an exercise of administrative discretion. That would be to apply the Convention as if it were already part of our law.

However, his Lordship added, following *Smith*,[37] that:

> there is a degree of overlap between proportionality and *Wednesbury* unreasonableness, at least in a field such as immigration control and respect for family life. . . . [In] judging whether a decision is unreasonable in the sense of being outwith the range open to a reasonable decision taker, the human rights context is important and the more substantial the interference with human rights the more a court will require by way of justification before it is satisfied that the decision is reasonable, in the sense of its being within that range.

In all of these ways, then, the courts had crafted the tools of a domestic human rights jurisdiction, in advance of the incorporation of Convention rights, by the 'incremental' development of the common law.[38] But this is not to say that judicial review was Convention-proofed before the Human Rights Act 1998 took effect. In fact, as an effective remedy for infringements of fundamental rights, it was deficient in a number of ways. Rabinder Singh, for example, remarked that the

> trouble with the common law is that it recognises liberty only as a 'negative idea': I am free to do whatever is not prohibited by some rule of law. Furthermore, it is axiomatic in our constitution that the common law is vulnerable to Act of Parliament.[39]

---

[36] *Abdadou v Secretary of State for the Home Department*, 1998 SC 504. See also, for example, *Kuma v Secretary of State for the Home Department*, Outer House, 5 Aug 1998, unreported; and *Booker Aquaculture Ltd v Secretary of State for Scotland*, [1999] 1 CMLR 35 (and see also 2000 SC 9 [First Division]), for an illustration of how fundamental rights may also come into play through the medium of European Community law. The latter has since been referred to the European Court of Justice for a preliminary ruling under Art 234 of the EC Treaty, *sub nom* Case C–20/00, *Booker Aquaculture Ltd v The Scottish Ministers*.

[37] *Smith*, above, n 31.

[38] See Sir John Laws, 'Is the High Court the Guardian of Fundamental Human Rights?' [1993] *PL* 59.

[39] R Singh, *The Future of Human Rights in the United Kingdom* (Hart Publishing, Oxford, 1997), 12.

The readiness of the courts to regard decision-makers as subject to constraints beyond those made explicit in a particular statute, especially in the field of fundamental rights, mitigated the effects of this but did not alter the essential truth of Mr Singh's point.[40] For that reason, the jurisdiction conferred on the higher courts to make declarations of incompatibility is an important step forward. Moreover, incorporation of Convention rights has helped to plug gaps in the common law. For example, the common law recognised no right of privacy as such.[41] In consequence, the applicants in *Smith* were obliged, ultimately, to seek their remedy in Strasbourg.[42] Had the Human Rights Act 1998 been in force at the time of their Court of Appeal hearing—or had the common law attached to the privacy interests of homosexual servicemen and women a weight commensurate to that attached to property interests or interests in bodily integrity—one suspects a different outcome would have been reached.

For Murray Hunt, the problem with pre-incorporation domestic jurisprudence was that it remained wedded to the substance/procedure distinction. He commented that:

> . . . as long as courts persist in exercising their review function by asking whether the Secretary of State has gone about his decision in the right way, courts are likely to defer to the Secretary of State's judgment wherever he can show that some sort of balancing exercise was carried out, without scrutinising the outcome of that balancing exercise for disproportionality as a proper human rights court would do.[43]

In other words, merely requiring a decision-maker to have regard to fundamental rights as a relevant consideration, without taking the further step of ensuring that full and proper regard was had to that consideration, fails adequately to address the human rights dimension to a given case. Nicholas Blake QC recognised this in stressing that, despite the legacy of *Brind*:

> . . . it should now be clear that the human rights protected in the Convention are in truth such relevant considerations in administrative law that the courts will require decision-makers to satisfy them that no decision inconsistent with these standards will be taken. In particular cases, this will require disclosure of evidence, adequate reasoning addressing the Convention criteria and relevant considerations emerging from the case law and, where necessary, primary judicial fact-finding. In those circumstances, judicial review would . . . become an effective remedy for the protection of human rights.[44]

It is apparent from the case law that Mr Blake's prescriptions are being heeded, as they must be if judicial review is to have the 'fullness of jurisdiction' neces-

---

[40] Which is reinforced by the response to 'objectionable' judicial decisions, as where the decision of the Court of Appeal in the *JCWI* case, above, n 20, was followed by the enactment of the Asylum and Immigration Act 1996.

[41] But see now *Douglas v Hello! Ltd* [2001] 2 All ER 289.

[42] *Smith and Grady v United Kingdom; Lustig-Prean and Beckett v United Kingdom* (1999) 7 BHRC 65.

[43] Hunt, above, n 26, 260.

[44] N Blake QC, 'Judicial Review of Discretion In Human Rights Cases' [1997] *EHRLR* 391, 403.

sary to constitute an effective remedy for breaches of the Convention rights. What is significant, however, is the ease with which developments driven by the Human Rights Act 1998 have dovetailed with domestic doctrine. A parallel may be drawn here between review for jurisdictional error and review under the Human Rights Act 1998 where it is alleged that a public authority has acted incompatibly with the Convention rights contrary to section 6(1) of the Act. In the first situation, it is well established[45] that an administrative decision may be invalid where the decision-maker has misconstrued the provisions empowering him to act or where, as Lord President Emslie put it in *Wordie Property Co Ltd v Secretary of State for Scotland*,[46] it is based on 'a material error of law going to the root of the question for determination.' This is not to say that the decision-maker must understand every condition of the exercise of his power 'correctly', the courts being the ultimate arbiter of correctness. Rather, as Lord Mustill put it in *R v Monopolies and Mergers Commission, ex parte South Yorkshire Transport Ltd*,[47] the question—normally—is whether the decision-maker's understanding fell within the 'spectrum of possible meanings . . . and permissible field of judgment' identified by the court. Where fundamental rights are in play, however, the courts will narrow the 'spectrum of possible meanings' to such an extent that only one answer to a given question of statutory interpretation may remain, and a decision taken on any other basis will be unlawful on that account. So much is clear from the decision of the House of Lords in *R v Secretary of State for the Home Department, ex parte Adan and Aitseguer*,[48] a case concerning the obligations of the Home Secretary under section 2(2) of the Asylum and Immigration Act 1996 in light of the Geneva Convention on the Status of Refugees.

Let us turn now to review under the Human Rights Act 1998. Generally speaking, this will involve a complaint that a public authority has acted, failed to act or proposes to act in a manner incompatible with Convention rights, contrary to section 6(1). Section 6(2), however, provides that this shall not be unlawful if, first, as the result of one or more provisions of primary legislation, the authority could not have acted differently; or, secondly, in the case of one or more provisions of, or made under, primary legislation which cannot be read or given effect in a way which is compatible with the Convention rights, the authority was acting so as to give effect to or enforce those provisions. While, in either event, the petitioner might seek to invoke the remedy of declaration of incompatibility, this would vindicate his rights only in the most abstract sense; his preference will be for a more concrete remedy against the relevant public

---

[45] See *Anisminic Ltd v Foreign Compensation Commission* [1969] 2 AC 147; *Watt v Lord Advocate*, 1979 SC 120; *R v Hull University Visitor, ex parte Page* [1993] AC 682; and see Lord Clyde and D J Edwards, above, n 19, para 22.18–22.43.

[46] *Wordie Property Co Ltd v Secretary of State for Scotland*, 1984 SLT 345.

[47] *R v Monopolies and Mergers Commission, ex parte South Yorkshire Transport Ltd* [1993] 1 WLR 23.

[48] *R v Secretary of State for the Home Department, ex parte Adan; R v Secretary of State for the Home Department, ex parte Aitseguer* [2001] 2 WLR 143.

authority. Tactically, this will produce a dynamic whereby both petitioner and respondent seek to avoid declarations of incompatibility and join battle instead on the correct interpretation of the primary or subordinate legislation under which the public authority is acting. In any case, the courts themselves are enjoined by section 3(1) to read and give effect to primary and subordinate legislation, so far as possible, in a way which is compatible with the Convention rights. For practical purposes, therefore, the issue in most cases will not be whether the legislation itself is incompatible with Convention rights but whether the public authority has exercised its discretion under legislation read so as to conform to the Convention rights in a manner inconsistent with those rights. And this, in effect, is an issue of vires or jurisdiction—something that is meat and drink to the supervisory jurisdiction already. Seen in this light, the Convention rights constitute, essentially, limits on the scope of discretionary powers, and in articulating and enforcing those limits the courts are not discharging a new and unfamiliar role. Indeed, the approach of the courts to statutory interpretation in the light of section 3(1) of the Human Rights Act 1998 may be *less* inexorable than that adopted by the House of Lords in *Adan and Aitseguer*. The Convention rights may, in particular cases, reduce statutory provisions to a single, Convention-proofed meaning. But where it is contended that a public authority has exercised its statutory discretion in a manner incompatible with, say, the right of privacy protected by Article 8 of the ECHR, the court will require to bear in mind the margin of appreciation allowed to public authorities in deciding whether and to what extent a competing public interest justifies an interference with the protected right. That consideration comes into play at the stage of guaging the substantive proportionality of an interference in the particular circumstances of the case before the court, but it must also feed into the initial, 'jurisdictional' question of whether, under the statute properly construed, the public authority had the power to interfere with protected rights in this way at all.[49]

A like parallel, or continuity, can be seen in the context of review for error of fact. Jurisdictional errors of fact have always been reviewable,[50] and the courts will intervene where material facts are found on the basis of no evidence.[51] That apart, as Lord Templeman put it in *R v Independent Television Commission, ex parte TSW Broadcasting Ltd*:[52]

> Judicial review does not issue merely because a decision-maker has made a mistake
> and it is not permissible to probe the advice received by the decision-maker or to

[49] For the overlap between review for illegality and review for unreasonableness/disproportion, see the judgment of Lord Phillips MR in *R (Javed) v Secretary of State for the Home Department* (hereafter *Javed*), (CA) Court of Appeal, Times, 24 May 2001, at para 57.

[50] See, for example, *R v Secretary of State for the Home Department, ex parte Khawaja* [1984] AC 74; *Tan Te Lam v Superintendent of Tai A Chau Detention Centre* [1997] AC 97.

[51] This is treated as amounting to error of law: see, for example, *Colleen Properties Ltd v Minister of Housing* [1971] 1 WLR 433; *R v Hillingdon London Borough Council, ex parte Islam* [1981] 3 WLR 942.

[52] *R v Independent Television Commission, ex parte TSW Broadcasting Ltd* [1996] EMLR 291.

require particulars or administer interrogatories or to cross-examine in order to discover the existence of a mistake by the decision-maker or the advisers of the decision-maker. An applicant for judicial review must show more than a mistake on the part of the decision-maker or his advisers.

Subsequent decisions suggested an emergent doctrine whereby a material error of fact, albeit 'non-jurisdictional' fact, would justify review.[53] It is probable that this tentative development will now become an established part of the supervisory jurisdiction, not least because, if it does not, judicial review might itself fail to satisfy the requirements of Article 6 of the ECHR. It is instructive, therefore, that in *R (Javed) v Secretary of State for the Home Department*,[54] both Turner J and the Court of Appeal held that, although historically reluctant to evaluate evidence when reviewing decisions of the executive, the courts have had a positive duty since the entry into force of the Human Rights Act 1998 to give effect to the ECHR and to ensure that there is an effective remedy in cases of suspected breaches of Convention rights. Therefore, where an executive decision requires to be reviewed on the facts, the court is competent to carry out that exercise once the relevant material is placed before it. In that case, the applicants successfully claimed judicial review of the Home Secretary's decision to include and retain Pakistan in the list of designated countries as a country in which it appeared to him that there was in general no serious risk of persecution, on the basis that such a conclusion was simply not justified by Pakistan's human rights record; and thus were able successfully to challenge the decision to reject their applications for asylum.

This is a significant departure from the traditional deference of the courts on review to findings of fact by the primary decision-maker, and one which extends the scope of review into areas once thought not to be its proper province. It stems not only from the obligation to furnish an effective remedy for breaches of the Convention rights, but also from a concern to ensure that the courts on review have the 'fullness of jurisdiction' necessary to fulfil the requirements of Article 6 of the ECHR. This entitles every person, in the determination of his civil rights or obligations or of criminal charges against him, to a fair and public hearing, within a reasonable time, before an independent and impartial tribunal established by law. The ECtHR has made clear[55] that Article 6 applies to

---

[53] See, for example, *R v London Residuary Body, ex parte Inner London Education Authority*, The Times, 24 July 1987; *R v The Parliamentary Commissioner for Administration, ex parte Balchin* [1998] 1 PLR 1; *R v Criminal Injuries Compensation Board, ex parte A* [1999] 2 AC 330; *Wandsworth London Borough Council v A* [2000] 1 WLR 1246. In the latter case, Stuart Smith LJ described the question whether error of fact qualified as a free-standing ground of review as 'difficult and elusive', adding, in particular, that 'the duty of anxious scrutiny imposed in asylum cases by *Bugdaycay* renders those cases an uncertain guide for other areas of public law.' This dictum suggests, nonetheless, that at least in that class of human rights case, the reviewability of errors of fact was becoming accepted; and see now, in particular, *R v Secretary of State for the Home Department, ex parte Turgut*, above, n 32.

[54] *R (Javed) v Secretary of State for the Home Department*, above, n 49.

[55] See, for example, *Ringeisen v Austria (No 1)* (1971) 1 EHRR 455.

any proceedings the result of which is 'directly decisive' for an individual's civil rights and obligations, whether or not final determination of the applicant's rights and obligations is the primary purpose of the proceedings and regardless of whether the decision-maker is a fully judicialised body in the normal sense of that term. However, where the function of determining civil rights and obligations is vested in an administrative, executive or professional body that is not a 'court of the classic kind,'[56] it is sufficient to secure compliance with Article 6 that the body is subject to subsequent control by a judicial body having 'full jurisdiction' and which does provide the guarantees of fair procedure.[57] It has been clear for some time, and certainly since the decision of the ECtHR in *Bryan v United Kingdom,*[58] that the supervisory jurisdiction, excluding as it did scrutiny of the merits of challenged decisions and having only limited scope to review findings of fact, might not always suffice to 'cure' procedural defects at the primary decision-making stage. In *Bryan* itself, the Court accepted that even though the court's jurisdiction on judicial review or a statutory appeal on a point of law was restricted, it was sufficient to correct the specific deficiencies of (planning) procedure there complained of. In contrast, however, the Court held in *Kingsley v United Kingdom*[59] that judicial review proceedings were insufficient to cure the risk of bias on the part of the Gaming Board of Great Britain in deciding to revoke the applicant's certificate of approval, and that his right to be heard by an independent and impartial tribunal had thereby been violated.[60]

The requirement of recourse to a court having 'full jurisdiction' should not, however, be understood as requiring, in all circumstances, a full right of appeal on the merits of every administrative decision. In *Kaplan v United Kingdom,*[61] the Commission held that to provide a right to a full appeal against any administrative decision affecting private rights would be inconsistent with the long-standing legal position in most of the signatory states. In *Bryan*, the ECtHR held

---

[56] The term is used by Lord Lester of Herne Hill QC and David Pannick QC in *Human Rights Law and Practice* (Butterworths, London, 1999), para 4.6.23 (a passage approved by Lord Macfadyen in *County Properties Ltd v The Scottish Ministers*, 2000 SLT 965 (hereafter *County Properties*)). See also *De Cubber v Belgium* (1984) 7 EHRR 236.

[57] *Albert and Le Compte v Belgium* (1983) 5 EHRR 533.

[58] *Bryan v United Kingdom* (1995) 21 EHRR 342.

[59] *Kingsley v United Kingdom* (Appl No 35605/97), *The Times*, 9 Jan 2001.

[60] This was because, where a complaint is made of a lack of impartiality on the part of the decision-making body, the concept of 'full jurisdiction' requires that the reviewing court not only considers the complaint but also has the ability to quash the impugned decision and to remit the case for a new decision by an impartial body. It is worth noting, in passing, that the 'real danger' test for bias in English law, prescribed by the House of Lords decision in *R v Gough* [1993] AC 646, was modified by the Court of Appeal in *In Re Medicaments and Related Classes of Goods (No 2)*, *The Times*, 2 Feb 2001, in order to bring it into conformity with the test applied by the ECtHR under Art 6. This followed the concession by the Court of Appeal in *Locabail (UK) Ltd v Bayfield Properties* [2000] 1 All ER 65; [2000] 2 WLR 870, decided before the entry into force of the Human Rights Act 1998, that the *Gough* test had not commanded universal approval in other jurisdictions, Scotland included (see *Doherty v McGlennan*, 1997 SLT 444), and that the 'reasonable apprehension' or 'reasonable suspicion' tests applied in Scotland and elsewhere might 'be more closely in harmony with the jurisprudence of the ECtHR.'

[61] *Kaplan v United Kingdom* (1980) 4 EHRR 64.

that in specialised areas of the law, such as planning law, it may be necessary and expedient for an administrative body to make findings of fact and to exercise discretionary judgment in relation to questions of policy; and that in such cases the requirements of Article 6 of the ECHR might be met by a right of appeal of a point of law or the individual's entitlement to seek a remedy by way of judicial review. Likewise in *ISKCON v United Kingdom*,[62] the Commission held that:

> it is not the role of Article 6 to give access to a level of jurisdiction which can substitute its opinion for that of the administrative authorities on questions of expediency and where the courts do not refuse to examine any of the points raised.

Despite these authorities, Lord Macfadyen distinguished *Bryan* in *County Properties*.[63] Given the circumstances which rendered the respondents 'not an independent and impartial tribunal'[64] and the nature of the issues which fell to be determined in relation to the applicant's case, his Lordship concluded that the Court of Session when seised of a statutory appeal under section 58 of the Town and Country Planning (Scotland) Act 1997 did not have the fullness of jurisdiction necessary to cure the defects of procedure at the earlier stages.[65] The Inner House subsequently reversed Lord Macfadyen's judgment in light of the House of Lords decision in the *Alconbury* case.[66] The joined appeals there considered by the House concerned applications for planning permission which had been 'called in' by the Secretary of State and appeals against planning decisions which the Secretary of State had 'recovered'. At first instance, the Divisional Court made declarations of incompatibility in respect of the relevant statutory provisions, having found it impossible to read and give effect to them in a manner compatible with Article 6 of the ECHR. This decision was overturned by a unanimous House of Lords, in which the speeches are notable for two things.

First, the speeches disclose a consciousness on their Lordships' part of the constitutional 'division of labour' between legislature, executive and judiciary, which, evidently, is not lightly to be upset. Lord Nolan, for example, states that his first reason for reversing the decision of the Divisional Court 'reflects the obvious unsuitability of the courts as the arbiters in planning and related

---

[62] *ISKCON v United Kingdom* (1994) 76-A DR 90.

[63] *County Properties Ltd v The Scottish Ministers*, above, n 56.

[64] '[What] is involved [here] is the respondents adjudicating on an issue between their own executive agency [Historic Scotland] and the petitioners' (per Lord Macfadyen, *County Properties*, above, n 56, at 974).

[65] See also, for example, *Tehrani v United Kingdom Central Council for Nursing, Midwifery and Health Visiting*, 2001 SLT 879. Lord Mackay held that there was no breach of Art 6(1) on grounds of want of independence and impartiality by a disciplinary tribunal from which there is a right of appeal to a court having full jurisdiction. His Lordship reserved his opinion, however, on the adequacy of judicial review or statutory appeal for this purpose. The authority of *Alconbury* may be less compelling in this situation than in *County Properties*, given the 'quasi-judicial' nature of the decision under review.

[66] *R v Secretary of State for ETR, ex parte Alconbury* [2001] 2 All ER 929.

matters. . . . [The] decision to be made . . . is an administrative and not a judicial decision.'[67] To similar effect is Lord Hoffmann, who observes, after a lengthy review of the case law, that the European jurisprudence

> does not require that the court should be able to substitute its decision for that of the administrative authority. Such a requirement would in my opinion not only be contrary to the jurisprudence of the ECtHR but would also be profoundly undemocratic. The 1998 Act was no doubt intended to strengthen the rule of law but not to inaugurate the rule of judges.[68]

Secondly, and relatedly, their Lordships make clear that, at least for the purposes of a case such as *Alconbury*, the 'supervisory jurisdiction of the court *as it has now developed'*[69] is sufficiently wide to pass muster under Article 6. In that regard, as Lord Slynn explains:

> It has long been established that if the Secretary of State misinterprets the legislation under which he purports to act, or if he takes into account matters irrelevant to his decision or refuses or fails to take account of matters relevant to his decision, or reaches a perverse decision, the court may set his decision aside. Even if he fails to follow necessary procedural steps—failing to give notice of a hearing or to allow an opportunity for evidence to be called or cross-examined, or for representations to be made or to take any step which fairness and natural justice requires, the court may interfere. The legality of the decision and the procedural steps must be subject to sufficient judicial control. . . . [In regard to the principle of proportionality] I consider that even without reference to the Human Rights Act the time has come to recognise that this principle is part of English administrative law . . . Trying to keep the *Wednesbury* principle and proportionality in separate compartments seems to me to be unnecessary and confusing. . . . [But] this principle does not go as far as to provide for a complete rehearing on the merits of the decision. Judicial control does not need to go so far. It should not do so unless Parliament specifically authorises it in particular areas.[70]

In light of such dicta, it is unsurprising to find that the reception of proportionality and the margin of appreciation doctrine has not greatly altered the intensity of substantive review. As we have seen, in the period immediately preceding the entry into force of the Human Rights Act 1998, the courts had so far developed the 'sliding scale' of judicial review as to subject the substantive outcomes in fundamental rights cases to a level of scrutiny that was, and is, functionally identical to that of the proportionality principle.[71] True it is, as Simon Brown LJ acknowledged in *Smith*, that incorporation of the Convention rights

---

[67] *R v Secretary of State for ETR, ex parte Alconbury* [2001] 2 All ER 929, at para 60, *per* Lord Nolan.

[68] *Ibid*, at para 129, *per* Lord Hoffmann.

[69] *Ibid*, at para 169, *per* Lord Clyde (emphasis added).

[70] *Ibid*, at paras 50–52, *per* Lord Slynn.

[71] For a particularly clear exposition, see the speech of Laws LJ in *Mahmood*, above, n 32, at 847: 'the application of so exiguous a standard of review [as the conventional *Wednesbury* principle in a case such as this] would . . . involve a failure to recognise what has become a settled principle of the common law, one which is entirely independent of our incorporation of the European Convention by the Human Rights Act 1998. It is that the intensity of review in a public law case will depend on

involves a change of emphasis that makes, or might have made, a difference in some cases, *Smith* itself not the least of them.[72] But the change of emphasis has hardly been revolutionary: the pattern of reasoning reflected in the jurisprudence of the ECtHR was discernible in domestic law prior to 2 October 2000. Some of the vocabulary in which the courts couch that reasoning is new: one term at least with which we are already familiar is the 'margin of appreciation', which denotes the area of discretion left to national authorities by the ECtHR. One rationale for the doctrine is that it is the natural deferential reflex of a multi-national court, which recognises the dangers of overriding too freely the substantive judgments of national authorities. It might be thought that this justification for the margin of appreciation cannot apply to the dealings between public authorities and the domestic courts of the United Kingdom. But the need to allow public authorities the free exercise of discretion within a sphere of reasonable possibilities is explicable on grounds which apply equally at the national level, and which we have touched on already. Simply put, there must in any constitutional system be an appropriate division of labour between the judicial, executive and legislative branches of the state, and the supervisory jurisdiction must respect that division. The margin of appreciation doctrine, like the sliding scale of review developed as a matter of domestic administrative law, allows the courts to calibrate the intensity of their intervention in a manner appropriate to the subject matter of the cases brought before them and the nature of the fundamental rights implicated therein. The point was well captured by Lord Hope in his speech in *R v Director of Public Prosecutions, ex parte Kebilene*:[73]

> The questions which the courts will have to decide in the application of [the Convention]will involve questions of balance between competing interests and issues of proportionality. In this area difficult choices may have to be made by the executive or the legislature between the rights of the individual and the needs of society. In some circumstances it will be appropriate for the courts to recognise that there is an area of judgment within which the judiciary will defer, on democratic grounds, to the considered opinion of the elected body or person whose act or decision is said to be incompatible with the Convention. . . . It will be easier for such an area of judgment to be recognised where the Convention itself requires a balance to be struck, much less so where the right is stated in terms which are unqualified. It will be easier for it to be recognised where the issues involve questions of social or economic policy, much less so where the rights are of high constitutional importance or are of a kind where the courts are especially well placed to assess the need for protection.

---

the subject matter in hand; and so in particular any interference by the action of a public body with a fundamental right will require a substantial objective justification.' See also, for example, *R v Secretary of State for the Home Department, ex parte Launder* [1997] 1 WLR 839 at 867, *per* Lord Hope of Craighead; *R v Lord Saville of Newdigate, ex parte A* [2000] 1 WLR 1855 at 1867, *per* Lord Woolf CJ.

[72] See below, n 74, and accompanying text.

[73] *R v DPP, ex parte Kebilene* [1999] 3 WLR 972; [2000] 2 AC 326 at 381. See also M Supperstone QC and J Coppel, 'Judicial Review After the Human Rights Act' [1999] *EHRLR* 301 at 316: 'the doctrine of the margin of appreciation is founded in the status of the [European] Court of Human Rights *as a court, and not merely as an international court*' (emphasis added).

The appropriateness and, indeed, legitimacy of judicial intervention is in large part a function of the limits which exist on judicial competence to resolve polycentric, substantive—at bottom, political—issues and choices. It was ever thus. The incorporation of the Convention rights sharpens domestic human rights jurisprudence in a number of ways, not least by drawing into judicial review rights (and European authority) not previously known to, or insufficiently recognised by, the common law.[74] Equally, as Lord Steyn put in *Daly*,[75] while there is an overlap between the traditional grounds of review and the principle of proportionality, and while most cases would be decided in the same way whichever approach is adopted, the intensity of review under the proportionality principle is greater inasmuch as it may require the reviewing court to assess the balance which the decision-maker has struck, not merely whether it is within the range of rational or reasonable decisions, and to consider the relative weight accorded to interests and considerations. But it does not involve the courts in a function intrinsically different from that which they were already accustomed to discharge in the context of the supervisory jurisdiction.

One point remains. It is often said that the central objective of the Human Rights Act 1998 is to encourage the growth in the United Kingdom of a 'culture of rights'. That will come about not solely, or even mainly, as a consequence of judicial decisions in litigated cases, but rather as a consequence of general shifts in the practice of public authorities in response to the duties laid on them by the Act. One important way in which the Act, and the courts on review, are likely to contribute to such a change of practice, and so to enhance the transparency and rigour of decision-making processes, is by requiring public authorities fully and properly to justify their decisions when those decisions impinge upon fundamental rights. As Lord Clyde noted in *Stefan v Health Committee of the General Medical Council*,[76] in which the Judicial Committee of the Privy Council considered the relevance of the existence of a right of appeal and/or the availability of judicial review to whether a duty to give reasons was to be implied into a statutory procedural code, there is still no general common law duty to give reasoned decisions. The courts have established that such a duty does arise in certain circumstances—where, for example, a decision is on its face and in view of the known facts irrational; or where the absence of reasons renders the decision unfair, either *per se* or because it frustrates the individual's ability or right to challenge the decision. Even before the entry into force of the

---

[74] For example, the Human Rights Act 1998 would have made a difference in *Smith*, above, n 31, not in the sense of allowing the court to adjudicate on the proportionality of the policy of the Ministry of Defence—that, effectively, the court was prepared to do—but in the sense of giving the applicants an explicit right to respect for their private life on which to found. By the same token, the right to respect for the home, family and private life, which imposes positive as well as negative obligations on public authorities, may in future be relied upon by persons adversely affected by decisions in the planning and environmental sphere: see, for example, *Lopez-Ostra v Spain* (1995) 20 EHRR 277.

[75] *R v Secretary of State for the Home Department, ex parte Daly* [2001] UKHL 26.

[76] *Stefan v Health Committee of the General Medical Council* [1999] 1 WLR 1293, 1300–01.

Human Rights Act 1998, then, a public authority wishing to avoid judicial censure was well-advised to provide reasons for its decisions. But where violations of Convention rights are complained of, the jurisprudence of the ECtHR *requires* that reasons be provided to justify such interference (assuming such interference is permissible at all). Moreover, if human rights are to merit more than mere lip service, a public authority whose decision is attacked on human rights grounds can no longer be allowed to get away with a simple averment that it took the human rights dimension into account. Rather, the courts should require a fully reasoned record which discloses that any human rights dimension was *properly* considered, and should be entitled to infer from the absence of such record that that crucial dimension was *not* properly taken into account. The interference with protected rights would therefore fall to be impugned as unjustified and unlawful. And if this happens in the field of fundamental rights, it is but a short step to requiring the provision of reasons for all administrative decisions, as a matter of the common law.

C. REMEDIES

It is perhaps curious that the remedy contained in section 4(1) of the Human Rights Act 1998, the declaration of incompatibility, excited such comment at the time of the Act's enactment. It is not a striking new departure, because the courts were already obliged to 'disapply' national legislation which was found to be incompatible with European Community law.[77] When doing so, no doubt consciously, the courts chose to use the language of 'incompatibility' rather than 'invalidity', so preserving a veneer of legal truth in the notion of the supremacy of Parliament.[78] This distinction is also captured by the Human Rights Act 1998 itself, which provides in section 4(6) that a declaration of incompatibility will not affect the validity, continuing operation or enforcement of the provision in respect of which it is given, and will not be binding on the parties to the proceedings in which it is made. For this reason, as has been seen, it is likely that most litigants, not to mention the government itself, will seek to avoid declarations of incompatibility as a hollow alternative to the possibility of having a violation of Convention rights stopped or compensated.

A person who satisfies the requirements of title and interest under the Human Rights Act 1998 may bring proceedings against a public authority if he claims that the authority is acting, or proposes to act, inconsistently with Convention rights; or he may rely on the Convention right or rights concerned in any legal proceedings.[79] In either event, if the court finds that the public authority respondent is acting, or proposes to act, unlawfully, it may grant 'such relief or remedy, or make such order, within its powers as it considers just and

---

[77] Case 92/78, *Simmenthal SpA v Commission* [1979] ECR 777.
[78] *R v Secretary of State for Transport, ex parte Factortame Ltd (No. 2)* [1991] 1 AC 603; *R v Secretary of State for Employment, ex parte Equal Opportunities Commission* [1995] 1 AC 1.
[79] S 7(1)(a) and (b).

appropriate'. The remedial powers of the Court of Session on judicial review are contained in rule 58.4 of Chapter 58 of the Rules of the Court of Session. This provides that the court may make any order

> that could be made if sought in any action or petition, including an order for reduction, declarator, suspension, interdict, implement, restitution, payment (whether of damages or otherwise) and any interim order.

There are restrictions on this discretion, perhaps most notably the exclusion of the remedy of interdict against the Crown in 'civil proceedings' under section 21 of the Crown Proceedings Act 1947. That exclusion was partially lifted following the decision of the European Court of Justice in *Factortame (No. 2)*.[80] In judicial review proceedings in England, the exclusion was wholly removed following the decision in *M v Home Office*.[81] There, on the basis that judicial review is the modern incarnation of 'proceedings on the Crown side of the King's Bench Division'— which are excluded from the scope of the term 'civil proceedings'—it was held that the remedy of injunction was competent against a Minister of the Crown 'acting in his official capacity' in the context of a claim for judicial review. The Second Division declined to follow this reasoning in *McDonald v Secretary of State for Scotland*.[82] In the light of the Human Rights Act, a prisoner at HM Prison Barlinnie sought, *inter alia*, declarator that an order ordaining the Scottish Ministers to transfer him to conditions of detention compatible with Article 3 of the ECHR might competently be made in judicial review proceedings, notwithstanding section 21 of the 1947 Act.[83] Affirming *McDonald*, it was held, first, that the reasoning in *M* simply did not translate into Scottish terms, turning as it did on peculiarities of English procedure. There was nothing in the 1947 Act to suggest that the supervisory jurisdiction of the Court of Session was not a 'civil proceeding'. Secondly, the arguments drawn from the incorporation of the ECHR met with a response that can fairly be described as trenchant. Lord Marnoch remarked that it 'serves absolutely no purpose to assert that the "rule of law" requires coercive orders to be granted against the Crown unless there can be shown a means of construing the [1947 Act] to that end.' Lord Hardie accepted that, even though unincorporated by the Human Rights Act, Article 13 of the Convention entitles individuals to an effective remedy in respect of breaches of their Convention rights. It does not, however, entitle one to a remedy of one's choice. As it is, the 1947 Act allows declaratory relief against the Crown, and 'to suggest that a declarator, coupled with an undertaking from the Scottish Ministers, is not an effective remedy because it is not coercive is plainly wrong.' If there is any comfort for intending litigants in this, it is to be found in Lord Weir's speech: while

---

[80]   *Factortame (No. 2)*, above, n 78.

[81]   *M v Home Office* [1994] 1 AC 377.

[82]   *MacDonald v Secretary of State for Scotland*, 1994 SLT 692. An interim order was made against the Crown, in the shape of the Keeper of the Registers of Scotland, in a case which involved a question of Community law and which was therefore covered by *Factortame*: *Miller & Bryce Ltd v Keeper of the Registers of Scotland*, 1997 SLT 1000.

[83]   *Scott Davidson v The Scottish Ministers*, Extra Division, 18 Dec 2001.

compelled by section 21's lack of ambiguity to agree that it included judicial review in Scotland, his Lordship noted his dissatisfaction with the outcome, not least since the immunity no longer obtains in England. Nevertheless, 'the only cure for this state of affairs lies in the hands of Parliament.'

A further point relating to remedies concerns damages. Section 8(2) of the Human Rights Act 1998 provides that damages may be awarded by a court having power to award damages or to order the payment of compensation. The Human Rights Act 1998 may therefore be regarded as creating a new 'statutory delict', although not, perhaps, a delict subject to the ordinary principles of reparation. First, a court may only award damages where it considers it 'just and appropriate' to do so. Thus, as Merris Amos has pointed out, proof of a violation of one's Convention rights will not *ipso facto* entitle one to a monetary remedy: more suitable redress 'may be obtained merely by quashing the decision or issuing an injunction to put an end to conduct incompatible with Convention rights.'[84] Secondly, in deciding whether an award of damages is necessary to afford just satisfaction to the applicant, the court is directed by section 8(3)(b) to consider the consequences of doing so. Amos suggests that this is likely to be interpreted as calling the courts' attention to the risks of opening the floodgates:

> to make an award of damages in respect of [an] act [at the instance of one applicant] may mean that hundreds, even thousands, of potential applicants will have a similar claims, representing a considerable strain on the public purse.[85]

Here as elsewhere, moreover, the courts must take into account the principles applied by the ECtHR in deciding whether to award damages and the amount of any award. But the jurisprudence of the ECtHR in this regard has been justly criticised by Alastair Mowbray as inconsistent, opaque and premised upon unarticulated moral judgements about the nature of different types of applicants.[86] In their joint report on damages under the Human Rights Act 1998,[87] the Law Commission and Scottish Law Commission accepted that *when* the ECtHR awards damages, it seeks to restore the applicant to the position he would have been in had the breach not occurred. But even they were driven to remark upon the lack of principle in the case law of the ECtHR as to whether and in what amount damages should be awarded. They conclude that the entry into force of the Human Rights Act 1998 will not require major changes to the law on damages in either jurisdiction, but on the basis that,

> where the courts . . . have established appropriate levels of compensation for particular types of loss in relation to claims in tort or delict, it would seem appropriate for the same rules to be used in relation to a claim under the Human Rights Act 1998.

---

[84] M Amos, 'Damages for Breach of the Human Rights Act 1998' [1999] *EHRLR* 178 at 181.
[85] *Ibid*, at 186.
[86] A Mowbray, 'The ECtHR' Approach to Just Satisfaction', [1997] *PL* 647 at 653.
[87] *Damages under the Human Rights Act 1998* (Law Com No 266, Cm. 4853; Scot Law Com No 180, SE/2000/182).

This would seem to suggest that, far from attempting to distil a body of principle from the jurisprudence of the ECtHR to guide the exercise of their remedial discretion under the Human Rights Act 1998, the courts should instead apply and adapt existing causes of action to complaints of breaches of the Convention rights. This may in turn trigger a re-appraisal of the delictual liability of public authorities in non-Convention cases, on the basis that, as Lord Woolf remarked in *M v Home Office*,[88] adaptation of existing remedies (in *M*, for the purposes of Community law) may generate pressure to reform the remedy more generally.

There is much to suggest that, here as elsewhere, the influence of the Convention is already being felt. Recent cases, such as *Barrett v Enfield London Borough Council*[89] and *Phelps v Hillingdon London Borough Council*,[90] represent a retreat from the highly restrictive stance on the negligence liability of public authorities adopted by the House of Lords in *X v Bedfordshire County Council*[91] and *Stovin v Wise (Norfolk County Council, third party)*.[92] This retreat owes much to the judgment of the ECtHR in *Osman v United Kingdom*,[93] where it was held that the striking out of the applicant's claim against the Metropolitan Police in *Osman v Ferguson*[94] amounted to a breach of the applicants' rights under Article 6 of the ECHR. There are, as Lord Browne-Wilkinson remarked in *Barrett*, difficulties with the reasoning of the ECtHR in the *Osman* case, and it is perhaps significant that in *Z v United Kingdom*[95] and *TP and KM v United Kingdom*,[96] the ECtHR found no breach of Article 6 in either case.[97] It did, however, find in the first case that the applicants' rights to freedom from inhuman and degrading treatment under Article 3 of the ECHR had been breached by the failure of the United Kingdom authorities to provide them with appropriate protection against the serious and prolonged neglect and abuse they had suffered at the hands of their parents. In the second case, the Court held that the applicants' rights under Article 8 were breached by the local authority's failure to disclose a video interview and its transcript, on the basis of which the child had been removed from her mother, to a court for determination in care proceedings. More importantly, the ECtHR found a breach of Article 13 of the ECHR in both cases. Given that the courts now regard themselves as obliged to furnish effective remedies for breaches of the ECHR, it is probable that both of these cases will cause the domestic courts to reconsider further their approach to the actionability of negligent exercises of (or failures to exercise) statutory powers.

---

[88] *M v Home Office*, above, n 80, 407.
[89] *Barrett v Enfield London Borough Council* [1999] 3 All ER 193.
[90] *Phelps v Hillingdon London Borough Council* [2000] 3 WLR 776.
[91] *X v Bedfordshire County Council* [1995] 2 AC 633.
[92] *Stovin v Wise (Norfolk County Council, third party)* [1996] AC 923.
[93] *Osman v United Kingdom* (1999) 25 EHRR 245.
[94] *Osman v Ferguson* [1993] 4 All ER 344.
[95] *Z and Others v United Kingdom* (Application No 29392/95), The Times, 31 May 2001.
[96] *TP and KM v United Kingdom* (Application No 28945/95), The Times, 31 May 2001.
[97] Both petitions were brought by the disappointed plaintiffs in two of the five joined appeals (the 'abuse cases') heard in *X v Bedfordshire County Council*, above, n 90.

7

The Swedish Experience of the ECHR Since Incorporation

IAIN CAMERON*

A. INTRODUCTION

THE SWEDISH STATUTE incorporating the European Convention for the Protection of Human Rights and Fundamental Freedoms (ECHR) entered into force on 1 January 1995.[1] The present chapter will look at what can loosely be termed the constitutional issues raised by incorporation of the ECHR in Swedish law. One of the most interesting features of the ECHR, like EC law, is that it is a separate, autonomous system of law which nonetheless, with incorporation, becomes a part of the national legal system. As such it cuts across national legal categorisations. But it is also an incomplete system. ECHR issues can arise under national law which have not (yet) arisen in the context of the ECHR system. Thus, studying the case law of other jurisdictions dealing with the ECHR can be of immediate benefit to one's own system, even leaving aside the long-term, indirect benefit to be gained by studying comparative constitutional law in general. For a variety of reasons, the Swedish system is likely to be of interest to Scottish and English public lawyers. While the political histories of the United Kingdom and Sweden have differed considerably, both have a strong attachment to parliamentary democracy. In both states the parties which have dominated government have tended to stress the 'self-vaccinating' function of periodic elections as regards risks of abuse of power, and to play down the need for constitutional protection of rights. Both states steadfastly refused for many years to incorporate the ECHR, mainly out of a fear that this would result in a shift of power to the courts and thus impede 'strong government'. While the

---

* Professor in Public International Law, University of Uppsala, Sweden. This chapter is an updated version of an article first published in (1999) 48 ICLQ 20.

[1] Lag (1994:1219) om den europeiska konventionen angående skydd för de mänskliga rättigheterna och de grundläggande friheterna [Act on the European Convention on Human Rights]. The law (and the accompanying amendment to the Instrument of Government, *Regeringsformen*, hereafter RF) entered into force on 1 Jan 1995. The law has been amended recently, with the incorporation of Protocol No 11 (Prop 97/98:107). Possible conflicts are between the law which incorporates the ECHR and another Swedish norm, not between the ECHR as such and a Swedish norm. For the sake of simplicity, however, I will refer simply to the 'ECHR'.

main focus of the chapter is directed at explaining the Swedish system, I will also draw some parallels with the British legislation incorporating the ECHR. However, much has already occured in the United Kingdom in general, and Scotland in particular, since the enactment of the Human Rights Act 1998, and I do not claim to be an expert on these developments.[2]

Before looking at the issues, I should note that translations are my own unless otherwise noted. As regards citation, references to the Swedish statute book (*Svensk författningssamling*, SFS) are by year followed by the relevant number. When I refer to the constitutional document, the Instrument of Government, I use the Swedish abbreviation, RF (*Regeringsformen*) followed by the chapter and section number (eg RF 11:14). Cases from the Supreme Court are cited from the semi-official series, *Nytt juridisk arkiv* (NJA) cases from the courts of appeal, from the official series *Rättsfall från hovrätterna* (RH) cases from the Labour Court from the official series *Arbetsdomstolens domar* (AD) and cases from the Supreme Administrative Court from the official series *Regerings-rättens årsbok*, (RÅ).[3] References to *travaux préparatoirers* are either to the number of the commission responsible for investigating the law, *Statens offentliga utredningar* (SOU) and the year of its report, or the draft bill put before parliament together with its accompanying documentation, (*proposition*, prop) or the report of the Parliamentary Committee on the Constitution on the bill (KU). References to Supreme Court cases and *travaux préparatoires* are made to the page number (*sida*, s)

B. THE CASES

Up to the time of writing (August 2001) there have been over 100 cases in the higher courts in which the ECHR was a significant issue, although in a large number of these it was still of secondary importance and only cursorily examined.[4] The published cases can give indications of the impact the ECHR is having on the ways in which judges and advocates think, but obviously cannot give more than a vague idea of the extent to which the human rights laid down in the ECHR are actually being respected in Sweden. It is not possible to determine the extent of the 'dark figure', namely cases in which the ECHR could have been relevant, or even decisive, to the judgment, but where the parties, or the court failed to take it up (notwithstanding the principle *jura novit curiae* which generally applies in Swedish procedural law). Nor, as regards comparative studies,

---

[2] So much has been written that I will not even attempt to list the most important Arts and books. For a valuable overview and analysis see D McGoldrick, 'The United Kingdom's Human Rights Act 1998 in Theory and Practice' (2001) 50 *ICLQ* 901.

[3] Supreme Administrative Court cases regarded as more important are found in the reference (ref) section, others in the note (not) section.

[4] District court cases and district administrative court cases are not published. The figure of 100 cases does not include administrative cases dealing with the lack of an oral hearing.

can much be read into the fact that courts in other states might have quoted ECHR case law in areas where Swedish courts have not. Obviously the extent to which a court is willing or able to rely on ECHR case law will depend on a number of factors, in particular the adequacy of the national system of protection of human rights and the ease (in law and fact) with which the courts are able to engage in constitutional review. Where Swedish law already fulfils, or even goes further than, the requirements of the ECHR, only Swedish law need, and probably will, be cited.[5]

The cases cover a large number of different issues, in different areas of law. For example, in family law, the issues have arisen of standing to challenge a decision on paternity and an administrative decision fixing the place of residence of children. In company law, issues have arisen of access to a court to challenge a decision on liquidation and the effectiveness of judicial remedies. In criminal law, issues have arisen of anonymous or absent witnesses, child witnesses in sexual abuse cases, use of video evidence, disqualification of judges, reopening of a trial held to be unfair and exceptional powers to investigate tax crime. Two criminal/administrative areas which have caused particular headaches for the courts are whether tax penalties and decisions to revoke drivers' licences are 'criminal' in nature. As regards other areas of administrative law, issues have arisen concerning deportation, compulsory detention of mental patients, trial within a reasonable time, access to a court to challenge administrative decisions and payment of church tax. In addition, there has been a relatively large number of cases concerning the right to an oral hearing in administrative cases. In civil law generally issues have arisen regarding execution of foreign judgments on defamation, which are allegedly in violation of freedom of expression, the proportionality of planning and expropriation decisions and regarding standing to challenge such decisions. In labour law, issues have arisen of disqualification of judges, negative freedom of association, challenge to security screening decisions, compulsory drug testing, freedom of expression and the *Drittwirkung* of the ECHR and denial of access to a court by means of an arbitration clause. As a survey of this case law is rather lengthy, and as my concern in the present chapter is what could be described as the 'constitutional' issues, I will not go through all these cases, but only those relevant to the present subject.[6]

---

[5] Eg extradition/deportation cases concerning refusal to deport because of a family connection, NJA 1996, s 365 and NJA 1997, s 172 or breaches of trade union representation rights, AD 2001, nr 33.

[6] I make a detailed survey up to 1998 in 'Swedish Case Law on the ECHR Since Incorporation, and the Question of Remedies' in I Cameron and A Simoni (eds), *Dealing with Integration* (Iustus Förlag, Uppsala, 1998) vol 2.

C. THE CONSTITUTIONAL STATUS OF THE ECHR AND THE COMPETENCE
TO RULE ON ECHR BREACHES

I will not deal with the history of the ECHR in Swedish law before incorporation, nor with the incorporation debate (such as it was).[7] Nor will I deal with
the general system of protection of constitutional rights in Sweden.[8] I have
already dealt with these subjects elsewhere. It is, however, necessary to say
something about the constitutional status of the ECHR in Sweden as compared
to the United Kingdom.

Unlike the United Kingdom, Sweden chose to incorporate the whole ECHR,
and its protocols, rather than simply the substantive rights and the general limitation provisions.[9] There is little explanation for this in the *travaux préparatoires*. The main reason appeared to have been that the other Nordic states had
incorporated the whole treaty or were planning to do so.[10] In practice, there
ought to be little difference between incorporating the whole ECHR or the
'operative' part of it, although the former method gives rise to the interesting
question as to whether the incorporation of the 'effective remedy' and 'just satisfaction' requirements in Articles 13 and 41 respectively provide Swedish courts
with the necessary procedural competence to award damages where the plaintiff's ECHR rights have been breached.[11] Only the ordinary courts may award
damages in Sweden, and it is not easy to obtain non-pecuniary damages from
the state. There has been at least one district court case in which the plaintiff
claimed damages for violation of her ECHR rights. However, in the case in
question, the plaintiff failed to prove such a violation and so the court did not
need to rule on the issue.[12] I consider that Swedish judges are not going to be
willing to create a remedy in damages in the absence of a much clearer go-ahead
from the legislature. The legislature is, in any event, going to have to create some
form of remedy in damages in the specific case of failure to provide a 'trial
within a reasonable time' following the Court's landmark judgment in *Kudla v
Poland*.[13]

The incorporation law provides that the ECHR is to have the status as an
ordinary statute. The problem with this was obvious: this statute could come
into conflict with other statutes. Accordingly, a provision was also added to the
constitution (RF 2:23) which lays down that 'a law or other regulation shall not
be issued in conflict with Sweden's obligations under [the ECHR]'. The British
discussion as to whether or not a parliament can bind its successors, procedu-

---

[7] See I Cameron, 'Sweden', in C Gearty (ed) *European Civil Liberties and the European
Convention on Human Rights* (Kluwer Law International, The Hague; Boston , 1997).
[8] See I Cameron, 'The Protection of Constitutional Rights in Sweden' [1997] *PL* 488.
[9] Sweden has ratified Protocols No 4, 6 and 7, but has not signed Protocol No 12.
[10] SOU 1993:40 s 126.
[11] I discuss this issue in more detail in Cameron, above, n 6.
[12] Uppsala district court, judgment in case nr T 3326–97, 8 June 2000 (unreported).
[13] *Kudla v Poland* No 30210/96, 26 Oct 2000.

rally or substantively, is not relevant to Sweden which has a written constitution and, naturally, a procedure for amendment of it. On the other hand, the rule in RF 2:23 was still regarded as controversial as it opens the way for a judicial encroachment of parliament's freedom of manouver, which is, if anything, even more jealously guarded in Sweden than the United Kingdom. Thus, the constitutional amendment was the subject of protracted discussions between the political parties. This is evident from the *travaux préparatoires* to the Act of incorporation. I should note here that, in contrast to the position in the United Kingdom, the *travaux préparatoires* to legislation are taken very seriously by the courts. This is particularly unfortunate in this case, as the *travaux préparatoires* to the Act of incorporation, being political compromises, are, on occasion, positively delphic. Every comma was the subject of debate between the political parties. By the time the bill was formally introduced to parliament, there was no room for changing anything in it. One thing was, however, made abundantly clear, namely that the rule in RF 2:23 was to be used sparingly, as a last resort. The courts were encouraged instead to solve the problem of possible conflicts with other Swedish norms by the application of certain principles of interpretation. These were named as *lex specialis*, *lex posterior*, the principle of 'treaty-conform' construction and a rather novel varient of it proposed by the Supreme Court when commenting on the legislative proposal, namely the principle that 'human rights treaties should be given special significance in the event of a conflict with other norms'.

There has been some discussion in doctrine as to the scope of the duty to engage in constitutional review and the sequence and extent of the interpretative operations to be performed before resort is made to it. This will be discussed further below. One point, however, should be noted here. RF 2:23 does not, as such, give the ECHR constitutional status. Nor does it, formally speaking, create a new category of laws midway between the Constitution and ordinary laws (although this is the position in practice). Formally the provision means that a law or other regulation which conflicts with the ECHR, also conflicts with the Constitution. As with all such conflicts, the normal restrictions in RF 11:14 apply on the power of the courts to engage in constitutional review.[14] This means that the courts, and administrative agencies, must refuse to apply legislation or subordinate legislation which conflicts with the ECHR, although where it is a statute or a government ordinance which allegedly breaches the ECHR, then the conflict with it must be 'manifest'. Accordingly, statutes or ordinances which conflict with the ECHR but do not manifestly conflict with it should thus be applied. No restriction applies to constitutional review of rules lower down in the hierarchy of norms, ie regulations promulgated by administrative agencies or local authorities.

---

[14] See further, Cameron, above, n 8, 502–12. Removal of the 'manifest' requirement has recently been proposed by a government commission, but for political reasons, change in this seems unlikely in the near future.

Thus, as regards the constitutional status of the ECHR, there are a number of similarities and differences between the Swedish, Scottish and United Kingdom parliamentary systems. In the Swedish and Scottish systems there is an explicit acceptance of the *lex superior* principle. However, the Scottish judges are given much more freedom to engage in constitutional review based on the ECHR. There is, however, an explicit difference as regards the scope of the bodies empowered to rule on the compatibility of the incorporated ECHR with other national law. In Britain, as in Sweden, all 'public bodies' are obliged to follow the ECHR. But in Britain only the superior courts may rule that there is an incompatibility between the ECHR and another national law. Whereas all legal systems recognising constitutional review have their own variants of it, it is possible to systematise these using a number of broad categories.[15] The British system could be said to be something of a hybrid, in that it is a diffuse, rather than concentrated, system of review (all the higher courts may rule on incompatibility). It is also 'concrete' review, in that it can only apply as a result of an actual dispute regarding the application of law between two parties, not indirect where no concrete dispute has yet arisen but someone or some institution wishes to challenge the legality of legislation or draft legislation ('abstract'). On the other hand, unlike other diffuse systems allowing only concrete review, such as the USA, Canada, Norway or, for that matter, Sweden, the ruling of the court that a breach of rights has occured is not determinative *in casu et inter partes,* but rather declarative.

In Sweden, unlike the United Kingdom, all courts *and administrative agencies* are in principle obliged to refuse to apply a norm which conflicts with the ECHR. Thus, it is an extreme diffuse system. But the scope of the power is diminished in proportion to the number of authorised users: the 'manifest' requirement, combined with Swedish legal culture, means that administrative agencies will never, and courts, even the highest courts, will only very rarely, refuse to apply a statute or ordinance on the basis that it breaches the ECHR. It should also be pointed out here that the effect of constitutional review of statutes or ordinances in the Swedish system—in the very rare cases where it has occured—is that the inferior norm is set aside only in the case at issue. It does not lapse as such. As such, while the ruling determines the issue between the parties, the impugned norm continues to be formally valid.

Finally in this section, the point can be made that the ECHR must be understood from the ECHR case law. Section 2 of the (UK) Human Rights Act 1998 expressly recognises this in that courts and tribunals are explicitly required to have regard to the ECHR *acquis,* at present growing at the rate of some 800

---

[15] On constitutional review see eg E McWhinney, *Supreme Courts and Judicial Lawmaking* (Martinus Nijhoff, Dordrecht; Boston, 1985), C Landfried (ed), *Constitutional Review and Legislation: An International Comparision* (Nomos, Baden-Baden, 1988), AR Brewer-Carías, *Judicial Review in Comparative Law* (Cambridge University Press, Cambridge, 1989) and DM Beatty (ed), *Human Rights and Judicial Review* (Martinus Nijhoff, Dordrecht, London, 1994). My way of categorising constitutional review follows that of Brewer-Carías, at 91–92.

judgments and 9,000 admissibility decisions per year. There is no such requirement in the Swedish statute. On the other hand, such a requirement is made
clear in the *travaux préparatoires* to the act of incorporation.[16] Bearing in mind
the great significance accorded to the *travaux préparatoires* to legislation in
Sweden, more or less the same result is achieved.

D. COEXISTING RIGHTS CATALOGUES

Another significant difference between the United Kingdom and Sweden is that
Sweden has a separate system of protection of constitutional rights. Indeed, it
has two systems of protection in addition to that of the ECHR. First, there is the
catalogue of rights set out in chapter 2 of the Instrument of Government; second, there is the constitutional protection of the printed media (the Freedom of
the Press Act, Tryckfrihetsförordningen, TF) and the electronic media (the
Freedom of Expression Act, Yttrandefrihetsgrundlag, YGL). The latter two acts
are *lex specialis* in relation to the former. The existence of a separate system of
protection of constitutional rights is obviously in line with the subsidiary nature
of the ECHR (Article 53). Indeed, viewed from this perspective, it is rather
strange to have a 'fall-back' or 'lowest common denominator' human rights
treaty as the only human rights statute in national law of general application.
One of the obvious difficulties with such an approach is that there is of no
'appeal' to Strasbourg if the British courts in fact go beyond the requirements of
the ECHR.[17]

A dual system of rights protection can have implications for the willingness of
the courts to interpret the ECHR dynamically. There may be less need to stretch
the wording of the ECHR, or 'anticipate' the Strasbourg case law, a point examined further below. It should also be recognised that there are bound to be problems when the same system contains different constitutional rights catalogues,
overlapping with one another. These were played down in the Swedish *travaux
préparatoires* which stated simply that the highest common denominator of
protection for the individual should apply.[18] But while this is obviously the correct general approach, the issue is complicated by the fact that rights often
involve balancing individuals' interests against each other, not simply against
state interests, eg the interest in freedom of expression and the interest in not
being defamed. Different rights catalogues can prioritise amongst interests in
different ways, either by formulating the rights differently, or through case law.
For example, the right to freedom of religion in RF Chapter 2 s 1 p 1, is absolute,
meaning no restrictions to it are permissible. This in turn entails defining its

[16] Rop 1993/94: 117 s 37. See also Ds 1997:25 s 49, produced as a result of the *Holm* case (see
below n 42) where it is stated that ECtHR cases are a source of law to be applied by the Swedish
courts.
[17] For more discussion of what can be termed the 'anticipation' problem see below.
[18] Prop 1993/94:117 s 37.

content (the protected area) in a very narrow fashion. For a male Sikh, the wearing of a turban is an important part of his religion. For an orthodox Jew or Muslim, it is important to be able to eat meat from animals killed in a particular way.[19] According to Swedish doctrine, neither of these ways of manifesting religion falls under s 1 p 1.[20] On the other hand, they do fall in under Article 9(1) and so restrictions in them have to be justified under Article 9(2).[21] The methodology the courts apply to approaching rights issues can also vary. For example, the Swedish courts and the ECHR organs have dealt very differently with the concept of what is a 'restriction' on human rights.[22]

E. ECHR MONITORING AND PREVENTIVE (LEGISLATIVE) CONTROL

As already mentioned, the Swedish legislator accepted constitutional review against the ECHR only very reluctantly. It was repeatedly stated in the *travaux préparatoires* that the primary responsibility for ensuring compliance with the ECHR was with the legislator. It might, then, have been expected that steps would be taken to ensure that legislation, and subordinate legislation, which raises issues under the ECHR is not passed without first having undergone expert scrutiny. This is not the case. On the other hand, the normal legislative process being long and rather open, ought to identify potential breaches. Put very briefly, the legislative process usually begins with a directive to a committee, consisting either of MPs or of civil servants, to investigate the need for new legislation. Committees dealing with legal questions are often assisted by, or even led by, external experts (eg academic lawyers). After the committee has reported, an opportunity is usually given for a cross-section of interest groups (often including the law faculties) to comment upon the merits of proposals before these are laid before parliament. The government then decides whether to propose legislation. If it does so, the relevant government department drafts a proposal. About 50 per cent of all proposals are sent to the Law Council, a group of prominent lawyers, mainly serving or retired judges from the highest courts. The Law Council comments on the technical aspects of the proposal, although it occasionally makes (guarded) criticism of the substance of it. The proposal is then submitted to parliament as a bill and considered by the relevant parliamentary standing committee. This committee then submits a report to parliament. The composition of this standing committee reflects the composi-

---

[19] For an ECHR case on this point, see *Cha'are Shalom ve Tsedek v France*, No 27417/95, 27 June 2000.

[20] See, eg H Strömberg, 'Hädiska tanker om religionsfrihet', in Rättsfonden, *Om våra rättigheter* (Almqvist and Wiksell, Uppsala, 1980).

[21] I would, however, argue that wearing a turban is a form of religious freedom of expression, and so protected by RF 2:1, p 1. Certainly if wearing a swastika badge or armband is a means of expression (NJA 1996, s 577), then so too is wearing a turban.

[22] I will not repeat the criticism I have made elsewhere of the narrow approach taken in the *travaux préparatoires* to RF and in some case law. See Cameron, above, n 8, 504–05.

tion of parliament as a whole so it is seldom that the vote in parliament goes against the proposal of the committee.

It can be seen from this very brief description of the Swedish legislative process that there are several points at which critical voices can be heard. The first of these is at the investigative stage. In this context one can point out that one of the standard directions to a committee is to consider in what way, if any, the changes it may propose are compatible with the constitution. As already mentioned, the ECHR as such does not have constitutional status. There is thus no general requirement for a committee to take it into account, although naturally the specific directive it receives may require it to do so. Another important stage is the scrutiny of the law faculties. A further safeguard is the Law Council. A brief survey I made of the minutes of Law Council meetings during 1998 disclosed several proposals in which the Law Council drew the attention of the government to possible difficulties relating to the ECHR. In each case, the Law Council contented itself with references to the ECHR itself, rather than European Court of Human Rights (ECtHR) case law. It should be noted here that the Law Council has no legal assistants and its membership changes every two years. The competence of the Law Council in the field of the ECHR thus depends wholly upon the knowledge the individual members have of it. Thus, it is by no means a totally reliable safeguard. A third, and last, stage at which ECHR issues can be raised is in the parliamentary committee which scrutinises the bill. Proposals relating to the constitution are sent to the Committee of the Constitution. Other committees can also refer a proposal to it for commentary. This committee has a small legal staff which is capable of making its own investigations. Independent investigations occur relatively rarely. One example where it happened was regarding a legislative proposal to close a nuclear power station. The political opposition inter alia raised the issue of the compatibility of this measure with Article 1, Protocol No 1, particularly whether it could be said to be 'in the public interest.'[23] The legal staff of the Committee on the Constitution, however, are not experts on the ECHR.

One weakness of the Swedish system is that the mechanisms for monitoring new Strasbourg case law concerning other states are deficient. The National Courts Administration Board now has a procedure for monitoring case law developments before the Court and the European Court of Justice (ECJ) and of disseminating judgments to Swedish courts. However, it is a single judge who has this task, so there is still a risk that cases which may have important implications are missed. There is no group, or person, in the Foreign or Justice Ministries given the job of checking whether a new case may cause problems for Swedish law. Having said this, there is no centralised monitoring of ECJ case law either. The procedural law and constitutional law units of the Department of Justice have most experience of dealing with ECHR and can, hopefully, be relied upon to pick up on the important ECHR cases and initiate a directive to a committee to inquire into the matter. This has occured before, eg regarding

---

[23] Prop 1996/97:22.

the implications of the Strasbourg case law for Swedish tax cases, although the commission of inquiry later produced a report recommending only minor changes, to bring the law in line with the *Funke* case.[24] The commission of inquiry chose, despite strong evidence to the contrary, to continue to classify tax penalties as administrative in nature, rather than as 'criminal' within the meaning of Article 6, and Protocol No 7, Article 4. The refusal to change the law ended up causing considerable problems for the Swedish courts.[25] A later commission of inquiry into tax penalties drew the correct conclusion that the teleological interpretative method most often applied by the ECtHR means that Swedish commissions of inquiry recommending legislation should not 'balance on the border' of what is permitted by the ECHR.[26] Such an approach can only serve to postpone problems, shifting them to the courts.

A few words should also be said about administrative agencies' knowledge, or lack of it, regarding the ECHR when they engage in rule-making and adjudication. I made a brief informal survey of some of those agencies which are most likely to come into contact with ECHR issues: the National Courts Administration, the Chief State Prosecutor, the National Board of Health and Welfare, the Ombudsman and the Chancellor of Justice. The Ombudsman is responsible inter alia for monitoring the administration on behalf of the parliament, the Chancellor of Justice, for monitoring it on behalf of the government. Of these bodies, it is the courts and the Ombudsman which have most contact with ECHR issues.[27] Only the National Courts Administration organises internal courses on the ECHR. No agency had a centrally placed person, or group, with ECHR monitoring as their special responsibility. None of the people I spoke to considered that the level of ECHR questions their agency faced in its daily work justified a specialist person or body. The work of all the above agencies is divided into different subject areas and each has only a small centralised co-ordination body, so it would admittedly be difficult to build in a meaningful centralised ECHR monitoring function.

In conclusion, on preventive monitoring, one can say that both the legislature and the major administrative agencies should do more to monitor the requirements of the ECHR when engaged in enactment of norms. This is particularly so in the light of the recommendation to this effect made in the Rome Resolutions on human rights, adopted by the member states of the Council of Europe in November 2000.[28]

---

[24] *Funke v France*, 25 Feb 1993, A/256–A, SOU 1996:116.

[25] See the judgments of the Supreme Court in NJA 2000 s 622 and the Supreme Administrative Court in RÅ 2000 ref 66.

[26] SOU 2001:25, at 331.

[27] I will not go into the Ombudsman's handling of ECHR issues since incorporation. For two examples of the Ombudsman examining the requirements of Art 8 in connection with telephone monitoring see JO 1995/96:29 and 97/98:115.

[28] Resolution concerning institutional and functional arrangements, (Rome Resolution) can be found in Human Rights Information Bulletin, No 50 and the Council website, posted at http://www.coe.int.

F. DRITTWIRKUNG

One of the interesting issues in the United Kingdom is the question of *Drittwirkung*, ie horizontal effect of the ECHR between individuals.[29] The requirement in section 6 of the Human Rights Act 1998 that all 'public bodies' have regard to the ECHR can involve them in applying the ECHR in adjudicating disputes between individuals. There is some ECHR case law on the subject of which bodies are part of the 'state', totally, or for certain defined purposes. Obviously, in the 1990s, many function of the state have been privatised. The ECHR organs appear, correctly, to have taken the view that it would be formalistic to deny the safeguards of the ECHR to these bodies when they are exercising public power.[30] As with Community law, however, new difficulties arise in drawing conceptually satisfactory boundary lines between wholly private bodies and partially public bodies. Nonetheless, the question of whether the ECHR should apply to individuals' relations *inter se* is separate from this issue, even if related.

To begin with it should be pointed out that the ECHR is a treaty regime, albeit of a special character, compliance with which functions, as with all treaties, on the basis of the rules of state responsibility.[31] On the other hand, the ECHR, once it has been incorporated into national law, is a national legal instrument. As a matter of constitutional law it is the national parliament which determines what formal status the incorporated instrument should have in the domestic legal hierarchy. And it is the national parliament, together with the national courts, which determine whether or not the incorporated ECHR is to be given any horizontal effect, direct or indirect. The scope of the ECHR at the level of national law need not be identical with its scope at the level of international law. If, of course, it is given a narrower scope by national courts, then cases will ultimately end in defeat in Strasbourg. But this will not be the case if the ECHR is given a more generous interpretation, whether as regards material rights or as regards procedural matters, eg the protected class of victim (standing) or the object(s) against which ECHR rights are guaranteed (only the state, or in certain circumstances, individuals too).

This, of course, is in theory. The Swedish legislature did not give any indications to the courts that they are to interpret the incorporated ECHR so as to give it horizontal effect. Nor is there any tradition of *Drittwirkung* to build upon as

---

[29] There have already been a large number of articles dealing with this issue. See, eg M Hunt, 'The "Horizontal Effect" of the Human Rights Act', [1998] *PL* 423, H W R Wade, 'Horizons of Horizontality' (2000) 116 *LQR* 217, N Bamforth, 'The True "Horizontal Effect" of the Human Rights Act 1998' [2001] *PL* 34, B Markesinis, 'Privacy, Freedom of Expression, and the Horizontal Effect of the Human Rights Bill: Lessons From Germany' (1999) 115 *LQR* 47.

[30] See, eg *Finska församlingen in Stockholm and Teuro Hautaniemi v Sweden*, No 24019/94, 85 DR 94 (1996) and the *Municipal Section of Antilly v France*, No. 45129/98, ECtHR 1999–VIII.

[31] This is a simplification. I will not go into the relationship between the concepts of material breach and state responsibility.

regards rights in RF.[32] Nonetheless, even if one accepts that the ECHR has no formal horizontal effect, the nature of the obligations contained in certain Articles in the ECHR sometimes requires the contracting parties to provide for rights for individuals which are exercisable against other individuals. The most obvious example of this is the right of access to a court to determine a dispute concerning civil rights or obligations, but even other rights can oblige states to engage in positive action. The issue is particularly interesting in Sweden because of the existence of powerful trade unions and because there are a few private companies which dominate certain branches of industry.

There have been a few cases so far before the Swedish courts in which the issue of *Drittwirkung* has been raised. In AD 1997, nr 57, the Labour Court rejected summarily a trade union's argument that Article 10 of the ECHR conferred horizontal rights, in this case on employees of a privately owned ambulance company who had sent a letter to the press criticising their employer and who were subsequently sacked. Admittedly, the direct issue before the court was whether there were reasonable grounds for dismissal (as if not, damages would have to be paid) and the ECHR argument was only of a subsidiary nature. Still, the court showed no awareness of the indirect *Drittwirkung* issue, ie by upholding the lawfulness of the dismissal, it, as a public body, was upholding a contract which restricted freedom of expression.[33]

In AD 1998, nr 17, the boot was on the other foot. Here it was a private employer who argued that it had a right derived from Article 11 (the right not to belong to an association) which was exercisable against a trade union. The background to this case was the judgment of the ECtHR in *Gustafsson v Sweden*.[34] In Sweden, many issues of employment law are regulated by collective agreement. The parties in the labour market are thus largely left free to use their economic muscle to force agreements on one another. However, it would seem to follow from the *Gustafsson* case that should trade unions try, by boycott or blockade, to force an employer to join an employer's association bound by a collective agreement, or to force him to be bound by this agreement independently, and should the trade unions not have legitimate reasons for taking this industrial action (ie the protection of their members' interests), then the state is obliged to provide the employer with a remedy before the courts. The courts must be entitled to review the reasonableness of the trade unions' action in the circumstances and order them to cease, or restrict, their industrial action where this is not reasonable/proportionate. An employer in the above circumstances affected by a trade union blockade or boycott is therefore entitled to

---

[32] I will not go into the debate concerning the desirability of giving provisions of Regeringsformen (RF) indirect drittwirkung. There are, interestingly, explicit rights for individuals exercisable vis-à-vis other individuals set out in TF and YGL.

[33] It should be pointed out here that under s 36 of the Contracts Act there is a general power for the courts to set aside, or vary, an unreasonable contract term in a concrete case. The plaintiff must, however, invoke this provision. As the employees had already been dismissed it was not an issue in the present case.

[34] *Gustafsson v Sweden* No 15573/89, 25 April 1996.

bring an action against the trade union in the courts relying upon Article 11 and the Swedish courts should, if all the above (admittedly very demanding) requirements are satisfied, issue an injunction or other such measure, notwithstanding the lack of specific statutory authority to do so. In AD 1998, nr 18, the Labour Court made it easy for itself by reaching the conclusion that the trade union had a legitimate basis for its actions in that the employment conditions in the company were not as advantageous to the workers as those provided by the collective agreement (particularly as regards overtime, which was not paid by the company). Accordingly, the union, which had two members working for the company, was entitled to take the blockade action. One judge dissented from this finding. While the trade union thus won in this case, the issue is by no means dead. Even the possibility that the ECHR gives the courts the possibility (indeed, duty) to intervene and determine whether a trade union blockade is proportionate or not has led to an overreaction from some Swedish trade union figures. One went so far as to call for the denunciation of the ECHR, mirroring the response of some right-wing MPs in the United Kingdom following the *McCann* case.[35]

Another, case similar to AD 1998, nr 18 was AD 2001, nr 1, where the majority of the Labour Court rejected the view that a collective agreement providing for an automatic deduction of salary on all employees, unionised and non-unionised, designed to cover the labour unions' costs in salary negotiations with employers, constituted an impermissible infringement of the negative right of freedom of association.

Finally, there have been two cases in which the Labour Court has rejected the view that compulsory drug testing by private employers constitutes a violation of Article 8. The Labour Court did not totally rule out that Article 8 could, exceptionally, be invoked in such cases, but found in the circumstances that the measures were justified by the nature of the employment in question in the first case, employees of a privately operated nuclear power station (AD 1998, nr 97), and in the second case, former offenders involved in care of 'problem' school children (AD 2001, nr 3).

G. THE IMPACT OF EUROPEN COURT OF HUMAN RIGHTS CASE LAW ON SWEDISH LAW

The most common complaints against Sweden can be divided into five broad areas: judicial review of administrative decisions, violations of property rights, taking of children into care, procedural safeguards in civil and criminal trials and matters concerning aliens. At the time of writing (August 2001) 49 cases have been referred to the Court and 45 judgments have been delivered (four

---

[35] *McCann and others v United Kingdom*, (1996) 21 EHRR 97. For the Swedish reaction see *Svenska dagbladet* 23 Feb 1998.

cases under Protocol No 9 referred to the Court by the applicants were not accepted). In 22 of the 45 judgments, at least one violation was found. In 14 cases, no violation was found. Eight cases were struck off the list. Several cases have been declared admissible during 2000 and 2001, concerning, inter alia, tax penalties and trial within a reasonable time.

The ECtHR's judgments in some of the above cases, eg the child custody cases, did not require changes to be in the law. On the other hand, even cases where Sweden was not found to have violated the ECHR have led to changes being made.[36] The most significant change occasioned by ECtHR judgments has been regarding the lack of access an individual had to a court to determine a dispute he or she has with the adminstration. Attention was drawn to the inadequacies of Swedish law in this respect by the ECtHR's judgment in *Sporrong and Lönnroth*.[37] The government of the day chose to ignore the warning, however, and Sweden paid the penalty for its legislative inaction when it lost, in quick succession, a number of cases on the issue in Strasbourg. beginning in 1987.[38] Legislation was accordingly introduced in 1988 which provides for a right of judicial review of certain administrative cases decided by an adminstrative agency or the government as a final instance of appeal. The law was initially passed for a trial period until 1991. It was made permanent in 1996. The law applies only to cases in which there is no other available judicial remedy and in which the administrative decision imposes a burden on an individual. The intention behind the legislation was to cover the category of 'civil rights and obligations' but this term was not used because it was considered that its unfamiliarity could cause Swedish lawyers difficulties. Instead, the law refers to the areas of public activity covered by RF 8:2 and 8:3. These provide that delegation of legislative power in certain areas—particularly those involving burdens for the individual—should be approved by statute. This has the consequence that, eg decisions to refuse permission to engage in a particular business activity, are subject to review whereas decisions to withold a benefit, eg a social security payment or admission to a higher educational course, are not. It has been pointed out that the exclusion of decisions involving benefits from review is not without difficulties, particularly in view of the *Deumeland* and *Feldbrugge* cases.[39] In addition to this general restriction, decisions by certain quasi-judicial tribunals and decisions concerning matters regarded as predominently of a policy nature

---

[36] The opinion of the dissenting minority in the *Leander* case (8 July 1987, A/116) concerning the inadequacies of safeguards on vetting checks by the security police was one of the factors behind the reform of the law made, eventually, in 1996. *Cruz Varas* (20 March 1991, A/201) led to an amendment of the Aliens Act (Ch 8 s 10a) allowing the government to issue a stay of execution in deportation cases where the Commission had requested this.

[37] *Sporrong & Lönnroth v Sweden* (1982) 5 EHRR 35.

[38] See *Pudas*, 27 Oct 1987, A/125-A, *Bodén*, 27 Oct 1987, A/125-B, *Tre Traktörer v Sweden* (1989) 13 EHRR 483, *Allan Jacobsson*, 25 Oct 1989, A/163, *Mats Jacobsson*, 28 June 1990 A/180A *Skärby*, 28 June 1990 A/180B, *Zander* 25 Nov 1993, A/279-B.

[39] *Deumeland v Germany*, 29 May 1986, A/100, *Feldbrugge v Netherlands*, 29 May 1986, A/99. See further the dispute between the Supreme Court and the Supreme Administrative Court noted below n 94.

are excluded from review, notwithstanding the direct impact these could have in the area of 'civil rights and obligations.'[40] Other changes made have included reforms of the rules on pre-trial detention (*McGoff*), on oral hearings in appeal courts (*Ekbatani*) and on the disqualification of judges in special courts (*Langborger*).[41] The issue of amendment of the Freedom of the Press Act was discussed as a result of the ECtHR's finding of a violation of the right to trial by an impartial tribunal in the *Holm* case.[42] However, the government, and later parliament, considered that the rare cases in which the composition of the jury was a problem could be dealt with by the courts applying the *Holm* case in conjunction with the general clause in chapter 4, section 13 of the Code of Judicial Procedure that provides for disqualification of judges and jury members.[43]

H. AVOIDING CONSTITUTIONAL REVIEW

(1) Generally

Before looking at the issue of constitutional review as such, it would be useful to take a closer look at the methods the legislator recommended to the courts as alternatives to their taking such an embarassing, and undemocratic, action. As already indicated, these were the *lex posterior* and *lex specialis* principles, the principle of 'treaty-conform construction' and the, amorphous, variant of this, that 'human rights treaties should be given special significance' in the event of a conflict. I deal with these in turn. I should stress, however, that the *travaux préparatoires* give no indication of the order in which these interpretative exercises are performed. What is clear, however, is that the method which advances a treaty-conform interpretation is to be preferred. The theoretical dividing line between the application of a treaty-conform construction and constitutional review is that the application of the former is designed to avoid, or deny, a norm conflict, whereas the application of constitutional review accepts it. The latter begins where the scope for applying the former ceases. But as shown below, the dividing line can be assumed to be drawn differently from state to state depending on a number of factors.

To begin with, as far as *lex posterior* is concerned, RF 2:23 is formulated as a duty on the legislature not to pass legislation in conflict with the ECHR. This might seem to indicate that this duty only applies prospectively. There would

---

[40] It is not by any means clear that all of these tribunals would satisfy the requirements of Art 6. Certainly, not all of them are regarded as 'courts' in Swedish constitutional law.

[41] Respectively, *McGoff* 26 Oct 1984, A/83, *Ekbatani* 26 May 1988, A/160 and *Langborger* 22 June 1989, A/ 155. For more detail on the legislative changes occasioned by these and other cases see I Cameron, 'Sweden' in R Blackburn and J Polakiewicz (eds), *The European Convention on Human Rights—The Impact of the ECHR in the Legal and Political Systems of Member States over the Period 1950–2000* (Oxford University Press, Oxford, 2001).

[42] *Holm* 25 Nov 1993, A/ 279–A.

[43] Prop 97/98:43, s 129–135.

thus be no duty to give the ECHR precedence as regards conflicts with pre-1995 legislation. But the *travaux préparatoires* contradict this interpretation, as does a case before the Supreme Administrative Court.[44] In this case, the plaintiff was a Finn who had been resident in Sweden in 1985. He was not a member of the Swedish Church, but he had nonetheless been obliged to pay Church tax for the year in question. The ECtHR in 1990 in *Darby v Sweden* had ruled that such a requirement was a breach of Article 9.[45] However, the law reform occasioned by the Commission admissibility decision in the case in 1988 had not been given retroactive effect and the tax authorities, and the lower courts, ruled that there was no basis on which the plaintiff's tax for 1985 could be adjusted. The Supreme Administrative Court, however, ruled that, as the ECHR has the status of Swedish law from 1995, and as no transitional provisions were made forbidding its application to cases arising before 1995,[46] it fell to be applied in the present case. The court thereafter referred to the *Darby* case and ruled that the plaintiff's tax for 1985 should be adjusted accordingly.[47]

But the *lex posterior* principle of course, means that legislation enacted after 1995 can be given precedence before the ECHR. This is, however, expressly excluded by RF 2:23. Is there, however, a way of avoiding the application of constitutional review in such cases? Of course, the preventive legislative safeguards are designed to minimise the risk of such conflicts, but as indicated above, some are bound to slip through. In such cases, the courts should then turn to the other principles of interpretation. In general, *lex specialis* can be a useful principle for avoiding norm conflicts, although it is rare that such norm conflicts are openly acknowledged in Sweden.[48] However, there are three major problems as regards using the *lex specialis* principle in relation to the ECHR. The principle, which is applied by the Strasbourg organs themselves,[49] is a means of identifying the most appropriate rule to be applied in a concrete dispute. However, *lex specialis* cannot really be used when the conflict is between two legislatures, or two norm systems. When both norm systems apply simulta-

---

[44] RÅ 1997 ref 6.

[45] *Darby v Sweden* A/187 (1991).

[46] This was not the case for the law enacting the new Instrument of Government in 1974 (1974:152), which contained provision for the continued validity of several laws and types of law which would otherwise have been invalid. Cf RÅ 1996 ref 57 (not involving the ECHR) where the absence of a transitional provision meant that the court felt unable to grant retroactive effect to legislation and so it once again ruled in the individual's favour and against the state.

[47] The issue of giving retroactive effect to ECHR judgments was considered by the ECtHR in *Marckx v Belgium* (1979) 2 EHRR 330. The ECtHR considered in this case that legal certainty ruled out giving retroactive effect to judgments in civil cases. On the other hand, the requirements of legal certainty are not necessarily so strong in administrative cases, at least where giving retroactive effect means the state losing. For an interesting discussion of this issue, see T Andersson, 'Blasting the Past or Cleaning the Slate?' (2001) 3 *Turku Law Journal* 5.

[48] For two examples see SOU 1995:115 s 99 (conflict between the Aliens Act and Care of Children Act) and AD 2000 nr 17 (conflict between security screening legislation and employment protection legislation). For a detailed treatment of the problems raised by the latter case, see I Cameron, *National Security and the ECHR* (The Hague, London, 2000), 204–12, 246–52, 291.

[49] See, eg *Enzelin v France*, 26 April 1991, A/202, ara 37.

neously, it does not help to identify the most specific rule: the conflict persists. It must be remembered that the incorporation act is no ordinary statute, but rather the insertion into Swedish law of a large body of law. The ECHR *acquis*, like EC law, permeates large areas of national law. Unlike EC law, however, it does not explicitly take precedence in the event of a conflict with national law. Instead, it applies *in parallel* with other national law. To put it another way, the ECHR, as interpreted by its case law, is largely a set of principles. As is well known, principles differ from rules in that a rule is either applicable or not, whereas several principles can apply simultaneously, all pulling in different directions. The process of applying these principles can be described as one of 'concretisation' rather than 'interpretation'. The general application of the ECHR means that for a national court it is not a question of deciding whether a rule contained in the ECHR or in another statute is the most appropriate and then applying it. Instead, the latter has to be applied in the light of the former. There is nothing really new about this, as in all states with a written constitution, statutes have to be applied in the light of the general rules set out in the constitution. Having said this, for a variety of reasons, the Instrument of Government is rarely referred to by Swedish courts. There is thus no great familiarity with this means of approaching cases. Even in other states which have specialised constitutional courts, the ordinary courts may be unfamiliar with such a way of working. It may be that British judicial culture, notwithstanding its lack of a written constitution, is more at home with this way of working than continental (and Swedish) judicial culture. Such a large issue is, however, outwith the scope of the present essay.[50]

The second, related, problem is that the *lex specialis* principle naturally cuts both ways: both for and against the ECHR. Other statutes are almost always going to be *lex specialis* in relation to the ECHR, even if the 'ECHR' is interpreted in the wide sense to include the ECHR *acquis*. There has already been at least two attempts in the higher courts to argue that a statute is *lex specialis* in comparison to the ECHR. In AD 1998 nr 17, the defendant argued that legislation requiring participation of the trade unions in company decision-making was *lex specialis*. This was, fortunately, rejected. In the second case, RH 2000:61, concerning whether or not a tax penalty was a 'criminal charge', Swedish tax law was stated to be *lex specialis* in relation to the ECHR, and applied. This second judgment in my view, is seriously wrong. The *lex specialis* principle should be a means of avoiding the—politically embarrassing—explicit application of the *lex superior* principle, not a means of undermining it. In other words, like the *lex posterior* principle, the *lex specialis* principle can only be applied in favour of giving precedence to the ECHR. Still, bearing in mind the confused, and confusing, *travaux préparatoires* to the incorporation act, it is

---

[50] For treatments of statutory interpretation in general in the United Kingdom and Sweden see the chapters in D N MacCormick and R S Summers (eds), *Interpreting Statutes, a Comparative Study* (Dartmouth, Aldershot, 1991) by Z Bankowski & N MAcCormick and A Peczenik & G Bergholz respectively.

difficult to be too critical of this mistaken decision of the Court of Appeal in RH 2000:61.

A third problem in using the *lex specialis* principle (which also applies to the *lex posterior* principle) concerns ordinances. These will often be *lex posterior* and will invariably be *lex specialis* in relation to the ECHR. As already mentioned, RF 11:14 applies to conflicts between hierarchically superior and hierarchically inferior norms. The effect of RF 11:14 is that, despite the fact that a statute is constitutionally superior to an ordinance, an ordinance which conflicts with it can be preferred as long as the conflict between it and the statute is not manifest. RF 11:14 also means that the principle of *lex specialis* (and *lex posterior*) cannot, formally speaking, be used to resolve conflicts between statutes and ordinances, whereas these principles *can* be used to avoid conflicts between norms on the same level, ie between statutes and statutes or between ordinances and ordinances.[51] This might seem to be a paradoxical result.[52] Constitutionally it can be explained by the fact that the government has its own primary area of legislative competence and does not simply exercise powers delegated by parliament. This is not usually a problem as an ordinance will usually consist of detailed rules, filling out a 'parent' statute. Possible conflicts between a statute and its implementing ordinance will simply be denied, 'interpreted away'. But, as already mentioned, the ECHR is of general application. Its area of application overlaps with many other statutes and ordinances. And there are no 'subsidiary' ordinances containing more detailed implementation rules for the ECHR. The result of all this is that there is no room for using *lex posterior* and *lex specialis* to resolve conflicts between the ECHR and ordinances. Instead, other principles will have to be used. It is obvious that the interplay between RF 11:14 and the ECHR as far as ordinances are concerned was not thought through properly.[53]

The remaining two principles will be treated together. As already mentioned, the principle that 'human rights treaties should be given special significance' in the event of a conflict was proposed by the Supreme Court in its comments on the proposal to amend the Instrument of Government. It was proposed as an alternative to what later became RF 2:23. As such, it was probably meant as a straight rule of precedence, unrestricted by the requirement of 'manifest' incompatibility in RF 11:14.[54] However, this was not

---

[51] Express rules giving a statute precedence over another in case of conflict are very rare in Swedish law. For an example see s 1 of the Privileges and Immunities Act (1976:661) as amended, regarding the Vienna Convention on Diplomatic Immunity.

[52] This point can easily be misunderstood. See, eg, U Bernitz, 'The Incorporation of the ECHR into Swedish Law—A Half Measure' (1995) 38 *GYbIL* 178, where it is stated that the ECHR, by virtue of its status as a statute, has precedence over ordinances.

[53] The constitutional protection from judicial review extended to government ordinances cannot be justified by reference to the primacy of the democratic will. I consider it to be an anachronism. The problems sketched out above provide another reason for abolishing it.

[54] This, in any event, is the conclusion of one prominent legal writer. H Strömberg, 'Europakonventionens genomslag i svensk rätt' [The Impact of the European ECHR in Swedish Law] (1996) 59 *FT* 19, 22–23.

accepted by the legislature.[55] Instead, the Supreme Court's proposal was simply added to the principles listed in the *travaux préparatoires* to be employed by the courts in an attempt to avoid constitutional review. No explanation was given for how this principle could be reconciled with RF 11:14. Nonetheless, the likely explanation is that the principle becomes the same thing as the principle of treaty-conform construction. Alternatively, it could be a form of turbo version of the principle, emphasising the 'especially important' character of human rights treaties, as opposed to other treaties. Arguably it could allow the straining of the plain language of a statute, but not contradicting it. A mere statement in the *travaux préparatoires* cannot go against the plain wording of the RF 11:14, so it is not open for the Swedish courts to rely on the principle to disregard RF 11:14 in cases of norm conflict with human rights treaties.[56]

I should stress again that the *travaux préparatoires* did not specify that the *lex specialis* and *posterior* principles should have been tried first. Indeed, the sensible approach to the exercise is first to apply the principle of treaty-conform construction, to identify what the ECHR case law prima facie demands in the specific case. Thereafter one would determine whether or not this conflicts with the interpretation usually given any other relevant statutes, or ordinances. If so, then the *lex specialis* and *lex posterior* principles would be applied. If these fail to achieve the desired result, the principle of treaty-conform construction would be returned to, in an effort either to avoid (ie reconcile) the prima facie conflict or to confirm it, before concluding (if necessary) with constitutional review. However, if one begins by engaging in constitutional review, as the Court of Appeal did in the above mentioned RH 2000:61, then it is easy to proceed to make a serious error, namely to believe that applying a statute which is more specific than the ECHR, one has 'solved' a conflict between the ECHR and that statute. This is a sure way of marginalising the effect of the ECHR in Swedish law.

---

[55] This lack of explicit acceptance in the *travaux préparatoires* has caused some commentators, mistakenly, to argue that the ECHR should *not* be accorded special significance in cases of conflict. Such an argument ignores the clear wording of RF 2:23, which states that the ECHR *has* precedence.

[56] To argue so builds upon a mistaken analogy with the position of EC law in Swedish law. The area of application of RF 11:14 was diminished by membership of the EU. The provision does not apply to conflicts between EC law with direct effect and national law. Legislative competence in the area covered by the EC has been transferred (competence to do so is set out in RF 10:5). Strictly speaking then, there is no norm conflict any more. (See, eg, RÅ 1997 ref 65, below). This is not the case here. There has been no transfer of legislative competence to the ECtHR. Here the conflict is between two national norms, the incorporated ECHR and another national norm. In the circumstances, the application of RF 11:14 to such a conflict could not have been excluded by a mere statement in the *travaux préparatoires*.

(2) Limits of the principle of 'treaty-conform' construction: relationship to constitutional review

The increasing internationalisation of the legislative process means that the principle of 'treaty-conform' construction[57] has achieved a new importance in many states, Sweden included. In the United Kingdom, section 3 of the Human Rights Act 1998 states that 'so far as it is possible to do so, primary legislation and subordinate legislation must be read and given effect in a way which is compatible with Convention rights'. It can be said that there are a number of factors influencing the willingness of Swedish courts to resort to ECHR conform construction.

The first is a very general point: the level of awareness amongst the legal profession that a legal problem has a 'ECHR dimension'. This depends partly upon the space devoted to human rights in the law degree and the legal journals, but probably more on the extent to which ordinary lawyers and judges come into contact with recognisably human rights issues in their day to day work. Study of the ECHR is obligatory for Swedish law students. On the other hand, it usually only consists of a seminar or two. Before incorporation, the ECHR tended to be part of the international law course. International law has been rather a neglected subject in Sweden. One practical reason for this is the fact that the act of transforming a treaty (which has been the usual practice in Sweden) can often, if not conceal the international origin of a statutory provision, at least reduce the significance of this. Of course, a common complaint of all international lawyers is the ignorance, timidity or even hostility their national courts show towards arguments made on the basis of international law, whether it is proving the existence of a rule of custom, interpreting an incorporated treaty or attempting to rely upon a provision of an unincorporated treaty to interpret national law. The view is often expressed that domestic courts miss highly relevant international law material when they decide cases, or if it is brought to their attention, play down its importance.[58] Be that as it may, the post-incorporation status of the ECHR as a part of constitutional law, and its insertion into the public law syllabus, has improved general awareness of it (even if constitutional law has also been a neglected subject).

But whereas it is one thing to be aware of a possible 'ECHR dimension', it is quite another to be on top of what the exact requirements of it are in a concrete case. These requirements are only made clear through the ECHR case law. In any specific issue, it will often be that the bulk of the case law will concern other

---

[57] I agree with van Gerven that the term 'construction' is better than 'interpretation' as it emphasises the active role which must be played by the judge. W van Gerven, 'The Horizontal Effect of Directive Provisions Revisited: The Reality of Catchwords', in D Curtin, *The Institutional Dynamics of European Integration. Essays in Honour of Henry G Schermers* (Kluwer Academic, Dordrecht, London, 1994) vol 2 at 345.

[58] See, eg, E. Benvenisti, 'Judicial Misgivings Regarding the Application of International Law' (1993) 4 *EJIL* 159.

states. It should be stressed that, under Article 46, Court judgments, formally speaking, are only binding for the respondent state. However, for the other state parties they are authoritative interpretations of their obligations under the ECHR. Obviously, it is highly desirable that Swedish courts apply where possible even judgments (and admissibility decisions) concerning other states. Still, the difficulties in doing so should not be underestimated. Courts in particular suffer from overwork and consequent lack of time. Most Swedes speak good English, although the fact that certain judgments are only available now in full-text in French is going to cause problems. But it is not simply a question of understanding a foreign language. The court will have to 'translate' a judgment concerning another state to the Swedish legal system. Admittedly, looking at foreign case law is no longer an exercise confined to courts grappling with issues in private international law. Membership of the EU has enabled, and obliged, the Swedish courts to interpret ECJ judgments and preliminary rulings concerning other states and apply them to the Swedish context. Still, the fact remains that there have been several important cases—in particular the tax penalty cases which I have already referred to—where the Swedish courts have been faced with vague or inconsistent case law, and, possibly with some relief, concluded that no definite conflict could be said to exist between the ECHR and Swedish law. Thus, there has been no need for the Swedish courts to engage in 'active' treaty-conform construction, let alone constitutional review.

One can say that, generally, a national court's ability to use ECtHR case law will depend in particular on how 'pedagogical' a judgment is, how well reasoned it is, and how consistent it is with previous case law. But improving the 'pedagogical' nature of the judgment is no simple issue. It goes to the heart of the Court's role in the system of European protection of human rights.[59] The Court has, understandably, been reluctant to behave too much like a constitutional court for Europe, for example, by overtly taking issues of national law up to a given level of abstraction, as the ECJ does in preliminary rulings, making it easier for courts in other states to identify and apply the rule emerging from its judgment, and/or spelling out more clearly for the national legislature what sort of changes are necessary in order to bring national law in line with the ECHR. But I consider that, under the pressure of a variety of factors, the Court *is* becoming more pedagogical in its judgments. In particular, the need to avoid case overload means that the Court must stress the subsidiarity of the Strasbourg system, and must therefore make its judgments less casuistic and more 'user friendly.'[60]

---

[59] I discuss this issue in greater detail in 'Protocol No 11 to the ECHR: The European Court of Human Rights as a Constitutional Court?' (1995) 15 *YbEL* 219.

[60] The *Kudla* case, above, n 13, is a graphic example of this. See also the Rome resolution (above n 28), which stresses subsidiarity, and the report to the Committee on Legal Affairs and Human Rights of the Parliamentary Assembly of the Council of Europe, Execution of Judgments of the ECtHR, Doc 8808, 12 July 2000. The Court and the Council of Ministers have recently created a liaison committee, designed specifically to deal with the issue of the changes which may be necessary in a state's law to bring it into line with a judgment.

For a number of reasons (language, accessibility of legislation, the harmonisation work of the Nordic Council), the judgments concerning foreign states which Swedish courts will usually find it easiest to understand are those concerning other Nordic states. But understanding the relevance of an ECtHR judgment is easiest for a Swedish court if there has been some reference to it, and its significance, in the *travaux préparatoires* to legislation. If a commission of inquiry has investigated the possible relevance the case can have for Swedish law and recommended law reforms but for one reason or another the parliament has not yet passed amending legislation, the courts can use the conclusions reached by the inquiry in interpreting Swedish law.[61] Similarly, where legislation has already been passed and the Law Council has commented upon the most 'ECHR friendly' way to interpret a proposal, this can naturally also be used.[62]

As regards the practical issue of physical access to sources, almost all Swedish courts are connected to the Internet. Swedish summaries of the collected Court case law have been published in a legal journal and summaries continue to be published regularly. The summaries up to 1996 are available in a database, when the work of summarising was discontinued for financial reasons. As regards more detailed scholarly works, a brief informal survey I made indicates that, at best, the majority of courts will have access to two or three textbooks on the ECHR.[63] Most judges are not used to looking at the original sources on the Court's Internet site, in particular admissibility decisions. This will seldom work to the disadvantage of an individual litigant, as the admissibility decisions normally disclose what is *not* in breach of the ECHR. It is, however, undoubtedly a waste of the Swedish courts' time to wrestle with an issue which has already been ruled as 'manifestly ill-founded.'[64]

Secondly, the constitutional procedure by which consent is given to a treaty is important, in particular, the extent to which the parliament has been involved in the procedure of ratification.[65] The courts do not want to come into conflict with parliament. Sweden and the United Kingdom are both 'dualist' states although too much should not be read into this, misleading, label. But unlike the United Kingdom parliament, the Swedish parliament has to give its consent before an instrument of ratification is deposited where the treaty in question

---

[61] See RÅ 1997 ref 97 (concerning tax investigations and Art 6).

[62] See RÅ 1996, ref 8 and RÅ 1997 ref 68 (concerning Art 5 and challenge to detention).

[63] P van Dijk and G J H van Hoof, *Theory and Practice of the European Convention of Human Rights*, 3rd edn (Kluwer Law International, The Hague, London, 1998), the introductory textbook by H Danelius, *Mänskliga rättigheter i europeisk praxis* (Norstedts, Stockholm, 1997) and D J Harris, M O'Boyle and C Warbrick, *Law of the European Convention on Human Rights* (Butterworths, London,1995). It can be noted here that the Swedish courts are not averse to citing doctrine. Opinions differ on the significance of such citations, ie whether they tend to indicate genuine influence on the court's legal reasoning or whether they instead serve as background information or simply as additional support for a conclusion which the court planned to reach anyway.

[64] See below regarding 'accidental anticipation'.

[65] The national courts are likely to be, and should be, unwilling to look at treaties which their state has not ratified, except in the special case where these can be seen as evidence of customary international law.

requires implementing legislation or involves substantial expenditure or is otherwise 'important' (RF 10:2). Interestingly, though, even where such consent has been given, as was the case for the ratification of the ECHR in 1951, the highest courts have ruled in a series of cases that legislation is still required where a treaty grants individuals rights or imposes duties. In comparison to the United Kingdom, the argument against letting a ratified but unincorporated treaty create rights for individuals appears not so much to be democracy (parliament has already expressed its consent) but legal certainty (*rättssäkerhet*). It can, of course, be argued that legal certainty is not a good reason for denying a right to an individual exercisable vis à vis the state, as opposed to another individual. Moreover, the coherence of the Swedish position is undermined a little by the wholescale incorporation of EC law, the incorporation rather than transformation of the ECHR and the fact that, being a EU member, some EC directives and a few EC treaties with third states can now have direct effect in the Swedish legal order. On the other hand, allowing unincorporated/untransformed treaties to create rights would mean that the Swedish courts would have to decide which rights in a treaty were sufficiently clear, complete, etc, to be self-executing. This would, in the Swedish legal tradition, be regarded as a usurpation of the role of parliament.[66] After all, most rights cost money, and in the end, it is the taxpayer who pays. Even if arguments could be found that the Swedish courts should take such a power, it is clear that this would lead to costs to society in the form of litigation, ineffective use of scarce judicial resources, and risks of conflicting findings in the administrative and ordinary courts. So, although this 'double dualist' stance has been criticised, it is unlikely to be changed in the near future.

A third factor heavily influencing treaty-conform construction is the way in which a statutory provision is drafted and the conception judges have of their own role. In the most extreme situation, when dealing with a ratified, but unincorporated/ untransformed treaty, there may be no national 'law' at all for the national court to construct in a treaty-conform way. There is thus a natural limit on the use of the principle.[67] Where there is a statutory provision, it must obviously give the court room for different courses of action. One example of this is when it is an optional (default) rule that is capable of being displaced by the parties to a dispute. In Sweden, such rules are fairly common in the area of civil procedure. Another example is where the rule explicitly gives discretion to the courts to solve problems on a case by case basis, eg the rules in the Code of

---

[66] Similar reasons are invoked for not incorporating, rather than transforming, treaties containing vague provisions. See, eg, a recent report on the legal position of the United Nations Convention on the Rights of the Child (SOU 1997:116). Cf the position taken by a Norwegian committee investigating the incorporation of human rights treaties (NOU 1993: 18).

[67] These two different types of situation can be compared to the situations where a national court is faced, respectively, with an incorrectly transposed EC directive and a totally untransposed directive. For an example of the difficulties this can cause a national court see *Webb v EMO Air Cargo (UK) Ltd* [1992] 4 All ER 929.

Judicial Procedure providing for the holding of oral hearings or the disqualification of judges. But the drafting of a provision is only part of the issue. The 'outer limit' of construction is determined not simply by the language but also by the judicial culture. Put crudely, the stronger the judicial branch is vis à vis the other branches, the more it can get away with. This is seen not simply in the extent of cases involving constitutional review, but also the 'covert' review of constitutional conform construction. In Sweden, while statutes are drafted in a general way, often leaving the courts wide discretion, there is no tradition of constitutional review or 'constitution conform' construction to build upon. It may be a generalisation, but construction tends not to be 'top down' but 'bottom up', ie the higher, more abstract, norm is constructed so as to fit in with the lower, more concrete norm.[68] The subjective approach to statutory interpretation—whereby the legitimate role of the courts is confined to discerning the intent of parliament—is strong in Sweden. Judicial philosophy and training discourages creativity and emphasises obedience to the will of the legislator as expressed in the *travaux préparatoires*.[69] This is changing slowly, partly as a result of the influence of EU membership. The lack of *travaux préparatoires*, and the fact that important parts of EC law are heavily case law based, tends to increase judicial discretion. The same factors apply, albeit to a lesser extent, as regards the ECHR system.[70] A 'spillover' effect on Swedish judicial attitudes on the lines of the British experience might therefore be expected.[71] As against this, the natural judicial predilection for concrete norms in the field of procedural law may operate against the ECHR having much of an impact. The ECHR contains rights without remedies. As already mentioned, the Swedish incorporation statute makes no mention of damages, or injunctions, or any other remedies. In some cases, it will nonetheless be possible to give the plaintiff the remedy he or she wishes, eg, the issue concerns access to a court and the obvious remedy is to grant standing or a criminal trial has not occurred within a reasonable time and the plaintiff can be given a reduction of sentence. But in many other cases there are no given national legal consequences following upon a finding of a breach. Swedish judges can thus be left with—for them—an unpleasantly large degree

---

[68]   This is recognised implicitly by the the *travaux préparatoires* to RF 11:14. See below. It is also evident in a number of cases in which RF is mentioned, if at all, as an afterthought.

[69]   See generally Cameron, above, n 8, 503–08.

[70]   Having said this, the fact that the ECHR regime is a case law system is not the same thing as saying that the legal culture(s) underlying it are the same as those applying in common law countries, in particular as regards the extent of legitimate judicial norm creation. It, like EC law, is heavily influenced by continental legal thinking.

[71]   See, eg, *M. v Home Office* [1994] 1 AC 377 per Lord Woolf: '[I]t would be most regrettable if an approach which is inconsistent with that which exists in Community law should be allowed to persist if this is strictly necessary' (at 422). I think 'spillover' is a better term than 'infection' (*smittoeffekt*) which has occasionally been used in Swedish doctrine. Calling EC/ECHR influence 'infection' is pejorative—it presupposes that the Swedish legal system is a healthy body which is contaminated by foreign bodies. As to the effect of EU membership on judicial attitudes towards constitutional review, see below.

of discretion. They are really being asked to complete a right, not simply to interpret it. Swedish judges are unfamilar with this.[72]

Fourthly, following on from this, it is interesting to compare the scope and extent of the duty of treaty-conform construction as it is expressed in EC law as compared to its scope and extent as regards national implementation of public international law. Beginning with the *von Coulson* case, the ECJ has laid down a duty on member states to interpret national law in accordance with EC law, whether passed before or after the national law in question.[73] The Swedish courts have already had occasion to apply this in a number of cases.[74] The principle is, in one sense, more powerful in EC law because of the greater possibility of intervention the ECJ has under the Article 234 procedure. There is no such procedure imposed on national courts to refer cases to the ECtHR for preliminary rulings. There is naturally a greater incentive on a national court to apply treaty-conform construction when the ECJ is breathing down its neck. The ECJ phrased this duty in *Marleasing* as requiring national courts 'as far as possible' to achieve an EC conform construction.[75] The exact limits of this duty have been the cause of some discussion although it is evident that even the ECJ accepts that it cannot require a court to make a construction *contra legem*, something which in the long term can only undermine respect for the law and the courts.[76] It should also be noted that the principle in EC law has functioned in a different way from the principle as it can apply in assisting the implementation of international law. In EC law, it has often been used as a substitute for horizontal direct effect of directives.[77] With the development of the principle of damages in *Francovich*, the principle has accordingly diminished somewhat in significance. There is not the same need to strain the language, as there is an alternative available. This alternative may well be lacking as regards a state's failure properly to implement an international law obligation. There may be a remedy in damages before the national courts in such a situation, but then again there may not. In Sweden, no such possibility exists today, although a change in the law has been proposed.[78]

But while there is no strong tradition of treaty-conform construction in Sweden, it is certainly not unknown. It was employed particularly in relation to the ECHR, before incorporation, but in later years it has made an appearance

---

[72] For a valuable discussion of this point from the perspective of EC law, see T Andersson, 'Effective Protection of Community Rights in Sweden', in Cameron and Simoni, above, n 6.

[73] Case 14/83, *von Coulson and Kamann v Land Nordrhein-Westfalen* [1984] ECR 1891, at para 26.

[74] See, eg NJA 1997 s 415, NJA 1997 s 299, although cf RH 1996:37 and NJA 1996 s 668. In the latter case, the Supreme Court interpreted a preliminary ruling extremely restrictively, some might say contrary to its spirit.

[75] Case C–106/89, *Marleasing SA v La Commercial Internacional de Alimentacion SA* [1990] ECR–I 4135 at para 8.

[76] See Case C–91/92, *Facine Dori v Recreb Srl* [1994] ECR–I 3325 at para 25. For the viewpoint of the British courts see, eg, *Duke v GEC Reliance* [1988] 2 WLR 359.

[77] See van Gerven, above, n 52.

[78] See Cameron, above, n 6.

in other areas: EC law of course, but even private international law.[79] But the mere invocation of the principle is no guarantee that it has any real significance when it comes to determining a case. If a court simply presumes that a law is in accordance with a treaty obligation ('bottom up' construction), it is not doing its job properly. Admittedly, it can be tempting to do this where the parliament at the time of ratification and/or incorporation stated its opinion that Swedish law was in accordance with the treaty in question. This was originally the case with the ECHR. The *travaux préparatoires* to the decision of the parliament to ratify the treaty stated clearly the opinion of parliament that there was 'harmony' between the two bodies of law. It was no real surprise that this was later employed in a number of judgments in the 1970s by lazy and/or timid courts to avoid examining what the ECHR really required.[80] There has been no such overt refusal on the part of the higher courts to look at the ECHR since incorporation, although there has been at least one example of a lower court doing so. In an unreported case from a county administrative court concerning custody of children, the court ruled that, since the *travaux préparatoires* to the act incorporating the ECHR had stated that the government's view was that the Care of Children Act (1990:52) was in accordance with the requirements of the ECHR, it would decide the issue only on the basis of the Act.[81] A similar approach was taken in 1995 by the Aliens Board (*Utlänningsnämnden*) as regards the Convention on the Rights of the Child. The Board expressed the view that, as the government was of the opinion at the time of ratification that Swedish law was in accordance with the Convention then that was the end of the matter.[82]

But these are extreme cases, and the correct approach to the scope of the principle in Swedish law is probably that which is set out in an important separate opinion to a Supreme Court case concerning the ECHR in 1992, before incorporation.[83] Justice Lind stated in this case that he considered that, where a treaty provision contained an argument for a particular construction of national law, then this should be followed, notwithstanding the fact that it might conflict with leading doctrine, or the *travaux préparatoires* to the legislation in question. Bearing in mind the status of both doctrine and *travaux préparatoires* in the Swedish legal system, this is an important and bold statement, even if it may fall short of the requirement ('so far as possible') in section 3 of the (UK) Human Rights Act 1998. According to Lind, the limits of the principle are the objective wording of the legislative provision being constructed. This limit also applies in the United Kingdom, but of course, as indicated above, whether or not wording

---

[79] For example, where treaties on private international law have been transformed or incorporated into Swedish law, eg RÅ 1996, ref 52 (Hague Convention on Abduction of Children, 1980).

[80] See in particular NJA 1974, s 423. For discussion see Cameron, above, n 6, 227–29.

[81] LR i Skaraborg 1995–02–22, Ö 1274–94, Ö 915–94 and Ö 3059–94. To be charitable some excuse for such action can be found in lack of time.

[82] Decisions in cases UN 73 and UN 274 (in H Sandesjö and K Björk (eds) *Utlänningsärenden—praxis*, supplement 1 (Fritz, Stockholm, 1995)).

[83] NJA 1992, s 532.

is 'objective' is itself a question of legal culture. To put it another way, judges know the boundaries when they see them. Interestingly, there have already been examples of post-incorporation cases in which a relatively bold approach has been taken to construction.[84] On the other hand, there have also been cases where the principle was not applied when I think it could have been.[85]

One general limitation on the principle follows from its purpose: to secure compliance with international obligations. This means that it should not be employed to secure an interpretation of national law that is not actually required by the ECHR, ie to interprete the ECHR more dynamically, or progressively, than the ECtHR itself does.'Anticipation' of the ECHR can, of course, be tempting for a national judge who wants to secure a given result in a case, particularly where a judge is forbidden to engage in overt constitutional review, as is the case in the Netherlands and the United Kingdom. Still, the purpose of the principle means that it is difficult to criticise a national court which refuses to go further in interpreting the ECHR in the absence of a clear precedent from the ECtHR.[86] Having said this, the line between anticipating ECHR case law (wrong) and applying existing case law to a new situation (right) can be very thin. Where national courts are afraid of correction in Strasbourg, there will be a tendency to err on the side of caution. A 'grey zone' could thus emerge which in one sense could be the mirror image of the margin of appreciation, ie the national court finds the state to be in violation of the ECHR when this is not actually required. But this is speculation. There is insufficient evidence of such an attitude in the Swedish courts. Indeed, as already mentioned, what evidence there is points in the other direction: that the Swedish courts, while not hostile to ECHR case law, want clear precedents before they are prepared to engage in 'active' treaty-conform construction.

In one substantive area at least, criminal law, Swedish legal culture places definite limits on the power of the courts to deny/avoid norm conflicts by resorting to the principle of treaty-conform construction. Of course, judicial *expansion* of the criminalised area by means of referring to a treaty is unacceptable.[87] In the Swedish criminal code the application of analogy reasoning in criminal matters is moreover excluded. But even a construction which is to the advantage of the individual can be ruled out if this involves going too far from the wording of the statute. This is illustrated by a recent case of constitutional review which concerned the Political Uniforms Act (1947:164). This statute makes criminal the wearing of any uniform or emblem which displays the wearer's political views. It was designed to be aimed at undemocratic groups (and in the concrete case

---

[84] Eg RH 1995:66 concerning access to a court to challenge an administrative decision liquidating a company.

[85] See the Administrative Court of Appeal judgment in the '*Lassagård*' case, below.

[86] As already mentioned, this was the approach of, inter alia, the Supreme Court judgment in the tax penalty case, NJA 2000, s 622.

[87] Cf Case 80/86, *Officier van Justitie v Kolpinghuis Nijmegen* [1987] ECR 3969. I leave aside the thorny question of whether this might be justifiable in extreme situations, such as that of the East German border guards. See Judgment of the BVerfG of 24 Oct 1996, (1997) 18 HRLJ 65.

was against neo-Nazis) but it is framed in general terms, to cover all possible political views, democratic and undemocratic. While its use in the concrete case was not, in my view, repugnant, the 'ordinary meaning' of the rule was not 'acceptable in a democratic society'. This ordinary meaning could technically, have been narrowed by a judicial ruling on the basis of either the *travaux préparatoires* or an independent judicial evaluative exercise based on the needs of society etc. But there is a greater societal interest in interpreting criminal law rules in accordance with the ordinary meaning to be given to the words of the rule. Following such a course of action would also have left an unacceptably large degree of discretion to the police and prosecutor in applying the law. The courts in Sweden have, traditionally, not had the necessary prestige (or mandate) to engage in overt rule-making on such a scale, (and, besides, in such a politically sensitive area). Thus, the court felt that the possibility of such a judicial narrowing of the scope of application of a criminal statute was ruled out. This was a matter for the legislature. The result was that the court invoked RF 11:14 and refused to apply the statute, acquitting the defendants.[88]

By contrast, in the United Kingdom, the greater flexibility of the common law means that the principle of treaty-conform construction has the potential to be a more powerful tool in the hands of a bold judge,[89] at least when the treaty in question has been converted in some way to national law.[90] It is interesting to speculate as to whether the British rules on declarations of incompatibility will encourage more treaty-conform construction or less. Only the higher courts may rule on incompatibility. Is it more reasonable to suppose that most lower court judges, faced with the alternative of letting an issue go on appeal to a higher court or attempting to settle it will be tempted to strain the wording of the statutory provision so as to read it to be compatible with the ECHR? Is it reasonable to suppose that the higher courts, faced with the alternative of ruling that an open conflict exists between the incorporated ECHR and another statute or avoiding that conflict will choose the latter option? This would mean concealing a norm conflict, which is arguably more of a judicial usurpation of power. Nor will it necessarily solve the problem for future litigants. On the other hand it will have the benefit of allowing the court to do what it thinks is justice in the concrete case before it, ie rule in favour of a litigant whose ECHR rights have been violated.

---

[88] RH 1997:47.

[89] See, eg, *Derbyshire County Council v Times Newspapers Ltd* [1993] QB 770 (CA), [1993] AC 534.

[90] The absence of such a 'go ahead' from parliament was cited as the main reason for not taking more judicial notice of the ECHR in, inter alia, *R v Secretary of State for the Home Department, ex parte Brind* [1991] 1 AC 696 and *R v Ministry of Defence ex parte Smith* [1996] 2 WLR 305.

As mentioned already, constitutional review is in general very rare in Sweden, and, for the reasons set out above, is likely to remain so. However, constitutional review has an important symbolic function, and so it is necessary to say something about it. First, however, a terminological point: by 'constitutional review' a British lawyer thinks about review of statutes. But as already mentioned, RF 11:14 provides a partial protection for both statutes and government ordinances from review in the courts.

Little need be said about the few cases in which the courts explicitly engaged in constitutional review. RH 1995:85 was a tragic case, concerning standing in paternity matters. The plaintiff wished to be recognised as the father of a child who had died in infancy. Chapter 3, section 5 of the Family Code states that applications to establish paternity may only be made in the name of the child by its guardian (usually the mother) or the social authorities. But the mother had committed suicide and the social authorities chose not to bring a paternity action. The Court of Appeal considered whether the right to family life under Article 8 could nonetheless grant the plaintiff standing to bring a paternity action. It concluded that, while there was Commission case law indicating that the putative father should have the possibility of establishing legal relations with his alleged child, in the absence of a clear authority from the ECtHR on the issue, it could not find that the exclusive right of standing bestowed by Chapter 3, section 5 was 'manifestly' in breach of the ECHR.[91]

In a case in 1996, an administrative court of appeal found invalid on the basis of Article 6 an ordinance on EC regulations relating to Agricultural Produce[92] which provided for no right of appeal to a court from an administrative decision to pay or not pay an agricultural subsidy.[93] The ordinance postdated the law on incorporation. The court also found—controversially and in indirect conflict with an earlier decision of the Supreme Administrative Court[94]—that the administrative courts, rather than the general courts, were competent to hear the appeal. In doing so the court felt that it also had to set aside, or rather, rewrite, section 14 of the Administrative Courts Act,[95] although in my opinion, this was not necessary, as it is doctrine, and the *travaux préparatoires*, which

---

[91] This was a hard judgment, but difficult to say conclusively that it was incorrect. See, in particular, *Nylund v Finland*, No 27110/95, 29 June 1999, where the ECtHR found that equivalent Finnish restrictions on proving paternity were not in breach of Art 8. Having said this, one important factor in *Nylund*, not present in the Swedish case, was the feelings of the child.

[92] 1994:1715.

[93] Decisions of 15/8/96 and 17/9/96 (not reported).

[94] RÅ 1995, ref 58. It was careful to distinguish the two cases, although in substance the two issues are the same. RÅ 1995 ref 58 went against an earlier judgment of the Supreme Court (NJA 1994, s 657). For a discussion of the conflict between the two supreme courts, see Cameron, above, n 7, at 254–55.

[95] 1971:289.

insisted that this rule meant that there must be a statute or statutory instrument bestowing competence on the administrative courts before they are competent to hear cases.[96] Thus, the principle of treaty-conform construction could have been used to avoid this apparent conflict. The use of constitutional review is also surprising in that it is difficult to employ Article 6 directly to set aside section 14. Article 6 demands only that one has access to *a* court, not an administrative court.

The case was appealed to the Surpreme Administrative Court. This court ruled that the right of access to a court, *as this is expressed in the general principles of EC law,* required the courts to provide a judicial remedy.[97] The Court also ruled that it was 'most appropriate' that the administrative courts took jurisdiction. As the conflict then, was between EC law and national law, the restriction on constitutional review in RF 11:14 did not apply. In fact, there was no conflict any more. The court's duty was to apply EC law. While the judgment was correct, it sheds no light on the issue of constitutional review on the basis of the incorporated ECHR as such (as opposed to the ECHR as a source of EC law).[98]

The third case in which a court explicitly[99] raised the question of whether a 'manifest' conflict existed has already been mentioned, namely RH 2000:61, concerning tax penalties. That such a penalty is a 'criminal charge' is now fairly clear. However, the case concerned whether the *ne bis in idem* rule in Protocol No 7, Article 4 prohibited a prosecution for tax crime, *after* the defendant had been punished for the same 'offence' by the imposition of a tax penalty. The Court of Appeal came to the conclusion that it was possible to have such a double 'prosecution'. The issue is of considerable significance, as around 100,000 tax penalties are issued each year, and these are occasionally followed by criminal prosecutions. The Court of Appeal may have come to the correct conclusion. A commission of inquiry has recently recommended that, in the future, it should not be possible to impose a tax penalty *after* a person has been prosecuted for the same act, as this is probably in breach of the ECHR, but that the reverse situation, ie that considered by the Court of Appeal, was possible.[100] Nonetheless, as I have already noted, the process by which the Court of Appeal reached its judgment can be heavily criticised on constitutional grounds.

---

[96] Partly as a result of this case, the rule was changed to allow appeal of administrative decisions to administrative courts unless otherwise provided by statute or ordinance (Administration Act, 1986:223, s 22a). However, a large number of such exceptions exist where appeal lies to higher administrative, or quasi-judicial bodies.

[97] RÅ 1997 ref 65. For the application of the principle of judicial remedies see Case C–97/91, *Borelli Spa v Commission* [1993] ECR I–6313. For a discussion see Andersson, above, n 67.

[98] For a discussion of the case see J Nergelius, 'The Impact of EC Law in Swedish National Law—A Cultural Revolution' in Cameron and Simoni, vol 2, above, n 6.

[99] It has been claimed that the 'manifest' requirement was a factor in RÅ 1999, ref 76, where the court upheld the legality of a controversial government decision to close the Barsebäck nuclear reactor.

[100] SOU 2001:25.

To turn now to the function constitutional review serves in the overall system of constitutional control, as mentioned the *travaux préparatoires* to RF 11:14 stress that constitutional review is a 'long stop', to be used, if at all, only in extreme situations. What little doctrine there is tends to support this. The absence of constitutional review is treated as an indication of the health (and proper functioning) of the political system.[101] As mentioned, the *travaux préparatoires* to the incorporation law also stress, repeatedly, that the primary responsibility for maintaining compliance with the ECHR remains with the legislature. There is some doubt as to what this means. It naturally cannot mean that the legislature has the *sole* responsibility, as then one can legitimately ask the question, what purpose is served by RF 2:23? Sweden in any event already has a duty under international law to amend legislation in breach of the ECHR. The whole point of the ECHR, RF 2:23 and indeed, of RF 11:14, is that they are aimed *against* the legislator.[102] I consider that the above statement in the *travaux préparatoires* should be read as simply asking the courts to refrain from engaging in *major* exercises of constitutional review, something which goes to the scope of the institute, rather than its existence.[103]

What, then, is a 'manifest' conflict in the context of the ECHR? I have earlier expressed the view that a conflict which cannot be reconciled by means of the principles of *lex posterior*, *lex specialis* and treaty-conform construction must, logically, be 'manifest.'[104] Still, as Holmes said, the life of the law is not logic but experience. The *travaux préparatoires* to RF 11:14 and RF 2:23, doctrine and case law give few clues as to what is a manifest conflict. The *travaux préparatoires* to RF 11:14 state that, in general, the more vaguely the superior rule is formulated, the less likely the conflict with an inferior rule will be manifest.[105] If applied this would allow review on the basis of such relatively clear provisions as those dealing with delegation of legislative competence (RF Chapter 8) but not those dealing with the majority of rights set out in RF Chapter 2, and by extention, the ECHR. The majority of rights in these two documents could be described as qualified rights, as opposed to absolute rights, ie they are capable

---

[101] See J Nergelius, *Konstitutionellt rättighetsskydd* [Constitutional Protection of Rights] (Norstedts, Stockholm 1996) at 701–03.

[102] Nergelius, *ibid*, however, expresses the view (at 685) that the effect of RF 11:14 is to emasculate RF 2:23 to the extent that it becomes a simple interpretative rule, giving only a weak precedence to the ECHR in the event of an apparent conflict between it and another Swedish norm. I do not agree with this. In the event of a conflict, the interest in giving the ECHR precedence should not be balanced against other interests. RF 2:23 clearly allows, indeed obliges, the courts to set aside statutes in concrete cases.

[103] Cf Danelius, above, n 63, 46: 'The debate in the *travaux préparatoires* hardly gives answers to this question [of how to handle conflicts] and the courts must therefore be considered to have considerable freedom in this respect to develop their case law in a way they consider appropriate'. Strömberg, above, n 54, at 23 argues that the lack of guidelines in the *travaux préparatoires* as regards the interpretative exercises which are to be performed means that constitutional review will be the dominant means of judging the compatibility with the ECHR and other Swedish law but this, I think, underestimates the Swedish judge's reluctance to engage in overt constitutional review

[104] Cameron, n 6, 240.

[105] See SOU 1978:34, s 109.

of being limited by a statute, albeit a statute which must satisfy certain proce-dural and substantive conditions. Similar views have been expressed in doctrine as to the inappropriateness of review on the basis of the general requirement (in RF 2:12 para 3) that a restriction in a qualified right be 'necessary in a democra-tic society' and proportional to the end to be achieved.[106]

The 'necessity' and proportionality requirements are expressed in the same way in inter alia Articles 8–11. The reason for this restrictive approach appears to be that it is inappropriate, in moral and social questions, that the democratic will of the people expressed through their representatives can be overruled by the courts. Obviously any constitutional review on the basis of rights involves 'trumping' the democratic will but where the constitution allows the legislature a choice of means, and it has fully debated the necessity and proportionality of a particular restriction, then this argument holds that there is little, or no, room for reaching a different conclusion from that drawn by the legislature. To use the ECHR terminology, the national courts should allow the legislature a margin of appreciation. Such an attempted distinction between the permissible scope of review of different types of rights can be criticised. The very idea of national courts applying the margin of appreciation doctrine can also be criti-cised on the basis that it is an international doctrine, to be used by an inter-national court, whose job is to apply a form of European low common denominator test.[107] The national courts should arguably apply a tougher test. This would undoubtedly be in line with the underlying idea of the ECHR as a subsidiary system (Article 53). Moreover, if the Swedish courts fail to look at the substance of an issue, it will be more difficult for the Swedish government to argue non-exhaustion of domestic remedies, or otherwise convince the ECtHR that an issue has been properly aired before it went to Strasbourg.[108] On the other hand, the ECHR in general, and Article 13 in particular, does not require contracting parties to create the institution of constitutional review, or, where this exists, to expand (or contract) its scope. Moreover, the fact is that even national constitutional courts tend to apply similar doctrines of judicial restraint, at least in social and economic areas.[109] Still, the consequence must be

---

[106] See Nergelius, above, n 101, 701–03; E Holmberg, 'På spaning efter rättigheter' [Looking For Rights] (1987) *SvJT* 653–76, at 662–64; B Bengtsson, 'Om domstolarnas lagprövning' [On Constitutional Review by the Courts] (1987) *SvJT* 229–47.

[107] See, eg T H Jones, 'The Devaluation of Human Rights under the European Convention' (1995) *PL* 430.

[108] Compare: 'One clearly should not take a case decided by the European Court through the application of the [margin of appreciation] doctrine as an authoritative statement that the ECHR does not give grounds for a claim that would extend further. As long as the European Court rests on a margin of appreciation, domestic courts should conduct an independent scrutiny in order to prove themselves worthy of the discretion left to them.' (M Scheinen 'International Human Rights in National Law' in R Hanski and M Suksi (eds), *An Introduction to the International Protection of Human Rights* 2nd edn (Institute for Human Rights, Turku, 1999), 422.

[109] See, eg, A von Brünneck, 'Constitutional Review and Legislation in Western Democracies' in Landfried, n 14.

that in the few cases where a margin of appreciation and/or the 'manifest' requirement is invoked by the courts, it will usually be worth the while of the losing party to take the issue to the ECtHR.

One other point can be mentioned here, even if it does not fit easily into either the category of *travaux préparatoires* or doctrine. This is the psychological impact of EU membership on judicial attitudes. I have mentioned the 'spillover' effect earlier in the context of encouraging more treaty-conform construction. EU membership can also, albeit more gradually, encourage more 'ordinary' constitutional review on the basis that it is easier for Swedish judges both to grasp, and openly acknowledge, that norms can be in conflict with one another. It is fair to say that when Swedish courts (possibly even all courts) find an applicable norm, they apply it. They do not normally go looking for other applicable, and conflicting, norms. But with EU membership there is no longer a single ominipotent source for all norms applicable in the domestic legal order. It becomes easier to accept that norms can, and do, conflict.

Bearing in mind the lack of guidelines, I submit that the likelihood of constitutional review is dependent on four factors. The first of these is the nature of the ECHR right at issue and the clarity of its breach. As already mentioned, some rules in the ECHR (eg Article 3) are framed in unconditional terms, although even here there will be areas of lack of clarity. The requirements of other Articles, such as Articles 5 and 6, are relatively clear and have furthermore been concretised by case law. But the prohibited restrictions which follow from Articles 8–11 and Protocol No 1 Article 1 are much less clear and can only be understood from the case law, and sometimes not even then. Admittedly, where the ECtHR says that Swedish legislation as such is in breach of the ECHR, then even the most cautious Swedish court will be able, indeed, obliged, to apply constitutional review in a subsequent case which is in substance identical to the earlier Strasbourg case. But it should be remembered that the ECtHR only rarely finds legislation as such in breach of the ECHR. It is more often a practice which is found to be in breach, eg the Swedish violations of Article 8 as regards child custody cases. The courts ought usually to be able to handle the latter case by reference to the principle of treaty-conform construction. A problem here, in terms of clarity of breach, is cases involving other states. As already mentioned, such cases have to be 'translated' to the national context. In any event, if 'anticipation' is unlikely as regards the principle of treaty-conform construction, it is even more unlikely here.

The second factor is the relationship in time between the ECtHR case law relied upon and the date of enactment of the Swedish statute or ordinance. Here one can speak of three different situations: existing legislation conflicts with old case law, new legislation conflicts with old case law, and existing legislation conflicts with new case law. As regards the first situation, bearing in mind the superficial nature of the work done, little trust can be put in the views expressed in the *travaux préparatoires* that existing Swedish legislation was in conformity with the ECHR.[110] Instead, conflicts with older legislation should be accepted and not explained away. As regards the second situation, where the legislator has considered the ECHR case law and reached a conclusion that new legislation is not in breach of the ECHR, the Swedish courts should be, and will be, very reluctant indeed to reach a different conclusion. But where the legislator has not considered the issue at all, then the conflict with the legislator disappears. There is no 'second guessing' the legislator when the legislator has not even 'guessed first.'[111] There is admittedly a problem where the legislator might have considered the issue, but not done so fully, or properly, but the quality of most Swedish legislation, and the openness of the legislative process ought hopefully to reduce such situations to a minimum.[112] The third situation is where new Strasbourg case law comes into conflict with existing Swedish legislation. Here one must again distinguish between cases concerning Sweden and cases concerning foreign states. As regards the former, the problem will usually be that the legislator will not have had time to act. As time does not stand still, the Swedish courts cannot stay an action or refuse to give judgment pending legislation. Here the risk of a conflict between the courts and the legislator is obvious.[113] It should also be noted that Sweden has no 'fast track' legislative amendment procedure similar to that provided for in section 10 of the Human Rights Act 1998. If, on the other hand, the legislator has had time to consider the matter and has deliberately refrained from acting, then the Swedish courts should be very cautious about reaching a different conclusion. As regards the latter, the problem is either that the implications of the case for Swedish law are not apparent, or that, bearing in mind the constraints on parliamentary time, the legislator has not yet had time to act.[114] In both these situations, constitutional review can be legitimate. Where, on the other hand, the legislator has had an opportunity to look at the case but has refrained from acting the Swedish courts should again be very careful about reaching another conclusion about the need for amendment of Swedish law than that of the legislator.

The third factor is the type of norm reviewed. Despite the fact that the same ('manifest') protection against review is extended to both statutes and ordinances, review of the latter will in practice often be less controversial. Even though, in the Swedish parliamentary system, the government (almost invariably) has the same political composition as the parliament, a distinction in

---

[110] SOU 1993:40. Although to be fair, doubts were expressed regarding the lack of a general right to an oral hearing (at 58) and the limited possibilities of obtaining damages from the state when a breach of the ECHR is committed (at 78).

[111] As E Smith writes, 'when the judge . . . discovers constitutional problems of which the legislator was not aware, it is not easy to see why the judge should not prefer the constitutional norm over the legislative one', *Constitutional Justice under Old Constitutions* (Kluwer Law International, The Hague, London, 1995) at 374.

[112] The 'proper consideration' test is most used in countries which emphasise the importance of *travaux préparatoires* in discerning the legislator's will—which suggests that it could be appropriate for Sweden (Smith, above, n 111, 375).

[113] See, eg *Vermeire v Belgium*, 29 Nov 1991, A/214–C.

[114] An example of this is RÅ 1996 ref 97, above n ??.

treatment can be justified by the lack of democratic scrutiny an ordinance receives and the fact that it is usually passed much faster than a statute.[115]

The fourth factor is the area of law concerned and the degree of political controversy surrounding the issue. As already pointed out, the room for using the principle of treaty-conform construction is less as regards criminal law. It should be noted that the Danish legislator was prepared to accept a greater degree of constitutional review by the courts in criminal matters.[116] To some it may seem wrong for a judge to take into account the degree of political controversy involved in a case, but I think that it is foolish to be blind to the political dimension of constitutional review.[117] On the other hand, the practical significance of the conflict between those who argue for parliamentary supremacy and those who consider that the courts' power to engage in constitutional review should be strengthened should not be exaggerated. Normally, the situations in which the courts will be engaging in constitutional review will be, politically speaking, rather trivial (although for the individual plaintiff they will, of course, be important).[118] In Sweden the issue of access to a court as regards review of administrative decisions is still problematic and there is clearly scope for (more) constitutional review here. As mentioned, the tax penalty cases caused considerable problems for the Swedish courts, even if these were, in the end, resolved without the need for constitutional review (or even active treaty-conform construction). The impartiality of certain courts containing lay judges representing special interests can also be questioned on occasion. The political repercussions of constitutional review in such cases would be small, or at any event, much less than the political repercussions of review in the area of trade union or property rights.[119]

J. CONCLUDING REMARKS

The significance of incorporation of the ECHR in Sweden should not be overestimated. It does, after all, provide for a minimum system of protection. There has been relatively little discussion in doctrine about the value or otherwise of incorporation. What discussion there has been has tended to focus on the issue of access to a court to determine civil rights and obligations and to treat the issue

---

[115] Thanks to Thomas Bull for useful comments on this point.

[116] For a brief discussion of the approaches taken by the Danish and Norwegian legislators see Cameron, n 7, 238.

[117] Of course, the interest in shielding the ordinary courts is one of the main arguments for establishing a specialist constitutional court.

[118] See the comments of F Sterzel, in *Rättsfonden, Författningsdomstolen och lagprövning* (Rättsfonden, Stockholm, 1991), at 88. A good example here is RH 1995:85 (above n 91).

[119] An interesting example of a recent judicial decision on property rights that was partly based on the ECHR was the interim decision of the Supreme Administrative Court ordering a stay of execution of the government's decision to close a nuclear power station (decision of 14 May 1998). This decision had major political implications for the ruling Social Democratic Party.

together with the principle of judicial remedies under EC law. Three controversial ECHR issues which have caused some doctrinal discussion are the implications of the *Gustafsson* case for trade union law, the question of the compatibility of the government policy to close all nuclear power stations with Article 1, Protocol No 1 and the issue of whether tax penalties are criminal penalties.

The legislative process ensures that in most cases, the Swedish legislator will adequately take account of the ECHR. More could be done as regards ensuring that administrative agencies, especially those in the 'front line' of possible ECHR violations, are aware of the requirements of the ECHR. As regards the case law since incorporation, this indicates that the Swedish courts are faithfully attempting to take the ECHR into account. The few deficiencies which have been revealed can probably be put down to lack of time, rather than hostility or indifference towards the ECHR. A development towards slightly greater independence in interpretation can be expected from the Swedish courts; mainly, however, under the influence of EC law rather than the ECHR as such. This development is likely to manifest itself, at least initially, in certain areas of the law: particularly in adminstrative procedural law (access to courts) rather than the (more controversial) field of civil liberties generally. The respect which Swedish judges accord the legislator means that the main way the ECHR will be used is in the form of treaty-conform construction rather than constitutional review. Nonetheless, the constitutional difficulties involved in avoiding review of ordinances means that a small increase in constitutional review can also be expected.

8

Private Rights, Private Law and the Private Domain

HECTOR L MACQUEEN* and DOUGLAS BRODIE**

A. INTRODUCTION

OVER THE YEARS before the passage of the Human Rights Act 1998 the European Convention for the Protection of Human Rights and Fundamental Freedoms (ECHR) impinged only from time to time upon the private law consciousness in Scotland.[1] Most conspicuous was the long-running debate about a law of privacy, and whether the ECHR supported the existence of a right to be let alone by virtue of the right to respect for private life contained in Article 8;[2] but this only served to emphasise the absence of discussion in the Scottish courts (in increasing contrast with the approach of their English counterparts[3]) about whether in developing the common law consistency with the ECHR should be sought. In the *Kaur* case in 1980 there was the understandable refusal of Lord Ross, sitting in the Outer House of the Court of Session, to use the private law doctrine of *jus quaesitum tertio* as a backdoor means of making the Convention an enforceable source of rights in Scots law.[4] In 1989 the

---

* Professor of Private Law, University of Edinburgh.

** Senior Lecturer in Law, University of Edinburgh.

[1] For general surveys of the ECHR and Scots law pre-incorporation, see W C Gilmore and S C Neff, 'On Scotland, Europe and Human Rights' in H L MacQueen (ed), *Scots Law into the 21st Century* (W Green, Edinburgh, 1996), 265–76; J Murdoch, 'Scotland and the European Convention' in B Dickson (ed), *Human Rights and the European Convention* (Sweet & Maxwell, London, 1997), 113–42; Lord Reed, in Lord Lester of Herne Hill and D Pannick (eds), *Human Rights Law and Practice* (Butterworths, London, Edinburgh and Dublin, 1999), ch 5.

[2] See, for full discussion of the Scottish and other authorities on privacy, M A Hogg, 'The very private life of the right to privacy' in *Privacy and Property*, Hume Papers on Public Policy, vol 2 no 3 (Edinburgh University Press, Edinburgh, 1994), 1–28.

[3] Notably in the context of defamation, for which see eg *Derbyshire County Council v Times Newspapers Ltd* [1993] QB 770 (CA), aff'd on other grounds [1993] AC 534; *Rantzen v Mirror Group Newspapers* [1994] QB 670 (CA); *Reynolds v Times Newspapers Ltd* [2001] 2 AC 127 (CA and HL); *McCartan Turkington Breen v Times Newspapers Ltd* [2001] 2 AC 277. Note also the influence of the ECtHR on the development of defamation: *Tolstoy Miloslavsky v United Kingdom* (1995) 20 EHRR 442.

[4] *Surjit Kaur v Lord Advocate* 1980 SC 319; commented upon by Gilmore and Neff, above, n 1, 266–67; Murdoch, above, n 1, 114–17.

Spycatcher litigation and its Scottish equivalent, *Lord Advocate v The Scotsman Publications Ltd*,[5] made use of Article 10 of the ECHR (freedom of expression) to develop the law of confidential information, albeit in a public law context. Finally, in 1996, in the *T, Petitioner* case,[6] the First Division of the Court of Session not only permitted adoption by a homosexual, but also over-ruled *Kaur* by declaring the legitimacy of use of the ECHR to assist in the interpretation of ambiguous domestic legislation. Adoption is, however, another subject in which private law relations arise in an essentially public law context.

In general, then, human rights had not been of central concern for a private lawyer in Scotland. Human rights law dealt essentially with the relationship between the person[7] and the State—that is, was a public rather than a private law matter. If private law is essentially concerned with relationships between individuals or other legal actors apart from the State, then a good working assumption seemed to be that human rights law would have little direct impact upon that arena.

Now, however, perceptions like these have at least to be reconsidered. For our part, we have read the ECHR; we have studied the Government's White Paper, *Bringing Rights Home: the Human Rights Bill*[8] and the Human Rights Act 1998; we have sallied into the *European Human Rights Reports* and 'surfed' on the website of the European Court of Human Rights (ECtHR);[9] we have dipped into the literature and the Parliamentary debates on the Human Rights Bill; and we have followed the early case law of the Court of Session, the High Court of Justiciary and the Privy Council since 6 May 1999 and of the English courts since 2 October 2000. And the words of John Keats on first looking into Chapman's Homer have come repeatedly to mind:

> Then felt I like some watcher of the skies
> When a new planet swims into his ken;
> Or like stout Cortez when with eagle eyes
> He stared at the Pacific—and all his men
> Looked at each other with a wild surmise—
> Silent, upon a peak in Darien.

There are admittedly some difficulties with this quotation: it was not Hernando Cortés (conqueror of Mexico) but Vasco Nuñez de Balboa who in 1513 became the first European to see the ocean later named the Pacific by Ferdinand

---

[5] *Lord Advocate v The Scotsman Publications Ltd* 1989 SC (HL) 122. For 'Spycatcher' see *Attorney General v Guardian Newspapers (No 2)* [1988] 3 WLR 776, [1990] 1 AC 109. The matter went on to the European Court of Human Rights: see *The Observer and The Guardian v United Kingdom* (1992) 14 EHRR 153 and *Sunday Times v United Kingdom (No 2)* (1992) 14 EHRR 229.

[6] *T, Petitioner* 1997 SLT 724, commented upon by Murdoch, 'Scotland and the European Convention' 136–41. See also Lord Hope of Craighead, 'Devolution and human rights' [1998] *EHRLR* 367–79 at 370–71.

[7] Note that where not inappropriate (eg right to marry) a legal person may claim Convention rights (eg to protection of property under Art 1 of the First Protocol).

[8] Cm 3782: October 1997.

[9] http://www.dhcour.coe.fr.

Magellan; while Darien has been a name of ill omen amongst Scots since their disastrous colonial venture there from 1698 to 1700. But we wish to draw, not upon Keats' historical accuracy or awareness of Scottish sensitivities, but upon the general sentiment evoked by the opening lines of the quotation, which seems, for the reasons about to be given, to be entirely apt to the occasion. For the essential thrust of this paper is that the impact of human rights law has transformed the *Weltanschauung* of the private as much as that of the public or the criminal lawyer in Britain.

In Scotland, it is also necessary to take account of the Scotland Act 1998 and the legislative competence of the Scottish Parliament established by that Act,[10] because that competence does not extend to passing Acts incompatible with any of the Convention rights.[11] Nor can the Scottish Parliament modify the Human Rights Act 1998, which is thus as entrenched in the new constitution as some of the Articles of the Acts of the 1707 Union or certain key sections of the European Communities Act 1972.[12] One important consequence of these limitations on the powers of the Scottish Parliament is that, while the Government brought the Human Rights Act 1998 into force on 2 October 2000, the Convention rights took effect in Scotland before the rest of the mainland United Kingdom, since the Scotland Act 1998 came into force on 6 May 1999. Further, the actings of the Scottish Executive (and in particular the Lord Advocate) became subject to Convention rights upon its formation on 20 May 1999, the limitation which has been at the root of most of the Scottish case law on the subject so far.[13]

B. HORIZONTAL EFFECT OF THE HUMAN RIGHTS ACT

The conclusion that the human rights legislation will have a fundamental impact upon private law, whether Scottish or English, is not a self-evident one

---

[10] See Lord Hope of Craighead, *Working with the Scottish Parliament: Judicial Aspects of Devolution*, Hume Occasional Paper No 54 (The David Hume Institute, Edinburgh, 1998); Lord Hope, above, n 6; R Reed, 'Devolution and the Judiciary' in The University of Cambridge Centre for Public Law (ed), *Constitutional Reform in the United Kingdom: Practice and Principles* (Hart Publishing, Oxford, 1998), 21–31; Lord Steyn, 'Incorporation and Devolution' [1998] *EHRLR* 153–56; A Miller, 'Human Rights and the Scottish Parliament' [1998] *EHRLR* 260–66.

[11] Scotland Act 1998, s 29(1)(d). See *A (A Mental Patient) v Scottish Ministers* 2000 SCI; 2002 SC (PC) 63 (right to liberty and the Mental Health (Public Safety and Appeals) (Scotland) Act 1999, asp 1), upheld by the Judicial Committee of the Privy Council 2001 SLT 1331 (PC).

[12] See Scotland Act 1998, Sch 4 para 1.

[13] *Ibid*, s 57(2). See eg *Starrs v Ruxton* 2000 JC 208 (temporary sheriffs); *Brown v Stott* 2001 SC (PC) 43; [2001] 2 All ER 97 (protection against self incrimination); *Clancy v Caird* (No 1) 2000 SC 441; 2000 SLT 546 (temporary judges); *County Properties Ltd v The Scottish Ministers* 2000 SLT 965, rev'd 2001 SLT 1125 after the decision of the House of Lords in *R v Secretary of State for ETR, ex parte Alconbury* [2001] 2 All ER 929 (planning inquiries as independent and impartial tribunals); *Lafarge Redland Aggregates Ltd, Petitioners* 2001 SC 298 (hearing within reasonable time and planning decision); *McIntosh v HM Advocate* 2001 SC (PC) 89 (drug traffickers confiscation order and presumption of innocence); *Millar v Dickson* 2002 SC (PC) 30 (retrospective effect of *Starrs v Ruxton*, waiver of Art 6).

at a first reading of the ECHR or the Human Rights Act 1998. Although the rights to which they extend include what look like private law subjects—for example, respect for private and family life (Article 8), the right to marry (Article 12), and the protection of property (Article 1 of the First Protocol)—the ECHR, reflecting its origins in a reaction to the horrors of Nazi Germany, is clearly aimed first and foremost at abuses of human rights perpetrated by the State or public authorities rather than by one private person against another such person. Under Articles 33 and 34, only States may be sued in the ECtHR. The wording of the texts conferring the substantive rights often appears to be expressly addressed to the State: thus, for example, the right to respect for private and family life in Article 8 prohibits interference with the exercise of this right by a public authority, while Article 10 declares that the right to freedom of expression shall be exercised without interference by public authority and regardless of frontiers. Section 6 of the Human Rights Act 1998 states that 'it is unlawful for a public authority to act in a way which is incompatible with a Convention right', but, just like the ECHR itself,[14] there is no provision stating in terms that it is unlawful for a private individual or legal person so to act. At first sight, therefore, the Act appears intended not to have horizontal, but only vertical effect, apparently confirmed by the express provision enabling victims of unlawful acts under section 6 to make claims against the public authority concerned.[15]

But once we move further into the detail of the Human Rights Act 1998, its potential horizontal effects, and the fundamental implications arising therefrom for private law, quickly become apparent.

(1) Statute

First is the impact of the Human Rights Act 1998 upon domestic legislation, the source of much modern private law.[16] Section 3(1) requires primary and subordinate legislation to be read and given effect in a way compatible with Convention rights, so far as it is possible to do so. There is nothing stated in the section to limit this requirement to legislation concerning public authorities.[17] It applies whenever the legislation was enacted,[18] so all existing statutory material is now subject to the ECHR. Primary legislation is, broadly speaking, Acts of

---

[14] Although see Art 17 of the ECHR, discussed below, see n 50.

[15] Human Rights Act 1998, s 7(1)(a).

[16] See in general *Brown v Stott* 2000 JC 328 for Lord Justice-General Rodger's valuable discussion of the application of the Act's provisions about statutes in conjunction with the provisions of the Scotland Act 1998, a matter not touched upon in the subsequent review of the case by the Privy Council (2001 SC (PC) 43).

[17] The duty of the court is reinforced by the fact that under s 6 of the Human Rights Act 1998 it too is a public authority obliged to act compatibly with Convention rights: see *Cachla v Faluyi* [2001] 1 WLR 1966 (CA).

[18] Human Rights Act 1998, s 3(2)(a).

the Westminster Parliament, while Acts of the Scottish Parliament (and of the Northern Ireland Assembly) are subordinate legislation,[19] reflecting the devolved status of these legislatures. Reinforcing the effect of section 3(1) of the Human Rights Act 1998, the Scotland Act 1998 provides that Acts of the Scottish Parliament are be read as narrowly as is required for them to be within the Parliament's legislative competence, ie inter alia, within Convention rights.[20] It is possible that the apparent difference between the expansive approach to interpretation encouraged by the Human Rights Act 1998 and the restrictive one of the Scotland Act 1998 may be more than a question of words chosen for the distinct contexts of establishing Convention rights over existing legislation, on the one hand, and defining a subordinate body's legislative competence, on the other. But it is quite clear, however, that Convention rights will henceforth be a factor in reading and applying all legislation, including legislation within the sphere of private law.

The new rules of statutory interpretation in the Human Rights Act 1998 and the Scotland Act 1998 go beyond anything in the existing rules on this subject, being 'less concerned with . . . textual analysis', and more with 'a process of moulding the law to what the Court believes the law should be trying to achieve.'[21] There is no prior need for the statute to be ambiguous;[22] section 3 will apply unless it is impossible to make the legislation ECHR-compatible. It is a moot point whether this interpretive process can extend as far as reading into a statute provisions which ought to be there.[23] The section seems likely to have a particular effect on the reading of pre-1998 statutes, since they were drafted and debated without human rights considerations necessarily at the forefront of either the draftsman's or Parliamentary thinking. New legislation, by contrast, will be so drafted and considered, and both Westminster and Edinburgh Ministers are now statutorily obliged to make statements when introducing new

[19] *Ibid*, s 21(1).

[20] Scotland Act 1998, s 101. R A Edwards, 'Reading Down Legislation under the Human Rights Act', (2000) 20 *Legal Studies* 353–71 at 357, n 28 suggests that the Scottish courts face a problem whether to apply s 101 or Human Rights Act 1998 s 3, given that the former was enacted after the latter.

[21] Lord Irvine of Lairg, 'The Development of Human Rights in Britain', [1998] *PL* 221–36 at 232–33; and see *Rights Brought Home*, para 2.7. See also Lord Lester of Herne Hill, 'The Impact of the Human Rights Act on Public Law' in The University of Cambridge Centre for Public Law (ed), above, n 10, 105–07 at 106; and, for critical comment, G Marshall, 'Patriating Rights—With Reservations: The Human Rights Bill 1998' in Beatson (ed), above, n 10, 73–78 at 80ff; idem, 'Interpreting Interpretation in the Human Rights Bill' [1998] *PL* 167–70; idem, 'Two Kinds of Compatibility: More About s 3 of the Human Rights Act 1998' [1999] *PL* 377–83; Lord Cooke of Thorndon, 'The British Embracement of Human Rights' [1999] *EHRLR* 243–260; Lord Irvine of Lairg, 'Activism and Restraint: Human Rights and the Interpretation process' [1999] *EHRLR* 350–72; Edwards, above, n 20; F A R Bennion, 'What Interpretation is "Possible" under Section 3(1) of the Human Rights Act 1998' [2000] *PL* 77–91; Lord Reed (ed), *A Practical Guide to Human Rights Law in Scotland* (W Green, Edinburgh, 2001), paras. 1.10–1.13.

[22] Unlike the previous Scottish common law position under *T, Petitioner* (above, n 6).

[23] See discussion in Edwards, above, n 20, 366–68.

Bills of which they are in charge, indicating their compatibility with, respectively, Convention rights [24] and devolved legislative competence.[25]

Section 4 of the Human Rights Act 1998 enables certain (but not all) courts to declare that a piece of primary (ie Westminster) legislation is incompatible with the ECHR, although such a declaration is not to affect the validity, continuing operation or enforcement of the Act in question, and is not binding on the parties to the proceedings in which it is made.[26] The theory is that, when Westminster is confronted with such a declaration, a special fast-track legislative procedure will be deployed to remedy the incompatibility.[27] In this way the supremacy or sovereignty of the Westminster Parliament, that keystone of the British constitution, is preserved or maintained in the face of what are effectively new judicial powers to scrutinise the vires of legislation.[28] But the position of Acts of the Scottish Parliament in relation to human rights is not so protected; as already noted, if incompatible with Convention rights, they are outwith the legislative competence of the Parliament and thus not law at all.[29]

An early instance of the impact of Convention rights upon statutory private law occurred in the copyright case of *Ashdown v Telegraph Group Ltd*.[30] The issue concerned the impact of the Article 10 right to freedom of expression upon the fair dealing defences to claims of infringement under the Copyright, Designs and Patents Act 1988. At first instance Sir Andrew Morritt VC held that the fair dealing provisions of the statute in themselves satisfied the requirements of Article 10 and that there was no need to bring section 3 of the Human Rights Act 1998 into play:

> the balance between the rights of the owner of the copyright and those of the public has been struck by the legislative organ of the democratic state itself in the legislation

[24] Human Rights Act 1998, s 19.

[25] Scotland Act 1998, s 31.

[26] For a declaration of incompatibility in relation to provisions of the Consumer Credit Act, see *Wilson v The First County Trust Ltd (No 2)* [2001] 3 WLR 42; 3 All ER 229 (CA), for which see further below, text to n 121. The First Division of the Court of Session considered whether to make a declaration of incompatibility in *S v Miller* 2001 SLT 531 (commented upon by I Jamieson, 2001 SLT (News) 137); it eventually did not do so because the Scottish Ministers had power under the relevant legislation to deal with the breach of Convention rights in question (*S v Miller (No 2)* 2001 SLT 1304).

[27] The procedure is set out in permissive terms in Human Rights Act 1998, s 10 and Sch 2.

[28] *Rights Brought Home*, paras 2.11–2.15. But, as always in this connection, see the observation of Lord President Cooper in *MacCormick v Lord Advocate* 1952 SC 396 at 411: 'the principle of the unlimited sovereignty of Parliament is a distinctively English principle which has no counterpart in Scottish constitutional law.' For other comment on the issue after not only the Human Rights Act 1998 but also the European Communities Act 1972 and devolution, see A W Bradley, 'Constitutional Reform, the Sovereignty of Parliament and Devolution' in Beatson (ed), above, n 10, 33–40; N Bamforth, 'Parliamentary Sovereignty and the Human Rights Act 1998' [1998] PL 572–82; V Bogdanor, *The Start of a New Song* Hume Occasional Paper No 55 (The David Hume Institute, Edinburgh, 1998).

[29] Scotland Act 1998, s 29(2)(d). And see *A (A Mental Patient) v Scottish Ministers* 2001 SCI; 2002 SC (PC) 63.

[30] *Ashdown v Telegraph Group Ltd* [2001] 2 WLR 967; 2 All ER 370 (Morritt VC); rev'd [2001] 4 All ER 666 (CA).

it has enacted. There is no room for any further defences outside the code which establishes the particular species of intellectual property in question (para 20).

The Court of Appeal concluded, however, that

> rare circumstances can arise where the right of freedom of expression will come into conflict with the protection afforded by the Copyright Act, notwithstanding the express exceptions to be found in the Act. In these circumstances, we consider that the court is bound, insofar as it is able, to apply the Act in a manner that accommodates the right of freedom of expression (para 45).

This view must be correct under section 3 of the Human Rights Act 1998. The court went on to observe that, at least in this case, the approach required could be fulfilled, not so much through examination of the statutory language as such, as by way of the remedies granted to enforce the legislation: in the particular case, by withholding the discretionary relief of an injunction and leaving the copyright owner to a damages claim or an account of profits (see paras 46 and 59). Further, while the statutory defences and the judicial precedents elaborating upon their application fell to be reconsidered in the light of Article 10, that did not require the defendant to be able to profit from the use of another's copyright material without paying compensation.

(2) Common law

Although clearly the new powers with regard to legislation are of considerable importance for all law in the United Kingdom, and therefore for private law as much as for any other branch of law, nonetheless private law is only in part legislative, and arguably its essence lies in unenacted or common law, produced by the decisions of the courts and the rationalisations of text writers. If we take the definition of Scots private law in the Scotland Act 1998—

the following areas of the civil law of Scotland—

(a) the general principles of private law (including private international law),

(b) the law of persons (including natural persons, legal persons and unincorporated bodies),

(c) the law of obligations (including obligations arising from contract, unilateral promise, delict, unjustified enrichment and negotiorum gestio),

(d) the law of property (including heritable and moveable property, trusts and succession), and

(e) the law of actions (including jurisdiction, remedies, evidence, procedure, diligence, recognition and enforcement of court orders, limitation of actions and arbitration)[31]

---

[31] Scotland Act 1998 s 126(4) (deploying the Justinianic or institutional scheme of persons, things and actions). Large areas of commercial and 'single market' law which can be seen as pertaining to private law, broadly conceived, are reserved to Westminster under Sch 5 of the Act, but it should be

—and reflect on the extent to which the law so defined is indeed a mixture of statute, judicial decisions and text writing, the obvious question is whether only its legislative elements are affected by the Human Rights Act 1998. The answer to be given to this question here is that the whole of private law, including the common law, will be subject to Convention rights, although the argument depends upon interpretation of the legislation rather than upon any direct statement to that effect within the four corners of the Human Rights Act 1998.

The argument starts from the Act's definition of a 'public authority', the bodies upon which, by section 6, it imposes a positive and legally enforceable duty to act in accordance with Convention rights. Under the Act, these include courts and tribunals.[32] If the courts cannot act in a way incompatible with a ECHR right, this would seem to extend their duties to observe the ECHR beyond the functions already discussed, namely, those of interpreting legislation in a way compatible with Convention rights and declaring legislation incompatible with a ECHR right.

The first obvious implication of the courts' responsibility as public authorities is for the law of actions, defined as part of private law by the Scotland Act 1998 (see above), and covering both the procedures followed by the courts and the remedies which they grant. There may be a major effect here on existing forms and processes. Article 6 of the ECHR entitles persons to a fair and public hearing in the determination of their civil rights and obligations.[33] Can *ex parte* procedures, or remedies not involving public procedure in a court room, such as summary diligence,[34] be denials of the right under Article 6? The English 'Anton Piller' order, under which a court may, without any notice to the defendant, enable a plaintiff to enter and inspect another's premises, to require the giving of information by that other even when self-incriminating, and to seize or record material potentially relevant to intellectual property infringements, has been

---

noted that ECHR rights are highly relevant to commercial interests: see further P Duffy, 'The Protection of Commercial Interests under the European Convention on Human Rights' in R Cranston (ed), *Making Commercial Law: Essays in Honour of Roy Goode* (Clarendon Press, Oxford, 1997), 525–42; M Smythe, 'Incorporation and its Implications for Business' [1998] *EHRLR* 273–91; C Gane, 'Business, Commerce and Human Rights' (1998) 43(10) *JLSS* 32–33; Sir Nicolas Bratza, 'The Implications of the Human Rights Act 1998 for Commercial Practice' [2000] *EHRLR* 1–13.

[32] Human Rights Act 1998, s 6(3)(a). It does not apply to private arbiters, mediators and the like, although courts enforcing arbitral awards and mediation agreements would presumably have to have an eye upon Convention rights.

[33] See for general accounts of Art 6: D J Harris, M O'Boyle and C Warbrick, *Law of the European Convention on Human Rights* (Butterworths, London, Dublin and Edinburgh, 1995), ch 6, or F G Jacobs and R C A White, *The European Convention on Human Rights* 2nd edn (Clarendon Press, Oxford, 1995), ch 8.

[34] For summary diligence see W A Wilson, *The Scottish Law of Debt* 2nd edn (W Green, Edinburgh, 1991), paras 19.5–6. A debtor's consent to registration for execution, the precursor of most summary diligence, presumably waives any Art 6 rights: *sed quaere* summary diligence on a negotiable instrument. It was reported in *The Scotsman*, 24 January 2001, that a sheriff had suspended the execution of a summary warrant to enforce business rates as a possible infringement of Art 6. For the summary warrant procedure see Wilson, *ibid*, para 19.7.

challenged in Strasbourg as a violation of Article 8 (respect for private and family life), and although the challenge was unsuccessful, reform of the procedure followed in 1994.[35] The Scottish equivalent to Anton Piller orders was also amended once the Human Rights Act came into force.[36]

Article 6 also has implications for the reforms of procedure designed to streamline the activities of the courts in the interests of efficiency and speedier despatch of business.[37] Article 6 says that a party to litigation is entitled to a hearing within a reasonable time. What is the significance of the requirement in relation to procedural rules known to be used tactically by lawyers to delay a case coming to court? On the other hand, can a judicially imposed timetable for litigation be too short to be reasonable? As part of an attempt to reduce the dispute culture in the construction industry, the Housing Grants, Construction and Regeneration Act 1996 introduced the special procedure of adjudication, allowing decision-making on disputes by adjudicators within a 28-day period. Do Convention rights apply? Are adjudicators 'courts or tribunals'? Do they 'determine' parties' rights and obligations? Are adjudication procedures fair? Attention has been drawn to the potential for tactical ambush by adjudication, leading to lack of time for the preparation of defences; the insufficiency of the 28-day period to determine complex issues of law and fact; the lack of publicity in the proceedings enabling the adjudicator to hear one party without the other being present; and the possibility that an adjudicator, while statutorily required to be impartial, need not be independent of both parties.[38] In *Austin Hall Building Ltd v Buckland Securities*,[39] however, it was held that an adjudicator was not a court or tribunal, and so, albeit subject to the rules of natural justice, not caught by Convention rights; although courts enforcing adjudications must apply Convention rights.

But the significance of the courts' obligation to act compatibly with Convention rights goes much further than the procedural and remedial aspects of their activities. It extends also to their substantive decision-making in cases, not just under statute, but also under the unenacted law, and so including the substantive private law of persons, obligations and property. The Human

[35] *Chappell v United Kingdom* (1990) 12 EHRR 1; Lord Chancellor's Department, Anton Piller Orders (Consultation Paper No 181, 1992); Practice Direction (Mareva Injunctions and Anton Piller Orders), 28 July 1994 (see (1994) 144 *New Law Journal* 1134). See further W R Cornish, *Intellectual Property: Patents, Copyright, Trade Marks and Allied Rights* 4th edn (Sweet & Maxwell, London, 1999), 80–85. Note also *Dabelstein v Hildebrand* 1996 (3) SA 42 (C), in which it was held that the South African equivalent of an Anton Piller order did not infringe the right to privacy in the interim Constitution of South Africa.

[36] See Administration of Justice (Scotland) Act 1972, ss 1 and 1A (added by Law Reform (Miscellaneous Provisions) (Scotland) Act 1985, s 19); Rules of Court ch 64; A MacSporran and A R W Young, *Commission and Diligence* (W Green, Edinburgh, 1995), paras. 2.34–2.49.

[37] See eg *The Reform of Civil Justice*, Hume Papers on Public Policy vol 5 no 4 (Edinburgh University Press, Edinburgh, 1997); *Justice and Money*, Hume Papers on Public Policy vol 7 no 1 (Edinburgh University Press, Edinburgh, 1999).

[38] M L Macaulay, 'Adjudication: Rough Justice?' 2000 SLT (News) 217–19.

[39] *Austin Hall Building Ltd v Buckland Securities* [2001] BLR 272 (Bowsher J, TCC). See also *Elanay Contracts Ltd v The Vestry* [2001] BLR 33 (TCC).

Rights Act 1998 itself provides in section 7 that not only may a person make a claim that a public authority is acting, or proposes to act, unlawfully under section 6 in proceedings against that authority, but also he or she may rely on Convention rights 'in any legal proceedings'[40]—that is, presumably, proceedings other than one brought directly against, or by, the public authority concerned. The definition of 'legal proceedings' for these purposes states that it 'includes—(a) proceedings brought by or at the instigation of a public authority; and (b) an appeal against the decision of a court or tribunal';[41] but this does not preclude a first instance action between two purely private persons not involving a public authority other than the court or tribunal before which the case is being heard. Indeed, section 11 of the Act seems to recognise that such an action might be a vehicle for an issue about Convention rights by providing that:

> a person's reliance on a ECHR right does not restrict . . . his right to make any claim or bring any proceedings which he could make or bring apart from sections 7 to 9.[42]

Finally it seems implicit in section 12 that courts are to give effect at least to the rights of freedom of expression and perhaps privacy in litigation between private parties. When a party is seeking relief affecting the exercise of the ECHR right to freedom of expression (Article 10)—say, wishing to invoke the Article 8 right to privacy or, as in *Ashdown v Telegraph Group*, claiming infringement of copyright, to prevent a newspaper from publishing a story—the court or tribunal considering the matter should have 'particular regard' to the importance of freedom of expression—that is, the newspaper's right should be treated as of especial weight in the balancing exercise to be conducted by the court.[43] More specifically, the court should not restrain publication before trial unless satisfied that the applicant is likely to establish at trial that publication should not be allowed,[44] and should also have regard to:

(1) the extent to which
   (a) the material in issue has, or is about to, become available to the public; or
   (b) publication is or would be, in the public interest; and
(2) any relevant privacy code.[45]

---

[40] Human Rights Act 1998, s 7(1)(b). See also s 22(4) for limitations on the retrospective effect of s 7(1)(b).

[41] Human Rights Act 1998, s 7(6).

[42] Human Rights Act 1998, s 11(b).

[43] Compare the jurisprudence of the European Court: see Harris, O'Boyle and Warbrick, above, n 33, 372–77.

[44] This may counter what is sometimes known as the 'Maxwell injunction', following the practice of the late Robert Maxwell, who is said to have frequently prevented the publication of information about him by the use of interlocutory injunctions against the publisher.

[45] Current examples of such self-regulatory codes protecting privacy are the Newspaper Industry Code of Practice, operated by the Press Complaints Commission, and the Broadcasting Standards Code, operated by the Broadcasting Standards Commission. See further below, n 166, for the privacy code of the PCC. A recent case on the BSC privacy code is *R v Broadcasting Standards Commission, ex parte British Broadcasting Corporation* [2000] 3 All ER 389, [2000] 3 WLR 1327.

There thus seems to be much to sustain the view that, in purely private litigation involving unenacted private law, a party could argue successfully that for the court as a public authority to apply the law in question would be incompatible with that party's Convention rights and so unlawful under section 6. This argument that the duty of the courts to respect Convention rights applies in private litigation can be further supported, on the basis of *Pepper v Hart*,[46] with an important statement by the Lord Chancellor in committee in the House of Lords:[47]

> We also believe that it is right as a matter of principle for the courts to have the duty of acting compatibly with the Convention, not only in cases involving other public authorities but also in developing the common law in cases between individuals. Why should they not? In preparing this Bill we have taken the view that it is the other course, that of excluding Convention considerations altogether from cases between individuals, which would have to be justified. We do not think that that would be justifiable; nor, indeed, do we think it would be practicable.

It is also true, however, that in the House of Commons the Home Secretary commented that 'Convention rights . . . would not be directly justiciable in actions between private individuals.'[48] The two statements can be reconciled by focusing on the concept of 'direct justiciability'. The Act does not enable one individual to sue another on the basis of infringement of Convention rights alone (direct justiciability); but it does allow Convention rights to be invoked in the context of litigation founded on other points, and for the law in question to be developed or restricted, as the case may be, by the obligation of the court to act compatibly with the Convention rights of the litigants.

Such an approach can also be justified by the jurisprudence of the ECtHR, which British courts must take into account under section 2(1) of the Human Rights Act 1998. The Court takes the view that, apart from protecting the individual against State action, there are Articles of the ECHR that oblige the State to protect individual rights even against the action of other individuals.[49] These are sometimes described as giving rise to positive obligations upon the State to take action to prevent the infringement of individual's rights by others. This approach rests ultimately on Article 17 of the ECHR, one of the Convention rights to which British courts must give effect.[50] It provides, under the heading 'Prohibition of Abuse of Rights', that:

---

[46] *Pepper v Hart* [1993] AC 593.
[47] HL Debs 24 Nov 1997, col 783.
[48] HC Debs 17 June 1998, col 406.
[49] See generally A Clapham, *Human Rights in the Private Sphere* (Clarendon Press, Oxford, 1993), 178–244.
[50] Human Rights Act 1998, s 1 and Sch 1. The importance of Art 17 in balancing apparently competing ECHR rights cannot be over-stated. In particular, it has important implications for any development of a law of privacy restricting press freedom. Just as the press should not abuse freedom of expression (Art 10) to destroy private life (Art 8), so the assertion of a right to privacy should not be allowed to destroy free speech. See further below, 168–71.

Nothing in this Convention may be interpreted as implying for any State, *group or person* any right to engage in any activity or perform any act aimed at the destruction of any of the rights and freedoms set forth herein or at their limitation to a greater extent than is provided for in the Convention [emphasis added].

The best-known examples of this approach in the Strasbourg jurisprudence are *Young, James and Webster v United Kingdom*,[51] which concerned 'closed shop' employment practices as a breach of the right to freedom of association even although the employer was taken not to be a State body, and *X and Y v Netherlands*,[52] dealing with the failure of the State to prosecute the perpetrator of a sexual assault upon a mentally incapacitated girl of 16, in contravention of Article 8. Other, more recent claims of this type occurred in the *Stedman*[53] and *Osman*[54] cases. The *Osman* case is discussed further below; in *Stedman*, the Commission, in finding that there was no violation of Article 11's freedom to manifest one's religion in worship when an employer dismissed an employee who refused to work on Sundays, nevertheless took the opportunity to reaffirm the doctrine of the State's liability for infringement of human rights committed by individuals within its territory as well as directly by its organs. In *Glaser v United Kingdom*,[55] a case concerned with a father's rights under Article 8 in his attempt to enforce contact orders made in private law proceedings between him and the mother of his children, the ECtHR said:[56]

> The essential object of Art 8 is to protect the individual against arbitrary interference by public authorities. There may, however, be positive obligations inherent in an effective 'respect' for family life. These obligations may involve the adoption of measures to secure respect for family life, *even in the sphere of relations between individuals*, including both the provision of a regulatory framework of adjudicatory and enforcement machinery protecting individuals' rights and the implementation, where appropriate, of specific steps.

Finally, in *Hatton v United Kingdom*,[57] where residents of the area around Heathrow airport complained that the noise of flights during the night destroyed their sleep and so constituted an intrusion upon their private lives contrary to Article 8, the ECtHR noted that 'Heathrow airport and the aircraft which use it are not owned, controlled or operated by the [UK] Government or by an agency of the Government' (para 95). Although the Government could therefore not be said to have interfered directly with the applicants' private life, it did have 'a positive duty . . . to take reasonable and appropriate measures to

---

[51] *Young, James and Webster v United Kingdom* (1982) 4 EHRR 38.
[52] *X and Y v Netherlands* (1985) 8 EHRR 235.
[53] *Stedman* (1997) 23 EHRR CD 168.
[54] *Osman v United Kingdom* (2000) 29 EHRR 245.
[55] *Glaser v United Kingdom* [2000] 3 FCR 193.
[56] *Ibid*, para 63 of the judgment.
[57] *Hatton v United Kingdom* Application no 36022/97, decision of 2 Oct 2001; The Times, 8 Oct 2001.

secure' (para 95) their rights under the Article, and had failed to take the appropriate steps to ensure that these rights were respected.

C. THE NATURE OF THE HORIZONTALITY—WEAK OR STRONG?

The provisions of the Human Rights Act 1998 just discussed have of course generated considerable debate since they first appeared in Bill form in 1997.[58] There is an argument that Convention rights cannot have horizontal effect in private law in so far as it is judge-made law. The essence of this argument is that the Convention rights are conceived and expressed as rights against the State or its manifestations only, and therefore have no relevance in adjudications of disputes between private parties. The content of the ECHR cannot be changed by the simple provision in the Human Rights Act 1998 that the courts are public authorities.[59] This position has been countered with the observation that many of the Convention rights are in fact couched in general terms rather than specifically against the State, and by the argument that opponents of horizontality are not taking enough account of what is involved in the transition from an instrument enforced in an international tribunal to a domestic statute enforced in national courts. If, as seems plain, section 3 of the Human Rights Act 1998 envisages statutes being made compatible with Convention rights, why should this not also be the case with the common law? Since the courts pre-incorporation were taking account of the ECHR in developing the common law, why should they not continue to do so post-incorporation?[60]

The view taken here is that Convention rights have horizontal effect in relation to private law, whether under section 3 when its content is statutory or under the section 6 duty of the courts as a public authority in relation to the common law. In the latter case, however, the legislative intent was clearly against direct horizontality in the sense that one private litigant could sue another purely and simply upon the basis of infringement of a ECHR right.[61] The horizontality under section 6 is therefore of an indirect nature;[62] but, as a

---

[58] For a convenient summary, see A J Bowen, 'Fundamental Rights in Private Law' 2000 *SLT* (News) 157–61.

[59] See Lord Justice Buxton, 'The Human Rights Act and Private Law' (2000) 116 *LQR* 48–65.

[60] See H W R Wade, 'Horizons of Horizontality' (2000) 116 *LQR* 217–24, and N Bamforth, 'The True "Horizontal Effect" of the Human Rights Act 1998' (2001) 117 *LQR* 34–41.

[61] Contrast the position in South Africa, where clause 8 of the 1996 Constitution states that the Bill of Rights applies to all law, and that the judiciary and natural and juristic persons (to the extent that the nature of the right and its correlative duty allow) are bound by it as well; and in Ireland, where breach of a constitutional right is a cause of action between private parties. On horizontality in South Africa, see A Cockrell, 'The Bill of Rights and Private Law: A threshold issue of "Horizontality" ' *Butterworths Bill of Rights Compendium* (Butterworths, London, 1997). See also A Fagan, 'Determining the Stakes: Binding and Non-binding Bills of Rights' in D Friedmann and D Barak-Erez (eds), *Human Rights in Private Law* (Hart Publishing, Oxford, 2002).

[62] This seems to be accepted in all the standard works on the Human Rights Act 1998: see Lester and Pannick, above, n 1, 31–32 ('an indirect but powerful influence upon private law rights and

number of commentators have pointed out, this gives rise to at least two possible approaches, which may be dubbed 'weak' and 'strong' indirect horizontality respectively.[63] The first involves the courts taking into account the values embodied in the Convention rights in applying and developing the existing law,[64] while the second compels them to make the existing law compatible with the ECHR,[65] the difference lying essentially in the degree to which the courts will be bound by the ECHR in handling private litigation.

Judicial opinion, expressed on and off the bench, has so far not plumped unequivocally between the two approaches to indirect horizontality and has indeed tended to deploy other metaphors to describe the effect they see coming. Thus, while Lord Cooke of Thorndon accepted in *McCartan Turkington Breen v Times Newspapers Ltd*[66] that 'in the field of communications the Act has "horizontal" effect', he has also written extra-judicially:

> [T]he Convention rights scheduled to the Act will prevail over the common law, in that the Courts will have the responsibility of adjusting the common law as far as may be necessary to give effect to such of them as are capable of application . . . When there is relevancy, it will be the duty of the Courts . . . to incorporate them into the common law. But this requires no new remedy. As is commonly the case with human rights instruments, the Act is not 'horizontally' applicable, in that it does not directly create rights between private individuals. What it requires is a process of interweaving the scheduled rights into the common law.[67]

In the published version of his Hamlyn Lectures, Sir Stephen Sedley endorsed Lord Cooke's image of interweaving but added another of his own, which he called the 'cascade effect' of the Act.[68] Both may however be seen as tending towards the strong version of indirect horizontality. Academic commentary discussing the issue has ranged widely across a spectrum of views: Murray Hunt

---

obligations'); J Wadham and H Mountfield, *Blackstone's Guide to the Human Rights Act 1998* 2nd edn (Blackstone, London, 2000), 29; S Grosz, J Beatson and P Duffy, *Human Rights: The 1998 Act and the European Convention* (Sweet & Maxwell, London, 2000), 91; R Clayton and H Tomlinson, *The Law of Human Rights* (Oxford University Press, Oxford, 2000), 232–38; Reed (ed), above, n 21, 19–24.

[63] See M Hunt, 'The "Horizontal Effect" of the Human Rights Act' [1998] *PL* 423–43; I Leigh, 'Horizontal Rights, the Human Rights Act and Privacy: Lessons from the Commonwealth' [1999] 48 *ICLQ* 57–87; G Phillipson, 'The Human Rights Act, "Horizontal Effect" and the Common Law: A Bang or a Whimper?' [1999] 62 *MLR* 824–49; T Raphael, 'The Problem of Horizontal Effect' [2000] *EHRLR* 493–511. See also D Oliver, 'The Human Rights Act and Public Law/Private Law Divides' [2000] *EHRLR* 343–55.

[64] As in Germany (see further B S Markesinis, 'Privacy, Freedom of Expression and the Horizontal Effect of the Human Rights Bill: Lessons From Germany' (1999) 115 *LQR* 47–88), Canada (see *Retail, Wholesale and Department Store Union v Dolphin Delivery* [1986] 2 SCR 573), New Zealand (see Lord Cooke, above, n 21) and South Africa under s 35(3) of its Interim Constitution of 1993 (see *Du Plessis v De Klerk* 1996 (3) SA 850), now superseded by the direct effect of the 1996 Constitution.

[65] See the dissenting judgment of Kriegler J in *Du Plessis v De Klerk* 1996 (3) SA 850.

[66] *McCartan Turkington Breen v Times Newspapers Ltd* [2001] 2 AC 277 at 299D.

[67] Lord Cooke, above, n 21, 258.

[68] Lord Justice Sedley, *Freedom, Law and Justice*, The Hamlyn Lectures 1998 (Sweet & Maxwell, London, 1999), 23–25.

argues that the courts as public authorities are 'under an unequivocal duty to act compatibly with Convention rights';[69] Clayton and Tomlinson in contrast state that

> the court is not *compelled* to develop the common law in line with Convention rights wherever it has the opportunity to do so: section 6(3) is a *prohibition* which enjoins the court from acting in a way which is inconsistent with Convention rights.[70]

Gavin Phillipson concludes that the Convention rights 'will figure only as principles to which the courts must have regard,'[71] the weight of each right in this context being variable; and Ian Leigh suggests that the Act does not formally change the approach to the ECHR which existed at common law (at least in England) before 1998 and is likely only to favour increasing judicial reference to it.[72]

Faced with such a variety of opinion, we ourselves take refuge in further metaphor in predicting future developments, informed as much as anything by an instinctive sense that the judiciary are more likely to be cautious than bold in responding to the requirements placed upon them as public authorities under section 6 of the Act, and also by the fact that the range of Convention rights probably having an impact upon private relationships is relatively narrow. It therefore seems to us that the speed, power and thoroughness of the horizontal impact of Convention rights is probably considerably over-stated in Sir Stephen Sedley's 'cascade' metaphor, but that at the other extreme the suggestions that nothing much has changed or that the Convention rights will provide only principles to which the courts must have regard are altogether too minimalist. We see Convention rights rather as likely to permeate the common law over time, consistently with its traditional case-by-case development under which the relevance of the rights to common and private law issues will gradually emerge for assessment and determination of compatibility questions. The implications for the future development of private law are therefore considerable, but will not occur with dramatic suddenness and all at once.

In the following sections of this chapter, we look at the potential impact of Convention rights upon some central areas of common law applying to private relationships, taking account where possible of developments since the Human Rights Act 1998 came into force. Property and family law are dealt with elsewhere in this volume, and our focus is therefore upon the law of negligence and contract. This is followed by some comments upon the development of the concept of privacy by the courts, which may well confirm that their probable approach in general is as we have just suggested.

---

[69] Hunt, above, n 63, 441.
[70] Clayton and Tomlinson, above, n 62, para 5.94.
[71] Phillipson, above, n 63, 848.
[72] Leigh, above, n 63, 82–83.

(1) Negligence

It seems very likely that the incorporation of the ECHR will stimulate change to the common law of negligence. A useful comparison may be made with the way in which the statutory background can influence the determination of whether or not a duty of care exists. By way of introduction, it may be suggested that Articles 2 (right to life) and 3 (against inhuman and degrading treatment or punishment) will play a particularly significant role in this process given that they concern the most fundamental of rights. The ECtHR has indicated that Article 2 'ranks as one of the most fundamental provisions in the Convention' and 'together with Art 3, it enshrines one of the basic values . . .'[73] These words are likely to strike a powerful chord with those judges who believe that negligence law has strayed from its 'traditional' values. In *Perrett v Collins*[74] Hobhouse LJ clearly regarded the decision in favour of the plaintiff as a reassertion of traditional values. There the plaintiff suffered personal injuries when the plane in which he was flying crashed. The denial of the existence of a duty of care to the plaintiff would represent

> a fundamental attack upon the principle of tortious liability for negligent conduct which had caused foreseeable personal injury to others. That such a point should be considered even arguable shows how far some of the fundamental principles of the law of negligence have come to be eroded.[75]

Indeed, the prima facie case for the plaintiff against the defendant was overwhelming:

> The denial of a duty of care owed by such a person in relation to the safety of the aircraft towards those who may suffer personal injuries, whether as passengers in the aircraft or upon the ground, would leave a gap in the law of tort notwithstanding that a plaintiff had suffered foreseeable personal injury as a result of the unsafety of the aircraft and the unreasonable and careless conduct of the defendant. It would be remarkable if that were the law.[76]

Such emphasis upon the duty to ensure the safety of others gains only further support from Articles 2 and 3 of the ECHR.

The most immediate impact of Convention rights will probably be in 'vertical' cases against public authorities; but the negligence liability of public authorities has often had major effects upon the law of negligence in general.[77] In *Osman v United Kingdom*[78] the ECtHR took the view that Article 2 could give

---

[73] *McCann v United Kingdom* (1996) 21 EHRR 97, para 147.
[74] *Perrett v Collins* [1998] 2 Lloyd's Rep 255
[75] *Ibid*, 257–58.
[76] *Ibid*, 259–60, per Hobhouse LJ.
[77] See for example the effect of *Anns v Merton LBC* [1978] AC 728 and *Murphy v Brentwood DC* [1991] 1 AC 398 upon liability for pure economic loss.
[78] *Osman v United Kingdom* (2000) 29 EHRR 245; and see L Hoyano, 'Policing flawed investigations' (1999) 62 *MLR* 912.

rise to 'a positive obligation on [public] authorities to take preventive opera-
tional measures to protect an individual whose life is at risk from the criminal
acts of another individual.'[79] In the event, the applicants failed in their Article 2
complaint on the facts. However, had the risk described been found to exist, the
scope of the duty derived from Article 2 was said to be as follows:

> Where there is an allegation that the authorities have violated their positive obligation
> to protect the right to life in the context of their above-mentioned duty to prevent and
> suppress offences against the person . . . it must be established that the authorities
> knew or ought to have known at the time of the existence of a real and immediate risk
> to the life of an identified individual or individuals from the criminal acts of a third
> party and that they failed to take measures within the scope of their powers which,
> judged reasonably, might have been expected to avoid that risk.[80]

One would expect Article 2 to be influential in future cases of negligence against
the police where they have failed to prevent harm being done to the pursuer's
person by a third party. Indeed already in *Gibson v Strathclyde Police*[81] Lord
Hamilton regarded the *Osman* ruling as pointing towards a finding that a duty
of care was owed by the defender. It is important to emphasise that *Gibson* did
not involve the police in their role in the investigation and suppression of crime,
but was rather a case about their civil functions, in which their failure had been
to ensure the safety of road users where a bridge over a river had been swept
away in a flood. A more radical consequence of *Osman* is that there may well be
a narrowing of the immunity set out in *Hill v Chief Constable*,[82] where it was
held that a duty of care does not arise in the exercise of the police function 'in
the investigation and suppression of crime.'[83] Were that immunity to be narrowed, this might result in the police owing a duty of care along the lines of the
obligation set out in *Osman*. What will be the consequences if the duty of care
owed by the police is reformulated in this way? In terms of adjudication the
practical result may well be that attention will shift to the question of breach of
duty. This is unlikely to present undue difficulties for the courts. Indeed, there
is already some evidence to suggest that the Scottish courts are more than comfortable in taking on board factors peculiar to public authority liability in negligence at the stage of standard of care rather than at the stage of duty.[84]

The judgment in *Osman* is confined to the criminal context but the reasoning
in the case can be readily extended to public bodies other than the police, such
as other branches of the emergency services. In the context of medical malprac-
tice and negligence liability, the NHS may also find itself in litigation centring
on the scope of Article 2. It is arguable, however, that Article 2 would have no

---

[79] *Osman*, above, n 78, at para 115.
[80] *Ibid*, at para 116.
[81] *Gibson v Strathclyde Police* 1999 SC 429.
[82] *Hill v Chief Constable of West Yorkshire* [1989] AC 53.
[83] *Ibid*, at 63, per Lord Keith.
[84] *Duff v Highland and Islands Fire Board* 1995 SLT 1362; *McCafferty v Secretary of State for Scotland* 1998 SCLR 379.

impact when a doctor was treating a private patient.[85] Nonetheless, if Article 2 is relevant to claims against NHS trusts, it seems likely that it will bring about a more fundamental change to the law of medical negligence. It is unlikely that domestic courts would wish to see the law of negligence imposing lower standards in the case of private medicine.

In *X v Bedfordshire*[86] the plaintiffs alleged that they had suffered parental abuse and neglect. They brought negligence actions against the council alleging that, despite being aware of the situation, it had failed to investigate the matter adequately or protect the plaintiffs from further harm. It was held that no duty of care was owed, public policy considerations weighing heavily. The claim in the *Bedfordshire* case proceeded to Strasbourg, where the applicants alleged that the local authority had failed to protect them from inhuman and degrading treatment contrary to Article 3 of the ECHR. In finding for the applicants, in *Z v United Kingdom*,[87] the ECtHR reiterated that 'Article 3 enshrines one of the most fundamental values of democratic society. It prohibits in absolute terms torture or inhuman or degrading treatment or punishment.'[88] The decision of the court confirms the stance of the Commission that there is a positive obligation on the State to take those steps that could be reasonably expected of them to avoid a real and immediate risk of ill-treatment contrary to Article 3 of which they knew or ought to have had knowledge.[89] Article 3 may thus require the State to intervene to protect citizens from ill-treatment administered by private individuals.[90]

The impact of *Z v United Kingdom* is likely to be that, in the field of child welfare, a public body with appropriate powers under statute is more likely to be held to be under a duty of care (however defined) to exercise them to protect vulnerable children. This may not alter significantly the development of UK law as, of late, the courts have in any event been less inclined to protect public bodies from the impact of negligence actions. This is the case even where the public body is operating within a statutory framework in the realm of education/welfare.[91]

In *Lopez Ostra v Spain*.[92] the ECtHR accepted that:

> . . . severe environmental pollution may affect individuals' well-being and prevent them from enjoying their homes in such a way as to affect their private and family life adversely, without, however, seriously endangering their health.[93]

---

[85] R Owen et al, in P English and R Havers (eds), *An Introduction to Human Rights and the Common Law* (Hart Publishing, Oxford, 2000), 137.
[86] *X v Bedfordshire County Council* [1995] 2 AC 633.
[87] *Z v United Kingdom* [2001] 2 FCR 246.
[88] *Ibid*, para 73.
[89] *Z v United Kingdom* Application No 29392/95 (10 Sept 1999).
[90] *A v United Kingdom* (1998) 5 BHRC 137 at 141.
[91] *Barrett v Enfield London Borough Council* [1999] 3 All ER 193.
[92] *Lopez Ostra v Spain* (1995) 20 EHRR 277.
[93] *Ibid*, para 51.

In determining whether any obligation was owed by the State by virtue of Article 8 '. . . regard must be had to the fair balance that has to be struck between the competing interests of the individual and of the community as a whole.'[94] The applicant argued that by virtue of its general supervisory powers the municipality had a duty to act. In finding for the applicant, the court noted that:

> . . . the State did not succeed in striking a fair balance between the interests of the town's economic well-being—that of having a waste treatment plant—and the plaintiff's effective enjoyment of her right to respect for her home and her private and family life.[95]

It is also worthy of note that in *Guerra and Others v Italy*[96] the ECtHR held that the effect of toxic emissions from a factory polluting the atmosphere in the applicants' homes fell within Article 8, observing:[97]

> Italy cannot be said to have 'interfered' with the applicants' private or family life; they complained not of an act by the state but of its failure to act. However, although the object of Art 8 is essentially that of protecting the individual against arbitrary interference by the public authorities, it does not merely compel the state to abstain from such interference: in addition to this primarily negative undertaking, there may be positive obligations inherent in effective respect for private or family life.[98]

It is already the case that the UK courts have been influenced by the cases mentioned in the preceding paragraph. In *Marcic v Thames Water Utilities Ltd*[99] the plaintiff claimed that the failure of the defendant to provide a proper drainage system involved both a common law nuisance and infringed his rights under Article 8 (and Article 1 of the First Protocol). He failed to establish that a nuisance existed at common law but, on the facts, the court held that there was a breach of Article 8(1). But could the authority's failure be justified in terms of Article 8(2), which permits action 'necessary in a democratic society in the interests of . . . the economic well-being of the country . . . for the protection of the rights and freedoms of others'? It was held that the economic well-being of the country as a whole was not in issue,

> since sewerage costs are financed from sewerage charges. No doubt sewerage charges have an effect on the economy of the country, but it has not been suggested that that is a significant consideration.[100]

---

[94] *Ibid.*
[95] *Ibid*, para 58.
[96] *Guerra and Others v Italy* (1998) 26 EHRR 357.
[97] *Ibid*, (para 58).
[98] See further the Heathrow night flights decision of the ECtHR, *Hatton v United Kingdom* (Appl no 36022/97) handed down on 2 Oct 2001 and also based upon Arts 8 and 13: The Times, 8 Oct 2001, discussed above, see text to n 57.
[99] *Marcic v Thames Water Utilities Ltd* [2001] 3 All ER 698.
[100] *Ibid*, para 92.

The defendant also failed to establish that the infringement of the complainant's rights could be justified by virtue of the need to protect the rights and freedoms of others.

Questions also arise as to the potential impact of Article 8 on the planning system in the UK. In *R v Lam*[101] there was held to be no duty of care in respect of the granting of planning permission. However, in *Kane v New Forest District Council*[102] the Court of Appeal indicated that the conferring of an immunity was not appropriate. A planning authority might well owe a duty of care not to, for instance, permit the construction of a foreseeably dangerous footpath. Simon Brown LJ regarded it as perfectly feasible for the planning authorities to have regard to 'private law interests' in the processing of planning applications. It seems likely that regard will, in future, also be had to the Articles of the ECHR including Article 8.

In *Osman* the applicants succeeded under Article 6.[103] They alleged that the dismissal by the Court of Appeal of their negligence action against the police on grounds of public policy amounted to a restriction on their right of access to a court. This ruling suggested that Article 6 might prove to be highly influential in negligence cases. However, if no duty of care was owed to the applicant one might have thought that no right existed which required to be determined in accordance with Article 6. The response of the Court was to say:[104]

> The common law of the respondent State has long accorded a plaintiff the right to submit to a court a claim in negligence against a defendant and to request the court to find that the facts of the case disclose a breach of a duty of care owed by the defendant to the plaintiff which has caused harm to the latter. The domestic court's enquiry is directed at determining whether the constituent elements of a duty of care have been satisfied, namely: whether the damage is foreseeable; whether there exists a relationship of proximity between the parties; and whether it is fair, just and reasonable to impose a duty of care in the circumstances.

What of the reference to a right to 'request the court to find that the facts of the case disclose a breach of a duty of care'? On one reading, this would appear to be at odds with the Scottish law of relevancy. It might mean that a duty of care case against a public authority could never be dismissed at that stage of court procedure.

Since *Osman*, however, the ECtHR, in *Z v United Kingdom*,[105] has revised its approach to this issue. Reverting to earlier case law of the Court, it has accepted that Article 6 (1) does not in itself guarantee any particular content for (civil)

---

[101] *R v Lam* [1997] 3 PLR 22.

[102] *Kane v New Forest District Council* [2001] 3 All ER 914.

[103] *Osman*, above, n 78. The ECtHR awarded each of the applicants £10,000 since they had been denied 'the opportunity to obtain a ruling on the merits of their claim for damages against the police'.

[104] *Ibid*, para 137.

[105] *Z v United Kingdom*, above, n 87.

'rights and obligations' in the substantive law of the Contracting States.[106] Article 6 requires that there be access to courts to adjudicate on disputes over civil rights and obligations which are arguably recognised by domestic law. However, that right is not infringed by the law of relevancy or, in England, 'striking out'. The approach in *Z* is incidentally in line with that taken in the Scottish case of *Crooks v Haddow*,[107] where the pursuer's complaint in respect of Article 6 met with the following rebuttal:

> If it is suggested that dismissal of his action deprived him of the opportunity of presenting evidence in support of his case, that is a consequence of the irrelevance of his pleadings. The dismissal of an action on the ground of the irrelevance of the pleadings does not constitute, in our view, a breach of either of the provisions to which he referred.

The court in *Z v United Kingdom* was happy to confirm the validity of relevancy procedures:[108]

> If as a matter of law, there was no basis for the claim, the hearing of evidence would have been an expensive and time-consuming process which would not have provided the applicants with any remedy at its conclusion. There is no reason to consider the striking out procedure which rules on the existence of sustainable causes of action as per se offending the principle of access to court. In such a procedure, the plaintiff is generally able to submit to the court the arguments supporting his or her claims on the law and the court will rule on those issues at the conclusion of an adversarial procedure.

The court in *Osman* had also suggested that the denial of the existence of a duty on the basis of the fair, just and reasonableness test was the conferral of an immunity; it was that conferral which led to the finding that Article 6 had been breached. However, the ECtHR is now satisfied,

> that the law of negligence as developed in the domestic courts since the case of *Caparo Industries plc v Dickman*, and as recently analysed in the case of *Barrett* includes the fair, just and reasonable criterion as an intrinsic element of the duty of care and that the ruling of law concerning that element in this case does not disclose the operation of an immunity.[109]

It therefore seems that the frosty reception of *Osman* in the House of Lords when considering the issue of barristers' immunity from negligence liability in *Arthur J S Hall & Co v Simons*[110] has had its effect in Strasbourg.

---

[106] *James v United Kingdom* (1986) 8 EHRR 123 at 157–58.

[107] *Crooks v Haddow* unreported, Inner House 1 March 2000, 2000 GWD 10–367. The paragraphs of the opinion are un-numbered.

[108] *Z v United Kingdom*, above, n 87, para 97.

[109] *Osman*, above, n 78, para 100.

[110] *Arthur J S Hall & Co v Simons* [2000] 3 WLR 543; 3 All ER 673 (HL). See further Lord Hoffmann, 'Human Rights and the House of Lords' (1999) 62 *MLR* 159–66, esp at 162ff.

(2) Contract

Much less than this can be said about contract law at present. The ECHR contains no commitment either to the freedom and sanctity of contract as a central value or to the protection of consumers or employees as an aspect of protection against inequality.[111] It is not easy to see in the Convention rights much that is immediately relevant to contracts. Here the fundamental concern of human rights law with public as opposed to private power at first seems to limit its potential scope. Nevertheless, Gerhard Lubbe has observed of the (now direct) horizontal application of the Bill of Rights in South Africa and the constitutionalisation of private law in that country, that 'it is clear in the first instance that henceforth open norms are to be informed by, or given content with reference to the fundamental rights.'[112] Where the law of contract deploys concepts such as 'reasonableness' or 'public policy', as for example with regard to unfair contract terms or illegal and immoral contracts, or where it gives remedies a discretionary character, as with specific implement or interdict, the judge as a public authority may well find at least broad guidance on occasion arising from consideration of the parties' Convention rights such as the prohibition of forced labour (Article 4), respect for private and family life (Article 8), freedom of conscience (Article 9), freedom of expression (Article 10) and freedom of association (Article 11). To take the question raised in a recent and controversial group of cases but answered rather differently in Scotland and England:[113] is it contravention of the right against 'forced labour', or of its spirit, for a commercial landlord to compel its tenant to carry on trading at a loss under a long lease? Convention rights may give added impetus to the development of further open-ended norms in contract law, such as the obligation of good faith between contracting parties increasingly discussed as part of both Scots and English contract law.[114] In Scotland the discussion really began in earnest as a result of the decision of the House of Lords in *Smith v Bank of Scotland*[115] that a wife could escape her obligations to her husband's bank under a guarantee (including the loss of the matrimonial home) if the bank, contrary to good faith, failed to ensure that she was given proper advice about the consequences of the guarantee at the time it was given. In other jurisdictions such as Germany the same

---

[111] Compare the Charter of Fundamental Rights of the European Union, which recognises, inter alia, freedom to choose an occupation and the right to engage in work (Art 15), freedom to conduct a business (Art 16), several employee rights (Arts 27–31) and a right to a high level of consumer protection (Art 38).

[112] G Lubbe, '*Ex Africa semper aliquid novi?*—The Mixed Character of Contract Law in The New South Africa' in J Smits (ed), *The Contribution of Mixed Legal Systems to European Private Law* (Intersentia, Antwerp/Froningen, 2001), 77–78.

[113] See *Highland and Universal Stores v Safeways Properties* 2000 SC 297 and *Cooperative Insurance v Argyll Holdings* [1998] AC 1.

[114] See A D M Forte (ed), *Good Faith in Contract and Property* (Hart Publishing, Oxford, 1999).

[115] *Smith v Bank of Scotland* 1997 SC (HL) 111. This essentially followed the earlier English decision, *Barclays Bank plc v O'Brien* [1994] 1 AC 180.

result has been reached by way of constitutional provisions protecting the autonomy of private individuals and interpreting that as requiring limitations upon freedom of contract where otherwise an unusually heavy burden would fall upon the weaker party in the relationship.[116] Again, the ever more flexible rules about interpretation of contracts, which at least in England now allow the courts to disregard the actual words used by the parties if satisfied from the overall context of the contract that this is not what the parties really meant,[117] can only be reinforced by the approach to statutory interpretation now allowed under section 3 of the Human Rights Act 1998 as the courts search where necessary for meanings compatible with Convention rights. In South Africa, for example, the word 'family' in an insurance contract has been read, having regard to the spirit of the Constitution and in particular its equality provisions, as including a same-sex partnership.[118] Turning to Article 6 and the right to a hearing, do some contract law doctrines, such as the requirement of intention to create legal relations to make an enforceable contract, or the rules making gambling debts unenforceable in the courts, have the effect of denying parties to lawful agreements of considerable value or social significance access to a forum in which their civil rights and obligations can be determined,[119] or will they be saved by the decision in *Z v United Kingdom*?[120]

It might be thought that human rights would be most likely to benefit the consumer, but *Wilson v The First County Trust Ltd*,[121] the first case in which a statute was subjected to a declaration of incompatibility under section 4 of the 1998 Act, shows that the ECHR may be a double-edged sword. The statutory provision in issue was section 127(3) of the Consumer Credit Act 1974, under which the court could not enforce an otherwise regulated consumer credit agreement where there was no document containing all the prescribed terms of the agreement signed by the debtor. Securities related to the loan were also unenforceable. W's loan agreement, which she had signed, mis-stated the amount of the credit given, so both it and a related security over her BMW car were unenforceable. The Court of Appeal took the view that this was a disproportionate response, given the absence of prejudice to any party in the mis-statement and having regard to the creditor's Convention rights under Article 6 (right to a hearing) and the First Protocol Article 1 (no deprivation of possessions except in the public interest and subject to law). The section could not be

---

[116] BverfG 89, 214–236 (= *NJW*, 47 (1994) 36–39); discussed by M Habersack and R Zimmermann, 'Legal Change in a Codified System: Recent Developments in German Suretyship Law' (1999) 3 *Edin LR* 272–93.

[117] See the speech of Lord Hoffmann in *Investors Compensation Scheme Ltd v West Bromwich Building Society* [1998] 1 WLR 896.

[118] *Farr v Mutual & Federal Insurance Co Ltd* 2000 3 SA 684 (C).

[119] For recent examples of invocation of these doctrines to dismiss claims in the courts, see *Ferguson v Littlewoods Pools Ltd* 1997 SLT 309 (football pools unenforceable: *sponsio ludicra* and no intention to create legal relations); *Percy v Church of Scotland* 2001 SC 757 (church minister has no contract of employment with church: no intention to create legal relations).

[120] See above, nn 87–89, 105.

[121] *Wilson v The First County Trust Ltd (No 2)* [2001] 3 WLR 42; 3 All ER 229 (CA).

rescued by construction under the powers conferred by section 3 of the Human Rights Act 1998.[122] While the policy aim, as determined from the legislative history of the 1974 Act, was legitimate, the means of achieving its goals was disproportionate and inflexible in disabling the court from consideration of all the factors in a case. The possibility of the creditor having an unjust enrichment claim against the debtor would go against the intention of Parliament in enacting section 127(3) in the form it had.[123] The case strongly suggests the need to review all consumer protection provisions that operate by way of making agreements wholly void or unenforceable for some failure of form or substance, and to replace them with judicial discretions which will allow Convention rights appropriate play along with the other factors which may be relevant.

Convention rights will also have to be considered in the legislative reform of the law: thus the Law Commission of England and Wales in proposing changes to the rules on illegal contracts in 1998 took care to note that its reforms were consistent with Convention rights.[124] The Commission, prompted by a case in the Court of Appeal about transfers of money to Iraq in breach of UN sanctions against that country, has since raised the question whether the present law may not be in breach of Article 1 of the First Protocol to the ECHR as arbitrary and disproportionate in its results.[125] *Wilson v First County Trust* provides another example of the problem. So Convention rights may drive reform in which the courts as well as law reform bodies play a role. The remedy of civil imprisonment for non-compliance with an order for the specific implement of a contract[126] is presently allowable under Article 5 ('No one shall be deprived of his liberty save . . . (b) . . . in order to secure the fulfilment of any obligation prescribed by law'), but would cease to be so if Article 1 of the Fourth Protocol to the ECHR ('No one shall be deprived of his liberty merely on the ground of inability to fulfil a contractual obligation') is eventually adopted by the United Kingdom.

(3) 'Gaps' in the common law

Pre-incorporation Strasbourg jurisprudence suggests that questions may be raised, not only about existing rules of private law, but also about the absence

---

[122] *Wilson v The First County Trust Ltd (No 2)* [2001] 3 WLR 42; 3 All ER 229 (CA). 'By "some other legitimate interpretation" we mean some interpretation of the words used which is legally possible. The court is required to go as far as, but not beyond what is legally possible. The court is not required, or entitled, to give to words a meaning which they cannot bear; although it is required to give to words a meaning which they can bear, if that will avoid incompatibility . . .' (para 42).

[123] The court here relied on *Dimond v Lovell* [2000] 2 WLR 1121 (HL).

[124] Consultation Paper No 154 Illegal Transactions: the Effect of Illegality on Contracts and Trusts (1998) para 1.23.

[125] Consultation Paper No 160, The Illegality Defence in Tort (2001) paras 1.5–1.8; *Al Kishtaini v Shanshai*, *The Times* 8 March 2001. The comments could equally apply to the Scots law on illegality in contract and delict.

[126] See W W McBryde, *The Law of Contract in Scotland* 2nd edn (Edinburgh, 2001), 623. In practice the remedy of imprisonment is never used.

of rules or the limits of their application.[127] In a case before the Commission decided in 1986, *Hughes v United Kingdom*,[128] the applicant's husband, a school cleaner, had been found collapsed at his place of work. He was immediately thought to have died, and a couple of hours then elapsed before he was taken to hospital and pronounced officially dead. His widow raised an action in tort against his employers, alleging negligent failure to take prompt emergency action which might have saved her husband's life. The cause of death was a coronary occlusion, and the evidence showed that, even if prompt action had been taken, the husband would still have died. The tort action was accordingly lost. The widow then made a claim under Article 2 of the ECHR (right to life), arguing infringement through the absence in English law of a 'duty to rescue'. The Commission rejected the claim without commenting on the basic proposition, because the existence of an express obligation to take emergency action would not have been of any avail to the deceased, leaving open the question about whether or not a gap in the law of tort could or did infringe Article 2.

How exactly will questions like the one in the *Hughes* case be dealt with in a domestic court if it forms the opinion that the existing law, whether by omission or otherwise, infringes the Convention rights of a party? The basis upon which it is suggested that the issue will arise is the duty of the domestic court as a public authority to act compatibly with Convention rights. But there is no procedure given in the Human Rights Act 1998 akin to that for declaring legislation incompatible with the ECHR to deal with situations where the issue is one about the unenacted law or concerns a supposed gap in the law, statutory or otherwise. Until now, when matters of this kind have come up in Strasbourg, the claim has been against the Government, on the basis of its failure to act. But if a party to a private action successfully takes a ECHR point of the kind being discussed, clearly the other party to the litigation cannot be made responsible for what may be done by the court deciding the case.

A further issue of relevance here is the Government's decision to leave out of the Human Rights Act 1998 Article 13 of the ECHR,[129] which provides that

> everyone whose rights and freedoms as set forth in this ECHR are violated shall have an effective remedy before a national authority notwithstanding that the violation has been committed by persons acting in an official capacity.

The significance of this omission, particularly when set alongside the inclusion of Article 17 and its prohibition of the abuse of rights by the State or any group or person, is far from clear. The Government has argued that, given the enactment of the Human Rights Act 1998 itself, express incorporation of Article 13

---

[127] Note also the South African case of *Janse van Reensburg v Grieve Trust* CC 2000 1 SA 315 (C), where the aedilician remedy of the *actio quanti minoris* was extended from the law of sale to the trade-in of motor cars, Van Zyl J invoking the constitutional principles of equality before the law as requiring equality of protection and benefit in the law as well as human dignity, equality and freedom.

[128] *Hughes v United Kingdom* Application 11590/85, decision of 18 July 1986, 48 D & R 258.

[129] See Human Rights Act 1998, Sch 1.

was unnecessary. It is also unclear how far the British courts will be able to make use of the European Court's doctrine of the 'margin of appreciation', by which the Court has recognised national derogations from Convention rights on the basis that Contracting States are in a better position than the Strasbourg judiciary to judge what the local requirements of public policy are in the pursuit of legitimate economic and social goals, unless their actions are manifestly unreasonable.[130]

The answers to many of these problems may be found in sections 8 and 9 of the Human Rights Act 1998. Section 9(1) enables a direct action to be brought against a court or tribunal which has acted contrary to Convention rights, but only by way of

(1) exercising a right of appeal;
(2) a petition for judicial review; or
(3) in such other forum as may be prescribed by rules to be made by the Secretary of State for Scotland.[131]

Some commentators have argued that this section does nor give rise to a cause of action or a right or a sanction against a court, and that it is therefore authority against courts giving any horizontal effect to Convention rights;[132] but it does seem to provide a remedy against a court while at the same time operating within the established norms of the judicial structures of the United Kingdom. Section 8 deals with awards of damages against an infringing public authority; but it is not very plausible to suppose that a court would order itself to pay damages to a party whose Convention rights it proposed to infringe. This may explain section 9(3) of the Act: 'In proceedings under this Act in respect of a judicial act done in good faith, damages may not be awarded otherwise than to compensate a person to the extent required by Article 5(5) of the Convention' (Article 5(5) applying only to victims of arrest or detention).

More interesting to the judge or court on the horns of a dilemma regarding Convention rights and the existing law is section 8(1), which provides that:

> In relation to any act (or proposed act) of a public authority which the court finds is (or would be) unlawful, it may grant such relief or remedy, or make such order, within its powers as it considers just and appropriate.[133]

If it is the court itself which is the public authority apparently being pressed by the existing common law (or the lack thereof) to an act incompatible with Convention rights, what happens? What relief, remedy or order is within the

---

[130] See Harris, O'Boyle and Warbrick, above, n 33, 12–15; Jacobs and White, above, n 33, 37, and in particular *James v United Kingdom* (1986) 8 EHRR 123.

[131] This will presumably involve the Judicial Committee of the Privy Council.

[132] Buxton, above, n 59, 57; Bamforth, above, n 60, 39.

[133] The rest of s 8 deals with the award of damages against a public authority, on which see also the Law Commissions' Report on Damages under the Human Rights Act 1998 (Scot Law Com no 180; Law Com no 266; Cm 4853), which provides guidance for court users on the Strasbourg jurisprudence on this subject.

court's powers? The House of Lords has several times made clear that, subject to the doctrine of precedent, there is judicial power to develop the unenacted law,[134] and the Court of Session has shown itself willing to follow the lead provided by their Lordships in this regard.[135] A particularly strong case for judicial activism arises when Parliament itself has pointed out the general direction in which the law should go.[136] The Human Rights Act 1998 is beyond cavil a powerful Parliamentary indication of the course that the judiciary should take in future right across the whole body of judge-made law. In Scotland it may be possible to move even further, into statutory law, thanks to the *nobile officium* of the Court of Session, its 'ultimate residuary equitable power to provide a remedy where justice requires it and to prevent unduly rigorous law working injustice.'[137] This power may be used in non-contentious proceedings in relation to procedures and machineries provided for under legislation in special circumstances that Parliament had not foreseen and by implication not dealt with.[138] Apart from such cases of statutory omission, the *nobile officium* can also be used to grant petitions for remedy where no other procedure is available. In *Law Hospital NHS Trust v Lord Advocate*,[139] for example, Lords Clyde and Cullen would both have been prepared to use the *nobile officium* to grant the petition enabling the PVS patient's treatment to be terminated had no other solutions existed.[140] All this suggests that the problems of unenacted law which is either inchoate or contrary to Convention rights, and those of at least some gaps in statute, can often be met by the existing powers of the courts acting under a generous interpretation of section 8(1).[141] The limits lie essentially at wherever the

---

[134] See most recently *Kleinwort Benson v Lincoln City Council* [1999] 2 AC 349, especially per Lord Browne-Wilkinson (dissenting) at 358G–H ('The theoretical position . . . that judges do not make or change law . . . is . . . a fairy tale in which no-one any longer believes. In truth, judges make and change the law') and Lord Goff of Chieveley at 375F–G (formerly thought by other judges that mistake of law doctrine too deeply embedded to be uprooted judicially, but 'a more robust view of judicial development of the law is, I understand, taken by all members of the Appellate Committee hearing the present appeals'). For a Scottish example of judicial innovation in an area of common law, see *Smith v Bank of Scotland* 1997 SC (HL) 111.

[135] See further H L MacQueen, 'Judicial Reform of Private Law' (1998) 3 *SLPQ* 134–58.

[136] *Erven Warnink BV v J Townend & Sons (Hull) Ltd* [1979] AC 731 per Lord Diplock at 743C–D ('Where over a period of years there can be discerned a steady trend in legislation which reflects the view of successive Parliaments as to what the public interest demands in a particular field of law, development of the common law in that part of the same field which has been left to it ought to proceed on a parallel rather than a diverging course'). See also the interesting arguments put forward in J Beatson, 'The Role of Statute in the Development of Common Law Doctrine' (2001) 117 *LQR* 247–72.

[137] D M Walker, *The Scottish Legal System* 8th edn (Edinburgh, 2001), 482; see also *ibid*, 203, 534, 560.

[138] *R v Kennedy* 1993 SC 417; *L, Petitioners (No 1)* 1993 SLT 1310.

[139] *Law Hospital NHS Trust v Lord Advocate* 1996 SC 301.

[140] *Ibid*, at 324 and 328–29. But this case now needs to be considered in the light of the Convention right to life (Art 2): see C Gane, 'Human Rights Bill: Impact on the law of Scotland' (1998) 43(5) *JLSS* 16–19 at 19.

[141] Arguably this will also fulfil the obligation under s 3(1) to read and give effect to primary legislation in a way compatible with Convention rights.

judicial power to develop the law stops.[142] And if this is right, then the absence of Article 13 of the ECHR from the Articles otherwise given effect by the Human Rights Act 1998 may prove not to be especially significant.

The best current example of the potential development of the common law into new areas as a result of the domestication of human rights in the United Kingdom is the law relating to privacy. In 1990 the Court of Appeal declared that there was no tort of privacy known to English law;[143] while if there was such a delict in Scots law before 1998 its nature and scope were quite obscure.[144] The right to respect for private and family life under Article 8 of the ECHR had however raised questions about this aspect of the laws of the United Kingdom, including the possibility that it was covered by other branches of the law, such as that on confidential information. Indeed, in January 1998 the Earl and Countess Spencer failed to persuade the European Commission of Human Rights that United Kingdom law did not provide protection against media intrusion into their private lives in accordance with Article 8, either because the law of breach of confidence was sufficient for the purpose or because the Spencers had failed to exhaust their domestic remedies under that law.[145]

In Scotland Lord Reed noted in a case in late 1998 that issues of privacy were a controversial area of the law, much discussed in the Parliamentary debates on the Human Rights Act 1998, and observed: 'As reference to that Act suggests, this is an area where the development of the common law should have regard to the European Convention on Human Rights.'[146] In November 2000 the film stars Michael Douglas and Catherine Zeta-Jones were married in New York. They had sold exclusive photography rights to *OK!* magazine, the results to be published in the UK. Unauthorised photographs were somehow taken by others at the wedding and sold to *Hello!* magazine for publication, also in the UK. The two stars and *OK!* sought an interim injunction against publication by *Hello!*. Because it was possible that the unknown photographer had been an intruder not bound by any obligation of confidence that had been incumbent upon other persons present at the wedding, the case had to be based upon a right of privacy. The Court of Appeal discharged the interim injunction which had been granted at first instance, but not on the ground that there was no law of privacy in England; rather the discharge was given on the basis that the balance of convenience favoured the defendants and the claimants' loss of privacy could readily be compensated by an award of damages after further trial, given that they had

---

[142] See most recently P Birks, 'Mistakes of law' (2000) 53 *CLP* 205 at 217–18, arguing that the limits of judicial change to the law lie in 'interpretive discipline', and citing Lord Goff's Maccabaean Lecture, 'The Search for Principle' (1983) 69 *Proceedings of the British Academy* 170, in support of this proposition.

[143] *Kaye v Robertson* [1991] FSR 62.

[144] See Hogg, above, n 2.

[145] See Application Nos 28851/95 and 28852/95, *Earl Spencer and Countess Spencer v UK* [1998] 25 EHRR CD 105, and Press communiqué issued by the Secretary to the European Commission of Human Rights.

[146] *Ward v Scotrail Railways Ltd* 1999 SC 255 at 261E–F.

already commercialised their privacy by selling exclusive rights to *OK!*.[147] The judgments thus recognised a protectable interest in privacy, and it remains to be seen how it will be evaluated when the case comes back for trial later in 2001 or 2002.

The real interest of the case for present purposes lies in the way the judges went about recognising a right to privacy and the impact of the Human Rights Act 1998 on the common law in this area. Brooke LJ clearly had doubts about whether the Act had a general horizontal effect making all Convention rights enforceable in litigation between private parties (see especially para 91 of his judgment). For him the case was covered, if not by the law of confidentiality as it had already developed, then by section 12 of the Act (see above) and the Code of Practice of the Press Complaints Commission. Keene LJ, although perhaps more open to a general horizontality (para 166), was likewise prepared to accept that the case could be covered by the law of confidence and section 12. Sedley LJ, unsurprisingly in the light of his already published remarks in the Hamlyn Lectures,[148] offered the boldest pronouncements in recognising horizontality in general and a right to privacy distinct from a right of confidentiality, even though he recognised that the latter had developed far towards the protection of privacy:

> What a concept of privacy does, however, is accord recognition to the fact that the law has to protect not only those people whose trust has been abused but those who simply find themselves subjected to an unwanted intrusion into their personal lives. The law no longer needs to construct an artificial relationship of confidentiality between intruder and victim: it can recognise privacy itself as a legal principle drawn from the fundamental value of personal autonomy. [para 126] . . . [I]f the step from confidentiality to privacy is not simply a modern restatement of a known protection but a legal innovation—then I would accept . . . that this is precisely the kind of incremental change for which the Act is designed. [para 129]

A further step towards a law of privacy in England and Wales occurred in *Venables and Thompson v News Group Newspapers Ltd*.[149] The 18-year old claimants had been convicted in 1993 (when both were 11) of the murder of James Bulger, a two-year old boy, and detained in separate secure units. Injunctions based upon laws protecting children and young persons and 'good against the world' as a result were in place restricting publication of information about the claimants, who had become eligible for Parole Board consideration of their reintegration into the community. They wished the injunctions to be continued into their adult lives so that there would be no publication of information about changes in their physical appearance since their detention, their new identities upon release into the community, their existing placements,

---

[147] *Douglas v Hello! Ltd* [2001] 2 All ER 289.
[148] See Sedley, above, n 68.
[149] *Venables and Thompson v News Group Newspapers Ltd* [2001] 2 WLR 1038; [2001] 1 All ER 908 (QB, Butler-Sloss P).

and all specific material relating to their time in the secure units. The case thus stood to develop the law in extending to adults protection previously available only to children, in terms of both the information to be protected and, since injunctions against the world were not generally competent save in children cases, the persons against whom the injunctions could be enforced. Dame Elizabeth Butler-Sloss, President of the Family Division of the High Court, granted the injunctions sought. She accepted that, although the case was one entirely between private parties, the court had an obligation as a public authority to act compatibly with the ECHR. This, however, did not require the court to create a free-standing cause of action based directly upon the ECHR.

> The duty on the court, in my view, is to act compatibly with Convention rights in adjudicating upon existing common law causes of action, and that includes a positive as well as a negative obligation. (para C4) . . . The Human Rights Act and the Convention do not, however, establish new law. They reinforce and give greater weight to the principles already established in our case law. (para C13) . . . The common law continues to evolve, as it has done for centuries, and it is being given considerable impetus to do so by the implementation of the Convention into our domestic law. (para F6).

The relevant cause of action here was the tort of breach of confidence. Article 10 of the ECHR and section 12 of the Human Rights Act 1998 highlighted the especial importance of freedom of expression, but this right could be restricted when the strict necessity of doing so, within the exceptions recognised by the Article and section 12, could be convincingly demonstrated. The judge was satisfied that publication of the information could lead to a real danger to the lives of the claimants, contrary to Article 2 of the ECHR, or expose them to the risk of torture or inhuman or degrading treatment or punishment, contrary to Article 3, and she noted that no exceptions to these rights were stated in the Articles. She cited the *Osman* case and the requirement placed upon public authorities to take measures within their powers to avoid real and immediate risks to the lives of individuals. Butler-Sloss P also recognised the potential relevance of Article 8 (private and family life). She was therefore prepared to extend the law of confidence and injunctions to deal with the case, although expressing doubt whether an injunction would have been appropriate had breach of Article 8 alone been involved.[150]

The cases on privacy to date confirm that the domestication of the Convention rights has an impact upon the development of the law in this area, and not just through Article 8. The cases also suggest strongly that for most if not all the judges concerned the way forward was not through recognition of a

---

[150] The injunctions were subsequently amended to ensure that Internet service providers (ISPs) would not be liable should the protected information about Venables and Thompson be published on websites established by customers of the ISPs (*The Times*, 11 July 2001). For another case discussing *Venables*, but in which an injunction was refused, see *Mills v News Group Newspapers Ltd*, unreported, 4 June 2001.

new cause of action arising under the ECHR but rather by way of elaboration of the existing law on breach of confidence. That said, the developments of the law of confidence to satisfy the requirements of the ECHR, in particular in the *Venables/Thompson* case, are by no means minor, and they cannot be presented as the court merely moulding the law to reflect the values inherent in the Convention rights. The approach is very 'positive', that is, about taking steps to ensure that Convention rights are respected, which in this context means developing the law to match ECHR requirements and not simply avoiding infringements of Convention rights. The texts of the rights are closely scrutinised along with the Strasbourg jurisprudence and the provisions of the Human Rights Act 1998, and the facts of the case analysed in the light of that scrutiny. The judgments thus bear all the hallmarks of a strong approach to indirect horizontality and are indicative, it is suggested, of the likelihood of a powerful impact upon the development of private and common law in the years ahead.

Perhaps in the light of this one could go further and to some extent follow Sir William Wade in questioning the ultimate validity of the distinction between direct and indirect horizontality.[151] It seems perfectly possible in the light of *Douglas v Hello!* and *Venables v News Group Newspapers* that a doctrine of privacy will be recognised apart from the law of confidential information, just as previously in the history of the law general concepts of negligence and unjust enrichment (and indeed of confidentiality) have emerged from previously inchoate collections of cases and juristic analysis, to take the courts in hitherto unexplored and, indeed, unknown directions. At that point it will cease to be necessary to remind the courts of their duties as public authorities under section 6 of the Human Rights Act 1998; instead litigants will be able to go directly to the authority, whatever it is, that upholds the general privacy doctrine. Indirect horizontality will by no means lose its overall significance; but as the law draws into itself the Convention rights so in each particular case of development of new rules and principles the concept will cease to play a role.

D. THE PRIVATE SPHERE AND FUNCTIONS OF A PUBLIC NATURE

A final argument about how the Convention rights may enter the private domain, or at any rate a domain which hovers uneasily between the private and the public, arises from the further definition of 'public authority' to include also 'any person certain of whose functions are functions of a public nature.'[152] This means that not all the person's functions need be public for the Human Rights Act 1998 to apply. The Government's White Paper, *Bringing Rights Home*, stated:

---

[151] Wade, above, n 60, 221–22.
[152] Human Rights Act 1998, s 6(3)(b).

The definition of what constitutes a public authority is in wide terms. Examples of persons or organisations whose acts or omissions it is intended should be able to be challenged include central government (including executive agencies); local government; the police; immigration officers; prisons; courts and tribunals themselves; *and to the extent that they are exercising public functions, companies responsible for areas of activity which were previously within the public sector, such as the privatised utilities.*[153]

During the Parliamentary progress of the Human Rights Bill, there was considerable debate about the scope of the proposed definition of 'public authority'. It is clear from the passage in the White Paper, quoted above, that privatised organisations can come under the definition. On 17 June 1998, the Home Secretary elaborated the point as follows:[154]

> We decided that Convention rights should be available in proceedings involving what might be very broadly described as 'the State' . . . we wanted a realistic and modern definition of the State so as to provide correspondingly wide protection against an abuse of human rights. . . . The principle of bringing rights home suggested that liability in domestic proceedings should lie with bodies in respect of whose actions the United Kingdom Government were answerable in Strasbourg.

The discussion nevertheless raises questions about how to identify the activities that will bring an organisation within the scope of Convention rights. In the Parliamentary debates, it was said that Railtrack would be caught in relation to its function of monitoring safety on the rail network, but not for its operations as a commercial property developer.[155] The Home Secretary also suggested that guidance will be found (1) in the Strasbourg jurisprudence insofar as it has identified those activities for which the State may be held responsible; and (2) in the law of judicial review.[156] In English law, judicial review has been seen as explicitly a matter of public law, with only public authorities being amenable to the process;[157] and Mr Straw summarised the position as follows:[158]

> The courts will consider the nature of a body and the activity in question. They might consider whether the activities of a non-statutory body would be the subject of statutory regulation if that body did not exist . . . ; whether the Government had provided underpinning for its activities; and whether it exercised extensive or monopolistic powers.

A difficulty with this approach may be, however, that the basis of judicial review is not the same in Scotland as it is in England, following the rejection in

---

[153] *Bringing Rights Home*, para 2.2 (emphasis supplied).
[154] HC Debs, 17 June 1998, col 406.
[155] HL Debs, 24 November 1997, col 811 (Lord Irvine of Lairg); HC Debs, 17 June 1998, col 409 (Mr Jack Straw).
[156] HC Debs, 17 June 1998, cols 406, 407–10.
[157] The approach is founded on the decision of the House of Lords in *O'Reilly v Mackman* [1983] 2 AC 237.
[158] HC Debs, 17 June 1998, col 410.

West v Secretary of State for Scotland[159] of the public law/private law distinction as a basis for the invocation of the supervisory jurisdiction of the court. In Scotland, it is said, any person or body to whom jurisdiction, power or authority is delegated by statute, agreement or any other instrument is susceptible to judicial review. So it seems that the procedure may provide only limited assistance in identifying those bodies that may also be challenged under the human rights legislation. To take an example: the Home Secretary cites the Football Association as an example of a body which would not be a public authority under the Human Rights Act 1998, since it is not judicially reviewable.[160] But in Scotland the Scottish Football Association has been subjected to judicial review.[161]

There is accordingly a degree of uncertainty as to how widely the courts will feel able to go in interpreting the 'functions of a public nature' which make a person a public authority for the purposes of the Human Rights Act 1998, especially in Scotland. The definition in section 6 does not prevent the possibility of Convention rights impinging upon persons operating principally within the private sphere. It has already been held, without apparent debate in the case, that a privatised water authority may be the target of a direct claim under the Act.[162] Given the curious mixture of statutory, publicly-funded, self-regulatory and privatised bodies which perform the governance of the United Kingdom, and the continuing developments in this area, this uncertainty is perhaps inevitable. But it raises questions about what will happen over time. For example, will a former public utility cease to be a public authority after a certain period in the private sector, especially where a former monopoly has been broken up into a group of competing companies, as in water, gas, electricity and rail? Another example of this may be provided by NHS Trusts.[163]

The discussion so far has concentrated on those bodies once wholly within the public sector but no longer in that position. Another problem case is that of bodies which have never been within the public sector but nonetheless perform what can be seen as public functions. The two examples giving rise to most discussion during the Parliamentary passage of the Human Rights Bill were the Press and the churches.

The Press, it was generally accepted in debate,[164] did not constitute a public body or bodies, and the direct impact of Convention rights upon Press activity would therefore be felt through the courts and the development of the law

---

[159] *West v Secretary of State for Scotland* 1992 SC 385.
[160] HC Debs, 17 June 1998, col 410.
[161] *St Johnstone FC v Scottish Football Association* 1965 SLT 171.
[162] *Marcic v Thames Water Utilities Ltd* [2001] 3 All ER 698.
[163] See further D Oliver, 'The Frontiers of the State: Public Authorities and Public Functions under the Human Rights Act' [2000] *PL* 476–93; also, in more polemical vein, A Clapham, 'The Privatisation of Human Rights' [2001] *EHRLR* 20–32. Note also the argument of Sedley, above, n 68, that the private power of large corporations and other private bodies may be brought within a rights regime.
[164] See in particular HC Debs, 2 July 1998, cols 534–63.

relating to privacy, in the manner already discussed,[165] and through the Press Complaints Commission, the body set up by the press itself to regulate Press activity and handle public complaints. The Commission, although the product of Press self- rather than governmental regulation, was finally taken to be exercising functions of a public nature and so to be required to uphold Convention rights in carrying them out, notably the right to respect for private life under Article 8.[166] But fears that all this would entail the Commission in necessarily condemning investigative journalism in the United Kingdom were allayed by the inclusion of what is now section 12 of the Human Rights Act 1998, described above.[167] These rules emphasise the need to balance competing Convention rights and, other things being equal, to prefer freedom of expression. The rules also articulate what is anyway the spirit of Article 17 of the ECHR, prohibiting the abuse of Convention rights to destroy or unduly restrict other Convention rights.[168]

Churches, while to be treated as private rather than public bodies with regard to issues about worship, administration of the sacraments, and admission to or expulsion from membership or ministry,[169] were thought to exercise public functions with regard to the provision of (1) marriage services and (2) education in church schools. Therefore churches might be vulnerable to claims that

[165] See above, 000.

[166] The PCC's Code of Practice contains the following provisions on privacy:

'3. Privacy
(i) Everyone is entitled to respect for his or her private or family life, home, health and correspondence. A publication will be expected to justify intrusions into any individual's private life without consent.
(ii) The use of long lens photography to take pictures of people in private places without their consent is unacceptable.
Note: Private places are public or private property where there is a reasonable expectation of privacy.'

The BBC newsreader Anna Ford failed to persuade the PCC that these rules were infringed by the publication of photographs in the *Daily Mail* and *OK!* magazine showing her in a bikini on a beach in Majorca with her then partner (the former astronaut David Scott), applying suncream to each other, because the beach was held not to be a private place. Her action for judicial review of this PCC decision also failed: *The Times, The Scotsman*, 1 Aug 2001. Contrast the decision of the PCC on 2 Oct 2001 about a similar complaint made by the author J K Rowling, where the fact that her 8-year-old daughter was photographed with her on a beach in Mauritius seems to have led the Commission to reach a different result. See generally http://www.pcc.org.uk.

[167] See 150 above.

[168] See for this balancing exercise in operation *Ashdown v Telegraph Group*, above, n 30; *Douglas v Hello!*, above, n 147; and *Venables and Thompson v News Group Newspapers*, above, n 149. For a pre-incorporation decision in which Lightman J balanced the freedom of expression of the press with a person's right under s 84 of the Copyright, Designs and Patents Act 1988 not to have a work falsely attributed to him, all within the spirit of Art 10 ECHR, see *Clark v Associated Newspapers* [1998] 1 All ER 959 at 965.

[169] But there seems to be nothing in the Human Rights Act 1998 to stop ecclesiastical courts and tribunals being seen as courts or tribunals bound to uphold ECHR rights as public authorities. Disciplinary proceedings, whether against ministers/priests or members, would therefore seem to be subject to the ECHR rights of the person charged. Thus there is room ultimately for consideration of ECHR rights in cases such as *Percy v Church of Scotland* 2001 SC 757, referred to above at n 119. This will however be affected by Human Rights Act 1998, s 13.

Convention rights to freedom of thought, conscience, religion, and expression (Articles 9 and 10), and to freedom from discrimination on grounds of religion (Article 14), were being infringed when, for example, a priest or minister refused to marry a couple on the grounds that they were not members of his church, or when a person was denied, or dismissed from, employment by a church on the basis that the religion which he or she practised (or did not, or had ceased to, practise, as the case might be) was not compatible with the teachings of that church. In effect, the problem was again one of the clash of Convention rights, and it was ultimately resolved by the inclusion in the Act of section 13, under which the right of a religious organisation to freedom of thought, conscience and religion (as distinct from the equivalent right of an individual) is to receive 'particular regard' from any court or tribunal determining a question arising under the Act and affecting that right. Once again, the spirit of Article 17, preventing the abuse of Convention rights tending towards their own destruction or diminution, is to the fore.

In conclusion, private law and persons acting in the private sphere will be deeply affected by the passage into law of the Human Rights Act 1998, although the exact nature and full scope of these effects will continue to be unclear for some time to come. The new rights will be of vital importance in the processes of law reform and legislation, and will therefore be of particular interest to the Scottish Parliament. Indeed, an early test is likely to be provided by the reform of land law and in particular the abolition of feudalism and rights of superiority, the replacement of real burdens, and the introduction of rights of access to open land along with a community right to buy, which have obvious potential to conflict with the right to protection of property in Article 1 of the First Protocol.[170] But the movement to a rights-based legal culture should not seem as unduly foreign to Scots lawyers as it does to at least some English ones. Brooke LJ observed in *Douglas v Hello!*: 'English law, as is well known, has been historically based on freedoms, not rights.'[171] But Stair, the father of modern Scots law, wrote in the seventeenth century that 'the formal and proper object of law are (*sic*) the rights of men',[172] and founded the whole of his celebrated *Institutions* around the concept of rights; an approach in which he was followed by later institutional writers such as Bankton[173] and Bell.[174] It would seem, therefore, that, in Scotland at least, rights are indeed coming home.

---

[170] See the Abolition of Feudal Tenure etc (Scotland) Act 2000; and the Title Conditions (Scotland) and the Land Reform (Scotland) Bills, both under public consultation at the time of writing prior to enactment by the Scottish Parliament. An important decision of the European Court of relevance to this reform is *James v United Kingdom* (1986) 8 EHRR 123.

[171] *Douglas v Hello!*, above, n 147, at para 64.

[172] Stair, *The Institutions of the Law of Scotland*, I.1.22. I have used the 6th edition by Professor D M Walker (Edinburgh and Glasgow University Presses, Edinburgh and Glasgow, 1981).

[173] Bankton, *An Institute of the Civil Law of Scotland* (Edinburgh, 1751–53), I.1.85. Bankton's *Institute* has recently been reprinted in three volumes by the Stair Society (University of Edinburgh, 1993–95).

[174] Bell, *Principles of the Law of Scotland* 10th edn (T & T Clark, Edinburgh, 1899), introduction, § 1. This statement is found in all previous editions of the work.

p 148—In *Karl Construction Ltd v Palisade Properties plc* 2002 SLT 312, a building contract case, Lord Drummond Young held that the court as a public authority had to ensure that its remedies conformed to Convention rights and that the automatic right to inhibition on the dependence upon raising an action in Scots law was incompatible with Article 1 of the First Protocol. With regard to 'horizontality', the judge observed that the applicability of Convention rights must extend 'at least' as far as the court's procedures and remedies (para 76). *Karl* was followed in *Fab-Tek Engineering Ltd v Carillion Construction Ltd*, Dunfermline Sheriff Court, 22 March 2002, 2002 GWD 132–390, with regard to arrestment on the dependence.

p 152—The decision of the ECtHR in *Hatton v UK* is to be reviewed before a Grand Chamber of the Court.

p 159—The Court of Appeal upheld the first instance findings on the applicability of Convention rights in *Marcic v Thames Water Utilities Ltd* [2002] 2 All ER 55 (CA), but found that the claimant did also have a case in nuisance. The Court's comments about Convention rights are brief: see para 105ff, especially para 116–118, where it is suggested that achieving a fair balance of interests may always require the payment of compensation to individuals whose rights under Article 8 and Article 1 First Protocol.

pp 168–171—The English courts continue to develop the law of breach of confidence to protect privacy in the light of Article 8 ECHR: see *Theakston v Mirror Group Newspapers Ltd* [2002] EWHC 137 (QB, Ouseley J); *A v B and C* [2002] 1 All ER 449 (Jack J); [2002] EWCA Civ 337; and *Campbell v Mirror Group Newspapers Ltd* [2002] EWHC 499 (QB, Morland J). On 17 April 2002 Butler-Sloss P, following her decision in Venables, granted a temporary extension of the injunction protecting the identity of the daughter of Mary Bell (who at the age of 11 in 1968 was convicted of the manslaughter of two small boys). The injunction was due to expire on the daughter's 18th birthday on 25 May 2002. A hearing on whether the injunction should be permanently extended for the daughter's lifetime is expected in June 2002 (*Times, Scotsman*, 18 April 2002). In Scotland note also *Nicol v Caledonian Newspapers Ltd*, Outer House, Lady Paton, 11 April 2002, 2002 GWD 13–417 (law of defamation and qualified privilege considered in light of ECHR Articles 8 and 10).

9

Charting the Impact of Rights and Equality Discourse on Canadian Family Law

SUSAN B. BOYD*

IT IS ALMOST two decades since the *Canadian Charter of Rights and Freedoms* (the "*Charter*")[1] was entrenched within the Canadian Constitution in 1982 as part of an effort to promote national unity by the then Prime Minister Pierre Elliott Trudeau. One impetus behind the introduction of the *Charter* was the inadequacies of the *Canadian Bill of Rights*.[2] The statutory bill of rights, enacted in 1960, was ambiguous as to its effect on inconsistent statutes, it was not applicable to the provinces, and its effectiveness in relation to federal statutes was questionable. In short, it lacked constitutional status.[3] By 1985, three years after the repatriation of the Canadian constitution, all *Charter* rights and freedoms were in effect in relation to both federal and provincial legislatures and governments.[4] The fact that the *Charter* applies to both federal and provincial legislatures is significant because in Canada's constitution, jurisdiction is divided between the federal and provincial governments. In some fields, notably family law, jurisdiction is divided, and for some legal issues (such as child custody law), jurisdiction is shared between the two levels of government.

---

* Professor of Law, University of British Columbia, Canada. I would like to thank Melinda Anderson, Darlene McBain, Ellen Schlesinger, Kim Stanton, and Nicole Todosichuk for their research assistance, and the University of British Columbia Faculty of Law and Hampton Committee for the Humanities and Social Sciences Research Grant for funding. Thanks also to Bill Black, Claire Young, and Margot Young for commenting on earlier drafts, and especially to Hester Lessard for assisting me in expressing the complexities of the application of the *Charter* to the family law field. An earlier version of this chapter was published as 'The Impact of the Charter of Rights and Freedoms on Canadian Family Law', (2000) 17 *Canadian Journal of Family Law* 293–331.

[1] *Canadian Charter of Rights and Freedoms*, Part 1 of the *Constitution Act*, 1982, being Schedule B to the *Canada Act* 1982 (UK) 1982, c 11. Sections of the *Charter* that are relevant to this chapter are provided in Appendix I.

[2] *Canadian Bill of Rights*, SC 1960, c 44; RSC 1970, C–5.7.

[3] See Peter W Hogg, *Constitutional Law of Canada*, 2nd edn (Carswell, Toronto, 1985) at 639–40, 650; Brian Dickson, 'The *Canadian Charter of Rights and Freedoms*: Context and Evolution' in Gerald A. Beaudoin and Errol Mendes (eds), *The Canadian Charter of Rights and Freedoms* 3rd edn (Toronto, Carswell, 1996) 1–2 at 1–6 to 1–7.

[4] See s 32 (1) of the *Charter*. The effect of s 15 on equality rights was suspended until 1985 by s 32 (2).

This chapter provides a snapshot of the substantively diverse ways in which the *Charter* has affected a significant field of Canadian 'private law'—family law. The first part assesses the general impact of the *Charter* on family law. The second part reviews the most significant court challenges to family law based on the *Charter*. The final part offers a brief case study of the impact of the equality/anti-discrimination provisions of section 15 on family law in order to illustrate the diverse effects that the *Charter* can have. This final part also reveals the evolving approach to equality and discrimination of the Supreme Court of Canada. Appendix I lists relevant sections of the *Charter*. Throughout the chapter, the complex and often contradictory ways in which rights discourse relates to legal regulation of familial relations are highlighted.

A. GENERALITIES: THE IMPACT OF THE *CHARTER* ON FAMILY LAW

There are no specific provisions on the right to family or the right to privacy, *per se*, in the *Charter*. It does, however, contain provisions on equality or freedom from discrimination (section 15), freedom of religion and freedom of expression (section 2), and the right to 'life, liberty and security of the person' (section 7), all of which have been invoked in the family law context. The rights and freedoms set out in the *Charter* are guaranteed 'subject only to such reasonable limits prescribed by law as can be demonstrably justified in a free and democratic society' (section 1). This section has been invoked to limit the impact of the *Charter* on some areas of family law.

The *Charter* applies only to situations where 'an element of governmental action [is] implicated in the litigation'.[5] Because court orders *per se* are not government action, there have been questions as to whether the *Charter* would have any significant effect on so-called 'private law', including family law, or on the common law generally. Apart from this 'state action' problem, there is also a deeply held view that there is something about family law, and familial relations, that makes application of the set of public values contained in the *Charter* more problematic than it might be, say, in criminal law. The rights paradigm—based as it tends to be on a liberal vision of 'the citizen' (liberalism's unencumbered individual)—does not apply easily to the family law field, where individual family members are encumbered with complex interdependencies, needs, and relations of care. Legal arguments based on either individual or group rights do not always work well in the context of the family, when the interests of parents, children, and government/community are often inter-related and/or all at stake in different ways. The powerful familial ideology that prevails in this field, with corresponding expectations that often differ for women and men, or for Aboriginal and non-Aboriginal people, complicates the

---

[5] S 32(1) of the *Charter*; *Retail, Wholesale and Department Store Union, Local 580 v Dolphin Delivery* [1986] 2 SCR 573.

rights framework, which is premised on formal equality, due process, and liberty/autonomy.[6] These values are not always seen as appropriate or workable in the familial context.

In 1991, one family law scholar noted that, for many of these reasons, Canadians were not likely to see 'the constitutionalization of everyday family life', at least in the short term.[7] Although he rightly noted that a false dichotomy is too often drawn between 'public' and 'private' spheres of life and law,[8] Stephen Toope argued that the reluctance of Canadian courts to apply the *Charter* to aspects of life that they considered private would inhibit *Charter* arguments in the family law field. Nonetheless, the *Charter* has affected family law in three different ways. First, some governments have reviewed and amended their legislation in order to ensure that statutory provisions comply with the *Charter*, as will be discussed later in the chapter. Secondly, direct con- stitutional challenges have been brought in the courts to statutory provisions on the basis that they violate *Charter* guarantees such as sex equality (s 15) or the right to 'life, liberty and security of the person' (s 7). Thirdly, the *Charter* has been invoked indirectly to argue that, even in the absence of the required element of government or state action, judges must nevertheless in this situation take into account the fundamental values that are enshrined in the *Charter*. This last aspect is important because many areas of family law involve the exercise of judicial discretion regarding the interpretation of concepts that originated in common law. Indeed, family law is a field that arguably involves more indeter- minative normative concepts and standards than many areas of law that are embodied in statutes. For example, judicial interpretation of the 'best interests of the child' standard in child custody statutes is known to produce results that vary enormously.[9] The relationship between the *Charter* and judicial discretion in relation to such concepts has been unclear and the Supreme Court of Canada remains divided on this issue, as will be seen below.

[6] See Hester Lessard, Bruce Ryder, David Schneiderman and Margot Young, 'Developments in Constitutional Law: The 1994–95 Term', (1996) 7 *The SCLR* (2d) 81–156 at 110; Stephen Toope, 'Riding the Fences: Courts, Charter Rights and Family Law', (1991) 9 *CJFL* 55 at 56–7. Mary Jane Mossman has argued that the concept of 'family' mediates the relevance of competing notions of 'individualism' and 'community' for women especially. Ideas of community and individualism are gendered in the context of family roles and relationships: 'Individualism and Community: Family as a Mediating Concept' in Allan Hutchinson and Leslie Green (eds), *Law and the Community: the End of Individualism* (Carswell, Toronto, 1988) 205.

[7] Toope, *ibid.*, at 96. Although now somewhat out of date, this article remains an excellent detailed treatment of the complexities of applying a rights paradigm in the family context.

[8] *Ibid.* For instance, the family has never been free from regulation by state and law: Susan B Boyd (ed), *Challenging the Public/Private Divide: Feminism, Law, and Public Policy* (University of Toronto Press, Toronto 1997).

[9] An extensive literature has developed on this point since Robert Mnookin's well-known article, 'Child-Custody Adjudication: Judicial Functions in the Face of Indeterminacy', (1975) 39 *L&CP* 226. Scholars who have examined the interpretation of the best interests test in relation to biases connected to gender, race, disability, class and sexual orientation have extended this analysis. See, for example, Marlee Kline, 'Child Welfare Law, "Best Interests of the Child" Ideology, and First Nations', (1992) 30 *OHLJ* 375–425.

It is now generally accepted in Canada that the introduction of the *Charter* has led to increased invocation of the language of rights and increased use of social context, social science studies, and statistics in legal argument generally, including in family law.[10] Since Toope wrote in 1991, there have been demonstrable—if often contradictory—effects of the *Charter* on family law arguments, judicial decisions, and statutory reform, regardless of the technical issue that the *Charter* applies only to government action and the complicating impact of familial ideology. Moreover, since the 1980s, cases dealing with discrimination based on sex and sexual orientation have become more prevalent. Indeed, the changes that have resulted from *Charter* challenges related to sexual orientation discrimination have arguably altered the face of family law in Canada. The next section of this chapter will review court challenges that have been brought in relation to a variety of family law statutes, in order to illustrate the impact of the *Charter*.

B.   KEY COURT CHALLENGES TO FAMILY LAW STATUTES USING THE *CHARTER*

This part reviews the most important and interesting court challenges to regulation of family relationships based on the *Charter*, starting with claims relating to 'adult' relationships and moving on to those related to children (although of course there is some overlap). The focus will mainly be on topics typically associated with family law (marriage, separation, child custody, child protection) that invoke familial concepts such as 'spouse'. Most challenges in the family law field brought by adults have been based on section 15 equality rights, whereas freedom of religion and liberty rights (ss 2 and 7) have been invoked mainly in cases related to parents and children. Indeed, *Charter* arguments in the family law context have been invoked most commonly in disputes involving children.[11] However, the emphasis on the best interests of the child principle is so intuitively attractive that it has not easily been displaced by *Charter* rights of parents. Where *Charter* challenges are successful, section 24, the remedial section of the *Charter*, and section 52 of the *Constitution Act, 1982*, permit courts a wide range of remedies including a declaration that an impugned section of a statute is unconstitutional and should be struck down or a 'reading in' of wording that saves the offending section.

---

[10] See, generally, David Schneiderman and Kate Sutherland (eds), *Charting the Consequences: The Impact of Charter Rights on Canadian Law and Politics* (University of Toronto Press, Toronto, 1997); in the family law context, see The Honourable Justice Claire L'Heureux-Dubé, 'Making Equality Work in Family Law', (1997) 14(2) *CJFL* 103–127; Alison Harvison Young, 'The Changing Family, Rights Discourse and the Supreme Court of Canada', (2001) 80 *Canadian Bar Review* 749–792. Young argues that family law can no longer be characterized as an area falling only within the domain of private law.

[11] Toope, *supra* n 6, at 95. Toope's observation remains true, although challenges by unmarried partners in relation to adult matters have recently increased, mainly as a result of challenges to the legal definition of 'spouse'.

(1) Marriage

The most overt challenges to the marriage laws have been made by same sex couples. However, opposite sex cohabitants have also brought *Charter* challenges in relation to benefits that accrue only to married spouses and, until recently, they enjoyed greater success than same sex cohabitants.[12] In *Layland v Ontario*,[13] a section 15 equality challenge by two gay men to the opposite sex requirement of marriage failed. The men had challenged the refusal of a City Clerk to issue them a marriage license. Previous cases had held that section 15 includes grounds of discrimination that are analogous to those explicitly listed, and sexual orientation had been declared to be an analogous protected ground of discrimination.[14] Nonetheless, the majority in *Layland* held that the *Charter* could not be invoked in order to bring about a change in the definition of marriage. The majority also held that the institution of marriage was intended to encourage the procreation of children and that this purpose could not generally be achieved in a homosexual union. The decision in *Layland* was not appealed.[15]

Most recently, the opposite sex definition of marriage is being taken up once more in Ontario in light of favourable precedent that has emerged since *Layland*.[16] In *Halpern v Toronto (City) Clerk*,[17] six same sex couples are asking

---

[12] *Miron v Trudel* [1995] 2 SCR 418 involved a s 15 challenge to the definition of 'spouse' in Ontario's *Insurance Act* which denied an unmarried opposite sex couple accident benefits that were available to legally married couples. Marital status was held to be an analogous protected ground of discrimination for the purposes of s 15 (1) and the impugned definition of spouse was found to violate s 15 and it was not saved by s 1. See also *Walsh v Bona*, (2000), 5 RFL (5th) 188, where the Nova Scotia Court of Appeal held that Susan Walsh was entitled to a division of matrimonial property upon the termination of her 10 year opposite sex common law relationship and that the province's *Matrimonial Property Act* which excluded common law relationships violated s 15 (1) of the *Charter*. In contrast, see the unsuccessful claim by a gay man in relation to old age security benefits in *Egan v Canada* [1995] 2 SCR 513. I shall discuss challenges by unmarried cohabitants to support law *infra*.

[13] *Layland v Ontario* (1993) 104 DLR (4th) 214 (Ont. Ct. of Justice, Gen. Div).

[14] *Andrews v Law Society of British Columbia*, [1989] 1 SCR 143; *Egan v Canada, supra* n 12.

[15] A decision was made by a collective of equality-seeking groups and individuals involved in the lesbian/gay movement not to appeal the *Layland* decision, due at the time to the jurisprudence and the composition of the Supreme Court of Canada. See also *Egan v Canada, supra* n 12, in which several judges of the Supreme Court of Canada held (in a non-family law context) that although sexual orientation is a protected ground of discrimination under section 15, the exclusion of same sex couples from benefits under the old age security legislation was not unconstitutional because it was legitimate to offer special protection to heterosexual couples.

[16] *M v H* [1999] 2 SCR 3 (discussed *infra* under *Spousal Support*) which found that same sex relationships are capable of being both conjugal and lengthy and that Ontario's *Family Law Act* should be expanded to include same sex cohabitants. Additionally, *Vincent v. Ontario (Ministry of the Attorney General)*, [1999] OJ No 4905 (QL) (Ont.Superior Court of Justice), found that Bill 5 passed by the province of Ontario as a result of *M v H* to recognise same sex benefits across various pieces of legislation, should have a retroactive effect in relation to the Ontario Human Rights Code to permit an ex-partner to bring an action before the provincial human rights commission. See also *LKF (Re)* [1999] BCJ No 819 (BC Provincial Court) (QL) where British Columbia's amendments to its *Family Relations Act* to include same sex partners in the definition of step-parent were found to have a retroactive effect in order to conform to s 15 (1) of the *Charter*. This allowed an ex-partner to claim today's standard of child support payments even though her same-sex relationship had dissolved before her partner was recognised in legislation as a step-parent.

[17] *Halpern v Toronto (City) Clerk* [2000] OJ No 3213 (Ont Superior Court of Justice) (QL).

the Clerk of the City of Toronto to issue them marriage licenses. Unlike in *Layland*, the Clerk did not refuse to issue the licenses, but decided to hold the matter in abeyance until it could get direction from the courts as to the constitutionality of the issue. A similar court battle is underway in the western province of British Columbia. In *Marriage Act (Can.) (Re)*[18] two same sex couples who had been refused marriage licenses by the Director of Vital Statistics initiated the challenge. Initially, the Attorney General of BC supported the position of the claimants, although it has since withdrawn. In January of 2001, the Attorney General of Canada attempted to have BCs standing dismissed. The Chief Justice of the BC Supreme Court ruled that because the federal government has the jurisdiction to define marriage, it thus 'governs the circumstances in which provincial officials are permitted to issue certificates of Marriage'. As a result, the province is implicated in circumstances that may constitute a breach of the *Charter* rights of some of its residents and a 'genuine' interest is created for which standing is required.

(2) Spousal Support

Successful challenges have been brought to spousal support provisions on the grounds that they discriminated against unmarried cohabitants and same sex cohabitants by excluding them from the protection of the legislation. Thus far, these challenges have been brought only in relation to provincial statutes related to support law and not to the federal *Divorce Act,*[19] which applies only to spouses who have been legally married. For instance, the Province of Alberta was challenged for its exclusion of unmarried opposite sex cohabitants from its spousal support provisions in a case where a woman who had been in a common law relationship of thirty years duration brought an action for support.[20] In 1998, the Alberta Court of Appeal held that the definition of 'spouse' for the purpose of spousal support provisions of the *Domestic Relations Act*[21] discriminated against common law partners in contravention of section 15(1) of the *Charter*. The definition of spouse was legislatively expanded to include common law opposite sex cohabitants.

The Ontario spousal support legislation has also been challenged, this time for exclusion of same sex cohabitants from its provisions. In *M v H,*[22] the breakdown of a ten-year lesbian relationship left one woman (M) in a vulnerable economic position. M wished therefore to claim financial support. In order to do so, she had to seek a court declaration that the definition of spouse in the spousal support section of the Ontario *Family Law Act*, which (in contrast to the

---

[18] *Marriage Act (Can.) (Re)* (2001), 13 RFL (5th) 418 (BCSC)
[19] *Divorce Act*, RSC 1985, c 3 (2nd Supp.).
[20] *Taylor v Rossu* (1998), 161 DLR (4th) 266 (Alta CA).
[21] *Domestic Relations Act*, RSA 1980, c D–37.
[22] *M v H, supra* n 16.

Alberta legislation) included married spouses *and* opposite sex unmarried cohabitants, should be expanded to include same sex cohabitants. M was successful in her section 15 challenge to this legislative definition at all court levels, including the ground-breaking decision of the Supreme Court of Canada. Cory and Iacobucci JJ, writing for six justices of the eight to one majority, accepted the argument that same sex relationships are capable of being both conjugal and lengthy. As a result of the Supreme Court of Canada's decision, Ontario passed (albeit grudgingly) Bill 5, *An Act to Amend Certain Statutes Because of the Supreme Court of Canada's Decision in M v H,*[23] which amended the *Family Law Act* as well as 66 other Ontario statutes recognising the same sex partner as a new category of relationship.

(3) Single Fathers and Financial Support

In the early days of the *Charter*, single fathers successfully challenged legislative provisions in Nova Scotia that provided government public assistance benefits to single mothers but not to single fathers.[24] Judges rejected the argument that benefits to single mothers should be characterised as an affirmative action program under section 15(2) of the *Charter*. The courts did not, however, extend the benefits to men and instead the provisions were struck down for single mothers as well. Regulations were eventually promulgated to extend eligibility to single fathers.

In contrast to these Nova Scotia cases, in *Shewchuk v Ricard*[25] a 'natural' father brought a section 15(1) sex equality challenge to British Columbia legislation that permitted single mothers to sue natural fathers for child support. The British Columbia Court of Appeal held that legislation allowing a single mother to sue the natural father of her child without providing a similar right for natural fathers constituted a *prima facie* case of discrimination under section 15(1), but that it was a demonstrably justified limitation under section 1 of the *Charter*. Judy Fudge argued that the apparent discrepancy between the Nova Scotia and the British Columbia cases could be explained by the fact that judges were willing to uphold legislation that privatised the costs of social reproduction, even if the legislation denied the formal equality of men and women.[26]

---

[23] SO 1999, c 6.

[24] See *Phillips v Attorney General of Nova Scotia* (1986) 34 DLR (4th) 633 and *Reference Re Family Benefits Act (NS)* (1986), 75 NSR (2d) 338 (NSCA). For an analysis of these cases, see Judy Fudge, 'The Privatization of the Costs of Social Reproduction: Some Recent *Charter* Cases', (1989) 3(1) *CJWL* 246–55.

[25] *Shewchuk v Ricard* (1986), 28 DLR (4th) 429 (BCCA). See also *Friesen v Gregory* (1986) 55 Sask. R 245 (Sask Unified Fam Ct.).

[26] Judy Fudge, *supra* n 24, at 250. The relevant statute, the *Child Paternity and Support Act* RSBC 1979, c 49, was repealed by SBC 1988, c 36.

(4) Single Mothers and Financial Support

In general, unmarried mothers have been successful in challenging restrictions on their ability to claim child support or bring filiation proceedings, as compared to married mothers. In *Milne (Doherty) and Milne v Attorney General of Alberta, Director of Maintenance and Recovery and Stadnyk*,[27] a mother of a child born out of wedlock and her child both sought a declaration that section 23(1)(b) of the *Alberta Maintenance and Recovery Act*, which terminated a father's obligation to pay child maintenance for children born outside of marriage when the mother married, was invalid due to its inconsistency with section 15(1) of the *Charter*. They were successful. A recent case has highlighted the role of social assistance in financial support of single mothers and its different definition of 'spouse' from family law. In *Falkiner v Ontario (Ministry of Community and Social Services, Income Maintenance Branch)*,[28] an Ontario court ruled against the province's effort to deny social assistance benefits to single parents once they started cohabiting with a person of the opposite sex. In what could be described as an attempt to reduce the number of benefit recipients, the word 'spouse' had been defined to include virtually any cohabitation, even where there was minimal economic interdependence between the cohabitants and even if they were not 'spouses' for the purposes of spousal support obligations. The legislation was found to violate section 15(1) of the *Charter* because its practical effect in most cases was to discriminate against women, in particular, single mothers.

In *Thibaudeau v Canada*[29] a divorced custodial mother argued unsuccessfully that the provisions in the *Income Tax Act* which required her to pay tax on child support that she received from her ex-husband were discriminatory under section 15(1). As I shall later explain, her failure can be explained by the fact that the male judges on the Supreme Court of Canada treated her as part of a post-divorce 'family unit' with her husband, whereas the two women judges, in dissent, treated her as an individual whose situation should be compared to that of her husband, who received a tax deduction for the child support he paid.

(5) Adoption

In the area of adoption law, complaints of discrimination based on section 15(1) have been quite successful. For example, natural fathers have successfully chal-

---

[27] *Milne (Doherty) and Milne v Attorney General of Alberta, Director of Maintenance and Recovery and Stadnyk* [1990] 75 ALR (2d) 155 (Alberta QB). For another case on unmarried mothers and child support, see *Panko v Vandesype* (1993) 45 RFL (3d) 424 (Sask Ct QB).

[28] *Falkiner v Ontario (Ministry of Community and Social Services, Income Maintenance Branch)* (2000) 188 DLR (4th) 52 (Ont Sup Ct of Justice).

[29] *Thibaudeau v Canada* [1995] 2 SCR 627.

lenged British Columbia *Adoption Act* provisions that did not require their consent to adoptions, whereas the mother's consent and that of a father who was married to the mother was required.[30] Some provincial adoption legislation[31] has been amended to reflect such concerns, although natural mothers and fathers are still not treated in a completely symmetrical manner.

In *Re K*, a successful section 15(1) challenge was brought to a statutory definition of 'spouse' that restricted stepparent adoptions to heterosexual couples only.[32] Four lesbian couples applied to adopt children already being raised by them. In each case, the children had been conceived by one of the lesbian partners through the use of artificial insemination and had been born during their relationships as a joint decision. In considering section 1 of the *Charter*, Nevins J found that there was no rational connection between the goals of the legislation (ensuring the best interests of children and establishing and protecting parent/child relationships) and the prohibition against adoption by homosexual couples.[33] He therefore held that the discrimination could not be justified under section 1. The Alberta government was faced with a similar challenge to the meaning of 'spouse' under the adoption provisions of its *Child Welfare Act*.[34] It then amended the provisions replacing 'spouse' with 'step parent'. *Re A*[35] then ruled that 'step parent' could include a same sex partner, thus allowing the applicants to successfully adopt the biological children of their respective partners. The 2001 decision of *Nova Scotia (Birth Registration No 1999–02–004200) (Re)*[36] saw the court reading in the term 'common-law partner' alongside the word 'spouse' so that the adoption provisions found in Nova Scotia's *Children and Family Services Act*,[37] would not offend the *Charter* by discriminating against either same sex or opposite sex common law couples.

---

[30] *NM v British Columbia (Superintendent of Family and Child Services)* (1986) 34 DLR (4th) 488 (BCSC)

[31] For instance the British Columbia *Adoption Act*, RSBC 1996, c 5, s 13.

[32] *Re K* (1995) 15 RFL (4th) 129 (Ont Ct Prov Div). In addition, the British Columbia *Adoption Act,* RSBC 1996, c 5 was amended to permit adoptions by 'one adult or 2 adults jointly' (s 29(1)). This language permits same sex couples to adopt. The language in s 29(2) is broad enough to permit stepparent adoptions by same sex partners.

[33] *R. v Oakes* [1986] 1 SCR 103 identified two central criteria in determining whether a limitation on a right or freedom is justified under s 1 of the *Charter*. First, the objective of the limiting measure must be of sufficient importance to warrant overriding the right. Second, the means chosen to achieve that objective must be proportional to the ends. The limiting measure must be rationally connected to the objective, minimally impair the *Charter* right in question, and not so severely trench on an individual or group that the legislative objective is outweighed by the abridgment of rights.

[34] *Child Welfare Act*, SA 1984, C–8.1.

[35] *Re A,* (1999), 2 RFL (5th) 358 (Alta Ct of QB)

[36] *Nova Scotia (Birth Registration No.1999–02–004200) (Re)* [2001] NSJ No 261 (NS Family Court) (QL)

[37] *Children and Family Services Act*, SNS 1990, C 5.

(6) Custody and Access

Some controversial court challenges have been brought in the field of child custody law, where the best interests of the child test renders application of rights discourse problematic. The sex equality guarantee in section 15(1) has been argued by fathers seeking custody or joint custody, and freedom of religion has been argued by access parents, especially fathers. In an early case, *Keyes v Gordon*,[38] a father appealed a sole custody award of the children to the mother and a small child support award. He argued that the *Charter* gave him, the children, and their mother a right to an order of joint custody in the absence of any evidence of bad character. He had refused to pay the nominal child support that had been awarded, arguing that 'because he is ready, willing and able to care for his children but has been denied custody of them (shared or otherwise) it is contrary to his constitutional rights to order him to pay maintenance for children "banished" from him'. The judge on appeal found that the primary consideration in child custody matters was the best interests of the children and that the *Charter* had in no way altered this principle. The father's claim for custody/joint custody was dismissed, as was his claim that he should not have to pay maintenance for his children if he was not allowed to share in their custody.[39]

The Supreme Court of Canada addressed the issue of whether the *Charter* applies to child custody law more directly in the 1993 cases *Young v Young* and *P(D) v S(C)*, widely acknowledged to be very confusing decisions by the Court.[40] Sections 2(a) and (b) on freedom of religion and expression (of the access parent) were mainly at issue. The Court decided that there could be some restrictions on a father's access where the father was discussing his religion with the children in a way that involved 'indoctrination, enlistment, or harassment having the aim or effect of undermining the religious decision made by the custodial parent'.[41] All Supreme Court judges agreed that the *Charter* applied to the legislative test for determining best interests of the child, but they left the issue of the application of the *Charter* to court orders unsettled. Most agreed that if the best interests test were interpreted properly, it would not violate the *Charter*, although Sopinka J emphasised that freedom of religious expression should be overridden only if its exercise would result in consequences involving more than inconvenience, upset,

---

[38] *Keyes v Gordon* (1985) 45 RFL (2d) 177 (NSSC, Appeal division).

[39] For a commentary by the mother, which shows that the father had used several court proceedings to 'harass' her, see Jane Gordon, Multiple Meanings of Equality: A Case Study in Custody Litigation, (1989) 3(1) *CJWL* 256–68.

[40] *Young v Young* [1993] 4 SCR 3; *P(D) v S(C)* [1993] 4 SCR 141. For reviews of these two cases, see Martha Bailey, 'Custody, Access, and Religion: A Comment on *Young v Young* and *DP v CS*', (1994) 11 *CFLQ* 317–49; Joel Bakan, Bruce Ryder, David Schneiderman and Margot Young, 'Developments in Constitutional Law: The 1993-94 Term', (1995) 6 *SCLR* 67 at 70–77; Nicholas Bala, 'Developments in Family Law: The 1993–94 Term: The Best Interests of the Child', (1995) 6 *SCLR* (2d) 453–474 at 454–68. Bailey, at 321-2, points out that the father 'won' in *Young*, but not in *P(D) v S(C)* because Mr Young had already given an undertaking under oath to limit his religious freedom when it came to his children. In *P(D) v S(C)* the father 'lost' but ended up in the same position as Mr Young because he had a court order that limited his religious freedom.

[41] *Young v Young, ibid*, at 110, *per* Iacobucci and Cory JJ.

or disruption to the child and, incidentally to the custodial parent.[42] Others were more inclined towards the view that section 2 did not protect conduct that violated the best interests of the child. Most judges also agreed that the interpretation of the best interests test should take into account the values of the *Charter*, but they disagreed on the manner and extent to which the *Charter* should affect the interpretation. These disagreements reflect wider differences of opinion concerning the proper interpretation of the best interests test.

In an access case in Alberta that generated a great deal of media attention, *Johnson-Steeves v Lee*, section 7 of the *Charter* was invoked by a mother arguing she had a right to decide what type of family she would create in which to raise her child.[43] An agreement had been made that Mr Lee would assist in the conception of, and financial support for, a child, but would not interfere with child's upbringing. The parents never lived together and slept together only in order to conceive a child. The Alberta Court of Appeal doubted that the *Charter* applied to this dispute between two private individuals, where there was no apparent state intervention. However, even if it did apply, section 7 did not create a right for a custodial parent to decide on a family model that excluded the other parent from the life of the child, especially where such a model was inconsistent with the best interests of the child (as was found at trial).[44] The Court affirmed an access order in favour of the father, who had been seeing the child from time to time.

A *Charter* right that could, in theory, be invoked by custodial parents who need or wish to relocate to another geographical area against the wishes of the access parent, has not in fact been influential. Mobility rights, entrenched in section 6 of the *Charter*, have not been argued explicitly in the custody context in support of the custodial parent's right to relocate.[45] Toope's assessment is that making a *Charter* argument would not strengthen a custodial parent's case because section 6(3)(a) makes the mobility right subject to 'any laws or practices of general application in force in a province . . .'. Thus, even if mobility rights were invoked, directly or as an interpretive principle, parental mobility would be restricted by the 'best interests of the child' principle that is so central to legislation on custody and access.[46] Indeed, in the *Goertz v Gordon*[47] case on relocation of a custodial parent that was decided by the Supreme Court of Canada, the mobility right was not explicitly invoked or discussed.

The role of children's rights in custody and access decisions remains unclear. For example, children too could argue 'freedom of religion' and that they are protected from discrimination on the basis of age in section 15(1). Yet children

---

[42] *Ibid*, at 107.

[43] *Johnson-Steeves v Lee* (1997) 33 RFL (4th) 278.

[44] Courts have decided that mothers can exclude a man from being acknowledged as the father of the child on the child's birth certificate: *Trociuk v British Columbia (Attorney General)* [2001] BCJ No 1052 (BC Court of Appeal) (QL), *Klreklewetz v Scopel* 2001, 13 RFL (5th) 408 (Ont Sup Ct of Justice). This, however, does not seem to affect a father's right to claim access or his responsibility to make child support payments.

[45] See Toope, *supra* n 6, at 90–95.

[46] *Ibid*, at 94.

[47] *Goertz v Gordon* [1996] 2 SCR 27.

are rarely represented in custody proceedings, nor are they typically parties in most custody disputes. Generally, it is parental rights under the *Charter* that are at issue. Yet parental rights may or may not coincide with children's rights or wishes. The Supreme Court of Canada has invoked children's rights in a variety of contexts; however, rather than emphasising children's autonomy rights, a paternalistic approach stressing children's right to be nurtured and cared for has usually been adopted.[48] Nonetheless, in *P(D) v S(C)*, discussed above, the Supreme Court upheld a trial judgment that recognised the capacity and right of a child who has reached the age of discretion to make decisions regarding religion. The court order had restricted the access father from involving the child in religious activities, but only until a court determined that the child was capable of deciding which religion she wished to adopt.[49] Some recognition of children's rights was therefore acknowledged.

(7) Child Protection Cases

In child protection law, section 7 guaranteeing 'life, liberty, and security of the person' and section 2 on freedom of religion have been invoked most frequently. Most challenges have been ultimately unsuccessful, with the courts tending to uphold state procedures and apprehensions.

In the early case *S(MK) v Nova Scotia (Minister of Community Services)*[50] two children were apprehended from the same family, one at birth and one at two years of age. The parents were of Aboriginal ancestry, poor, and young (approximately seventeen and twenty-one when the children were apprehended). There were allegations of child and spousal abuse. Both parents invoked *Charter* arguments. On a procedural issue, they argued that section 7 had been violated, as there had been no emergency when the children were apprehended. They also argued discrimination on the basis of race, ethnic origin, colour, and economic status under section 15(1). All arguments were dismissed: even if the *Charter* was breached it would have been justifiable under section 1 of the *Charter*, with the 'best interests of the children' standard being paramount and superseding parental rights. A similar reasoning was echoed, this time by the Supreme Court of Canada, in *Winnipeg Child and Family Services v K.L.W.*[51] The child apprehension procedure set out in Manitoba's *Child and Family Services Act*[52] allowed KLW's child to be apprehended a day after it was born. KLW argued that the warrantless apprehension of her child in a non-emergency situation infringed her rights under section 7 of the *Charter*. The majority of the court, however, disagreed, ruling that children's lives and health trumped parental rights to freedom from state intervention.

---

[48] Martha Bailey, 'Developments in Family Law: The 1994–95 Term', (1996) 7 *SCLR* (2d) 327–65 at 351.

[49] See M Bailey, *ibid*, at 327–31 for further discussion.

[50] *S(MK.) v Nova Scotia (Minister of Community Services)* [1988] NSJ No 302 (NS Co Ct).

[51] *Winnipeg Child and Family Services v KLW* [2000] 2 SCR 519

[52] *Child and Family Services*, SM 1985–86, c 8.

The Supreme Court of Canada made an important, if complicated, decision in 1994 in *B(R) v Children's Aid Society of Metropolitan Toronto*.[53] A child was born prematurely with many health problems. Her parents consented to medical treatment except for blood transfusions, to which they objected for religious reasons. The child was found to be in need of a blood transfusion (although evidence was conflicting on this issue) and she was apprehended for seventy-two hours in order that consent could be given. The parents appealed the wardship orders on the question of whether the Ontario statutory provision defining 'child in need of protection', together with various powers and procedural provisions in the statute, offended sections 2(a) or 7 of the *Charter*. Their appeal was dismissed. A complex decision from a divided Supreme Court of Canada was nonetheless unanimous that section 7 was not breached because the state had acted in a manner consistent with fundamental justice. However, a plurality of four judges felt that the section 7 liberty right was broad enough to include the right to nurture a child, care for its development, and make decisions for it in fundamental matters such as medical care. In relation to section 2, a majority held that although the legislative scheme contravened the parents' religious right to choose medical treatment, it was nonetheless justified under section 1.

This case raised a potential conflict between the rights of the state (child protection authorities), parents, and children. It ultimately showed that the *Charter* rights of freedom of religion and liberty could not seriously constrain the ability of the state to intervene in families to protect children. However, several judges acknowledged that such rights were held by parents. Moreover, despite the ultimate loss by the parents in this case and others like it,[54] it can be argued that, as a result of heightened scrutiny of state action in the *Charter* era, 'better evidence' is now required to justify infringement of parental rights. Some governments have enhanced procedural safeguards in relation to the apprehension of children in child protection law,[55] including those in relation to the issue of consent to medical treatment raised in the *B(R)* case. Some governments have also introduced quite elaborate legislative statements of the rights of children in care.[56]

Procedural issues appear to have become the focus of attention in child protection cases. A case involving whether a government-funded legal aid lawyer

[53] *B(R.) v Children's Aid Society of Metropolitan Toronto* [1995] 1 SCR 315.

[54] In *Re Children's Aid Society of Metropolitan Toronto and TH et al.* (1996) 138 DLR (4th) 144 (Ont Ct Gen Div), an appeal based on ss 2(a) and 7 of the *Charter* failed even where both a 13 year old girl and her mother (the custodial parent) refused to agree to medical treatment for a life threatening condition that required that she have a blood transfusion. For a different result in an earlier case, see *Children's Aid Society of Metropolitan Toronto v K* (1985), 48 RFL (2d) 164 (Ont Prov Ct Fam Div).

[55] See, for example, British Columbia's *Child, Family and Community Service Act*, RSBC 1996, c 46, s 29.

[56] For example, British Columbia's *Child, Family and Community Service Act*, RSBC 1996, c 46, s 70, lists rights such as reasonable privacy and to be consulted and to express their views, according to their abilities, about significant decisions affecting them.

190   Susan Boyd

should be available to a parent fighting attempts by a government agency to take custody of her children was heard by the Supreme Court of Canada in 1998. A mother had argued that legal aid services violated the fundamental justice guarantee in section 7, and her equality rights under section 15, by refusing to fund a lawyer to represent her. Jeannine Godin lost in the lower courts in New Brunswick, but won at the Supreme Court of Canada.[57] A bare majority of the Court of Appeal had decided that section 7 did not encompass the integrity of the family and that there was no discrimination on enumerated or analogous grounds in section 15. In contrast, the Supreme Court decided that both Godin's and her children's rights to security of the person under section 7 were violated as a result of the lack of state-funded counsel in the particular circumstances of this case, where effective parental participation in the hearing could not be obtained without legal representation. Three justices also held that the parent's liberty interest under section 7 was triggered, not only her security of the person. It was felt that the parent's decision-making and other attributes of custody are protected under the liberty interest of section 7. Moreover, the principles and purposes of the section 15 equality guarantee must be taken into account when considering section 7 issues. In this case, gender equality issues were raised because women, especially single mothers, are disproportionately and particularly affected by child protection proceedings.[58]

This part of the chapter has reviewed the main court-based *Charter* challenges to family law. Overall, although the *Charter* has had a definite impact on family law, and some statutes have been amended as a result, the jurisprudence on rights and claims in the family law context is characterised by some degree of contradiction and ambiguity.[59] For example, although most Supreme Court judges agree that parental rights are protected to some degree by the section 7 liberty interest, in the final result, *Charter* challenges to child protection laws and procedures by parents (often parents from a non-conforming religious community) tend to fail, usually because the facts of the cases indicate that the government authorities acted in a manner consistent with the principles of fundamental justice (see s 7).[60]

[57] *New Brunswick (Minister of Health and Community Services) v JG* (1997), 145 DLR (4th) 349 (NBCA); (1995), 131 DLR (4th) 273 (NBQB); (1999), 177 DLR (4th) 124 (SCC).
[58] A distinction has been drawn between child protection proceedings (public state intervention) and child custody proceedings (private dispute between two parties): *Miltenberger v Braaten* [2000] SJ No 599 (Sask Unified Family Court) (QL) where it was found that the mother's s 7 *Charter* rights to liberty and security of the person were not violated with her inability to qualify for state-appointed counsel to represent her in a child custody dispute between herself and the child's father, even though she faced the possibility that she would lose custody and that she did not have the financial means to retain private legal counsel.
[59] See Hester Lessard, 'Liberty Rights, the Family, and Constitutional Politics' in David Schneiderman (ed), *Canadian-American Constitutional Law* (Centre for Constitutional Studies, Edmonton, forthcoming). See also Lessard et al., *supra* n 6, at 113, writing in relation to s 15 equality challenges by gay or lesbian couples to discriminatory legislation.
[60] Even if a *Charter* right is infringed, it is still possible to save the challenged law under s 1 which allows for 'such reasonable limits prescribed by law as can be demonstrably justified in a free and democratic society'. S 7 includes limiting wording within itself: 'Everyone has the right to life, liberty

The next section offers a case study on the ways in which the equality guarantees in section 15 of the *Charter* have been used, increasingly over the past decade, to introduce social context into both statutory reform and judicial decision-making. In this field as well, contradictions can be identified in relation to the impact of the *Charter*.

C. THE IMPACT OF SECTION 15 EQUALITY GUARANTEES ON FAMILY LAW

(1) Legislative Reform Inspired by the Equality Guarantees

The *Charter* has been invoked not only through court challenges to family laws, but also through legislative reform. One of the early effects of the *Charter* was that federal and provincial governments reviewed their legislation to see whether statutes were in conformity with the *Charter*. The equality section 15 was suspended for three years to permit this review.[61] The objective was to try to avoid unnecessary and expensive court challenges to legislation. In general, governments tended to take a formalistic and simplistic approach to equality in their reviews instead of examining the larger social, political, and legal context in order to determine whether differential treatment results in inequality or whether identical treatment might, in a particular context, result in inequality or foster disadvantage.[62]

In the province of Saskatchewan, for example, the Review Committee, which was not composed of people who understood the complexity of women's issues or human rights issues generally,[63] took a formal equality approach and looked for laws that were overtly discriminatory on their face. The Committee tended to focus on a rather simple model of gender equality by ensuring that all laws applied 'equally' to both men and women. The strategies offered by the Committee were also very basic and arguably missed the complexity and difficulty that we now know characterises anti-discrimination law. The Committee recommended, for example, that spousal support provisions be altered so that women and men in opposite sex relationships both owed support obligations to each other and judges were able to award support to husbands in appropriate cases. This legislative move—eventually adopted throughout Canada—arguably overlooked the fact that in reality, women are far more likely to be financially dependent on their male spouses than the other way around.

and security of the person and the right not to be deprived *thereof except in accordance with the principles of fundamental justice*' (emphasis added). For a detailed study of the application of the s 7 liberty interest to family laws concerning parental rights, including the *B(R)* case, see Hester Lessard, *ibid.*

[61] See s 32(2) of the *Charter*.

[62] See Wilson J in *R v Turpin* [1989] 1 SCR 1296 at 1331–32. For a discussion of the evolution of equality jurisprudence in the Supreme Court of Canada, and the tension between formal and substantive approaches to equality, see Lessard et al, *supra* n 6, at 87–99 and Margot Young, 'Sameness/Difference: A Tale of Two Girls', (1997) 4 *RCS* 150–66.

[63] Salina Shrofel, 'Equality Rights and Law Reform in Saskatchewan: An Assessment of the *Charter* Compliance Process', (1985) 1(1) *CJWL* 108–18 at 110.

One author argued that the Saskatchewan Committee made false assumptions about the actual status of the average woman.[64] Thus the law reforms resulting may or may not have addressed the inequalities of women and men in a meaningful way. Shelagh Day expressed the difficulty in an early cautionary note: 'Amendments to definitions of "dependants" and provisions for husbands to make financial claims on their wives can give the false impression that men and women are on an equal economic footing. This juridical equality may obscure the fact of women's continuing economic dependency and vulnerability'.[65] Fortunately, equality jurisprudence in areas such as support law has begun to redress this problem, as will be seen below in the discussion of the *Moge* case.

As a result of the review of legislation, most family law statutes in Canada now are facially neutral in terms of gender; that is, men and women in opposite sex relationships have reciprocal rights and obligations for the most part. As I will explain below, the primary way in which the *Charter* is now invoked in terms of sex equality as between men and women is therefore with regard to judicial *interpretation* of statutory provisions on issues such as spousal support. Because sex equality has been dealt with in legislation, at least in a formal manner, the main way in which family law statutes now seem to violate the *Charter* section 15(1) equality guarantees is through their exclusion of same sex cohabitants, and sometimes opposite sex cohabitants.

Most, but not all, provincial family law statutes now include not only married couples, but also unmarried opposite sex cohabitants in their provisions on spousal support, child support, and child custody and access.[66] As mentioned above, a 1998 section 15 challenge to the Alberta statute that excluded unmarried opposite sex cohabitants from the spousal support definition of 'spouse' was successful in proving discrimination on the basis of marital status (*Taylor v Rossu*).[67] Common law opposite sex partners are now included in the definition.

Provincial laws that have continued to favour married spouses or simply made no reference to common law relationships (whether opposite or same sex), particularly in relation to the division of property upon the dissolution of a relationship or upon the death of one partner, have recently been the subject of *Charter* litigation. In some cases, legislative reform has followed. In the 2000 decision of *Walsh v Bona*,[68] the Nova Scotia Court of Appeal found that the province's *Matrimonial Property Act*, which excluded common law partners from the definition of spouse, was unconstitutional. It prohibited the claimant from obtaining an equal division of assets after her opposite sex common law relationship of ten years broke down. The Atlantic province has since revised its *Vital Statistics Act* to enable individuals to register as domestic partners,

---

[64] Salina Shrofel, 'Equality Rights and Law Reform in Saskatchewan: An Assessment of the *Charter* Compliance Process', (1985) 1(1) *CJWL* 108–18 at 110.

[65] Shelagh Day, 'The Charter and Family Law' in Elizabeth Sloss (ed), *Family Law in Canada: New Directions* (Canadian Advisory Council on the Status of Women, Ottawa 1985) 27–61 at 52.

[66] See Winifred H Holland and Barbra E Stalbecker-Poutney (eds), *Cohabitation: The Law in Canada* (Carswell, Toronto 1990, loose-leaf updated in 1999).

[67] *Taylor v Rossu, supra* n 20.

[68] *Walsh v Bona, supra* n12.

whether same sex or opposite sex. Once registered, various legal rights and duties apply to the partners, including matrimonial property law. In terms of the division of an estate upon the death of one partner who leaves no will, the Saskatchewan case of *Ferguson v Armbrust*[69] found that the word 'spouse' in the province's *Intestate Succession Act*, as well as its *Administration of Estates Act*, should be interpreted broadly to include a common law partner. The court found that if 'spouse' were not interpreted broadly, it would offend the *Charter*. In a similar 2001 case involving a same sex common law couple, an Alberta court struck the provisions defining spouse as between opposite sex couples but did not feel comfortable reading into the impugned *Intestate Succession Act* provisions that would render the Act constitutional.[70]

Discrimination on the basis of sexual orientation has been argued increasingly by lesbians and gay men who want legal recognition of their relationships, and of rights and responsibilities flowing from those relationships analogous to those that unmarried opposite sex cohabitants receive. Some governments have amended their legislation without waiting for a *Charter* challenge to be made, while others have been more resistant to change. The important and successful section 15 *Charter* challenge in *M v H* to the Ontario *Family Law Act* provisions on spousal support, arguing that the definition of 'spouse' should be expanded to include same sex cohabitants, was described above.[71] The Supreme Court of Canada indicated that there could be implications for many other statutes that distribute benefits, rights, and responsibilities on the basis of a definition of 'spouse'. In fact, this probable consequence was a key reason why the Ontario Government resisted the *Charter* challenge.[72] That Government eventually passed amendments (Bill 5, discussed under *Spousal Support*) but rather than expanding its definition of 'spouse' it created a separate category of 'same sex partner'. The federal government also acknowledged the decision's impact on federal legislation that extends benefits to non-married couples. It passed Bill C–23 *An Act to Modernize the Statutes of Canada in Relation to Benefits and Obligations* to extend the same benefits to same sex partners, but cautioned that this did not mean that same sex couples were legally recognised as 'married'. In 1997, British Columbia was the first Canadian province to amend its *Family Relations Act* to include same sex cohabitants in child custody, spousal support, and child support provisions, having chosen not to await the decision of the Supreme Court of Canada.[73] Québec has passed omnibus legislation since the *M v H* decision to treat same sex cohabitants equally with unmarried

---

[69] *Ferguson v Ambrust* (2000), 187 DLR (4th) 367 (Sask Crt QB). See also *Grigg v Berg Estate* 2000, 31 ETR (2d) 214 (BCSC), where although there was a will, the living partner brought a successful *Charter* application against the *Wills Variation Act* which had prohibited common law partners from making claims against the estate for greater support.

[70] *Johnson v Sand* [2001] AJ No 390 (Alta Surrogate Crt) (QL)

[71] *M v H, supra*, n 16. Note that sexual orientation was read into the *Charter* as an analogous protected ground of discrimination in *Egan v Canada* [1995] 2 SCR 513.

[72] 'Same-sex ruling appealed', *The Globe and Mail* (14 Feb, 1997), A4.

[73] *Family Relations Act*, RSBC 1996, c 128, s 1 am. by *Family Relations Amendment Act, 1997*, SBC 1997, c 20 [Bill 31, 1997].

heterosexual cohabitants (but not with married couples). Nova Scotia, Manitoba and Saskatchewan have also made some amendments. However it should be noted that while most provinces have made initial changes, these amendments may not have remedied all previously denied rights.[74] Further *Charter* challenges and legislative reform will undoubtedly ensue.

(2) The Charter's Impact on Judicial Discretion: The Example of Sex Equality

As mentioned above, most family law statutes are now gender neutral on their face, treating male and female opposite sex spouses the same way in relation to spousal support, child support, child custody, and matrimonial property division. In other words, female and male spouses have reciprocal rights and obligations in these fields. Yet the influence of the *Charter* and equality jurisprudence has not stopped there.

In order to understand this point, we must return to the vexed question of the extent to which the *Charter* applies to family law. Section 32 of the *Charter* states that the *Charter* applies to the legislature and government of Canada and each province. This technical legal requirement of government action in order that the *Charter* be invoked, particularly when combined with the powerful familial ideology that dominates in this field, has meant that Supreme Court decisions in this field have been uncertain and unclear. The 1986 *Dolphin Delivery* case[75] seemed to make it clear, for awhile, that 'government' only referred to the executive and administrative branches, and not the judicial branch. For some time, then, it was thought that the *Charter* had no direct application to court orders that were not linked to government action in some other way, to the common law, or to purely private litigation. However, *Dolphin Delivery* did suggest that courts are bound by the *Charter* and that they should develop the law in all fields in a manner that was consistent with *Charter* values.[76] This suggestion allowed some room for *Charter* influence on private law and this opening expanded further with the Supreme Court of Canada's interpretation of the section 15 equality guarantee in the *Andrews* case.[77]

In general, the Supreme Court of Canada has shifted away from a formalistic approach to equality, which, in the sex equality context, effectively posited a goal

[74] Nova Scotia's amendments failed to address the adoption provisions in its *Children and Family Services Act* which restricted adoption to married couples. These inadequacies had to be subsequently challenged, see *Nova Scotia (Birth Registration No.1999–02–004200) (Re)*, *supra* n 36. British Columbia had to address the inadequate reach of its first amendments by later passing the *Definition of Spouse Amendment Act* 1999 SBC c 29. Prior to its coming into force, other matters still had to be resolved by litigation, see *Grigg v Berg Estate*, *supra* n 69)

[75] *Dolphin Delivery*, *supra* n 5.

[76] *Ibid*, at 603. For a discussion of how the Supreme Court of Canada has extended the reach of the *Charter* to the common law in the more recent cases *Canadian Broadcasting Corp v Dagenais*, [1994] 3 SCR 835 and *Hill v Church of Scientology of Toronto* [1995] 2 SCR 1130, see Lessard et al., *supra* n 6, at 144–54.

[77] *Andrews v Law Society of British Columbia* [1989] 1 SCR 143. See Kate Sutherland, 'The New Equality Paradigm: The Impact of *Charter* Equality Principles on Private Law Decisions' in David Schneiderman and Kate Sutherland (eds), *Charting the Consequences: The Impact of Charter Rights on Canadian Law and Politics* (University of Toronto Press, Toronto 1997) 245.

of making women the same as men wherever possible. The court now takes, on the whole, a more complex substantive equality approach,[78] although in any given case, individual judges may apply it differently.[79] Until recently there has been no consensus on the Court in relation to approaches to discrimination.[80] Although there remain differences of opinion on the Court in relation to the appropriate interpretation of section 15(1), the 1999 *Law v Canada* decision suggests that there is general consensus as to the basic principles relating to the purpose of section 15(1) and the proper approach to equality analysis.[81] In that case, Iacobucci J. stated the purpose of section 15(1) for the Court as follows:

> In general terms, the purpose of s 15 (1) is to prevent the violation of essential human dignity and freedom through the imposition of disadvantage, stereotyping, or political or social prejudice, and to promote a society in which all persons enjoy equal recognition at law as human beings or as members of Canadian society, equally capable and equally deserving of concern, respect and consideration.[82]

One of the most significant aspects of the equality decisions of the Supreme Court has been the emphasis, when determining whether a group was disadvantaged, not only on the context of the law that was subject to the challenge, but also on the context of the place of the group in the entire social, political and legal fabric of society. As Wilson J. put it for a unanimous Supreme Court in *R v Turpin*:

> Accordingly, it is only by examining the larger context that a court can determine whether differential treatment results in inequality or whether, contrariwise, it would be identical treatment which would in the particular context result in inequality or foster disadvantage. A finding that there is discrimination will, I think, in most but perhaps not all cases, necessarily entail a search for disadvantage that exists apart from and independent of the particular legal distinction being challenged.[83]

The role of social context in judicial treatment of family law has become increasingly apparent and, indeed, as Wilson J. illustrates, a substantive equality approach necessitates such a contextual analysis. The current position on the *Charter* and private law is that an order of a court in, for example, a custody or access dispute, may not itself be government action that can be challenged directly by invoking the *Charter*. However, the Supreme Court has tended to adopt an approach that the development of the common law, and court orders made under statutes in the context of private litigation, should be made in a manner

---

[78] In fact, Kate Sutherland suggests that it is the embracing of substantive rather than formal equality by the Supreme Court of Canada that has rendered the public/private distinction that the Court articulated in *Dolphin Delivery* more fragile: Sutherland, *ibid*. See, the decision in *Law v Canada* (1999), 170 DLR (4th) 1, where the whole Court adopted an approach to equality, albeit not in a family law context.

[79] See, for example, *M v H, supra* n 16.

[80] Lessard et al., *supra* n 6, at 89–99.

[81] *Law v Canada, supra* n 78, at para 5. See Craig D Bavis, '*Vriend v Alberta, Law v Canada, Ontario v M. and H.*: The Latest Steps on the Winding Path to Substantive Equality', (1999) 37 *ALR* 683–714.

[82] *Law v Canada, ibid*. at para 88.

[83] *R v Turpin, supra* n 62, at 1331–1332. See also *Law v Canada, supra* n 78, at para 30.

consistent with the fundamental values enshrined in the *Charter*, including equality. In the spousal support area, for example, the Court has moved from a formalistic approach based on a belief that spouses should be treated as equals at marriage breakdown regardless of whether they were in fact equally positioned,[84] to a more nuanced approach to equality that takes into account the reality of women's economic inequality at the time of relationship breakdown.

In the 1992 case of *Moge v Moge*,[85] the Supreme Court of Canada suggested that judicial notice be taken of the phenomenon of women's impoverishment on divorce, and the benefits that men often gain in their earning capacity due to the unrecognised work of their female partners in the home. In so doing the Court was influenced by the factum of the intervenor,[86] the Women's Legal Education and Action Fund (LEAF), which urged that the spousal support provisions in the *Divorce Act* must be guided by the *Charter* guarantees of sex equality.[87] Although the Court did not acknowledge explicitly that the spousal support provisions must be interpreted and applied in a manner consistent with constitutional equality standards, L'Heureux-Dubé J implicitly did so when she articulated for the majority of the Court a model of equitable sharing of the economic consequences—both disadvantages and advantages—of the marriage and/or its breakdown. This approach is known as the compensatory model of spousal support. Although compensation is not the only principle that provides a basis for support, the *Moge* case was important in establishing its significance.

The general emphasis in *Moge* on the feminisation of poverty and the economic advantages and disadvantages arising from marriage or marriage-like relationships has been followed in subsequent Supreme Court of Canada cases on constructive trusts[88] and child support, albeit without unanimity of judicial opinion in the latter case. In L'Heureux-Dubé J's concurring judgment in the child support case *Willick v Willick* (but with only McLachlin J and Gonthier J concurring with her), she stated:

> Given the profound economic impact on the parties that may follow from differing interpretations of the Divorce Act's support provisions, it follows that in the present

---

[84] See, for example, *Pelech v Pelech* [1987] 1 SCR 801. Ironically, the majority decision, much criticised by feminist legal scholars, was written by the first female judge on the Supreme Court of Canada, Madame Justice Bertha Wilson. See eg Martha Bailey, '*Pelech, Caron*, and *Richardson*: A Case Comment', (1989) 3(2) *CJWL* 615–33; Brenda Cossman, 'A Matter of Difference: Domestic Contracts and Gender Equity', (1990) 28 *OHLJ* 303–80.

[85] *Moge v Moge*, [1992] 3 SCR 813.

[86] An intervenor is a third party that is permitted to make arguments in order to assist a court in its deliberations. Leave of the court to participate by showing special knowledge related to an aspect of the case must be obtained.

[87] See especially paras 32–44 of the Factum of the Women's Legal Education and Action Fund (LEAF) in *Moge v Moge*, in Women's Legal Education and Action Fund, *Equality and the Charter: Ten Years of Feminist Advocacy Before the Supreme Court of Canada* (Emond Montgomery Publications Limited, Toronto 1996) 323. For a discussion of this case, see Alison Diduck and Helena Orton, 'Equality and Support for Spouses', (1994) 57(5) *Mod L Rev* 68–702.

[88] *Peter v Beblow* [1993] 1 SCR 980. In this case, McLachlin J wrote for the majority of judges, while Cory J wrote a concurring judgment (for L'Heureux-Dubé and Gonthier JJ). Both judgments cited the *Moge* case in their analyses.

case, as it did in Moge, supra, this Court should seek to assure itself that its preferred interpretation is consistent with Charter values of substantive equality rather than with the values of formal equality . . . .[89]

These decisions tend to take into account the value of the child-rearing responsibilities that are typically undertaken by custodial parents, usually mothers, after relationship breakdown, and the economic difficulties often faced by the custodial parents. Thus, a number of Supreme Court judges have effectively interpreted spousal support provisions of the *Divorce Act* 'within a framework that recognises the impact of the continuing gender-based division of labour during marriage and after separation on women's economic status and ability to become self-sufficient'.[90]

This substantive equality approach to spousal support has been widely applauded by women's groups. However, it should be put in perspective.[91] Even though most provincial statutes incorporate some attempt to equalise property entitlements of both spouses at the time of family breakdown, barriers remain to women's ability to obtain spousal support: once the property has been divided, courts tend to view spouses as 'equal' and expect them to be self-sufficient, regardless of whether property has in fact been equally divided or whether the economic positions of the spouses have in fact been equalised. For example, in relation to the division of property upon marital breakdown, the majority of the Supreme Court of Canada in *Boston v Boston*[92] ruled against the spousal support phenomenon known as 'double dipping'. It was ruled that where a spouse receives assets on equalisation in exchange for part of her former spouse's pension entitlement, it is unfair to allow the payee spouse to receive support payments derived from the part of the pension income portioned into the original equalisation. The dissenting judgment noted the repercussion of the majority's ruling will be a greater divergence of living standards between the former spouses. Spousal support awards are made in only a minority of divorces and this pattern has been so for many years.[93] Thus, despite the influence of the substantive equality approach to support, formal equality still retains significant influence.

[89] *Willick v Willick* [1994] 3 SCR 670 at para 52.

[90] See para 44 of the LEAF Factum in *Moge, supra* n 87.

[91] See Mary Jane Mossman, '"Running Hard to Stand Still": The Paradox of Family Law Reform', (1994) 17 *DLJ* 5. Carol Rogerson has provided a detailed study of case law since the *Moge* decision, arguing that although the landscape of spousal support has been transformed, confusion remains about the implications of the compensatory model and enormous variations exist in the quantum of support awarded: 'Spousal Support After *Moge*', (1997) 14 *CFLQ* 281–387.

[92] *Boston v Boston* [2001] SCJ No. 45 (QL). See also *Collins v Canada* (1999), 178 FTR 161 (Fed Ct Trial Division), where the Federal Court of Canada refused to find a provision of the *Old Age Security Act* in violation of s 15 (1) of the *Charter*. Although it discriminated by denying spousal allowance to separated spouses of pension earners, it was a reasonable limit as these single spouses could apply for provincial social assistance.

[93] In the year following separation, only 5% of women without children receive support payments while 35% of women with children receive support (child and spousal) payments. See Diane Galarneau and Jim Sturrock, 'Family Income after Separation', (1997) 9(2) *Perspectives on Labour and Income* 18 at 21–22; Diane Galarneau, 'Income after Separation—People without Children', (1998) 10(2) *Perspectives on Labour and Income* 32 at Table 4.

Furthermore, the substantive equality approach has not been adopted consistently in the family law context. In the child support case mentioned above (*Willick*), Sopinka J writing for the majority noted that a literal approach could produce the same result as a contextual approach in that particular case.[94] Although he acknowledged the relevance of spouses being in unequal positions with regard to their ability to pay, his contextual approach was considerably narrower than that of L'Heureux-Dubé J in her concurring judgement. Sopinka J also responded directly to, and resisted the need for, L'Heureux-Dubé J's lengthy consideration of the inadequacy of child support awards and the gendered nature of family breakdown. He said that use of the *Charter* as an interpretive tool was problematic where other rules of construction made the legislative intention clear.[95]

Moreover, a substantive equality approach was not adopted by a majority of the Supreme Court of Canada in *Thibaudeau*, the case mentioned earlier where a divorced custodial mother challenged the *Income Tax Act* provisions requiring her to pay tax on child support payments received. She failed in part because the Court chose to look at the 'post-divorce family unit' as the relevant unit of comparison rather than looking at divorced women as compared to divorced men. Since the divorced couple as a whole benefited from the tax rules on child support (the inclusion/deduction scheme), no disadvantage was identified by the majority of the Court. The two women judges on the Court dissented. McLachlin J said:

> The fact that no disadvantage results for the couple as a whole in most cases is no bar to concluding that the provision imposes prejudicial treatment on one of its members, the custodial parent.[96]

As well, the majority of the Court felt that if there was a problem, it was a problem for family lawyers to deal with (by 'grossing up' the amounts of child support to take account of taxation) and not a problem with the *Income Tax Act*. In actual fact, the taxation scheme for child support was amended by the federal government after the *Thibaudeau* case, so the *Charter* challenge had an indirect effect after all.[97]

Arguably, a substantive equality approach similar to that taken in *Moge*— recognising women's primary responsibility for the care of children and that interpretation of the best interests of the child test should not impose a detrimental burden on women[98]—could be taken in the child custody field; indeed

---

[94] *Willick v Willick, supra* n.89. See also the separate concurring judgments of L'Heureux-Dubé and Sopinka JJ in *B(G) v G(L)* [1995] 3 SCR 370; and the judgment of McLachlin J in *Moge*, where she emphasised that the case was 'first and last, a case of statutory interpretation' (para 102).

[95] Martha Bailey has pointed out that Sopinka J is inconsistent in his approach to whether the *Charter* should be used as an interpretive tool. He was strongly supportive of this approach in the *Young v Young* case on freedom of religion and child custody and access law. See M Bailey, 'Developments in Family Law: The 1994–95 Term', *supra* n 48, at 335. Sopinka J is no longer on the Court as a result of his death.

[96] *Thibaudeau v R* [1995] 2 SCR 627 at 717.

[97] *Income Tax Act*, RSC 1985 (5th Supp.), c 1, s 56 (1)(b) amended by SC 1997, c 25, s 8 (1); and s 60 (b) amended by SC 1997, c 25, s 10 (1).

[98] See para 23 of the LEAF Factum in *Goertz v Gordon*, in *Ten Years of Feminist Advocacy*, *supra* n. 87, at 477.

the Constitutional Court of South Africa took a similar approach (albeit not in a custody case) in *President of the Republic of South Africa and Another v Hugo*.[99] However, Canadian courts have not taken such a clear substantive equality approach in the custody field. Judges *have* resisted fathers' arguments that the sex equality guarantees mean that there should be a joint custody presumption in child custody law, noting that in cases of contested custody the best interests of the children are paramount.[100] In fact, courts appear to be quite vigilant in protecting their discretion in this field, particularly when they are interpreting the principle of the best interests of the child. Nonetheless, at a more general level, it is clear that judges do acknowledge some of the fathers' rights arguments that they should have more contact with children, always justifying this trend by reference to the children's interests.[101] Indeed some authors argue that rights discourse now inappropriately dominates the field of child custody[102] and that a formal equality approach to the issue is too often applied, as evidenced by the rising popularity of joint custody orders.[103]

Having reviewed recent public hearings on child custody and access law in Canada,[104] I would say that rights discourse is alive and well in this field: despite the supposed focus on a child-centred approach, parental rights discourse is often in evidence. Moreover, fathers' rights discourse may be more palatable than what is perceived to be mothers' rights discourse. The one Supreme Court of Canada judge who has attempted to bring a substantive equality analysis to child custody law remains a minority voice. L'Heureux-Dubé J has argued that the responsibility of primary caregiving and being a custodial parent should bring with itgreater legal deference to that parent's decision-making authority.[105] The 1996 Supreme Court of Canada decision on relocation of custodial parents (*Goertz v Gordon*)[106] demonstrates that her approach is a

[99] *President of the Republic of South Africa and Another v Hugo* (1997), CCT 11/96 (Const Ct South Africa) 38.

[100] *Keyes v Gordon* (1985) 45 RFL (2d) 177 (NSCA). The father in this case had argued that he had a constitutional right to joint custody. See text at n 28 above for discussion.

[101] In a 1998 case, a father who had never lived with the child (approximately one year old at time of judgment), and who lived in New York City whereas the mother and child lived in Ottawa, was awarded joint custody and access rights against the protests of the mother: *Hildinger v Carroll* [1998] OJ No 2898 (QL) (Ont Ct of Justice, General Division).

[102] Karen M Munro, 'The Inapplicability of Rights Analysis in Post-Divorce Child Custody Decision Making', (1992) 30 *ALR* 852–899.

[103] See Susan B Boyd, 'From Gender Specificity to Gender Neutrality? Ideologies in Canadian Child Custody Law' in Carol Smart and Selma Sevenhuijsen (eds), *Child Custody and the Politics of Gender* (Routledge, London 1989) 126 at 136–48.

[104] In 1998, a Special Joint Committee consisting of Senators and Members of Parliament reviewed custody and access law, as a result of the protests of fathers' rights groups in 1997: these groups said that if fathers had to pay child support under the new child support guidelines in the *Divorce Act*, then they should be able to see their children more frequently. See the Report of the Special Joint Committee on Child Custody and Access, *For the Sake of the Children*, Joint Chairs The Honourable Landon Pearson and Roger Galloway, MP (Dec 1998) (available on http://www.parl.gc.ca).

[105] *Young v Young, supra* n 40.

[106] *Goertz v Gordon, supra* n 47. See Susan B Boyd, 'Child Custody, Relocation, and the Post-Divorce Family Unit: *Gordon v Goertz* at the Supreme Court of Canada', (1997) 9(2) *CJWL* 447–68.

minority one, although in actual practice, some courts do take primary caregiving into account.

Overall, then, in its application to family law, section 15 of the *Charter* has facilitated the introduction of a social context analysis into judicial determinations especially of economic issues. The desirability of this approach remains somewhat controversial and its impact in fields such as child custody law remains uncertain.

D. CONCLUSION

In conclusion, the *Canadian Charter of Rights and Freedoms* has had tangible effects on family law: first, through the reviews of legislation to ensure that it conformed to the *Charter*; secondly, through the court challenges that have been brought to statutory provisions that are problematic when subjected to *Charter* scrutiny; thirdly, through the indirect effect that the introduction of the *Charter* has had on Canadian courts and legal argument and discourse generally. As a result of the increased use of intervenor status, groups such as the Women's Legal Education and Action Fund[107] have appeared before courts to make contextual arguments that the litigants to a case may not be prepared or able to make. In fact, the Government of Canada has provided funding to a Court Challenges Program that enables equality seeking groups, or an individual from a historically disadvantaged group, to prepare arguments related to equality rights and federal (not provincial) legislation or actions. Both parties and intervenors can be funded under this programme.

As we have seen, even when the *Charter* is not invoked explicitly, some judges have attempted to interpret common law principles and to render decisions in familial disputes in a manner that is consistent with the fundamental values embodied in the *Charter*.[108] Indeed, some would say that the legal system, legal argument, and in particular the judiciary, has been altered quite significantly as a result, not least due to the increased use of social science evidence in the *Charter* adjudication process. Many judges have attended 'judicial education' programmes which often emphasise the social context of law, including racial and sexual inequality. Moreover, even when *Charter* challenges have failed to persuade a court, in some instances legislation has been changed by a government nonetheless (as in the *Thibaudeau* case). Despite the fact that it is characterised as a realm of 'private law,' Canadian family law has not escaped the reach of this *Charter*-influenced legal world.

---

[107] Not all intervenors are 'progressive' or equality seeking groups. For example, 'REAL' Women of Canada intervened in the *M v H* case on lesbian spousal support claims, arguing against expansion of 'spouse' to include same sex couples.

[108] It seems, however, that the courts are more deferential to the common law than they are to governments in applying *Charter* principles: see David Schneiderman and Kate Sutherland, 'Conclusion: Towards an Understanding of the Impact of the Charter of Rights on Canadian Law and Politics' in David Schneiderman and Kate Sutherland (eds), *Charting the Consequences: The Impact of Charter Rights on Canadian Law and Politics* (University of Toronto Press, Toronto 1997) 343 at 347.

10

Incorporation of the European Convention on Human Rights: What Will it Mean for Scotland's Children?

LILIAN EDWARDS*

A. INTRODUCTION

WHAT DIFFERENCE, if any, will the incorporation of the European Convention for the Protection of Human Rights and Fundamental Freedoms (ECHR) make to the legal rights, remedies and status of Scotland's children? More than one in five people in Scotland are children or young persons under the age of 18, a not insubstantial portion of the population. Yet the otherwise heated debate pre-incorporation of the ECHR on how a Bill of Rights was likely to affect the legal culture of the United Kingdom until recently remained remarkably reserved on this point. This seems odd, given that child law in general, and childrens' rights in particular, have never had a higher profile either at the international or the domestic level. In Scotland, as in England and Wales and other Western nations, the late 1980s and 1990s were a period of dynamic growth and change in the law relating to children and parents. We saw the emergence of what has been termed 'child-centred' law in the shape of the Children Act 1989 in England and more recently, the Children (Scotland) Act 1995 in Scotland. Simultaneously, the issue of children's rights attained a high profile among policy-makers, with considerable attention devoted in particular to meeting the demands of the leading international instrument in the area, the United Nations Convention on the Rights of the Child (the 'UN Convention').[1] It is now standard practice in policy documents relating to child law to pay ritual obeisance to the articles of the UN Convention and in particular to Article 12, which guarantees the child a participatory voice in decisions affecting his or her interests. In Scotland, the UN Convention was considered and allowance made for it in the *Review of Scottish Child Care Law* (1991), the Scottish Law

---

* Senior Lecturer in Law, University of Edinburgh.

[1] Adopted 28 November 1989, reprinted in (1989) 28 *ILM* 1448, and ratified by the UK on 16 Dec 1991.

Commission *Report on Family Law* (1992)[2] and the White Paper *Scotland's Children* (1993),[3] all of which made important contributions to the eventual shape of the Children (Scotland) Act 1995. Scotland now has a special Minister for Children and Education (currently Jack McConnell MSP) and an express Child Strategy Statement[4] which requires that future legislative and policy initiatives originating from the Scottish Executive be checked for compliance with the interests of children and, especially, the UN Convention. On the academic front, the last few years have seen two editions of one book entirely devoted to assessing how Scots law measures up to the UN Convention[5] and an extensive debate around the area.[6] We have also grown used to seeing dicta referring to the UN Convention in child law cases such as the influential House of Lords access case *Sanderson v McManus*.[7]

All this activity around the UN Convention—a global document—rather than the ECHR—our leading regional human rights document—was in some ways slightly bizarre. It would perhaps have seemed more natural for the ECHR to have been the focus for the children's rights lobby, especially after the spotlight was placed on it by the prospect of incorporation from the time of the first Blair election victory. The European Convention has after all always had the significant advantage over the UN Convention that it has teeth, in the shape of the possibility of individual complaint to the European Court of Human Rights (ECtHR). Incorporation has made it an intrinsic part of domestic law which can be freely called upon without the cumbersome need to go all the way to Strasbourg. Throughout the United Kingdom, since the passing of the Human Rights Act 1998, government departments have been required to review draft legislation to ensure it complies with the ECHR, and a declaration of compatibility to this effect must be made when the legislation is promulgated.[8] Furthermore in Scotland, the competence of the Scottish Parliament to legislate is constitutionally limited by the duties imposed in the ECHR.[9] Since the Human Rights Act 1998 came into force throughout the UK, it has been possible for Westminster legislation to be declared incompatible with the ECHR and then speedily amended by a fast-track procedure,[10] and courts are under an

---

[2] Scot Law Com No 135 (1992).

[3] Cm 2286 (1993).

[4] Available at http://www.scotland.gov.uk/frame2l.htm.

[5] A Cleland and E Sutherland (eds), *Children's Rights in Scotland* 2nd edn (W Green, Edinburgh, 2001); 1st edn (W Green, Edinburgh, 1996).

[6] See inter alia K Marshall, *Children's Rights in the Balance: the Participation–Protection Debate* (Stationery Office, London, 1997); K Tisdall, *The Children (Scotland) Act 1995: Developing Policy and Law for Scotland's Children*, (Stationery Office, London, 1997); L Edwards and A Griffiths, *Family Law* (W Green, Edinburgh, 1997), ch 4; K Marshall 'The Scottish Parliament and the Rights of the Child' in A Miller (ed), *Human Rights: A Modern Agenda* (T & T Clark, Edinburgh, 2000).

[7] *Sanderson v McManus* 1997 SC (HL) 55. For discussion see text of n 85.

[8] Human Rights Act 1998, s 19.

[9] Scotland Act 1998, s 29(2)(d).

[10] Human Rights Act 1998, s 4(2) and s 10 and Sch 2.

obligation if necessary wholly to re-interpret common law principles and rules so that they can become compatible with the Convention.[11]

The UN Convention on the Rights of the Child, by contrast, has the status only of an ordinary international treaty, not binding in domestic law, and is enforced only by the obligation on state parties to submit reports on compliance to a central UN Committee on the Rights of the Child. Although the UN Committee's response in 1995 to the UK's first report on implementation was trenchantly critical,[12] there were hardly tidal waves of appalled public opinion as a result. The ECHR would thus seem a far better bet for making serious headway in the fields of children's rights, and indeed has already had significant domestic impact prior to the arrival of the Human Rights Act 1998, in particular in the field of corporal punishment; such punishment was outlawed in state-supported schools, following the case of *Campbell and Cosans v United Kingdom* in 1982[13] and more recently, the case of *A v United Kingdom*,[14] in which a nine-year old boy sought redress in Strasbourg because UK law had failed adequately to prosecute his stepfather for the savage beatings he had suffered, has re-opened the entire debate about the legitimacy of corporal punishment of children even within the family home.[15] It is notable that a decision of the ECHR has aroused frantic governmental activity in this area, whereas the recommendations made in a Report of the Scottish Law Commission on the matter have languished unimplemented as too controversial since 1992.[16]

Yet if one looks at the genesis of the Human Rights Act 1998, there was initially a surprising silence on the issue of how it might affect the rights of children. The UK White Paper on the incorporation of the ECHR, *Rights Brought Home: the Human Rights Bill*,[17] nowhere mentioned that incorporation might have implications for children, although mention was made both of the rights of parents (in relation to the education of their children) and of spouses. The children's rights lobbying community seem, as noted above, to have focused their indefatigable activity principally upon the UN Convention, even although its provisions when cited in domestic courts have merely rhetorical strength. There seemed a degree of surprise that the ECHR even applied to children. There was very little written on how the ECHR interacted with children's rights in the UK prior to the enactment of the Human Rights Act 1998 and even those who addressed the issue seemed to feel constrained to start with such

---

[11] Human Rights Act 1998, s 6(3) and s 8(1).

[12] See comment in J Grant, 'Could Do Better: The Report on the United Kingdom's Compliance with the Convention on the Rights of the Child' 1995 *JR* 534 and Marshall, *Children's Rights in the Balance*, above, n 6, 28–29.

[13] *Campbell and Cosans v United Kingdom* (1982) 4 EHRR 293.

[14] *A v United Kingdom* (1999) 27 EHRR 611 (decision of European Court of Human Rights), see further text to n 25 below.

[15] See *The Physical Punishment of Children: A Consultation* (Scottish Executive Justice Department, Edinburgh, Feb 2000); and news release of 6 Sept 2001 that the Scottish Parliament plans to legislate to ban entirely smacking of children under 3.

[16] See Scot Law Com No 135, above, n 2, para 2.67 ff.

[17] Cm 3782 (1997).

apparently unnecessary statements as 'Human rights are not for adults only. Children, too, are protected by human rights'.[18]

The absence of a children's rights dimension around the time of implementation of the ECHR seemed all the odder given the relatively uncritical approbation which generally seems to meet the whole idea of rights for children—as Freeman has famously said, 'Children's rights [have] become something of a hurrah idea. We all claim to be in favour.'[19] It is little known, for example, but also arouses little surprise, that more accessions have been made by states to the UN Convention than to any other international human rights instrument.[20] It seems remarkable then that so little attention was paid to the children's rights implications of the ECHR prior to incorporation.[21]

The answers to these conundrums, it is often suggested, lie in the origins of the ECHR in the aftermath of World War II and the experience of living under Nazi and Stalinist totalitarian regimes.[22] As such it was primarily aimed at protecting the individual citizen's rights from arbitrary interference by the *state*. Children's rights, however, are most often impaired *not* by state interference, but by the acts of those individuals who protect, guide or represent the child, most significantly, their parents. Children, depending on their age and circumstances, lack the physical competence, and economic and social power to act on their own, and so their rights and freedoms are crucially dependent on the assistance and attitude of adults. The attitude of both state governments and defenders of human rights has often been that children's rights are guaranteed not by the state, but by their parents; the rights of children being seen therefore as a private, not a public responsibility.[23] In fact, however, this simply means that children's rights are more likely to be infringed by parents than directly by state organs.

This, however, is not the whole of the problem. The ECHR, it is often said, has been interpreted as a living instrument and its case law has the potential to transcend its origins. The jurisprudence of the ECtHR makes it clear that states can have *positive* obligations imposed on them to intervene where the rights of

---

[18] L Smith,'Children, Parents and the European Human Rights Convention' in J Eekelaar and P Sarcevic (eds), *Parenthood in Modern Society* (Martinus Nijhoff, Dordrecht, 1993).

[19] M Freeman, *The Rights and Wrongs of Children* (Pinter, London, 1983), 6.

[20] 191 countries have acceded, the notable exception being the United States. See S Kilbourne, 'The Wayward Americans—Why the US has not Ratified the UN Convention on the Rights of the Child' (1998) 10 *CFLQ* 243.

[21] Texts which considered the issue prior to the enactment of Human Rights Act 1998 included Smith, above, n 18; Children in Scotland, *Children's Rights = Human Rights?*, (Children in Scotland, Edinburgh, 1998); G Douglas, 'The Family and the State under the European Convention on Human Rights' (1988) 2 *IJLF* 76; J Liddy 'The Concept of Family Law under the European Convention on Human Rights' [1998] *EHRLR* 15.

[22] See eg A Miller, 'The European Convention on Human Rights: What Does It Mean for Children in Scotland?' in *Children's Rights = Human Rights?*, above, n 21; Smith, above, n 18, 450; J Fortin, 'The HRA's Impact on Litigation Involving Children and their Families' (1999) 3 *CFLQ* 237, at 239–40.

[23] See M. Minow, 'Rights for the Next Generation: A Feminist Approach to Childrens' Rights' (1986) 9 *HWLJ* 1.

individuals are threatened by the actions of other individuals—the so-called 'horizontal effect.'[24] It can for example be a breach of a child's rights under Article 3 if a state does not pass laws sufficient to restrain a father from violently punishing his child.[25] It can be a breach of a child's rights *and* a father's rights to respect for their family life if the state does not provide laws adequate to persuade the mother that she should allow the father contact with the child pursuant to a legitimate court order.[26] The most pressing remaining problem with ECHR jurisprudence, however, is that it does not seem to have developed a full awareness of the fact that because children are dependent on adults, usually their parents, *conflicts* will inevitably arise between the rights and wishes of children and those of their parents, which will need to be resolved.

To take an example, a child's right to choose his or her own religion (guaranteed by Article 9) inherently conflicts with the child's *parents'* right to insist that a child is brought up in the family creed (which may be seen as part of the right to respect for family life[27]). In child abuse cases, the child's right to freedom from ill-treatment under Article 3, may conflict with the parents' rights to respect for privacy and family life under Article 8, and the parents' due process rights under Article 6 may make investigation of the abuse almost impossible. The Convention makes little attempt to anticipate or resolve these conflicts, even where they present themselves most obviously. For example, Article 2 of the First Protocol (to which the UK is a signatory) demands respect by the state for the *parent*'s right to determine how their children should be educated. There is no 'exemption' clause demanding that the state balance the rights of (say) the sufficiently mature child to make their own choices in this area.

This raises a connected problem. At the time the Convention was drafted, children were still largely seen as the objects rather than the subjects of legal processes, with the main aim of the law being to protect them, rather than to award them autonomous rights. It is unsurprising therefore that children are never explicitly named as the holders of rights within the ECHR, nor is there any explicit mention of the welfare principle as a restriction on parental rights. By contrast, the UN Convention, drafted rather later—1989 rather than 1950—is self-consciously 'child-centred'. Unlike the ECHR, the UN Convention not only adopts as a central tenet the primacy of the child's best interests (in Article 3), but more importantly, adds to the child's right to be protected the more modern notion of the right to participate, and grapples with the problem of conflicts between the rights of parent and child as the child matures and develops his or her own wishes. Article 5 of the UN Convention in particular expressly provides

[24] See further M Hunt, 'The "Horizontal Effect" of the Human Rights Act' [1998] *PL* 423; and MacQueen and Brodie's discussion of how horizontal effect has operated in UK case law post-incorporation elsewhere in this volume (141 ff.)

[25] See *A v United Kingdom,* above, n 14, discussed below.

[26] See *Glaser v United Kingdom* [2000] FCR 193.

[27] See eg *Hoffmann v Austria* (1993) 17 EHRR 293 (although that case involved intra-parent conflict rather than parent–child conflict).

that whilst parents have responsibility for the direction and guidance of their children, it must be *provided in a manner consistent with the evolving capacity of children*. Neither the ECHR itself nor its subsequent interpretative case law has yet developed this idea of the incremental growth in competence and rights of the child as he or she matures, an idea which is found in many domestic legal systems and which has pervaded English and Scottish child law as a break on paternalistic action ever since the case of *Gillick v West Norfolk and Wisbech Area Health Authority* reached the House of Lords.[28]

The Children (Scotland) Act 1995, in particular, explicitly requires, first, that the sufficiently mature child[29] be given a chance to express a view to which due regard must be given by the court, when a court order is sought relating to parental rights and responsibilities in respect of that child (s 11(7)), and secondly, that any person (not just a court) must, when reaching a major decision relating to a child, have regard to that child's views (s 6). Furthermore in relation to the particular area of medical consent, it has been accepted since *Gillick* in both Scotland and England that the consent of a sufficiently mature child cannot be vetoed by parents. There is then a serious danger that incorporation of the ECHR might actually set back the progress that has been made in domestic UK child law in allowing children participation as well as protection rights.[30] This is sometimes described as a conflict between 'rights' discourse[31] and 'welfarism' or 'utility,'[32] but it might also be seen merely as a conflict between two different versions of rights-speech. Either way, many commentators agree that the rights emphasis the ECHR brings with it is unlikely to be good news for children unless it is employed extremely skilfully by children and their advocates. As Fortin has argued,[33] unless the various judges of the United Kingdom show willingness to interpret the provisions of the ECHR in a child-centred way, the result may well be that parents will use the new instrument to pursue their own rights at the expense of those of their children.

Finally, the ECHR and the UN Convention deal with different categories of rights and emphasise different aspects of rights. The ECHR, like most human rights instruments of its vintage, is only concerned with civil/political rights and not with social/economic rights. For adults, civil and political rights are central to securing the autonomy they need to shape the rest of their lives. But for children, lacking autonomy and the ability to amass resources independently, social

---

[28] *Gillick v West Norfolk and Wisbech Area Health Authority* [1986] 1 AC 112.

[29] Sufficient maturity is presumed when the child is 12 or over (s 11(10)).

[30] Article 53 of the ECHR prohibits the Convention being used in ways which might derogate from existing rights guaranteed to individuals under another international agreement to which the State is party. However it says nothing about the Convention implicitly reducing the rights guaranteed by a state's domestic law.

[31] See discussion in Susan Boyd's contribution to this volume.

[32] See further Herring, 'The Human Rights Act and the Welfare Principle in Family Law—Conflicting or Complementary?' (1999) 11 *CFLQ* 223.

[33] J Fortin, *Children's Rights and the Developing Law* (Butterworths, London, Edinburgh, Dublin, 1998), 260–62.

and economic rights involving claims *to* resources, such as rights to health or leisure, rather than the rights to be left free *from* interference which are typical of the ECHR, are arguably far more important.[34] Again, the UN Convention stands in stark contrast to the ECHR in dealing with the full gamut of social/economic rights (though of course how far they are then implemented by states is another story).

The difficulties for children of a lack of positive participation rights to add to the protective freedoms from interference which are characteristic of the ECHR, are particularly apparent when looking at the right of access to legal representation;[35] a right which is clearly crucial to the securing of their rights by children who in their nature cannot generally navigate the legal process without adult representation. The most obvious and natural representative of a child is his or her parent or parents. Yet as we have stated, it is more than probable that the opposition to, or infringement of, a child's rights comes from that parent or parents themselves. Children therefore must be assured of access to independent legal representation, or all other human rights they might theoretically claim will become illusory. One of the central planks of the UN Convention is Article 12, which both guarantees that the child will have the right to express views in civil and administrative proceedings affecting that child, and also expressly states that this right may be exercised directly or via a representative. There is no equivalent right in the ECHR. Such guarantees for children must be found if at all in Article 6 of the ECHR which guarantees rights to due process and a fair hearing. In the jurisprudence of the ECHR however (discussed below), Article 6 has rarely been used to justify the rights of children against their parents and, in one of the few cases involving Scots children, has arguably acted positively to reduce rather than increase the rights guaranteed children as the cost of guaranteeing rights of parents.[36] However there are signs in the recent ECtHR cases following the English House of Lords case of *X v Bedfordshire*[37] that Article 6 guarantees of access to justice can be used to provide sauce for the gosling as well as the goose—although so far only in relation to actions against the state, not parents or family. Meanwhile the first domestic Scottish case on the children's hearings process and its conformity to Article 6, *S v Miller*,[38] has already had reverberations which have sent shockwaves through the entire system. It remains to be seen to what extent British judges will choose to view Article 6 as guaranteeing explicit rights of representation to children in the civil courts, where problematic cases often arise when eg parents claim they can adequately represent

---

[34] It is interesting to note that the new South African Constitution (1996), one of the most extensive in the world, guarantees children economic rights to family care, basic nutrition, shelter, basic health care etc, and declares the child's best interests to be paramount, but says nothing about participation rights (Article 28).

[35] See also the problem of confidentiality encountered in the *Dosoo* and *McGrath* cases, discussed below at text to nn 109–11.

[36] See the discussion of *McMichael v United Kingdom* (1995) 20 EHRR 205 at nn 73–76.

[37] Discussed at text to n 93.

[38] *S v Miller* 2001 SLT 531.

their childrens' views, and so legal aid should not be wasted on independent representation.[39]

What we find then is a paradox. The UN Convention is well suited to advancing the interests and rights of children but almost wholly lacks teeth in terms of domestic enforceability. The ECHR is far from the ideal starting point for pursuing the interests *or* rights of children but has an excellent international enforcement mechanism and has been incorporated into domestic law. To misquote the well-known aphorism, if one was looking to promote the rights of children in UK domestic law by the use of international human rights standards, one would not start from here.[40]

B. THE CHILD-RELATED JURISPRUDENCE OF THE STRASBOURG COURT

Notwithstanding the problems surveyed above, a substantial jurisprudence *has* been developed in the ECtHR and Commission which relates to issues affecting children. It is worth briefly surveying this case law to see if in practice the ECHR can be of benefit to children even if the instrument itself does not formally talk of their rights. Much of this jurisprudence derives from Article 8, which requires states to respect the right to family life, and from Article 14, which forbids all types of discrimination. It can loosely be divided into seven main areas:[41]

(i) *cases where a child has been taken into care by the state on welfare grounds* eg because parents (or one parent) are an unfit carer or unable to cope. Parents or other relatives may then argue that they are being denied rights to have care of or contact with the child contrary to Article 8. The ECtHR has consistently recognised that child and parent have as part of family life a right to mutual enjoyment of each other's company and this can only be terminated by the state where the means used are proportionate to a legitimate aim or are 'necessary in a democratic society.'[42]

---

[39] See further L Edwards, 'Hearing the Voice of the Child: Notes from the Scottish Experience' in C J Davel (ed), *Children's Rights in a Transitional Society* (Protea, Pretoria, 1999), 54–55.

[40] It should be noted that there also exists a European instrument of later vintage than the ECHR which is relevant: the European Convention on the Exercise of Childrens' Rights (ECECR). This was adopted by the Council of Europe on 8 Sept 1995 and has been signed by 13 member states but only ratified by two. The UK has so far done neither, and thus it can be ignored for the current purposes of this article. However even if the UK does at some point sign and ratify, and the Convention comes into force (which it will on three ratifications), the general view of commentators is that the ECECR gives only very weak protection to childrens' rights, particularly when in conflict with parental rights. See further C Sawyer 'One Step Forward and Two Steps Back: the European Convention on the Exercise of Childrens' Rights' (1999) 11 *CFLQ* 151.

[41] See for some excellent summaries of the area, Douglas, above, n 21; D Feldman 'The Developing Scope of Article 8 of the European Convention on Human Rights' [1997] 3 *EHRLR* 265; D Feldman, *Civil Liberties and Human Rights in England and Wales* (Clarendon Press, Oxford, 1993), ch 11, S Farran, *The UK Before the European Court of Human Rights* (Blackstone, London, 1996), ch 8; S Grosz, 'Article 8', in S Grosz, J Beatson, and P Duffy, *Human Rights, the 1998 Act and the ECHR* (Sweet & Maxwell, London, 2000).

[42] See eg *W v United Kingdom* (1987) 10 EHRR 29.

(ii) *cases where an intra-parental or family dispute*—most commonly divorce—*has resulted in one side losing custody of, or contact, with a child, possibly by court order.* In principle the ECtHR has refused to recognise that denial of residence (custody) to one parent on breakdown of the parental relationship infringes the right to respect for family life under Article 8, since in any event in these cases, one parent would have to accept a degree of separation from their child.[43] However, there is *still* room to make claims under Article 8, combined with Article 14, where the issue of contact or care is affected by discrimination, principally where such discrimination arises because the child's parents were not married to each other.[44] Procedural rules forbidding *any* unmarried father from applying for contact, eg, would clearly be contrary to Article 14.

(iii) *cases other than those in (i) and (ii) above, where discrimination is alleged contrary to Article 14 in respect of the parent's relationship with the child* eg where it affects issues such as succession rights, or title to sue. An interesting and influential case is *Soderback v Sweden*,[45] where the Commission agreed that an unmarried father's right to respect for family life had been violated because he, unlike a married father, did not have to give consent for the adoption of the child by the mother and her new husband.

(iv) *cases involving the rights of parents, teachers or other carers to use corporal punishment on children.* Claims are made under Article 3 (which prohibits the use of inhuman or degrading treatment or punishment), and also under Article 8.[46]

(v) *cases where family unity or reunion is threatened by the deportation of family member(s), or refusal of immigration rights to family member(s).* A multitude of claims have been made under this head under Article 8, although in the majority of cases the state is found to have acted within its margin of appreciation.[47] The plea may also be a two-edged sword, as a state may legitimately meet a demand for family unity under Article 8 by deporting the whole family rather than just one member.[48]

(vi) cases involving *rights of access by parents and children to public records relating to family life* eg of social work involvement with the child. Successful claims have been made under Articles 8 and 14, notably in the

---

[43] *X v Sweden,* Appl No 172/56.

[44] The leading case on discrimination in relation to parental relationship with children born outwith marriage is *Marckx v Belgium* (1979) 2 EHRR 330. See for an interesting analysis of how unmarried fathers might use ECHR jurisprudence to bolster their rights in English law, A Bainham, 'When is a Parent not a Parent? Reflections on the Unmarried Father and his Child in English Law' (1989) 3 *IJLF* 208.

[45] *Soderback v Sweden* 33124/96 [1998] EHRR 342.

[46] See eg *Campbell and Cosans v United Kingdom,* n 13; *Y v United Kingdom* (1992) 17 EHRR 238.

[47] See eg *Gil v Switzerland* (1996) 22 EHRR 93. An unusual case where Art 8 was successfully asserted in this field is *Meheni v France,* Case No 85/1996/704/896.

[48] See eg *Jaramillo v United Kingdom,* Appl No 24865/94.

leading cases of *Gaskin v United Kingdom*[49] and *McMichael v United Kingdom*[50] (discussed below).

(vii) cases involving *the rights of children to education* (including the right to special types of education, not to be excluded from school, to be educated in conformity with particular religious or other beliefs, etc). A number of claims have been made by parents acting for or with their children in this area, under Article 2 of the First Protocol to the ECHR, which states that no person shall be denied the right to education. Article 2 is however problematic in a childrens' rights context, since (as has been noted above) its second sentence guarantees *parents*' rights to make choices about the education of their children, while saying nothing about a *child's* right to such choice. It has been suggested that this will be a particularly fruitful area for litigation post-incorporation, as at present the English and Scottish educational systems offer remarkably little in the way of rights substantive or procedural to children *or* parents.[51] For example, until recently there was no opportunity for a child to appeal against the decision to exclude that child from school (although *parents* did have such a right[52]), and even such rights of parental choice of schooling as do exist in the UK have often been seen as effectively unenforceable.[53] Recent legislation rushed through the Scottish Parliament may have inelegantly plugged some of the more obvious human rights gaps.[54] However, it is still dubious if this Article will be much used to assert the rights of children as different actors to their parents. Cases under this Article brought to Strasbourg seem almost invariably to have been instigated by parents, and the main difficulty which impedes success seems to be the state's protestations that it is restricted in what educational choices it can offer by issues of resources.[55] The rights of children *per se* are rarely if ever raised. In education, however, particularly in relation to special needs education cases,[56] it may be that child-parent conflict is not as major an issue as it may be in all the other categories.

What even this most cursory survey reveals is more bad news: that these cases are overwhelmingly concerned, both in practice and in formulation, with the

---

[49] *Gaskin v United Kingdom* [1990] 1 FLR 167.

[50] *McMichael v United Kingdom*, above, n 36.

[51] Statistics of calls made to the helpline at the English Child Law Centre based at Essex University indicate that the highest number of enquiries were made about education-related disputes. This is thought to reflect the lack of access to legal representation, or local authority ombudsmen, currently offered by the UK law in this area. Anecdotal evidence from the Scottish Child Law Centre also places education at the top of their enquiry list.

[52] See Education (Scotland) Act 1980, s 28H.

[53] See eg *Harvey v Strathclyde Regional Council* 1989 SLT 612.

[54] See the Standards in Scotland's Schools etc Act 2000, s 41.

[55] This is particularly so because of the UK's reservation to Art 2 of the Protocol which is preserved in the Human Rights Act 1998, s 15. See eg *X v United Kingdom* (1978) 14 DR 179, and the special needs cases cited at n 56 below.

[56] See eg *Family H v United Kingdom* (1984) 37 DR 105; *Graeme v United Kingdom* (1990) 64 DR 158: 21 EHRR 104.

rights of *parents*, and not of *children*. The issues they deal with are (to name but a few)

— whether a *father* can be treated less well than a *mother* in relation to the award of access or care rights merely because he is or was not married to the mother;
— whether *parents* can be arbitrarily denied access to a child in care;
— whether a *parent* has a right to read confidential reports prepared by social workers concerning their child;[57]
— whether a *parent* has the right to remain in a country despite (say) criminal behaviour or illegal entry, so as to stay in touch with his or her children;
— whether a *parent*, rather than a cash-strapped local authority, should have the last word on what education a special needs child should get.

Although in some of the cases surveyed above, children are joined as applicant parties, very few cases indeed involve a *child* asserting a right which is in contradistinction to the right of a parent, and fewer still involve a child independently bringing the proceedings in question without the representation of a parent. Some of this, of course, is simply to do with practical concerns. The logistical and financial problems involved in taking a case to Strasbourg are intimidating for an adult, let alone a child. Furthermore, it was only recently that the law in Scotland and England was clarified to remove any doubt that a child had independent capacity to hire a solicitor and seek legal aid in civil matters.[58] Unsurprisingly, only a handful of cases has been brought to the Commission by children in their own right. There have of course been some notable exceptions, particularly in the area of corporal punishment, such the recent case of *A v United Kingdom*,[59] discussed above.[60] Nevertheless on the whole a jurisprudence has been generated which, as the Council of Europe itself recognised by commissioning a special report on the matter in 1987,[61] is adult-oriented, parent-centred, and fails adequately to consider children's rights.

A classic example of how this operates can be seen by looking at the most famous UK corporal punishment case, *Campbell and Cosans v United Kingdom*,[62] where the application was made jointly by the *parents* of children who had been caned at school, and the *children* themselves. No violation of

---

[57] This is drawn from the *McMichael* case, above, n 36. However in *Gaskin v United Kingdom*, above, n 49 the case did relate to the child's own rights (having attained adulthood) to access records of his foster care.

[58] See in Scotland, Age of Legal Capacity (Scotland) Act 1991, s 2(4A) and (4B) (as inserted by the Children (Scotland) Act 1995) and in England, Children Act 1989, s 10(8), and Family Proceedings Rules 1991 (SI 1991 No 1247) r 4.7.

[59] *A v United Kingdom* [1998] EHRLR 82 (Commission); violation upheld by Court, 23 Sept 1998, see n 14.

[60] X had been charged with assault but escaped conviction on the defence of reasonable chastisement under English law.

[61] J Eekelaar and R Dingwall, *Human Rights* (Report to the Council of Europe) (Council of Europe, Strasborg, 1987).

[62] *Campbell and Cosans v United Kingdom*, above, n 13.

Article 3 was proven as the punishment was insufficiently severe to amount to 'inhuman or degrading treatment'. However, the parents succeeded in winning the day on the basis of Article 8, as the school, by caning their children against their 'philosophical objections', had interfered with their rights as part of their family life to make decisions relating to parental rights in respect of their children. Eventually, the UK government, faced with a potential scenario where some children could be legally caned and others not, according to the whims of their parents, decided it was only practical to comply with the judgment by banning corporal punishment in state-funded schools entirely. It is entirely consonant with the parent-centred nature of ECHR jurisprudence that a case which is sometimes seen as a victory for children's rights, was in fact constructed entirely by concern for *parental* rights.

It is of course possible for the ECtHR to consider as relevant children's rights, even within the ambit of cases brought to assert the rights of parents by plaintiff parents. However in most cases brought by parents, the court and Commission seem most commonly to assume that the children's interests are identical with their parents. The court has repeatedly asserted in cases concerning parent's claims that parent and child have a 'mutual interest in the enjoyment of family life.'[63] The issue of conflict between parents and child's interests—eg the idea that children might wish to *cease* contact their parents—is thereby rendered invisible. Another practical point is that the court simply has little *opportunity* to consider the interests of children. There is no procedural requirement on the ECtHR or Commission to hear submissions presenting the view of the child who is not a party, nor to appoint some equivalent of a curator *ad litem* to speak to the child's interest, and it may often be in the interests of neither parent nor state to present the child's side.[64]

There *is* much evidence in recent years of an awareness that children have interests that must be taken into account as much as the Convention rights of their parents in deciding whether a state has acted correctly. In *Olssen v Sweden (No 2)*,[65] parents whose children had been removed due to lack of care claimed the state had breached their Article 8 rights in failing to take sufficient measures to *reunite* them with their children, who were now apparently happily settled with new foster parents. The ECtHR expressly noted that where contact with the natural parents would harm or interfere with the rights of the *children*, the authorities had to strike a fair balance between the child's and parent's rights. This appears to be the first occasion when the court acknowledged that Article 8 requires such a balancing exercise.[66] This approach has been followed up in

---

[63] See eg *Berrehab v Netherlands*, (1988) 11 EHRR 322; *Anderson v Sweden* (1992) 14 EHRR 615.

[64] Interestingly, in *Z v United Kingdom* and *TP and KM v United Kingdom*, discussed below, Professor Geraldine van Bueren, Director of the Programme on International Rights of the Child, University of London, was given leave to intervene and submit a written brief.

[65] *Olssen v Sweden (No 2)* (1994) 17 EHRR 134.

[66] See comment in C Barton and G Douglas, *Law and Parenthood* (Butterworths, London, 1995), 38.

subsequent cases such as *Hokkanen v Finland*,[67] *Glaser v United Kingdom*,[68] and especially *Elsholtz v Germany*[69] where the ECtHR went so far as to suggest that 'particular importance must attach to the best interests of the child which, depending on their nature and seriousness may *over-ride* those of the parent.' (emphasis added)

There remains a danger however that both the Strasbourg and UK courts may, in positively attempting to promote the progress that domestic law has made in safeguarding and prioritising the *interests* of children, fail to notice and thereby dilute the *rights* of children. This may in fact be the most significant drawback arising from the introduction of Strasbourg case law into the Scottish courts. In *Johansen v Norway*,[70] for example, the issue was, as in *Olssen*, whether there had been violation of the rights of a mother whose daughter had been taken into care, access terminated and the child settled permanently with foster parents. The ECtHR found the mother's Article 8 rights to respect for family life were not violated. In reaching this decision, emphasis was laid on the fact that the child's *interests* lay in establishing secure and undisrupted bonds with the foster parents. The protection of the interests of children was accepted by the court as a legitimate aim of the state justifying their interference with the mother's rights. What the court *could* have done (possibly in addition) was to have constructed a similar argument but by reference to the *rights* of the child to, as well as her interest in, a secure and nurturing family life. However this would have been a very radical step given the overwhelming bent of Strasbourg jurisprudence. Again we are in a lose/lose situation, where a step towards welfarism impedes the growth in rights accorded children, but a strengthening of rights discourse for parents may impede both the rights *and* welfare of children. This point is pursued further in the next section.

C. HARMFUL EFFECTS OF ECHR JURISPRUDENCE ON CHILDREN'S WELFARE AND RIGHTS IN DOMESTIC LAW?

So far we have indicated that incorporation of the ECHR into domestic law may 'open a Pandora's box'[71] unless judges are prepared to work on ECtHR jurisprudence to make it less paternalistic and more child-centred. Even this does not take us out of the woods however. It can be argued that the effects of incorporating the Convention may be positively *harmful* for children's interests.

To take a key Scottish example, Alan Miller has suggested that the children's hearings system may be damaged rather than improved by attempts to bring it

---

[67] *Hokkanen v Finland* (1996) 1 FLR 289.
[68] *Glaser v United Kingdom* [2000] FCR 193.
[69] *Elsholtz v Germany* [2000] FLR 497. *Elsholtz* was cited with approval by the Inner House in *White v White* 2001 SLT 485, a domestic case where a father was appealing against not being allowed contact with his 8-year-old daughter.
[70] *Johansen v Norway* (1997) 23 EHRR 33.
[71] See Fortin, above, n 22, 255.

into line with the ECHR or to 'Strasbourg proof it.'[72] Miller cites the example of the case of *McMichael v United Kingdom*[73] which is thus far the only case related to the hearings' system to have gone to Strasbourg. In *McMichael*, the son of unmarried parents was referred to a children's hearing. The hearing decided that the son should be placed with foster parents because of lack of parental care. The parents complained that they had not received copies of reports which the children's panel had seen, and thus had not been sufficiently involved in the decision-making process to protect their interests. The ECtHR agreed that their rights to respect for their family life (Article 8) and to a fair hearing (Article 6) had been violated. As a result, the rules of procedure of the hearings system were altered to give all *parents* of children before a hearing (not the children themselves[74]) the right to see any and all reports circulated to panellists.[75] At first brush, this seems like ordinary natural justice upheld. But the implications are less desirable. What *McMichael* means is that any information relating to a child which that child might wish to remain confidential—preferences as to with which parent the child would like to live, for example, or details of abuse or sexual history—can no longer be guaranteed any degree of privacy.[76] The result is that an ECtHR decision which upholds the rights of *parents* may have had seriously detrimental consequences for the interests and rights of *children*.

Miller's forebodings may have been justified when one comes to look at the seminal domestic case of *S v Miller*,[77] where the Inner House was asked to consider if the children's hearings system as a whole was fundamentally compatible with the ECHR, and, in particular, if the bar on legal aid for representation at the hearing was justifiable in terms of Article 6.[78] The stance in principle of the hearings' system ever since it was conceived in the Kilbrandon Report has been that the regular presence of lawyers at the hearing would conflict with the informal, welfare-centred and child-focused nature of the hearing process. As a result no provision for access to legal aid was made, although lawyers did sometimes appear on a *pro bono* basis, and aid was, of course, available if either the grounds of referral or the disposal was questioned and the case referred to the sheriff court or higher court. Nevertheless, in *Miller* the Inner House (having first found that hearing proceedings *were* concerned with 'the determination of . . . civil rights and obligations' as required for Article 6(1) to be applicable),

---

[72] See Miller, above, n 21.

[73] Above, n 36.

[74] Until practice was changed in 2001 following the *S v Miller* case—see below n 77.

[75] Children's Hearings (Scotland) Rules 1996, r 5(3).

[76] A parent can be excluded from a hearing (Children (Scotland) Act 1995, s 46(1)) so it appears that a child could in theory at least give *oral* testimony to the panel in confidence. However, this is not the case as the person excluded then has a right to have the substance of what occurred in their absence conveyed to them by the panel chairman.

[77] *S v Miller* 2001 SLT 531.

[78] For a fuller account of the *Miller* case see L Edwards, '*S v Miller:* The End of the Children's Hearings System as we Know it?' 2001 *SLT (News)* 187.

went on to conclude that 'without the possibility of [free] legal representation . . . the essence of the right of access would appear to be materially impaired' (para 79). As a result, free legal representation is to be introduced to the hearings' system, although at the time of writing no decision has yet been made by the Scottish Executive as to how exactly this should be done.[79]

The consequences of this enormous change in the system have yet to emerge. On the one hand, there was a clear gap in natural justice when children might effectively be accused of offences at the hearing without access to lawyers who could explain exactly what the law said, eg that defences such as provocation or self-defence were available to them.[80] To add insult to injury, Lord President Rodger correctly pointed out that children referred to the hearing as a client group were those likely to be most in need of free representation, being by nature of their immaturity likely to be ignorant, uncommunicative, shy and possibly mentally or physically handicapped. To go on denying legal aid and yet to comply with Article 6,

> one would have to be able to say that in no case could a child ever be unable to conduct his own case effectively before the hearing. I am unable to say this (para 36).

Yet the danger is that introducing legal representation to the hearings system may eventually destroy it as a unique welfare-centred tribunal, studied and praised as such throughout Europe. It is hard to see how the current character of the hearing could survive if both child referred, child's parents and perhaps even the Reporter and the panellists were to be legally represented in, say, a referral on grounds of the sexual abuse of the child in the home.[81] A great deal will rest on how the target set by Article 6 is to be accomplished and suggestions of a trained coterie of child advocates, possibly not even lawyers, providing representation, rather than a legal aid free-for-all for criminal lawyers do seem promising. Miller's thesis in general, however, seems to have the potential to come horribly true.

A similar problem can be observed in the current Scottish emergency child protection system. Under the Social Work (Scotland) Act 1968, a child could be removed by a place of safety order, obtainable from a Justice of the Peace as well as a court, in situations where their welfare was seen to be at risk, and that order could then only be challenged up to a maximum of seven days later at a children's hearing (at least initially). Following Lord Clyde's enquiry into the

---

[79] See also *S v Miller (No 2)* 2001 SLT 1304 where the Inner House agreed that no declaration of incompatibility needed to be made since steps could be taken under existing legislation to introduce access to legal representation at the hearing. See further comment by Jamieson at 2001 *SLT (News)* 137.

[80] It was suggested in *Miller* that this gap could be met by the panel chair-person. However this contention was rejected as children's panellists are themselves not legally qualified.

[81] It should be noted that no decision has yet been made as to whether Article 6 requires free legal representation to be available to any other actor than the child at the hearing. But in this writer's opinion it is inevitable such a development will occur at least in relation to 'relevant person' (usually, the child's parent(s)).

Orkney child abuse debacle of 1991,[82] the government was made forcefully aware that the system as it stood probably did not meet the due process demands of Article 6 of the ECHR, particularly because there was not necessarily any immediate hearing at, or appeal to, a court rather than a lay tribunal (the hearing) for parents seeking the return of their children. As a result (along with other causal factors) a new emergency protection system was introduced in Part II of the Children (Scotland) Act 1995, with the intention that it be more satisfactorily 'Strasbourg proofed'. However as a consequence it is considerably more complicated than the old system, almost to the point of incomprehensibility for both parents and children; and in particular, one knock-on effect of providing parents with various opportunities to seek remedies from a court has been that the entire time-scale of emergency protection has been extended, with the likely result that children removed from home are likely in future to spend more time in emergency care not less.[83] Again, a reform designed to protect the formal Convention rights of parents is most likely to have deleterious effects on the welfare (and rights) of children, while so far the anecdotally reported uptake on the new rights by parents has been small.

What these examples illustrate is a general threat that the ECHR, with its parent-centred jurisprudence and its emphasis on 'rights' discourse rather than welfare, may potentially prove incompatible with, and damaging to, the principles of modern domestic family law. Such issues have already arisen in Canada, where the Charter of Rights has been used extensively by parents to promote their rights and freedoms, even where these did not necessarily coincide with the rights or wishes of children.[84] In modern child legislation such as the Children (Scotland) Act 1995 and the Children Act 1989, the emphasis is on the welfare as paramount, and, to a lesser extent, on the rights and wishes, of the *child*; relatively little emphasis is on the rights of the *parent*. The 1995 and 1989 Acts de-prioritise the idea of parental rights and largely replace them with that of parental responsibilities; rights are given to parents only to enable them to fulfil their parental responsibilities. Thus, for example, parents owe their children the responsibility to maintain contact, rather than as formerly, having the right to contact (then called access). The Strasbourg jurisprudence, by contrast, looks startlingly different and somewhat antiquated. It is full of cases in which parents claim to have *rights* to which states are not giving due respect, mainly under Article 8. The ECHR might well provide ammunition to parents who are determined to persuade a court that they should have their 'rights' in old fashioned style, rather than, as the 1995 Act demands, regarding the welfare of the child as paramount and the rights of parents as secondary to their responsibilities. There are already warning signs in domestic case law that parents, particularly parents who are handicapped and frustrated by the current law—

---

[82] *Report of the Inquiry into the Removal of Children from Orkney 1991*: HC Papers 1992–1993, No 195.

[83] See further Miller, above, n 22, 13.

[84] See Susan Boyd's contribution in this volume.

principally fathers who are not married to the mother of their child—are will-ing to use any advantage going, including a 'rights' approach, to fight their cor-ner. In a celebrated recent Scots case, *Sanderson v McManus*,[85] an unmarried father was denied access to his son on the grounds he had not proven that access would be *positively* in the welfare of the child. His main argument against this conclusion basically boiled down to the assertion that as a natural father he had a *right* to maintain links with his child. Although this argument was eventually rejected by every court up to and including the House of Lords, it secured a fair amount of support along the way, notably from Lord McCluskey in the Inner House. In *Sanderson*, the appeal to rights failed—although not without a strug-gle. (Indeed, despite the father's lack of success, dicta from *Sanderson* have sub-sequently been lifted out of context and used imaginatively to promote the rights of fathers, a development which few would have anticipated and which shows the strength of the father's rights lobby.[86]) Incorporation of the ECHR, including Article 8, may however strengthen such arguments and in so doing both erode the welfare principle and weaken consideration of the *child* concerned.[87]

There are early signs in the Scots cases decided so far—especially the import-ant Inner House case of *White v White*[88]—that the courts are resisting manfully the wholesale use of rights arguments to obtain results prejudicial to the welfare of the child[89]—but again it remains to be seen how successful this strategy will be. In *White*, Lord President Rodger confidently declared that a system of fam-ily law where the child's welfare was paramount was wholly compatible with the ECHR, citing the Strasbourg case of *Elsholtz* mentioned above. Yet it may be questioned, inconvenient though it is, if it is really the same to say, as the Strasbourg court occasionally has, that the child's welfare may *infringe on* the Convention rights of the parents, as to say the child's welfare is *paramount*. No doubt case law will soon let us know.[90]

Within the child protection field, the issue is not so much the erosion of the rights of the child in favour of the rights of the parent, but rather the erosion of the principle that the welfare of the child is paramount, even if in order to meet that need, normal rules of natural justice must be viewed as of secondary

---

[85] See above, n 7.
[86] See further L Edwards, 'Life after *Sanderson v McManus*—What Next?' 1998 *SLT (News)* 299.
[87] UK fathers have already attempted to go to Strasbourg to combat domestic court decisions about access: see eg *Whitear v UK*, Appl No 28625/95, [1997] EHRLR 291 (rejected by Commission).
[88] *White v White* 2001 SLT 485.
[89] See also *City of Edinburgh v D and F* 2000 GWD 31–1210 (adoption).
[90] Morag Wise suggests in her chapter on Human Rights and Family Law in Lord Reed (ed), *A Practical Guide to Human Rights Law in Scotland* (Edinburgh, 2001) that: 'while there is certainly a difference in emphasis between the relative interests to be taken into account, the [European] Court has not shied away from upholding decisions to restrict parental rights where the welfare of the child so demands.' Again this writer feels this slightly fudges the issue; restricting parental rights is not equivalent to recognising welfare as paramount. See also for reflections from an English per-spective, A Vine 'Is the Paramountcy Principle Compatible with Art 8?' 2000 *Fam Law* 826; Herring, above, n 32.

importance. The *McMichael* case is but the tip of the iceberg here. The childrens' hearings system, defiantly welfare-centred as it is, has already been found in some respects procedurally lax by Strasbourg standards, as we have seen in the *Miller* case, but it is also often very successful in respecting, and indeed, promoting, the interests of children and families. In recent months, it has been suggested following the successful challenge to the legitimacy of temporary sheriffs,[91] that childrens' Reporters are similarly under threat, since they can be seen as quasi-judicial officials appointed by the Executive and insufficiently independent from it.[92] Many other conventional aspects of childrens' hearings procedure may also be brought to book in the years to come by desperate parents seeking any means to topple particular hearing or court decisions about their children. As in criminal law, this is an area where those involved will use whatever ammunition they have to hand to save their cause, no matter what damage they cause the institution as a whole at the same time. As this writer has suggested above and elsewhere, it may be doubted if the childrens' hearings system can survive the onslaught of incorporation whole, with its Kilbrandon purposes intact. If it does not, it will be children more than parents who will probably suffer as a result.

D. POSITIVE ASPECTS OF THE ECHR FOR CHILDREN'S RIGHTS?

Finally, not to be unduly negative, there is of course scope for creative lawyers to use the ECHR, particularly after incorporation, to further the interests of children. Two areas in particular have already been explored in recent cases, to greater or lesser degrees of success.

(1) The child's right to claim damages in respect of negligent acts by social workers

This issue was brought to the fore in *X v Bedfordshire*,[93] where in several conjoined cases, children and parents sought damages in respect of negligence by social workers and other public welfare employees such as child psychologists. In some of the cases, the negligence alleged was that a child had been taken into care without due cause; in others that a child had negligently *not* been taken into care, even although social workers knew that abuse was occurring or likely to occur. In all cases, however,[94] the House of Lords refused, on policy grounds, to find that a duty of care was owed by the social work authorities to the children

---

[91] *Starrs v Ruxton* 2000 JC 208.
[92] Oddly, this point was raised but not pursued in *S v Miller*.
[93] *X v Bedfordshire County Council* [1995] 2 AC 633.
[94] Some of the claims in conjoined cases against *education* employees were however allowed to stand.

concerned, or to their parents. Hence no damages were available. The so-called 'public law hurdle' was invoked to justify imposing what was effectively an exclusionary rule barring action by parents and children against social workers performing statutory duties. It was not 'just, fair and reasonable' to impose a duty on social work authorities enforceable by the public for failing to fulfil their statutory duties. Effectively, the result of *X v Bedfordshire* was that it became impossible in UK law for children who had suffered as a result of social workers' negligence in welfare duties to make civil claims for damages in negligence. Although alternative remedies of criminal injuries compensation, judicial review or complaint to a local authority ombudsman might be available, they would not necessarily provide the desired remedies of adversarial process, publicity and hard cash.[95]

In this case, however, the House of Lords was not the end of the line. In Strasbourg, claims were made by the *X v Bedfordshire* plaintiffs that the UK had failed to allow them access to justice as required by Article 6, and in various cases, had also failed to prevent a breach of Articles 3 and 8. This strategy effectively side-stepped the 'public law hurdle' and instead invoked the precedent of *Osman v UK*[96] in which the ECtHR had previously declared that such bars in principle to a hearing in English tort law so as to protect public authorities were invalid under Article 6.[97] The applications claiming violations of Articles 3, 6, 8 and 13 were declared admissible by the Commission in 1998[98] and in September 1999 the Commission's Report again upheld the view that there were violations of Articles 3, 6, 8 and 13.[99] At this stage, it looked as if the rights of children to justice under the ECHR had, quite radically, taken precedence over the policy upheld by the highest UK civil court, that public bodies should be protected against claims arising from their exercise of discretionary statutory duties.

The final result in the European Court has however been somewhat surprising compared to the earlier stages. In *Z and others v United Kingdom*[100] and *TP and KM v United Kingdom*,[101] a Grand Chamber of the ECtHR rather unexpectedly admitted that the judgment in *Osman* had been based on 'an understanding of the [English] law of negligence which has to be reviewed in the light

---

[95] See further L Edwards, 'Suing Local Authorities for Failure in Statutory Duty: Orkney Reconsidered after *X v Bedfordshire*' (1996) 1 *Edin LR* 115; R Bailey-Harris and M Harris 'The Immunity of Local Authorities in Child Protection Functions—is the door now ajar?' (1998) 10 *CFLQ* 227.

[96] *Osman v UK* [1999] 1 FLR 193.

[97] It appears that recourse to the ECtHR was also contemplated by the parents involved in the Orkney crisis but was forestalled by private cash settlements made by the Government (see *Scotsman*, 5 March 1996).

[98] *TP and KM v United Kingdom*, Appl No 28945/95, *Z v United Kingdom*, Appl No 29392/95 [1998] EHRLR 624.

[99] *TP and KM v United Kingdom*, 10 Sept 1999, Report of the Commission. See also *Z and Others v United Kingdom*, Appl No 29392/95, 10 Sept 1999, Report of the Commission.

[100] *Z and others v UK* 10 May 2001, ECHR, Appl No 29392/95.

[101] *TP and KM v United Kingdom* 10 May 2001, ECHR, Appl No 28945/95.

of the clarifications made by the domestic courts.'[102] It seemed that the application of the 'just, fair and reasonable' test to decide if a duty of care was owed was not, after all, a blanket immunity denying title to sue and therefore infringing Article 6—but rather an aspect of the substantive law of determination of whether a duty of care existed, and as such, was allowable, so long as some kind of adversarial argument took place in court as to whether a duty of care existed or not (evidence of facts did not however need to be led). The claims under Article 6 allowed hitherto were thus thrown out. As a result the two cases which had been conjoined were decided in a different way. In *Z*, which was a case where children had been abused by their mother over years and the social work authorities had *not* intervened, the court found that the state was substantively responsible for not having taken more positive steps to stop a breach of Article 3 occurring—the inhuman treatment which the children had suffered at the hands of the mother. They were therefore entitled to a remedy before a national authority according to Article 13, which the UK courts had denied them. Damages of £320,000 were awarded to the four plaintiff children. By contrast, in *TP and KM*, a case where the children had been taken *into* care wrongfully as a result of negligence by social workers, no Article 3 violation had occurred, but the right to respect for family life had been infringed (Article 8) and so again under Article 13 a remedy of damages had to be provided. Leaving aside the issue of how the result was reached, the ECtHR has thus enabled children wronged by social workers to have a remedy in national law where none was before provided, a remarkable achievement.[103] (It should be noted however that this rights based approach has still at no point persuaded either the House of Lords or the ECtHR to consider the child's *welfare* as relevant in this particular area of tort/delict law.)

(2) The child's participation in civil justice

As already noted above, serious efforts have been made in the last few years, particularly within the Children (Scotland) Act 1995, to allow children better access to justice in civil proceedings. In particular, the 1995 Act, as already cited,[104] requires that the views of children be given due regard when court proceedings are instructed which affect their interests—notably, when one of their parents decides to divorce the other; and gives children who have a general understanding of what it means the right, if they wish, to hire their own lawyers, and become independent litigants.[105] However there are signs, particularly from

---

[102] The House of Lords had to some extent already retrenched from the position adopted in *X v Bedfordshire* in *Barrett v Enfield London Borough Council* [1999] 3 All ER 193, pending the final view taken by the ECtHR.

[103] See further C Moodie 'Suing Social Work Authorities' [2001] *Fam LB* 52.

[104] See above, text accompanying n 18.

[105] See above p 207.

the much noted judgment of Sheriff Bell in *Henderson v Henderson*,[106] that the participation of children in what have hitherto been perceived as 'adult' actions may be discouraged because the child's presence is seen as undesirable, unnecessary or expensive—perhaps because they might hear evidence that might upset them, or their evidence is similar to that of one or both parents, or can be supplied at less cost and aggravation by reports or third parties. There is also some evidence that a similar view may sometimes be taken by the Legal Aid Board, whose financial support will of course usually be a crucial prerequisite to a child's litigation.[107] Another hurdle for children, especially in actions where there is a conflict of interest with a parent, may be that without assurances of confidentiality, they will find themselves unable to present their views fully or to pursue actions against their parents in court. It is well known that young children find it difficult to criticise or indict a parent publicly, especially in the intimidating atmosphere of a courtroom, and therefore their right to be heard may be dependent on rights of confidentiality.

Article 6 of the ECHR, which provides that 'everyone is entitled to a fair and public hearing' may potentially be of great use here in ensuring that a child's *formal* rights of participation are not reduced in effectiveness by administrative, financial or judicial hurdles. *Airey v Ireland*[108] makes it clear that the Convention is intended to guarantee, not rights that are theoretical or illusory, but rights that are practical and effective. On the other hand however, Article 6 might also be used by parents (or other litigants) to fight off any such claims of right by children. There is already a fascinating Scottish example of how such battles might be constructed in the cases of *Dosoo v Dosoo*[109] and *McGrath v McGrath*.[110] In *Dosoo*, two children aged 14 and 12 were interviewed by a sheriff to establish whether they wanted to have continuing contact with their father. The children were afraid of their father, and only agreed to give evidence if it was kept confidential and not shown to him. The sheriff agreed to seal the record of their views (as the 1995 Act allows) but the father sought to be informed of the contents, claiming that otherwise his rights to a fair hearing under Article 6 of the ECHR, and in particular to know all the testimony against him, were being breached. Remarkably, the sheriff however took the side of the children, stating that if she were to violate their privacy she would be failing to comply with Article 12 of the UN Convention on the Rights of the Child (discussed above), which guarantees the child the right to speak 'freely'. (One might have thought she would be more conscious of the fact that on incorporation the ECHR would clearly take precedence over the UN Convention.) An

---

[106] *Henderson v Henderson* 1997 Fam LR 120.
[107] See unpublished report for The Scottish Office, F Kean, *Research Into the Uptake of Civil Legal Aid by Children Under 16 and its Implications for Solicitors* (1997), which found that of 844 applications made by children under 16 for civil legal aid in 1996/97, around a third were rejected; a surprising result given that most children will satisfy the resources requirements.
[108] *Airey v Ireland* (1979) 2 EHRR 305.
[109] *Dosoo v Dosoo* 1999 GWD 13–586.
[110] *McGrath v McGrath* 1999 SLT (Sh Ct) 90.

immediately subsequent sheriff court case, *McGrath v McGrath*, however, took the opposite decision, not so much out of deference to Article 6, as to prior English and Scottish precedent. The sheriff summed up the case admirably, stating that 'the practicalities involved in reconciling the right to a fair hearing and a child's right to express his views are . . . of immense difficulty'.[111] *Dosoo* also demonstrates graphically how the rights of adults under the ECHR may come into direct competition with the rights more closely tailored for children of the UN Convention. Child advocates must hope that they can use Article 6 to fight as well for children as adult advocates may use it to fight against their cause. Again, 'rights' discourse proves a two-edged sword.

E. FINAL THOUGHTS

In conclusion then, incorporation of the ECHR for those concerned with the rights and interests of children may be both a curse and a blessing. On the one hand, there is a danger that existing rights of children, and advances that have been made towards a child-centred family law, may be prejudiced by a more robust 'rights culture' for *parents* which the ECHR may usher into Scottish and English legal culture. In this respect, the Canadian experience does sound a warning bell. On the other hand, the ECHR may prove to be an immensely powerful and flexible tool for lawyers who wish to use it to pursue the interests of children. It may be particularly useful in areas outwith traditional family law, where although the interests of children are crucially affected, the welfare principle is not paramount. We have already discussed one such area from the law of negligence above in relation to *X v Bedfordshire*, and how the ECHR has provided an opportunity to highlight the rights of the child—or at least the 'client'—in an area whose jurisprudence was previously dominated by policy concerns about the liability implications for public authorities. Another key area where the interests of children are arguably neglected by the existing law is, paradoxically, the Child Support Act 1991.[112] Although this Act ostensibly asserts that 'Children Come First,'[113] in fact the interests of children are not paramount in relation to the maintenance assessments made under the Act but need merely be given 'regard.'[114] One enterprising father has already attempted, admittedly with little success, to persuade the Commission that his right to respect for family life under Article 8 was prejudiced by the Child Support Act assessment made against him, in that the level of assessment did not take into account how far he had to travel to visit his children and how prohibitively

---

[111] *McGrath v McGrath* 1999 SLT (Sh Ct), 93.
[112] Which is in the process of being replaced by a similar but simpler scheme in the Child Support, Pensions and Social Security Act 2000.
[113] The title of the preceding White Paper: Cm 1263, 1990.
[114] S 2 of the Child Support Act 1991.

expensive this was; consequently, he asserted, his rights of access to his child were prejudiced.[115] Although the father in this case lost, the case illustrates well how many areas of hitherto settled law may be turned on their head by a thoughtful use of ECHR principles. Children in their turn, could conceivably contest child support assessments on the grounds that they are being robbed of their right to 'mutual enjoyment of family life' with their absent fathers. For children, (or those representing them), rights under Article 8 to respect for family life might usefully be employed in other non-welfare-centred areas with little in the way of a children's rights' 'angle', such as *inter alia* domestic violence law, child abduction law, criminal law and labour law. At the time of writing, for example, the age of eight as the age of criminal responsibility is under fire partly as a result of the ECHR.[116] The incorporation of the ECHR is thus both a boon and a threat to children's rights: only the future will tell which influence will emerge as the strongest.

---

[115] *Logan v UK*, Appl No 24875/94, 6 Sept 1996.
[116] See Scottish Law Commission Discussion Paper No 115, Age of Criminal Responsibility (Sept 2001).

11

Attitudes to Sexual Identity and Practice: The Impact of Human Rights Law in the Scottish Courts

MARTIN A HOGG*

THE SCOTTISH COURTS are traditionally conservative in matters of sexual mores, reflecting a conservatism still rooted in portions of Scottish society.[1] Yet whilst some Scots evidently find the subjects of sexual identity and sexual practice uncomfortable topics, the incorporation into national law of the European Convention for the Protection of Human Rights and Fundamental Freedoms (ECHR) through the Human Rights Act 1998 is already requiring our courts to consider these issues along with others raised by the Convention rights.

In what follows, consideration will be given to whether any assistance is afforded to Scottish courts by the case law of the European Court of Human Rights (ECtHR) in the determination of disputes concerning rights relating to sexual identity and practice. Has the judicial culture of the Court been restrained or active in promoting rights in this area? These questions will be considered in the context of five principal issues: (1) transsexualism, (2) same-sex partnerships, (3) sexual practice, (4) employment discrimination against homosexuals, and (5) adoption and custody proceedings. These are the issues which have pre-occupied the Court in recent years.

It will become evident from the following discussion that the Scottish courts have thus far seldom had occasion to turn their attention to issues of sexual identity and practice, and that the incorporation of the ECHR presents them with an opportunity to reflect changing social attitudes in these areas and encourage the sluggish machinery of the legislature. Whether they are given the chance to take up this opportunity will depend upon the actions pleaded before them. However, even if given such an opportunity, their traditional conservatism suggests that they may be reticent to promote rights in a radical way.

* Lecturer in Law, School of Law, University of Edinburgh. This chapter is dedicated to The Equality Network and its many supporters, and to the memory of Peter Duffy QC (1954–1999).
[1] As the public debate concerning the repeal of section 2A of the Local Government Act 1986 (commonly referred to as 'clause 28') demonstrated.

A. TRANSSEXUAL CASES

There are many helpful articles explaining the phenomenon of transsexualism for those who are not familiar with the medical aspects of gender.[2] Cases concerning transsexuals brought before the ECtHR have concentrated in the main either on the right of transsexuals to have their post-operative sex officially recognised, or their right to marry persons of the opposite sex to their post-operative sex. The claims of the applicants in such cases have focused in particular on Article 8 (respect for private and family life) and Article 12 (the right of marriage) of the ECHR. In some cases, these Articles have been pled in conjunction with Article 14 (non-discrimination).[3]

At first blush, Article 8 would not seem to provide a particularly helpful ground to such applicants, for how is the private or family life of a transsexual affected by a decision not to change a birth certificate or the failure to achieve proper civil recognition of change of sex? If such applicants want changes made to public documents, which they will show to others, is the failure to have such changes not about embarrassment suffered in *public* settings? The answer may partly be that it is the fact of having undergone an intimate, personal medical procedure that the applicant wants to keep private, but also partly that the ECtHR has shown itself activist in interpreting the concept of private life widely. Privacy has been found applicable in public situations into which an aspect of someone's personality has been introduced, and to situations which appear to raise issues more akin to personal autonomy rather than privacy. Following *B v France*,[4] the concept has been considered to include situations where an individual is required to reveal their pre-operative gender in a public setting, such as in official application forms or in court, and to cover a statement of gender on civil status documents.

In the two best-known actions against the United Kingdom, *Rees v United Kingdom*[5] and *Cossey v United Kingdom*,[6] the ECtHR held that the defendant state was not required to alter birth certificates to reflect a post-operative sex change. However, the court arguably failed to take proper account of the full argument of *Rees* and *Cossey*, which was not just about failing to alter historical birth certificates, but about a failing by the state *in general* to put in place measures to take account legally of their change of sex.[7] This point was made

---

[2] See, for instance, J K Mason, 'United Kingdom v Europe: Current Attitudes to Transsexualism' (1998) 2 *Edin LR* 107

[3] Article 3 (inhuman or degrading treatment) has occasionally been pleaded, but not successfully.

[4] *B v France* (1993) 16 EHRR 1.

[5] *Rees v United Kingdom* (1986) 9 EHRR 56.

[6] *Cossey v United Kingdom* (1990) 13 EHRR 622.

[7] The real crux of the complaint was put more forcefully by the complainants in *Sheffield & Horsham v United Kingdom* (1999) 27 EHRR 163, a fact the court recognised when it said: 'the applicants have formulated their complaints in terms which are wider than those invoked by Mr Rees and Miss Cossey since they contend that their rights under Art 8 of the Convention have

forcefully by Judge Martens in his dissenting judgement in *Cossey*, who noted that the 'very existence of such a legal system must continuously, directly and distressingly affect [transsexuals'] private lives.'[8] The court's answer in both cases was that due to the lack of common ground amongst the Contracting States, the law was in a transitional state, and the Contracting States must therefore be allowed a wide margin of appreciation.[9] Surprisingly, 12 years after the decision in *Rees*, the same conservative attitude was still being adopted by the court in its most recent judgment in this area, *Sheffield & Horsham v United Kingdom*,[10] despite a strong argument from the minority that the time has come to compel action by Contracting States.[11] It is note-worthy, however, that this conservative attitude is now barely commanding a majority in the Court.[12]

As regards Article 12 (the right to marry), the *Commission* in *Cossey* took the view that while Article 12 refers to traditional heterosexual marriage, where a male/female transsexual is now living as a post-operative woman and has been socially accepted as such, she must have the right to marry.[13] The ECtHR, *per contra*, said that the traditional concept of marriage had *not* been abandoned, and that this was sufficient reason for the continued adoption of biological cri-teria.[14] Such an attitude may fairly be characterised as 'restrained'. It means that the bizarre situation may exist where a male/female transsexual, having the out-ward appearance of a woman, would be perfectly entitled to marry a woman (hardly the 'traditional concept of marriage'), whereas a female/male trans-sexual, having the outward appearance of a man, would not be so entitled.[15]

As the foregoing indicates, the ECtHR has not been particularly activist in applying rights in this area, though in the more recent case of *B v France* the court did find the defendant state to be in breach of Article 8 in refusing to recog-nise the applicant's current status as female.[16] However, the court stressed that its conclusions were based upon the refusal of the French Government to alter civil status documents, not the historical birth certificates which were the subjects of the *Rees* and *Cossey* cases. This leads to the unwelcome situation that in states with a higher degree of social control through the use of civil sta-tus documents (for instance, identity cards), transsexuals may have the right to

---

been violated on account of the failure of the respondent State to recognise for legal purposes gen-erally their post-operative gender' (para 53).

[8] *Cossey v United Kingdom*, above, n 6, at 650.

[9] *Ibid*, at 639–40 and *Rees v United Kingdom*, above, n 5, at 64.

[10] *Sheffield & Horsham v United Kingdom* (1999) 27 EHRR 163.

[11] The comments of the minority in *Sheffield & Horsham v United Kingdom* are discussed below.

[12] The majority against a breach of Art 8 was only two (11:9).

[13] *Cossey v United Kingdom*, above, n 6, 635.

[14] *Ibid*, 642.

[15] Though, as discussed below, such a marriage would be voidable under Scots law.

[16] The court held, partly in the light of the number of official French documents which required sex to be stated, that B was faced with a daily situation which was not compatible with respect for her private life, even given the state's margin of appreciation.

have their change of sex officially recognised, but not so in states with a more laissez-faire attitude to such documents.[17]

The English courts have recently followed the ECtHR's conservative line with respect to birth certificates. In the case *R v Registrar General of Births, Deaths and Marriages for England and Wales, ex parte P & G*,[18] the Queen's Bench Division not only upheld the view that the birth register cannot be changed to accommodate gender reassignment surgery, but also reaffirmed the authority of *Corbett v Corbett*,[19] the case that is the foundation of the position adopted by English law that sex is determined at the moment of birth and judged on biological criteria.

However, in the sphere of employment rights at least, there has at last been improvement in domestic law. The first sign of a more radical judicial attitude in Britain towards the status of transsexuals came in the 1998 industrial tribunal decision, *Sheffield v Air Foyle*.[20] In this case, Ms Sheffield, a male/female transsexual, had been turned down for a pilot's job. The industrial tribunal hearing her claim for sex discrimination held that 'the applicant has been treated less favourably on the grounds of her transsexuality *and this amounts to less favourable treatment on the grounds of sex*.'[21] The radicalism of this decision, however, was not home-grown, as the industrial tribunal was merely following the lead given by the European Court of Justice (ECJ) in *P v S*, where it had been held that Cornwall County Council, which had made a male/female transsexual redundant, had breached European Directive 76/207/EEC on equal treatment. The ECJ held that the discrimination suffered by P was based on the ground that when she announced her intention to undergo gender reassignment she was treated unfavourably by comparison with persons of the sex to which she was deemed to belong before undergoing such gender reassignment. The ECJ said that to tolerate such discrimination would be tantamount to a failure to respect the dignity and freedom to which she was entitled. The decision embodies a more radical approach than that shown in the judgments of the ECtHR, and with its reference to basic principles of dignity and freedom, it looks more to the spirit of the legislation.[22]

As a result of the decision of the ECJ in *P v S*, the British Government decided through legislative action to put the matter beyond dispute. Discrimination against transsexuals in various employment situations has now been outlawed by extending certain provisions of the Sex Discrimination Act 1975 to cover those who have undergone, are undergoing, or who intend to undergo, gender

---

[17] See further on this point, D Feldman, *Civil Liberties and Human Rights in England and Wales* (Clarendon Press, Oxford, 1993), 509.

[18] *R v Registrar General of Births, Deaths and Marriages for England and Wales, ex parte P & G* [1996] 2 FLR 90.

[19] *Corbett v Corbett* [1971] P 83, [1970] 2 All ER 33.

[20] *The Times*, Home News section, 1 June 1998.

[21] *Ibid*, emphasis added.

[22] A defender of the ECtHR might plead that it has been constrained by the margin of appreciation doctrine.

reassignment.[23] This legislative change has already been enforced by an employ-ment tribunal.[24] It has also been reported in the press that the Army will now allow soldiers who undergo gender reassignment surgery to remain in their posts.[25] However, concern has been expressed at some of the exceptions to the provisions.[26] It remains to be seen whether the legislative restrictions placed by the Government upon *P v S* will be deemed acceptable.

In addition to Ms Sheffield's action before the industrial tribunal, she also raised an action against the United Kingdom before the ECtHR, alleging a breach of Articles 8, 12 and 14.[27] Her claim was that the *general state of law* in the United Kingdom in relation to the status of transsexuals disclosed a lack of respect for her private life. The Commission's view,[28] noting that Ms Sheffield was subject to a 'real and continuous risk of intrusive and distressing enquiries and to an obligation to make embarrassing disclosures,'[29] was that there had been a breach of Article 8 of the ECHR[30] and that the United Kingdom should be obliged to modify its existing legal system. The ECtHR, adopting a conserv-ative stance, held that Articles 8 and 12 had *not* been violated.

On Article 8, the ECtHR restated the traditional argument upholding the importance of the birth certificate as an historical document. On the wider issue of the general failure by the state to recognise the rights of the complainants, the court made three main points, *viz*: (i) there were still no conclusive findings on the medical doubts relating to transsexualism; (ii) there was still no common approach amongst the Contracting States as to how to deal with the legal

---

[23] See the Sex Discrimination Act 1975, new s 2A (as inserted by the Sex Discrimination (Gender Reassignment) Regulations 1999, SI 1999/1102). Other new sections have been added to the Act, including ss 7A, 7B, and amendments have been made to others, including ss 6 and 8. These changes came into force on 1 May 1999.

[24] Decision of the Employment Tribunal in *DA v Suffolk County Council*, 22 Dec 1999, where it was held that Suffolk County Council had unlawfully discriminated against the applicant (a male to female transsexual) by prohibiting her from continuing to work as a day care officer with a female client, following an objection by the client's mother.

[25] See, for instance, *Daily Telegraph*, 2 Aug 1999, discussing the case of Sgt Major Joanne Rushton (previously Joe Rushton), a pre-operative male to female transsexual, who had undergone hormone replacement therapy.

[26] Including the fact that the new section 2A will not apply (i) where a person's sex is a genuine occupational qualification for their job and the employer can show that his treatment is reasonable (by reference to provisions of the Act or to any other relevant circumstances); or (ii) if a limitation is imposed to comply with the doctrines of a religion or to avoid offending the religious susceptibil-ities of a significant number of the religion's followers. Surprisingly, perhaps, a male to female trans-sexual priest in the Church of England was supported by her bishop and permitted to continue in her parochial post: see *Church Times*, News, 23 June 2000. However, more recently and in contrast to this decision, it has been reported that a hospital chaplain in the Church of England diocese of Chichester who is seeking male to female gender reassignment has been asked to resign his position by his Bishop: see *Church Times*, News, 13 July 2001.

[27] *Sheffield & Horsham v United Kingdom,* above, n 10.

[28] The Commission referred specifically to the decision of the European Court of Justice in *P v S*.

[29] *Sheffield & Horsham v United Kingdom,* above, n 10, 177.

[30] The Commission so found, by 15 votes to 1. They also held that it was unnecessary to consider the Applicant's separate complaint under Articles 12, 13 and 14.

repercussions of transsexualism;[31] and (iii) the applicants had not suffered sufficient detriment to tilt the balance in their favour.

These points were all refuted forcefully in the various dissenting judgements:

(i) On the first point, various dissenting judges responded to the alleged lack of consensus on the aetiology of transsexualism by pointing out that the majority had failed to take into account the acceptance by the medical profession of gender dysphoria as a recognised medical condition. Even if the causes of this were not agreed, '(r)espect for privacy rights should not . . . depend on exact science.'[32]

(ii) The 'common approach' to legal repercussions was heavily criticised on the grounds that 'the Court need not wait until every Contracting Party has amended its law in this direction before deciding that Article 8 gives rise to a positive obligation to introduce reform.'[33] Judge van Dijk, in his dissent, neatly pointed out that the margin of appreciation, so often used to stand in the way of activism in this field, could in fact be used against the state here. For, as he put it, if other Contracting States have found ways to overcome the legal problems caused by transsexualism, the very diversity of their approach is a facet of the margin of appreciation, but one which supports change, albeit change within a framework of the individual State's choosing.[34]

(iii) On the balancing issue, Judge van Dijk commented:

> In applying the fair-balance test, and as an element thereof the proportionality test, the majority should have . . . taken into account, on the one hand, that the detriment to the first applicant is not limited to the specific incidents advanced by her . . . but consists of a continuous risk of being forced to reveal her post-operative gender . . . and, on the other hand, that the Government have not made out any plausible arguments that the interests of third parties referred to by the majority cannot be met in another less distressing way.[35]

As for Article 12, the ECtHR did no more than restate the traditional arguments in *Cossey* and *Rees* on the heterosexual nature of marriage, and the right of contracting states to determine the criteria for ascertaining gender for the purposes of marriage.[36]

---

[31] The majority opinion does raise some interesting questions. If respect for privacy allows transsexuals to keep their original gender a secret, how are insurance companies, for one, to discover a fact which may affect their risk assessment?

[32] Joint partly dissenting opinion of Judges Bernhardt, Thor Vilhjalmsson, Spielmann, Palm, Wildhaber, Makarczyk and Voicu: *Sheffield & Horsham v United Kingdom,* above, n 10, 202.

[33] *Sheffield & Horsham v United Kingdom,* above, n 10, 201.

[34] *Ibid*, 209.

[35] *Ibid*, 208. Among the intrusive incidents cited by Ms Sheffield were the requirements to disclose gender when standing surety, and when making an application under the Data Protection Act 1984. She also cited various circumstances covered by the Perjury Act 1911.

[36] Paras 62–70.

In its conservative decision in *Sheffield*, the ECtHR relied not only on *Cossey* and *Rees* but on its more recent decision in *X, Y & Z v United Kingdom*.[37] In that case, the court held that the Registrar General's refusal to register the natural mother of a child and her female/male transsexual partner as the joint parents of the child did not breach Article 8 of the ECHR. This was despite the fact that prior to the administration of AID treatment to the mother, her partner, the female/male transsexual, had been required to make an acknowledgement of paternity by the hospital in terms of the Human Fertility and Embryology Act 1990.[38] Whilst considering that de facto family ties bound the three applicants, mother, partner and child, it noted that there was no common European standard regarding the award of parental rights to transsexuals. Thus, the respondent state had to be afforded a wide margin of appreciation. This restatement of the traditional argument gave support to the conservative view in *Sheffield*.

What do all the above judgments mean for the rights of transsexuals before the Scottish courts? Consideration of that question would be incomplete without also considering the attitude of the United Kingdom Government and the Scottish Executive. Signs of a change of heart in domestic policy[39] may be seen in the recent report of the Home Office's Inter-Departmental Working Group on Transsexual People.[40] Whilst the majority of the areas covered in the report fall within the jurisdiction of the Scottish Parliament (eg the right to marry, birth certificates), as the Scottish Executive participated in the Working Group, the recommendations contained in the report will no doubt be influential on legislative proposals for Scotland.[41]

The Working Party presented no firm recommendations to the Government but presented various options. On the issue of birth certificates, they considered two possible options:

(a) to allow registrars to issue a short form birth certificate showing a person's new name, with no indication of their sex; or
(b) to offer transsexual people new short form certificates showing both their new name and their new sex.

The Working Party noted that:

---

[37] *X, Y & Z v United Kingdom* (1997) 24 EHRR 143.

[38] S 28(3): 'where a man, who is not married to the mother, is party to the treatment which results in the sperm being placed in the woman, he shall be deemed to be the father of the child.'

[39] Attitudes towards transsexuals in Scottish society at large may arguably have begun to change even before the publication of the Home Office Working Party report. In Sept 1998, it was reported in the press that a male to female transsexual was, for the first time, to serve a prison sentence in a women's prison.

[40] Published 26 July 2000.

[41] The Report noted that 'The work of the Inter-Departmental Working Group covers some matters which have been devolved to the Scottish Parliament, the Northern Ireland Assembly and the National Assembly for Wales. It will be for these administrations . . . to consider the Working Group's Report and decide whether, how and when these matters will be taken forward in their jurisdictions.' (Report, p 5). As well as the Scottish Executive, the Working Party included representation from the General Register Office for Scotland.

[i]n both cases the birth register would be noted to show change of name but would also continue to record the facts as at birth. Any full certificate would show the original details, together with a note in the margin of the registration.[42]

However, crucially, the report added that:

The ability to acquire a new certificate of this sort would ease a transsexual person's position in certain (fairly limited) circumstances. But, as at present, it would not constitute evidence of a person's identity and they would still for all legal purposes be of their birth sex as recorded on the full certificate.[43]

Change of legal status would be required as a pre-requisite to effectively undertaking certain legal acts (such as marriage). Again, the Working Group made no recommendations on this issue, but merely noted certain implications should change of sex be fully legally recognised. On the question of the marriage of transsexual persons, the Group did not directly address the question of whether a transsexual person should be entitled to marry a person of the same birth sex as themselves, but the Group's discussion of the possibility of granting full legal recognition to a change of sex would seem to imply the permissibility of this. The one marriage issue highlighted by the Group was the effect of recognition of a sex change on an *existing* marriage. Allowing this would be to permit a same sex marriage to exist, a position the group considered to be anomalous if same sex marriages were not generally to be recognised. They thus noted that

legislation providing for the grant of recognition of a transsexual person's new gender for all legal purposes could include a requirement that any subsisting marriage must have been ended or will be treated as ended from the date of the grant of official recognition.

A more progressive recommendation might have been to encourage recognition of same sex partnerships in general, something which would prevent the need to dissolve existing marriages.

The Report published by the Working Party may herald the beginning of a change of heart towards transsexual persons in the United Kingdom, though we must await the outcome of any consultation process for fear of making any overly-optimistic predictions. In the meantime, the following tentative comments may be made:

(1) In the absence of legislative change, the Scottish and English courts are unlikely to change their traditional view of the register of births in the light of the Human Rights Act 1998.

(2) English courts are not likely to change their minds about the determination of sex for the purposes of marriage. Whilst Scottish courts are not bound by *Corbett v Corbett* there is as yet no evidence to suggest that they will take a

---

[42] Report, 19.
[43] *Ibid*, 19.

different view, and their traditionally conservative attitude suggests otherwise. This is despite sound arguments that the existing Scots law of marriage does penalise transsexuals in a way which is contrary to Article 12.[44] The potential for change exists, however, and if a male/female transsexual were to raise an action in Scotland against the Registrar General arguing that the state's failure to register her marriage to a male was a breach of her ECHR right to marry, a case could be put on the basis of the more up-to-date scientific and social attitudes to transsexualism. A Scottish court, notionally free of the chains of *Corbett v Corbett*, would in theory be able to adopt a new view of the civil recognition of gender reassignment surgery and recognise a marriage in these circumstances. The power of such an argument would have been enhanced if the Commission view in *Sheffield v United Kingdom* had been upheld by the Court, but even if it had, then the practical likelihood is that a Scottish court will not take so radical a step. A further push from Strasbourg or from Holyrood may be required.

(3) Whilst advances have now been made to the employment law rights of transsexuals in the United Kingdom, some of the exceptions permitted under the Sex Discrimination Act may yet be open to challenge as unduly restricting the ambit of *P v S* and as still breaching the terms of the ECHR.

B. SAME-SEX PARTNERSHIPS[45]

The ECtHR has not required the Contracting States to grant legal recognition to same sex partnerships. Two articles of the Convention might have been thought relevant here: Article 8 (family life) (perhaps taken together with Article 14), and Article 12 (marriage). As will have been evident from the above discussion of the transsexual cases, the attitude of the ECtHR is that Article 12 is only concerned with heterosexual marriage. There is no evidence of any impending change in the attitude of the court to the interpretation of Article 12, and in this we may fairly characterise its attitude as restrained. This, of course, is matched by the attitude of the English courts, as exemplified by *Corbett v Corbett*.

As regards Article 8, the ECtHR, while recognising in *X, Y and Z* that the social unit of a post-operative female/male transsexual, a woman, and her child, could constitute a de facto family unit, have so far refused to recognise the

---

[44] See, *inter alia*, the arguments of Kenneth Norrie set out in 'Transsexuals, the Right to Marry and Voidable Marriages in Scots Law' 1990 *SLT (News)* 353. Norrie argues that a male to female transsexual in the position of Ms Cossey, being permitted under Scots law only to marry a woman, would at best be able to contract a voidable marriage in Scots law (being unable to achieve the penetration required of a biological male). This legal limitation of her right to marry, under a voidable marriage alone, may be argued, says Norrie, to breach Article 12 of the ECHR.

[45] On this and other issues related to homosexual equality, see for instance Robert Wintemute, *Sexual Orientation and Human Rights* (Oxford University Press, Oxford, 1995), and Peter Duffy QC, 'A Case for Equality' [1998] *EHRLR* 134.

relationship of homosexual couples as being part of family life.[46] These differing conclusions seem somewhat incongruous, given that in *X, Y and Z* the court
said:

> [T]he notion of 'family life' in Art 8 is not confined solely to families based on mar-
> riage and may encompass other de facto relationships . . . When deciding whether a
> relationship can be said to amount to 'family life', a number of factors may be rele-
> vant, including whether the couple live together, the length of their relationship and
> whether they have demonstrated their commitment to each other by having children
> together or by any other means.[47]

Apart from the reference to having children together (and presumably this could
include adoption, or artificial insemination of one member of a lesbian couple),
it is not clear why this statement could not in principle apply to same-sex couples. However, the case law of the ECtHR is against this: in *Kerkhoven v
Netherlands*,[48] the court took the view that same sex relationships do not fall
within the definition of family life. In his recent dissenting judgment in *Sheffield
& Horsham v United Kingdom*, Judge van Dijk lamented the fact that this attitude to Article 12 'has the unsatisfactory consequence that it denies to, or at least
makes illusive for, homosexuals a right laid down in the Convention', but such
a view remains very much in the minority, at least as regards the published views
of the court.

It would seem that if a challenge to state failure to grant legal recognition of
same sex relationships is going to arise, it is unlikely to come via Article 12, or,
unless the ECtHR ignores existing jurisprudence, through the 'family life'
provision of Article 8.[49] However, there may be an argument based upon the
'private life' element of Article 8, or perhaps Article 8 taken together with
Article 14. Given that, at least since *Dudgeon v UK*,[50] private homosexual
behaviour between two adults has been considered a matter of private life, then
arguably the right of a homosexual couple to have their partnership recognised
officially could be seen as a breach of Article 8, or at least Article 8 taken
together with Article 14. Article 8(2) might be raised against such a view, the justification being the protection of public morals or the protection of the institution of marriage, but could such an argument be sustained for much longer?

The answer of a Scottish court might be, however, that failure to recognise
such partnerships is a legitimate choice by Parliament, and that the issue would

---

[46] *X, Y and Z,* above, n 37.
[47] *Ibid*,166.
[48] *Kerkhoven v Netherlands* unpublished, Appl No 15666/89.
[49] However, as the Scottish Parliament has now abolished section 2A of the Local Government
Act 1986, the provision which prevented local authorities from promoting the teaching in any maintained school of the acceptability of homosexuality as a pretended family relationship, it may reasonably be argued that Parliament's view is that homosexual relationships may constitute a family
unit. An argument before a Scottish court that the failure to recognise same sex relationships is a
breach of the 'family life' provision of Article 8 may thus be strengthened.
[50] *Dudgeon v UK* (1981) 4 EHRR 149.

require legislation.[51] In reply, however, while it is true that no legislative provision has directly provided for recognition of same sex partnerships, they have at least been given indirect recognition within the provisions of the Adults with Incapacity (Scotland) Act 2000, which gives same sex partners of incapacitated persons the right to make decisions concerning their medical treatment[52], and within the provisions of the Housing (Scotland) Act 2001. [52a]

C. SEXUAL PRACTICE

Recently, the issue of sexual practice has been raised before the ECtHR in cases concerning the criminality of acts between consenting sado-masochists and the age of consent for male homosexuals.

In the former issue, brought before the court in the case of *Laskey, Jaggard & Brown v UK*,[53] its attitude was restrained. The applicants, who had been convicted before an English court on various charges of assault and unlawful wounding in respect of injuries inflicted for sexual gratification, pleaded Article 8 of the ECHR, but the ECtHR found unanimously that the Article had *not* been violated. The attitude of the court was restrained in two respects: first, in that it failed to criticise the English courts' inconsistent attitude in the treatment of homosexual accused such as Laskey, compared to the more favourable treatment of heterosexual accused in similar cases (as in *R v Wilson*[54]); second, it expressed a conservative view of privacy in the case, opining that whilst the state had not disputed the 'private life' aspect of the case, given that 'so many' men were involved the court might otherwise have been disposed to doubt that the case did raise an issue of privacy. This view contrasts rather oddly with the ECtHR's wider interpretation of privacy in the transsexual cases.

Despite these criticisms, it is likely that the Scottish courts would reach a similarly conservative conclusion as the House of Lords in such a case, following the principle in *Smart v HM Advocate*.[55] The conservative attitude of Scottish and English courts towards minority sexual practices in general is apparent from the cases.[56]

---

[51] There is no statutory provision stating in simple terms that marriage is restricted to heterosexual couples. However, in terms of s 6(1) of the Marriage (Scotland) Act 1977, the district registrar may only complete a Marriage Schedule for a couple who wish to marry if there is no legal impediment to the marriage. Section 5(4) of the Act states that there is a legal impediment where 'both parties are of the same sex'. Thus, for regular marriages, this section effectively prohibits same sex marriages.

[52] See the Adults with Incapacity (Scotland) Act 2000, asp 4, s 87(1), (2).

[52a] See the Housing (Scotland) Act 2001, asp. 10, s 108.

[53] *Laskey, Jaggard & Brown v UK* (1997) 24 EHRR 39.

[54] *R v Wilson* [1996] 3 WLR 125.

[55] *Smart v HM Advocate* 1975 (JC) 30.

[56] For instance, in the criminal law, one may note the somewhat colourful comments of Lord Dunpark in *Elliott v HM Advocate* 1987 JC 47 where, directing the jury that they might convict the accused of culpable homicide rather than murder if they believed that he had been provoked by fear of a 'homosexual assault', he said: 'I direct you that if your view of such of the accused's evidence as you accept it is that the acts of [the deceased] were likely so to provoke a normal, sober, heterosexual man, putting it colloquially, to see red, so that he acted in the way in which the accused

The equalisation of the age of consent has finally been achieved legislatively,[57] but only after the protracted failure by the United Kingdom over several years to follow a clear lead from the European Commission that failure to implement this change was a contravention of the ECHR. The Commission's view was expressed in 1997 in the case *Sutherland v UK*,[58] to the effect that the different ages for homosexual and heterosexual consent in the United Kingdom was a violation of Article 8 when considered with Article 14.

The problem in achieving this change domestically was that while the House of Commons repeatedly voted in favour of amending the law to equalise the age of consent, in direct contrast the House of Lords repeatedly voted to thwart such a change. The United Kingdom Government was eventually compelled to use the Parliament Acts to force the change through against the will of the House of Lords. The House of Lords' stance has served to reinforce the view held by some that it is irredeemably conservative on matters of sexual practice.

Recently the ECtHR has been activist in respect of a third issue in this area, namely the legislative provision that homosexual acts between consenting males are permissible only if there are no more than two men present.[59] There is no equivalent of this provision in respect of heterosexual persons, or indeed in respect of homosexual females. This provision, which in England and Wales is found at section 13 of the Sexual Offences Act 1956, was the subject of challenge before the Court. In *ADT v United Kingdom*,[60] a homosexual man, who had been convicted of gross indecency under the English provision, in respect that he had engaged in consensual sexual activity with up to four other men at one time, brought an action against the United Kingdom[61] alleging breach of Articles 8

---

said he would act, or in the way in which the accused said he himself had acted in this case, in that event you may return a verdict of culpable homicide.' The terminology itself seems designed to bolster the view of 'normal' heterosexuality and to reinforce fears of homosexual predatory behaviour. An example of general anti-homosexual comments may be seen in the comments of Lord Justice-General Emslie in *Wilson v HM Advocate* 1987 SCCR 217. Two men accused of murder had been engaged in mutual masturbation when discovered by the victim. Lord Emslie described the sexual acts as 'disgusting homosexual practices', a description which was wholly irrelevant to the case and seems simply to express his distaste for homosexual behaviour. The biased attitude of the English courts, particularly in relation to sentencing, is detailed at length by D Selfe and V Burke in *Perspectives on Sex, Crime and Society* (Cavendish, London, 1998), *passim*.

[57] In the Sexual Offences (Amendment) Act 2000, c 44, s 1(3) of which altered the Criminal Law (Consolidation) (Scotland) Act 1995 and reduced the age of homosexual consent in Scotland from 18 to 16. This legislative change was technically within the competence of the Scottish Parliament and not Westminster, but the Scottish Parliament agreed to let Westminster pilot the change in order that the unaltered Bill could benefit from use of the Parliament Acts. Removal of Scotland from its legislative effect would have prevented this possibility.

[58] *Sutherland v UK* (1997) 24 EHRR CD 22. The case was eventually dropped by the applicant in March 2001 following the legislative equalisation of the age of consent in the United Kingdom.

[59] In Scotland, the relevant provision is s 13(2)(a) of the Criminal Law (Consolidation) (Scotland) Act 1995.

[60] *ADT v United Kingdom* (2000) 31 EHRR 803, available at http://www.dhcour.coe.fr/Hudoc2 doc2/. The judgment was not appealed against by the UK.

[61] Somewhat incongruously, whilst the Government was defending the Sexual Offences Act before the ECtHR, the Home Office was in the process of preparing a report on sexual offences which recommended that the law 'should not treat people differently on the basis of their sexual

and 14. In its judgment, handed down on 31 July 2000, the ECtHR agreed that Article 8 had been violated, and found it unnecessary to consider the Article 14 argument. The court sought in its judgment to play down its comments about the scope of 'private life' in *Laskey,* and stated clearly that

> the applicant has been the victim of an interference with his right to respect for his private life both as regards the existence of legislation prohibiting consensual sexual acts between more than two men in private, and as regards the conviction for gross indecency.[62]

In order to give effect to this decision in Scotland, the Scottish Executive included within the Convention Rights (Compliance) (Scotland) Act 2001 a section abolishing the offence.[63] This legislative change will obviate the need for judicial advancement of the law in this area.

D. EMPLOYMENT DISCRIMINATION AGAINST HOMOSEXUALS

What of discrimination in the workplace, either against prospective employees or existing employees: is the ECHR relevant?

Article 14 (non-discrimination) would seem to be relevant, but it must be pleaded in conjunction with another Article.[64] The most likely Article to be conjoined is Article 8 (respect for private life), on the basis that to discriminate in an employment setting against an individual on the basis of their sexuality is to fail to respect an intimate matter of their personality.[65]

Following the decision in a recent appeal before the Court of Session, it has been confirmed that domestic employment protection legislation does not prevent discrimination on the grounds of sexual orientation,[66] and Community law prohibiting such discrimination has yet to be implemented domestically. In an

---

orientation'. The Report, entitled *Setting the Boundaries*, concluded that 'We could see no public policy justification for the criminal law entering into private consensual activity, which was causing no harm to those involved.'

[62] *ADT v United Kingdom,* above, n 60, 808.

[63] The relevant provision is contained within Part IV of the Convention Rights (Compliance) (Scotland) Act 2001, s 10.

[64] See S Livingstone, 'Article 14 and the Prevention of Discrimination in the European Convention on Human Rights' [1997] *EHRLR* 25.

[65] This is the Article around which the pleadings in *Smith and Grady v United Kingdom* were built (see n 76). Lord Kirkwood, in his opinion in *Clark v MacDonald* (Court of Session, 1 June 2001) stated that 'The Convention does not contain any free-standing right not to be discriminated against. While Article 14 has been held by the European Court of Human Rights to prohibit discrimination on the ground of sexual orientation, it does so only when taken along with one of the substantive rights and freedoms which are guaranteed under the Convention, and there is no Convention right or freedom which relates specifically to employment' (at para 10). This comment wholly fails to appreciate the way in which the existing provisions of the Convention, such as Art 8, have been found by the Court to apply to employment settings.

[66] *Clark v MacDonald,* Inner House, Court of Session, 1 June 2001. Although, following the decision of the House of Lords in *Malik v BCCI* [1998] AC 20, it could be argued that discrimination against existing employees on the grounds of sexual orientation would be in breach of the implied obligation of trust and confidence which exists between employer and employee.

English decision from 1998, the (UK) Sex Discrimination Act 1975 was interpreted in such a way as not to include sexual orientation within the definition of 'sex.'[67] A radical attack on this view was however mounted from Scotland by Lord Johnston, sitting in the Employment Appeal Tribunal. His Lordship's decision in *MacDonald v Ministry of Defence*,[68] was to the effect that the dismissal of a homosexual man from employment in the armed forces on the grounds of his sexual orientation was in breach of the provisions of the Sex Discrimination Act 1975. This decision was taken before the full implementation of the Human Rights Act 1998, but Lord Johnston held that 'if United Kingdom domestic legislation is ambiguous in the context of a potential Convention Right, the Convention may rule as between the two or more interpretations.'[69] He thus opted for a wide interpretation of the term 'sex' as including sexual orientation, seeing this as in accordance with the spirit of recent decisions of the Court. In particular he found the ECJ's decision in *Grant v South West Trains*[70] to be of little assistance.

The impact of the case on its particular subject matter was overtaken by the repeal of the ban on homosexual persons serving in the armed services,[71] but the radical implications of Lord Johnston's ruling for the interpretation of the Sex Discrimination Act 1975 in other employment cases was clear. However, the groundbreaking decision was overturned by the Inner House.[72] All three appeal judges agreed that the context of the word 'sex' in the Sex Discrimination Act 1975 indicated that it was intended to mean gender alone and did not include sexual orientation,[73] and they were of the view that the Human Rights Act 1998 did not require a different meaning to be attached to the word.

Interestingly, however, Lord Prosser would still have found in favour of the respondent. In his opinion, the proper comparison to be made with the treatment of the respondent was not with a homosexual woman in his circumstances, but rather:

---

[67] *Smith v Gardner Merchant* [1998] 3 All ER 852. Though the Court of Appeal concluded that a claim might arise under the Sex Discrimination Act 1975 if a homosexual man could show that a homosexual woman would have been treated differently.

[68] *MacDonald v Ministry of Defence*, Decision of 6 Oct 2000.

[69] *Ibid*, para. 22.

[70] *Grant v South West Trains* [1998] ECR 621, [1998] ICR 449.

[71] See below, n 74.

[72] *Clark v MacDonald*, above, n 61. The opinions of the Inner House were handed down on 1 June 2001.

[73] Lord Prosser did however make the following interesting comment in relation to the effect of s 3(1) of the Human Rights Act 1998 on statutory interpretation: 'Odd though it may seem, a court is in my opinion required by this section to impose upon legislation meanings which were clearly never intended by Parliament when it chose the words which it used. And without actually so deciding, I am prepared to assume that if a particular reading appears possible looking at a particular provision in isolation, one might have to adopt that meaning notwithstanding that it produced discrepancies or illogicalities when compared with other provisions, perhaps even in the same statute' (at para 28). Lord Prosser did not believe that such a course of action was possible in the instant case however.

Within the statutory context, the 'same' circumstances referred to in section 5(3) must be actually the same, in direct objective or descriptive terms. If one is faced with a man wanting or having a partner of a given gender, a comparison must in my opinion be made with a woman having or wanting the same—a partner of that same gender.

In other words, Lord Prosser would compare the circumstances of a man with or seeking a male partner with a woman with or seeking a male partner. So doing, he concluded that a heterosexual woman would have been treated differently than the applicant, and thus the applicant had been discriminated against on the grounds of his sex, meaning gender.

For Lord Prosser, then, the key lay in the statutory interpretation, not of the word 'sex', but of the words 'relevant circumstances' and 'same' circumstances. Are we to characterise this approach as radical, and one which actively promotes rights, or is it merely an unexceptional interpretation of a statutory provision, albeit with radical implications? Without knowing the judicial motivation, the issue is hard fully to determine, but given his Lordship's dismissal of the relevance of the ECHR to the case, the safest view is perhaps that his approach is a standard interpretative one, albeit radical in effect. In any event, Lord Prosser's view was in the minority and the current approach to the interpretation of the Sex Discrimination Act 1975 remains conservative.

(1) Convention arguments relating to workplace discrimination

If ECHR arguments have been thought by Scottish courts to be irrelevant to the interpretation of the Sex Discrimination Act 1975, what about their impact on a free-standing basis? The argument that the ECHR might render unlawful employment discrimination based upon sexual orientation was one which found favour in the eyes of Sir Thomas Bingham MR in a 1996 English decision concerning the dismissal of homosexual persons from the armed forces, *R v Ministry of Defence ex parte Smith*.[74] He said:

> [T]o dismiss a person from his or her employment on the grounds of a private sexual preference, and to interrogate him or her about private sexual behaviour, would not appear to me to show respect for that person's private and family life.[75]

The issue of employment discrimination came before the ECtHR for judgment in the joined cases of *Smith and Grady* and *Lustig-Prean and Beckett*, which concerned the United Kingdom's ban on homosexual persons serving in the armed forces. The court's decision in these cases was handed down in September 1999.[76] The conclusion, that the ban on homosexual persons serving

---

[74] *R v Ministry of Defence, ex parte Smith* [1996] QB 517, [1996] 1 All ER 257, [1996] 2 WLR 305.
[75] *Ibid*, [1996] QB 517, at 558G.
[76] *Smith and Grady v United Kingdom; Lustig-Prean and Beckett v United Kingdom* (1999) 7 BHRC 65. The judgments are available on the ECtHR's website at: http://www.echr.coe.int/eng/ Judgments.htm.

in the armed forces was in breach of Article 8,[77] was unsurprising. The British Government's own position had become increasingly untenable, given its decision to allow serving transsexual personnel in the armed forces to remain at their posts.[78] Following the judgments, the British Government announced that it was lifting the ban,[79] and it has recently been reported that one of the personnel previously dismissed has now applied to re-enlist.

The ECtHR's decision, however, strictly covers only *employment* within the *armed forces*. It does not cover the dismissal of volunteers, nor does it compel the Government to legislate against blanket employment bans on homosexual persons in other professions,[80] or against employers who, while having no explicit policy, in practice dismiss workers found to be homosexual. For protection against such behaviour, recourse will have to be had to a European Community Directive.

(2) European Community law

The European Council has adopted a Directive which outlaws discrimination in the workplace on the grounds of, amongst other things, sexual orientation.[81] Whilst the British Government supported the implementation of this Directive, pressure was brought to bear on them by at least one conservative group opposed to its implementation.[82]

The adoption of the Directive has radically altered the prior jurisprudence of the ECJ.[83] In a case also concerning dismissal of homosexuals from the armed

---

[77] And, in the *Smith and Grady* case, also of Article 13 (no effective domestic remedy) in conjunction with Article 8. The ECtHR considered that an argument based upon Article 14 in conjunction with Article 8 did not add anything to the argument based upon Article 8 *simpliciter*.

[78] The argument that this issue was different from that of sexuality was unconvincing, given that both homosexuality and transsexualism touch on the issue of gender identity.

[79] As announced by the Secretary of State for Defence, Geoffrey Hoon, in the House of Commons on 12 Jan 2000.

[80] The ban on practising homosexuals within the ordained ministry of many Churches is the clearest case.

[81] Council Directive Establishing a General Framework for Equal Treatment in Employment and Occupation, 2000/78/EC. The Directive was enacted pursuant to Article 13 of the Treaty establishing the European Community, which states:

> Without prejudice to the other provisions of this Treaty and within the limits of the powers conferred by it upon the Community, the Council, acting unanimously on a proposal from the Commission and after consulting the European Parliament, may take appropriate action to combat discrimination based on sex, racial or ethnic origin, religion or belief, disability, age or sexual orientation.

[82] Namely, the Christian Institute. See its report on the draft Directive, European Threat to Religious Freedom, available at http://www.christian.org.uk/EUthreatToReligiousFreedoms_FORTHEWEB.pdf

[83] Until the adoption of new Art 13 of the Treaty establishing the European Community, the ECHR's provisions were arguably more flexible than European Community law on sex discrimination, given the reference in Art 14 of the ECHR not just to 'sex' but also to 'other status' in the list of criteria in relation to which discrimination is impermissible.

forces, *R v Secretary of State for Defence ex parte Perkins*,[84] referred to the ECJ on the question of whether such dismissal was in contravention of the Equal Treatment Directive,[85] the Administrator of the ECJ invited the Queen's Bench Division to consider whether it still wished to refer the case in light of the ECJ's decision in *Grant v South West Trains*.[86] The decision in *Grant* was to the effect that sexuality did *not* fall within the definition of sex for the purposes of the Equal Pay Directive.[87] In the decision of 13 July 1998 by the Queen's Bench Division in *Perkins*, Mr Justice Lightman held that the ruling in *Grant* must also apply to the Equal Treatment Directive, and that the reference to the ECJ must therefore be withdrawn.[88]

The adoption of the Council Directive on equal treatment will obviate the need to rely on the uncertain attitude of the ECtHR in this area.[88a]

E. ADOPTION AND CUSTODY PROCEEDINGS

The other issue of discrimination worth brief consideration concerns adoption proceedings. Pre-eminently, one may cite the Scottish case, *T, Petitioner*,[89] in which the First Division of the Court of Session concluded that the homosexuality of a male applicant seeking to adopt a child raised no fundamental question of principle, sexual orientation being only one of the circumstances to be considered by the court. Whether this decision is activist or not may be disputed.[90] What is of interest, is that, in his decision, Lord President Hope commented that had his view been that the intendment of the Adoption Act excluded a man living in a homosexual relationship, the ECHR would *not* have helped the petitioner, because respect for family life in Article 8 of the ECHR does not extend to homosexual relationships, nor would respect for private life ground such a complaint.[91]

The first point, as to the notion of 'family life' in so far as this concerns a homosexual person's relation to his or her partner, is supported by the decision

---

[84] *R v Secretary of State for Defence ex parte Perkins* [1997] IRLR 297.
[85] Council Directive 76/297/EEC, OJ 1976 L39/40.
[86] *Grant v South West Trains*, above, n 70 (Judgment of 17 Feb 1998, Case C–249/96).
[87] Directive 75/117/EEC, OJ 1975 L45/19. Interestingly, the Human Rights Committee established under Article 28 of the United Nations International Covenant on Civil and Political Rights (ICCPR) concluded in *Toonen v Australia* (1994) IHRR 97 that the term 'sex' in the ICCPR included sexual orientation. The ECJ, having to discuss the matter as one of sex discrimination, said in *Grant*: 'Since the condition imposed . . . applies in the same way to female and male workers, it cannot be regarded as constituting discrimination directly based on sex' (at para 28). However, it might be said that since some female workers (those having female partners) were treated differently to some male workers (those having female partners), discrimination did exist between the treatment of some men and some women.
[88] *Perkins*, above, n 84.
[88a] Implementation is to occur by 2 Dec 2003.
[89] *T, Petitioner* 1997 SLT 724.
[90] It has been said that it is a perfectly ordinary example of statutory interpretation.
[91] *T, Petitioner*, above, n 89, 734E–G.

in *Kerkhoven*. However, as it relates to a homosexual person's relationship with his or her child (which was the issue in *T, Petitioner*), it may be argued to have been overtaken by the ECtHR's recent decision in *Salgueiro* (see below). Whilst in adoption proceedings, the child will not normally be a pre-existing member of the adopter's family, it can be argued that the right to adopt is an aspect of 'family life'.

As regards 'private life', there is a respectable argument that a state prohibition on adoption by persons in a homosexual relationship would constitute an infringement of the right to privacy.[92] As noted earlier, the wide bounds to the notion of privacy set by the ECtHR might support such an argument. While it is correct that the ECHR does not confer a right to adopt children, it would at least be arguable that a blanket ban on adoption by homosexuals in such a position could amount to a violation of Article 8, perhaps taken together with Article 14. The argument that such a blanket ban was justified by Article 8(2) would be unlikely to succeed in today's moral climate, though there is no reason why someone's sexual behaviour could not amount to good grounds to refuse adoption in an *individual case*.

As no such blanket ban exists, such an argument is academic. However, the current legislative policy of the United Kingdom not to grant *joint* adoption orders to homosexual couples in stable relationships could be open to challenge. Arguably, such failure can, when considered alongside the failure of the United Kingdom to recognise same-sex partnerships, be argued to amount to a failure to respect private life.[93]

The relevance of sexual orientation in child custody decisions (and, by extrapolation, in adoption proceedings also) was the subject of the recent decision of the ECtHR in *Salgueiro da Silva Mouta v Portugal*.[94] The case concerned a homosexual man who was denied custody of his child on the ground, inter alia, of his sexual orientation. The Portuguese Court of Appeal had noted in its decision: 'The child should live in . . . a traditional Portuguese family' and that:

> it is not our task here to determine whether homosexuality is or is not an illness or whether it is a sexual orientation towards persons of the same sex. In both cases it is an abnormality and children should not grow up in the shadow of abnormal situations.

The ECtHR held that such considerations by the Portuguese Court of Appeal amounted to a violation of Article 8 taken in conjunction with Article 14. Article 8 had been violated in respect that there had been interference with his right to family life.

Most recently, some suprising developments have occurred in the area of parental rights and responsibilities under the Children (Scotland) Act 1995,

[92] On the basis that it would represent an unjustified investigation by the authorities into the individual's relationship and domestic circumstances.
[93] It was reported in the press in May 2002 that the Prime Minister was considering tabling amendments to the English Adoption and Children Bill to permit joint adoption awards to unmarried heterosexual couples and same sex couples.
[94] *Salgueiro da Silva Mouta v Portugal* Decision of 21 Dec 1999.

developments led by the Sheriff Court. In March 2002 Sheriff Duncan at Glasgow Sheriff Court awarded a male homosexual sperm donor parental rights and responsibilities under the Act in relation to the child in question, but was not willing to extend such rights to the lesbian partner of the child's mother.[95] Sheriff Duncan, having reviewed the relevant ECHR material, commented that she 'did not think that [the lesbian partner] fell within the scope of "family" which was envisaged in making an order in terms of Section 11 of the Children (Scotland) Act 1995, for parental rights. That seemed to be an extension of the rights stated in ECHR.' Very shortly thereafter, however, this view was directly contradicted when, in April 2002, Sheriff McPartlin at Edinburgh Sheriff Court granted parental rights and responsibilities to a lesbian couple in relation to each other's children.[96] The implications of this rapid development of the notion of family by the shrieval bench are unclear. If the same approach is adopted by the Court of Session, it may well drive a coach and horses through the more conservative attitude of the ECtHR in relation to 'family life'. Such a development would be a remarkable one for the conservative Scots judiciary.

F. CONCLUSION

What can be concluded from the above discussion on the attitude of the ECtHR to sexual identity and practice and the possible approach of Scottish courts to these areas?

The theme underlining the above discussion has been the extent to which states can permissibly discriminate against persons who breach gender assigned roles, and how courts have reacted and will react to this. Such issues make some people feel uncomfortable, and this attitude has no doubt affected the ECtHR also, partly explaining its restrained attitude. The court has in general, however, been dynamic and active in the way it has interpreted the concept of privacy in order to bring these matters within its justiciability. This has opened up areas to consideration by the court that would otherwise have been blocked to it. It has used the concept of privacy in a flexible way, though perhaps not always in a way that retains the coherence of the concept of privacy that some privacy purists would prefer.[97]

---

[95] *Pursuer v Defender* in the case of Child A, 6 March 2002. The decision is reported on the Scottish Courts Service Website: www.scotcourts.gov.uk

[96] Unreported, April 2002.

[97] For instance, in *Sheffield & Horsham v United Kingdom*, above, n 10, Judge Van Dijk, in his dissenting judgment, said: 'I would not characterise the issue of the legal status of post-operative transsexuals as one of minorities, but rather as one of privacy: everyone's right to live one's own life as one chooses without interference, and everyone's right to act and be treated according to the identity that corresponds best to one's innermost feelings, provided that by doing so one does not interfere with public interests or the interests of others.' The freedom described by Judge van Dijk would be argued, by a privacy purist, to be an issue of liberty and not of privacy at all, even if the individual has his privacy infringed from time to time in the exercise of that liberty.

On the other hand, this definitional activism has not been matched in all cases with a forward thinking attitude in the *application* of the rights. In many cases, due to its acceptance of the margin of appreciation argument, the ECtHR has lagged behind the Commission. The court has failed to require states to recognise same sex partnerships or the right of transsexuals to marry, by maintaining a conservative view of traditional marriage despite changes in attitudes in many Contracting States. The court has recognised as a family unit a social grouping of a transsexual, a woman, and the woman's child, but not a same sex couple.

With such reticence by the court to take the Contracting States to task for their failure to take positive action to protect the rights of transsexuals and homosexuals,[98] it is hard to predict how far the Scottish courts will deal with these matters. Whilst our courts have been generally conservative in the past, the approach of Lord Johnston in *MacDonald* and of the Sheriffs in recent parental rights cases may suggest that change is in the air and that our courts will rise to the challenge. The Human Rights Act 1998 presents the opportunity for challenges in the courts to both the United Kingdom and Scottish governments' policies in these areas, and, as the issue of temporary sheriffs shows, the Convention gauntlet is already being picked up by lawyers.

Whilst change is more likely to come from the Strasbourg, Westminster and Edinburgh Parliaments, the very act of raising before the courts issues of respect for sexual identity and practice in a ECHR context, may itself increase the pressure for legislative change, even if the change itself does not come as a direct result of such court action.

---

[98] Indeed, some members of the old ECtHR feared that its conservatism would set a bad example for the new court. In his judgement in *Sheffield & Horsham v United Kingdom*, above, n 10, Judge van Dijk said of the decision of the majority: 'I deem it highly regrettable that the present Court has not used this very last opportunity to [review its previous case law on Article 8], thus giving clear guidance on what I consider to be the right direction in this area to the new Court' (at para 7).

12

Medical Law and Human Rights: Passing the Parcel Back to the Profession?

GRAEME LAURIE*

A. INTRODUCTION

THIS CHAPTER USES the example of the discipline of medical law to assess the impact of incorporation of the European Convention for the Protection of Human Rights and Fundamental Freedoms (ECHR) on domestic law, and in particular the impact of Article 8 which guarantees respect for private and family life, home and correspondence. The focus on Article 8 is appropriate for a number of reasons, not least of which is the fact that the majority of issues that are central to medical law fall within the realm of private and family life. More broadly, however, as a nascent discipline in its own right that continues to seek proper direction, medical law may well serve as a testing ground for the development of the 'rights culture' that many have predicted for Scotland and the rest of the United Kingdom as a result of incorporation of the Convention.

The chapter begins with a survey of the discipline of medical law as it is today in Scotland, and more generally in the United Kingdom. In particular, three seminal Scottish cases are examined which reflect the discipline's current state of development. These cases have also been criticised for their lack of sensitivity to human rights. The cases are then analysed in light of the jurisprudence of the European Commission on Human Rights and the European Court of Human Rights (ECtHR) to determine whether and how medical law might be affected by the incorporation into domestic law of the ECHR rights. Finally, the ruling of the Court of Session in *A v The Scottish Ministers*[1] will be considered. This was the first time the Court had been called upon to determine whether an Act of the Scottish Parliament had been passed within the competence of the Parliament, and most notably, whether the Act complied with the rights

* Senior Lecturer in Law, University of Edinburgh. The author would like to thank Professor Kenyon Mason and Catriona Drew for invaluable comments and assistance on earlier drafts of this paper. The usual disclaimer applies.

[1] *A (A Mental Patient) v Scottish Ministers* 2001 SC 1; 2002 SC (PC) 63.

protected under Article 5 of the ECHR. The Act in question is the Mental Health (Public Safety and Appeals) (Scotland) Act 1999, which was the first Act passed by the Scottish Parliament after its re-constitution in July 1999. This ruling, and the subsequent appeal to the Privy Council, serve as very clear indicators of how the courts might take to their task as gatekeepers of human rights in Scotland and as such represent important markers for the shape of things to come.

The conclusion of this chapter is that no radical changes are anticipated for medical law in the near future. Indeed, as we shall see, in some respects the guidance offered from Strasbourg on fundamental rights central to the discipline is unhelpful and represents a far less sophisticated state of affairs than already exists at home. This having been said, the possibility to develop medical law at the domestic level certainly exists in theory. It is doubtful, however, whether much advance will be made in practice in the medico-legal sphere using human rights arguments, given the relatively languid attitude of the UK courts when it comes to challenging the authority of the medical profession.

B. CONTEMPORARY MEDICAL LAW

Medical law is a young discipline, having been established in law schools in the United Kingdom in the mid-1970s. Parallel developments have occurred throughout the jurisdictions of the Western world, but in the UK the advance of medical law has arguably been hampered by the absence of clear legal protection of certain 'fundamental rights' which are considered to be the stalwarts of the discipline and which elsewhere are enshrined in law. Inter alia, these are:

— the right to life,
— the right to respect for personal autonomy,
— the right to privacy, and
— the right to reproduce and found a family.

Although the discipline has by no means floundered in the UK, the form which it takes departs—significantly in some cases—from that found in other jurisdictions. Respect for the autonomy of the patient has been relatively slow to emerge as the courts have dealt with controversial areas, such as refusal of treatment,[2] advance directives,[3] forced caesarean sections[4] and force feeding,[5] in a piecemeal, and at times haphazard, fashion. To an extent this is under-

---

[2] *Re T (adult: refusal of treatment)* [1992] 4 All ER 649.
[3] Only first recognised (tentatively) in 1994 in *Re C (mental patient: medical treatment)* [1994] 1 All ER 819. See also now, *Re AK* (2000) 58 BMLR 151.
[4] Compare *Re S (adult: refusal of medical treatment)* [1992] 4 All ER 671, *Re MB* [1997] *Fam Law* 542; [1997] 2 FCR 541 and *St. George's Healthcare National Health Service Trust v S (No 2): R v Louize Collins & Ors, Ex Parte S (No 2)* [1998] 3 WLR 936, [1998] 3 All ER 673.
[5] *Riverside Mental Health Trust v Fox* [1994] 1 FLR 614.

standable because the courts have been faced, on the one hand, with arguments about autonomy which have no grounding in the existing law, and on the other by powerful medical evidence suggestive of a more paternalistic approach.[6] When autonomy-based arguments have proved to be of limited use, as in cases involving children or incapax adults, the British courts have with few exceptions fallen back on the medical profession to decide how such patients should be treated.[7] The broad and undefined parameter which is used requires that patients be treated in their own best interests, as determined, primarily, by the medical profession itself.[8]

Difficult decisions involving the end of life, such as the withdrawal of feeding and hydration from patients in persistent vegetative state, have similarly been dealt with by reference to the concept of 'best interests'. And, once again, the British courts have been content to leave such matters to be determined by clinicians. Indeed, in *Airedale National Health Service Trust v Bland*[9] the House of Lords eschewed argument based on 'fundamentals' such as privacy and autonomy in favour of an approach which allows the medical profession to establish not only the limits of its own duties to patients but also the point at which continued alimentation can be deemed 'futile' and the patient allowed to die.[10]

The Scottish judiciary has not been called upon often to address itself to medical law issues. When it has, in the main, it has followed the lead of the English courts. And, while the means by which the Scottish courts have reached various end points have occasionally differed, the same has rarely been true of the

---

[6] For example, in *Re T*, above n 2, the court paid lip-service to the 'right' of the patient to refuse treatment but then held that she was incapable of exercising such a right because of undue influence from others, even though there was no clinical reason to doubt her mental capacity.

[7] A series of cases involving non-treatment of neonates perfectly illustrates this phenomenon, see: *In re J (a minor)(wardship: medical treatment)* [1990] 3 All ER 930; *In re J (a minor)(medical treatment)* [1992] 4 All ER 614; *Re C (a baby)* [1996] 2 FLR 43 and *Re C (a minor)(medical treatment)* [1998] 1 FLR 384. The only exception to this is *Re T (a minor)(wardship: medical treatment)* (1997) 35 BMLR 63, in which the Court of Appeal took the extraordinary step of respecting the decision of the parents of a young child not to put him through a liver transplant despite the fact that there was overwhelming medical evidence that the operation would be successful, and in the knowledge that without the operation the child would die.

[8] The English Court of Appeal has issued guidelines on how to deal with an incapax patient which endorse the use of the 'best interests' test. Significantly, the guidelines focus primarily on procedural issues and do not give any guidance on how 'best interests' are to be established, see *St. George's Healthcare NHS Trust*, above, n 4. In Scotland, the Adults with Incapacity (Scotland) Act 2000 rejects the use of the 'best interests' test to determine how incapax adults should be treated. And yet, while provision is made for the appointment of proxy decision-makers to stand in the shoes of such adults in many scenarios, the powers of such persons are limited in the context of medical treatment decisions. For example, there is no requirement to approach a proxy if treatment is to be withdrawn, and a refusal of treatment by a proxy can be overridden by a second medical opinion in all cases. The sole recourse is an appeal by the proxy to the Court of Session. The net effect, however, is to continue to 'medicalise' the decision-making process in respect of incapable persons. For comment, see G T Laurie and J K Mason, 'Negative Treatment of Vulnerable Patients: Euthanasia by Any Other Name?' 2000 *JR* 159.

[9] *Airedale National Health Service Trust v Bland* [1993] AC 789.

[10] See J K Mason and G T Laurie, 'The Management of Persistent Vegetative State in the British Isles' 1996 *JR* 263.

decisions ultimately taken.[11] Thus, in real terms the 'rights' of patients north of the border have not differed significantly from those south of it. This may, of course, be set to change as a result of the re-establishment of the Scottish Parliament. Indeed, in its first year the Parliament passed two Acts which have a direct bearing on patients rights: the Mental Health (Public Safety and Appeals) (Scotland) Act 1999 (asp 1) and the Adults with Incapacity (Scotland) Act 2000 (asp 4). The former immediately ran into controversy with questions raised over its compliance with the ECHR and is accordingly discussed below. The latter is the subject of comment elsewhere,[12] but also merits consideration here in terms of its robustness against a potential human rights challenge. Undoubtedly, these measures and others like them will re-mould the legal landscape in Scotland in respect of patients' rights, but for the moment the current state of medical law in the United Kingdom can be said to be characterised by the following features:

— grudging acceptance of the right to self-determination, including the right to refuse treatment;
— dominance by the 'best interests' test where patient competence is in doubt;
— undue deference by the courts to the medical profession to determine what should be meant by 'best interests';
— serious reluctance on the part of the courts to intervene in the assessment of best interests; and,
— perhaps most surprisingly of all, the rarely qualified surrender by the courts of the responsibility for deciding the scope of duty of care of the medical profession to its patients, and the linking of this with the assessment of best interests.

C. WILL INCORPORATION OF THE EUROPEAN CONVENTION CHANGE ANYTHING?

In determining the extent to which the incorporation of the European Convention on Human Rights might influence the rights of patients and the development of medical law as a discipline in Scotland, we can examine three seminal cases and consider whether, and how, the outcome might have been different if a 'human rights approach' had been adopted. These cases concern issues at the beginning and the end of life—the ethico-legal coalfaces of the medical lawyer—and the problem of the incapax adult.

In *Kelly v Kelly*[13] the estranged husband of a pregnant woman was unsuccessful in preventing an abortion of their fetus. He argued that the fetus had the right in law to be protected from civil wrongs as a legal person and that, as the

---

[11] See G T Laurie, '*Parens Patriae* Jurisdiction in the Medico-Legal Context: The Vagaries of Judicial Activism' (1999) 3(1) *Edin LR* 95.
[12] See Laurie and Mason, above, n 8.
[13] 1997 SLT 896; 1997 SCLR 749.

person's father, he was entitled to defend that right. The basis of the Inner House decision was that the fetus had no legal rights whatsoever while it remained in the womb. No historical precedent existed which could lead the court to a different conclusion and support was drawn from a plethora of foreign jurisdictions which hold the same at common law.

Although wholly in keeping with the terms of the Abortion Act 1967 (as amended), this decision denies any rights to the fetus and to the prospective father to protect it. Yet, it should not be thought as a result that the judgment is a vindication of any 'right' of the woman, for the 1967 Act makes the availability of an abortion wholly dependent on finding medical practitioners who are willing to certify that the conditions of the Act have been met.[14] There is no 'right', as such, to an abortion in the United Kingdom.

In *L, Petitioner*[15] the Outer House of the Court of Session authorised the sterilisation of a 32 year-old autistic woman on the request of her mother. It was the first case of its kind in which the proposed action had been challenged in Scotland. The court considered it to be in the woman's best interests to be sterilised both to protect her from the sequelae of menstruation (she had been on drug contraceptives since the age of 13) and for contraceptive purposes. This was so despite the fact that there was no real risk that she would become pregnant. The Court did not lay down any guidelines on how 'best interests' are to be determined in such cases, nor could it draw on guidelines offered in other cases. The speculative risk of continuing with drug-based contraception overshadowed the proceedings, in which there was no reference to the ward's *rights*, fundamental or otherwise. In particular, the court made no attempt, as has happened in other jurisdictions, to distinguish between therapeutic and non-therapeutic intervention. In Canada, for example, the Supreme Court has refused to authorise non-therapeutic interventions because of the necessary interference which this entails with fundamental rights of privacy, including the right to reproduce.[16]

In *Law Hospital NHS Trust v Lord Advocate*[17] a bench of five judges authorised the withdrawal of feeding and hydration from a patient in persistent vegetative state (PVS) on the basis of the 'best interests' test. The formulation of that test followed the decision of the House of Lords in *Airedale National Health Service Trust v Bland*[18] in that the court handed power to the medical profession to decide when it is in a patient's best interests no longer to be kept alive. Moreover, it did this by reference to the test for medical negligence: if a responsible body of medical opinion considers that continued treatment is futile, then there is no continuing duty to treat that patient and they may be

---

[14] 1967 Act s 1(1). For comment see J K Mason, *Medico-legal Aspects of Reproduction and Parenthood* 2nd edn (Ashgate, Aldershot, 1998), ch 5.

[15] 1996 SCLR 538.

[16] *In re Eve* [1986] 2 SCR 388.

[17] *Law Hospital NHS Trust v Lord Advocate* 1996 SC 301; 1996 SLT 848; 1996 SCLR 491.

[18] Above, n 9.

allowed to die. In this case 'treatment' was artificial feeding and hydration which, when withdrawn, led directly to the death of the patient by starvation. Such a formulation of the best interests test has implications not only for those who might seek to have treatment continued in future cases but also for those who would argue that the decision to end life should be for the persons concerned alone.

These cases demonstrate the amorphous nature of the 'best interests' test, and, correspondingly, the wide-ranging discretion of the medical profession in respect of their dealings with patients.

D. 'CONVENTIONALISING' SCOTTISH MEDICAL LAW

Seen from a human rights perspective, however, these rulings potentially invoke several Articles of the ECHR and raise a number of questions, the resolution of which could have significant consequences for the discipline of medical law and patient rights.

(1) *Kelly v Kelly*: Article 2 and the protection of the right to life

(a) The interests of the fetus

The ECHR guarantees in Article 2 that everyone's right to life shall be protected by law and that no one shall be deprived of his life intentionally.[19] The question therefore arises of the status of the fetus and whether it qualifies as 'someone' for the purposes of the Convention.

Neither the Commission nor the ECtHR has definitively answered this question.[20] Indeed, the ECtHR has always declined to address the issue.[21] In *X v United Kingdom*,[22] the Commission noted that the term 'everyone's' is not defined in the Convention, and that in almost every instance where it occurs the context dictates that it can only be read to refer to a person already born.[23] This

---

[19] Art 2 states: '(1) Everyone's right to life shall be protected by law. No one shall be deprived of his life intentionally save in the execution of a sentence of a court following his conviction of a crime for which this penalty is provided by law. (2) Deprivation of life shall not be regarded as inflicted in contravention of this article when it results from the use of force which is no more than absolutely necessary: (a) in defence of any person from unlawful violence; (b) in order to effect a lawful arrest or to prevent the escape of a person lawfully detained; (c) in action lawfully taken for the purpose of quelling a riot or insurrection.'

[20] Note, however, that in Austria where the Convention has the status of constitutional law it has been held that Art 2 does not cover unborn life: decision of 11 Oct 1974, Erk Slg (Collection of Decisions) No 7400, EuGRZ (Europaische Grundrechtezeitschrift) 1975 at 74. See *X v United Kingdom* (1988) 10 EHRR 81 at para 5.

[21] See, for example, *Open Door Counselling Ltd and Dublin Well Woman Centre Ltd v Ireland* (1992) 15 EHRR 244, at paras 63 and 66.

[22] *X v United Kingdom* (1988) 10 EHRR 81.

[23] The term occurs in Arts 1, 2, 5, 6, 8, 9, 10, 11, and 13.

is even the case in the context of Article 2 itself, if one has regard to the exceptions permitted in paragraphs 1 and 2.[24]

By corollary, the Commission has ruled on the permissibility of abortion in a number of cases. As a result, and by exhaustion, it has left us with an area of potential protection for the fetus. For example, in *X v United Kingdom* it held that a husband could not prevent a termination at 10 weeks when this was permitted within UK legislation as 'medically indicated'. More liberal still, the Commission ruled as inadmissible a claim by a partner to prevent an abortion at 14 weeks on social grounds.[25] However, what the Commission has refused to do is to rule that a fetus has no right to life in the later stages on pregnancy. At the same time, it has determined that there can be no *absolute* right to life for the fetus because of the obvious conflict that would arise if the woman's life were in danger. In such cases, the woman's life will trump. Arguably, however, this reasoning may mean in future cases that abortion at the later stages of pregnancy might only be justifiable in cases of danger to the life of the woman. Thus, justifications on the basis of handicap of the fetus might become questionable and subject to challenge under Article 2.[26]

(b) The interests of the father

In *X v United Kingdom* and *H v Norway* the Commission ruled that the prospective father of a fetus has standing under the Convention because he is directly affected by any decisions affecting his fetus. Thus Mr Kelly's case would have been competent in Strasbourg. However, any argument that he could have made would have been very unlikely to succeed. A submission that the termination interfered with his right to family life under Article 8(1) would be defeated because of the justifications under Article 8(2); either on the grounds of the health of 'the mother' or to protect 'the rights of others', namely, the woman herself.[27] The Commission has ruled, for example, that the continuation of the

---

[24] Above, n 19.

[25] *H v Norway*, unreported. The ECtHR ruled in *Open Door and Dublin Well Woman v Ireland*, above, n 21, that measures to restrict freedom of expression under Art 10 (offering of information and counselling on abortion abroad) were not automatically justified where the State considered that the life of the unborn was at stake. In each case the Contracting Parties must act in a manner which is compatible with their range of obligations under the Convention. Thus any measures which sought to restrict Art 10 freedom had to be justified in accordance with Art 10(2). On the facts of the case, although it was argued that restriction of speech was necessary for the protection of morals, the ECtHR held that to impose a perpetual injunction on those seeking to offer advice and counselling was disproportionate to the aim sought.

[26] This is currently permissible in the UK at any point in the gestation period, under s 1(1)(d) of the 1967 Act.

[27] Art 8 reads: '(1) Everyone has the right to respect for his private and family life, his home and his correspondence. (2) There shall be no interference by a public authority with the exercise of this right except as is in accordance with the law and is necessary in a democratic society in the interests of national security, public safety or the economic well being of the country, for the prevention of disorder or crime, for the protection of health or morals, or for the protection of the rights and freedoms of others.'

pregnancy principally raises issues for the woman's *private life* which impact substantially more directly on her than does an interference with the father's *family life* under Article 8(1).[28] Indeed, the Commission has gone further and ruled that his right to respect for family life does not extend to a right to be consulted on the termination.[29] This is in keeping with the US position where the abortion decision is seen, at least in the first trimester, to be solely a question for the woman.[30]

(c) The interests of the woman

One should not take from this, however, that the self-determination of the woman entitles her to a 'right' to abortion under the Convention. Indeed, the Commission has expressly ruled out any claim that there exists a right to abortion *simpliciter*. In *Bruggemann and Scheuten v FRG*[31] it was argued that the absence of an unfettered right to choose abortion within the first 12 weeks of pregnancy was a breach of Article 8(1) as an unjustifiable interference with private life. Despite holding that it did not find it necessary to decide whether the unborn child is to be considered 'life' in the sense of Article 2, or whether it could be regarded as an entity under Article 8(2) which could justify interference 'for the protection of others', the Commission ruled that not every aspect of regulation of termination of pregnancy constituted an interference with private life. Indeed, it held that the decision to abort was not one that was solely within the realm of the private life of the woman. Consequently the Commission opined that the State had not interfered at all with the private life of the woman by prohibiting abortion on demand.

This ruling is interesting for a number of reasons. First, it sheds further light on the protection given to fetal interests. Although Article 2 may not necessarily be the basis for protecting a 'right' as such, fetal interests are not entirely disregarded when it comes to determining the limits of Convention rights for women. Indeed, the weight which such interests are accorded is considerable given that the Commission held that there was no interference with the woman's private life. Put another way, this means that no *fundamental* right had been infringed. Had such a right been violated this would require strong justification under Article 8(2). To hold, however, that there is no interference under Article 8(1) is to deny the right to self-determination in the abortion decision. The right to an unfettered choice of terminating a pregnancy is not, accordingly, part of the protected rights under private life.

To bring this back to the UK, the absence of a 'right' to choose an abortion under the 1967 Act is unlikely to be redressed through incorporation. Primarily,

---

[28] *X v United Kingdom*, above, n 22, at para 27.
[29] *Ibid*.
[30] *Roe v Wade* 93 S Ct 705, (1973) and *Planned Parenthood of South Eastern Pennsylvania v Casey* 112 S Ct 2791, (1992).
[31] *Bruggemann and Scheuten v FRG* [1977] 3 EHRR 244.

the decision in *Bruggemann and Scheuten* fell to be considered in light of the margin of appreciation. When the decision was delivered in 1977, a wide range of views on abortion persisted throughout the Contracting States, and all states put limits on the availability of the procedure. No clear consensus had emerged. The applicants argued that although matters differed between countries, the relevant legislation was moving steadily towards recognition of self-determination of women. This submission was nonetheless rejected, and the Commission upheld a wide margin of appreciation for Contracting States to determine for themselves the limits of their abortion laws. Today, although attitudes have moved even further in the direction of women's rights, a broad range of approaches still persists.[32] It is therefore highly unlikely that any future case challenging restrictive abortion laws along the lines of *Bruggemann and Scheuten* would succeed.

(d) Information disclosure

Before leaving issues at the beginning of life, it is interesting to consider the ruling in *LCB v United Kingdom*[33] in which the ECtHR considered the question of whether a positive obligation was imposed on the state to inform the applicant's father that he might have been exposed to radiation as a serviceman serving on Christmas Island during the nuclear tests of the late 1950s. The applicant claimed, inter alia, violation of Article 2 on the grounds that the failure to inform of the risk materially contributed to her developing life-threatening leukaemia at the age of four. It was argued that failure to inform prevented pre- and post-natal monitoring which could have led to earlier diagnosis and treatment of the illness. Although the ECtHR held that there was no violation of Article 2 because there was insufficient evidence to indicate either that the father had been irradiated to a dangerous level or that at the relevant time the State had any reason to believe there was a causal link between irradiation and leukaemia in off-spring, it did opine that *had* relevant information pertaining to risk been available,

> the State could have been required to take steps in relation to the applicant if it had appeared likely at that time that any such exposure of her father to radiation might have engendered a real risk to her health.[34]

Here the ECtHR purports to impose a positive obligation on the state to take measures to protect not just an existing fetus, but also future generations; that is, not just the yet-to-be born but also the yet-to-be conceived. In relying on Article 2, the ECtHR issued the dictum in the interest of *future* persons, rather

---

[32] For a review of the diverse approaches to abortion regulation both in Europe and beyond see, Department for Economic and Social Information and Policy Analysis (Population Division); *Abortion Policies: A Global View*, 3 vols (United Nations, New York, 1995).

[33] *LCB v United Kingdom* (1999) 27 EHRR 212.

[34] *Ibid*, at para 38.

than, for example, under Article 8 when the need for information could easily be framed as an aspect of the private life of *existing* persons, ie those exposed to the risk.[35] Moreover, the interest which is at stake, or so it would seem from the wording of the judgment, is not simply one concerning 'life' itself, but rather one concerning 'quality of life.'[36] Thus, acts performed or omitted prior to a person's birth, which in some way affect their quality of life at a later stage, might be the object of a successful subsequent action by the person concerned. What, for example, would be the position if the state failed to inform prospective parents of appreciable risks of harm to their progeny from congenital or genetic disease when a therapy or cure was available? A ruling in favour of disclosure could have a significant impact of the need for population screening programmes.

But might more invidious arguments be made? For example, might it be put that a pregnant woman's acts during pregnancy could be curtailed if these are likely to affect the 'quality of life' of the fetus or her future child, and that the state's obligation under Article 2 requires action to be taken? Certainly, Article 2 does not seem to permit any exceptions which might be relied upon by the woman to excuse her behaviour, save, of course, the one clear exception that her own life was in danger (but in such cases a termination would be more likely than continuation of the pregnancy). But, the consequent interference which such an approach would have with other rights of the woman, such as the right to respect for her private life under Article 8, would also have to be considered. And, while it would seem from the above discussion in respect of a father's rights that no one would have sufficient standing to sue while the woman was pregnant, the recognition of rights for future persons nevertheless raises the prospect of 'new' actions and remedies in medical law. For example, if parents did not heed a state warning in respect of potential birth defects and produced a child which suffered from a fore-warned harm would the child have any remedy against the parents themselves? Would there be an obligation on the state to provide such a remedy if none existed?

At present the so-called *wrongful life* action is not available in the UK to children born with a disability. This action amounts to an argument that it would have been better not to be born at all rather than to be born with the handicap. The English Court of Appeal has refused to recognise the remedy on policy grounds,[37] and the Scottish courts have indicated that this precedent would be followed if ever such a claim were lodged in Scotland.[38] Moreover, in England and Wales, liability on the part of a mother is guarded against by the Congenital

---

[35] The particular 'right' requiring respect being the right to informed choice in reproduction.

[36] At several points in the judgment the ECtHR talks of the 'health of the applicant' and 'diminishing the severity of her disease' (see paras 38, 40 and 41). Historically the Commission has always required a threat to life itself under Art 2: see *De Varga-Hirsch v France* No 9559/81, 33 DR 158 (1983) and *M v FRG* No 10307/83, 37 DR 113 (1984).

[37] *McKay v Essex Area Health Authority* [1982] 2 All ER 771.

[38] *Anderson v Forth Valley Health Board* 1998 SLT 588; 1998 SCLR 97.

Disabilities (Civil Liability) Act 1976,[39] although liability of the father is not affected. Furthermore, the Act precludes liability for a health care professional if either or both parents know of the risk of the child being born disabled prior to conception.[40] No equivalent statute exists in Scots law, and there are no authorities directly in point. In all likelihood, however, the Scottish courts would again follow the English approach. Yet, the prospect of the absence of a remedy for the child raises the spectre of horizontal effect of the Convention.

The Commission and the ECtHR have ruled in respect of many Convention Articles that a positive obligation can be imposed on the state to ensure that adequate remedies exist when individual A's human rights have been violated by individual B's conduct. Thus, in *X and Y v The Netherlands*[41] the Dutch Government was held to be in violation of Article 8 because Dutch law did not permit the victim of sexual assault or her father to bring an effective criminal prosecution against the assailant. This was so even although civil remedies were available. In discussing the nature of Article 8 obligations the ECtHR said: '[t]hese obligations may involve the adoption of measures designed to secure respect for private life even in the sphere of the relations of individuals between themselves' (para 23). In similar fashion, the denial of a remedy for a seriously handicapped child may entail human rights violations on the part of the United Kingdom. This is not to say, however, that the wrongful life action would require to be adopted. Indeed, it would be ironic if it were, given that the basis of a human rights argument in this context would be Article 2 (protection of the right to life) and the basis of the wrongful life action is, essentially, that it would have been better never to be born. None the less, such argument as is offered here might require the adoption of other remedies, or the lifting of prohibitions on suits against certain parties, in order to respect fully the rights of 'future' persons under Article 2.

The acceptance in *LCB v United Kingdom* of a positive obligation to provide information about risk has also been upheld in the context of 'existing' persons in the case of *Guerra and Others v Italy* on the basis of Article 8.[42] The risk here came from toxic chemicals produced by a factory situated within a kilometre of the Italian town of Manfredonia. The inhabitants were held to have a right to 'essential information' relating to the work of the plant under Article 8 in order to assess meaningfully the risks of continuing to live in the town. Similarly, in *McGinley v United Kingdom* the ECtHR confirmed that where a state engages in hazardous activities which might have hidden adverse consequences on the health of those involved, Article 8 requires that an effective and accessible

---

[39] 1976 Act, ss 1 and 2. The only exception to this concerns harm caused while the mother is driving a motor vehicle. In such cases compulsory motor insurance ensures recovery which will not disrupt familial relations.

[40] 1976 Act, s 1(4).

[41] *X and Y v The Netherlands* (1985) 8 EHRR 235.

[42] *Guerra and Others v Italy* (1998) 26 EHRR 357.

procedure be established to enable such persons to seek relevant and appropriate information.[43]

These cases imposing positive obligations on the state to ensure that adequate information is given to people to allow them to make truly autonomous choices have clear implications for medical law. Central to that discipline is the notion that the right to self-determination is only meaningfully exercised through *informed* consent. The problem lies in deciding how much information is to be given. In the UK this matter has long been decided by the medical profession[44]—how much information would a responsible body of medical opinion disclose?—although more recent jurisprudence[45] indicates a gradual shift away from this position towards one in line with other jurisdictions where a more patient-oriented test is applied.[46] In like manner, what we perhaps see in the above Convention cases is the beginning of an acceptance of the centrality of self-determination to human rights which are crucial to the protection of the personality. However, before this is of any assistance to the development of domestic patient rights, a greater elucidation is required of how much information must be given, or rather, can be expected or demanded as part of the rights in question. In *Guerra*, for example, no indication was offered of what constituted 'essential information' necessary to respect the private lives of the inhabitants, nor was any guidance or test provided on how to determine the extent of disclosure required.

Information disclosure is crucial to the realisation of meaningful rights in the health care context. Cases such as these are encouraging, in that they reflect a similar ethical basis to that which underpins western medical law. They are found wanting, however, for their lack of precision on the parameters of the right in a practical setting. Indeed, domestic jurisprudence in this context is considerably more sophisticated, and will scarcely benefit from rulings such as these in their current form.

(2) *L, Petitioner*: Articles 8 and 12: private life, family life and the right to marry and to found a family

We can deal with Commission and ECtHR jurisprudence concerning sterilisation fairly briefly. To the knowledge of this writer there has only ever been one case before the Commission, which is unreported.[47] The case was dismissed because it appeared that the subject of the application had consented to the

---

[43] *McGinley v United Kingdom* (1999) 27 EHRR 1. In the present case the UK had fulfilled its obligation.

[44] Classically, see *Sidaway v Governors of Royal Bethlem Hospital* [1985] AC 871.

[45] For example, *Pearce v United Bristol Healthcare NHS Trust* (1998) 48 BMLR 118.

[46] Compare the position in Australia, Canada and certain American states: *Rogers v Whitaker* (1992) 67 ALJR 47, *Reibl v Hughes* [1980] 2 SCR 880 and *Canterbury v Spence* (1972) 464 F 2d 772 (DC Cir).

[47] Appl No 1287/61, unreported.

operation, and the Commission merely mentioned in passing that in certain circumstances a sterilisation operation might be contrary to Article 2. This is an interesting point for future generations, but no exegesis is offered. Nothing, however, was said about the rights of subjects of sterilisation and it is to this issue that we now turn.

The threat of removal of an individual's capacity to reproduce invites challenge under the ECHR on at least two grounds. First, as a potential invasion of (bodily) privacy under Article 8(1) and, second, as an interference with the right to marry and to found a family under Article 12.

(a) The right to marry and to found a family

Let us deal first with the protection accorded by Article 12.[48] It is important to note that this Article embodies a unitary right, not two separate rights.[49] Jacobs and White comment thus:

> [I]t seems from the wording of the Article that only married couples can claim the right to found a family. If the Article had been worded 'Everyone has the right to marry and to found a family', it might have been easier to infer that unmarried people also had the right to found a family.[50]

This view is substantiated by the jurisprudence of both the Commission and the ECtHR.[51] It would seem to indicate that for the adult incapax who is unlikely ever to marry, Article 12 is an unattractive prospect for protecting their reproductive capacity. But the notion that only married couples can claim the right to found a family under Article 12 should not go unchallenged. If this is true, for example, does it follow that only married persons can experience interference with this aspect of 'the' right? Surely if the right is to have meaningful content we must accept that one can interfere *today* with a person's ability to exercise their rights *in the future*. If an unmarried woman is sterilised without her consent, de facto she is deprived of the physical capacity to found a family. Thus, at no point in the future will she be able to exercise the 'unitary' right of marrying and founding a family. As a matter of logic, such action must be a violation of the aspect of the right pertaining to the founding of a family,[52] even if the interference in question is not actionable until later; in this case, until after marriage. Yet, even if this is accepted, the benefits for the adult incapax are limited.

---

[48] Art 12 states: 'Men and women of marriageable age have the right to marry and to found a family, according to the national laws governing the exercise of this right.'

[49] In *F v Switzerland* 18 December 1987, Judgment 21/1986/119/168 the ECtHR speaks only of '*the* fundamental right of a man and a woman to marry and to found a family' (at para 32, emphasis added).

[50] F G Jacobs and R C A White, *The European Convention on Human Rights*, 2nd edn (Clarendon Press, Oxford, 1996), 177.

[51] *Rees v United Kingdom* (1986) 9 EHRR 56.

[52] The Commission has ruled that 'the right to found a family is an absolute right in the sense that no restrictions similar to those in para (2) of Art 8 of the Convention are expressly provided for': *X v United Kingdom*, (1988) 10 EHRR 81, para 106.

Although it should not be assumed that an individual who is incapacitated in respect of some aspects of her life will always be so affected so as not to be able to marry at some future date, this will, unfortunately, be the case in many circumstances. If then the above interpretation is correct, it would indeed seem that Article 12 is unhelpful in protecting the reproductive rights of the incapax. The 'right to reproduce', if it is to be protected at all, must be found elsewhere.[53]

Some hope might lie in Article 8, but not in the right to respect for family life for this right protects only *existing* family life and not *future* family life. This, then, leaves 'private life.'[54]

(b) The right to respect for private life

Privacy is an amorphous concept which has come to represent different things to different people. As one commentator has rightly observed: 'Privacy, like an elephant, is more readily recognised than described.'[55] In the United States privacy has been relied upon extensively to champion family and individual rights, particularly in the medical sphere. It is the basis of a woman's right to abortion[56] and the right to access to contraception,[57] and it has even been used in certain states to justify the withdrawal of care to allow patients to die.[58] Privacy in this sense, however, has come to be conflated with autonomy and liberty,[59] and has become an unwieldy beast requiring taming.[60]

The first thing to note about the 'right' under Article 8 is that it is merely a right to respect, and more notable still, it is a right to respect for private life. For most of us 'private life' is undoubtedly broader than 'privacy' *in se* and this is a view shared by the Commission and the ECtHR. 'Private life' has been held not

---

[53] The nature of such a 'right' is undoubtedly negative. That is, it is a right not to experience interference with one's capacity to reproduce, rather than a right to be assisted to reproduce, which is a positive right. A similar view prevails in the United States. While in *Skinner v Oklahoma* (1942) 316 US 535 the Supreme Court laid down that the right to procreate is 'fundamental to the very existence and survival of the race', it was noted subsequently in *Poe et al v Gerstein et al.* 517 F 2d, 787, 795 (1975) that '*Skinner* . . . did not guarantee the individual a procreative opportunity, it merely safeguarded his procreative potential from state infringement'. In similar fashion, in the UK, the Court of Appeal has recently rejected the argument that Art 12 requires assistance from prison authorities to allow a prisoner access to artificial insemination facilities in order to procreate with his wife, see *R v Secretary of State for the Home Department, ex parte Mellor* [2001] 3 WLR 533, [2001] 2 FCR 153.

[54] It is interesting to note that the nature of the rights under Art 8 and the jurisprudence from the Commission and the ECtHR is such that it forces us to push for an expansionist approach towards the most amenable concept, *viz*, privacy.

[55] Taken from JB Young (ed), *Privacy* (John Wiley, Chichester, 1979), 5.

[56] *Roe v Wade*, above, n 30.

[57] *Griswold v Connecticut* 381 US 479 (1965) and *Eisenstadt v Baird* 405 US 438 (1972).

[58] This was recognised by the Supreme Court of New Jersey in *In re Quinlan* 70 NJ 10 (1976), 355 A 2d 647. On the facts of that case, however, the court did not sanction withdrawal.

[59] See J Wagner DeCew, 'The Scope of Privacy in Law and Ethics' (1986) 5 *Law and Philosophy* 145.

[60] The US Supreme Court itself has moved away from a privacy analysis towards a liberty analysis in the context of medico-legal cases: see *Cruzan v Director, Missouri Department of Health* 110 S Ct 2841 (1990).

only to include a right to control personal information[61] (often heralded as the core interest in 'privacy'), but also involves protection of spatial privacy interests[62] such as physical and moral integrity,[63] the freedom to develop one's personality[64] and to establish and maintain personal relationships.[65] It should be observed too that protection is not merely restricted to the 'inner circle' of life, but straddles the public/private divide. Thus, it has been held also to protect professional and business activities.[66] Lastly, it has been affirmed as encompassing both negative and positive obligations, that is, not merely a right not to be interfered with but, in certain circumstances, a right to have assistance in the fulfilment and enjoyment of one's private life.[67] All of these elements have conspired to make Article 8 one of the most politically useful Articles of the Convention.

From the medico-legal perspective the expansionist nature of 'private life'— and indeed 'family life'[68]—is particularly significant given that Article 8 is the most likely candidate for the protection of the autonomy-based interests that are so central to the discipline of medical law. Thus, although we do not as yet have a ruling from the Commission or the ECtHR on the acceptability of non-therapeutic non-consensual sterilisations, there is much scope for argument.

If we return to *L, Petitioner*, for example, it could be posited that if non-consensual sterilisation is seen to interfere with private life under Article 8(1), as most would undoubtedly agree, then the only defensible ground upon which it can be justified under Article 8(2) is in relation to the health of the individual in question; that is, for therapeutic purposes. Non-therapeutic sterilisation then becomes very difficult to justify, even within a rubric of 'best interests'. Unfortunately, the margin of appreciation which states currently enjoy has led the Strasbourg authorities to demonstrate considerable deference to the notion of 'best interests' where this is used in national law.[69]

Importantly, in the context of the UK law, the discretion accorded to the medical profession in using the 'best interests' test has been unprecedented. Indeed, from the perspective of Scots law in particular, it may even be arguable that the justifications which would normally legitimise interferences under Article 8(2) are not 'in accordance with the law' as this has been determined in Strasbourg.[70]

---

[61] *Niemietz v Germany*, (1992) 16 EHRR 97.

[62] For a theory of spatial privacy interests, see GT Laurie, *Genetic Privacy: A Challenge to Medico–legal Norms* (Cambridge University Press, Cambridge, 2002).

[63] *X and Y v Netherlands*, above n 41.

[64] *Gaskin v United Kingdom* (1989) 12 EHRR 36.

[65] *Beldjoudi v France*, (1992), Series A, vol 234–A.

[66] *Niemeitz v Germany*, above n 61.

[67] *Guerra and Others v Italy*, above n 42.

[68] On this see D Feldman, 'The developing scope of Article 8 of the European Convention on Human Rights' [1997] *EHRLR* 265.

[69] For a discussion of this in the context of minors see, DJ Harris, M O'Boyle, and C Warbrick, *Law of the European Convention on Human Rights*, (Butterworths, London, 1995), 350–53.

[70] For the text of Art 8, see above n 27.

This provision requires that there be a clear foundation in the law for the interference, that it must be knowable, that outcomes must be foreseeable and that there must exist, at least, some means of fettering or checking any excessive discretion which is given to any body or bodies to take decisions which potentially affect human rights under the Convention.[71] As Harris *et al* have noted, 'the usual complaint . . . is not that there is no national law but that the national law is too general in the scope of the powers that it confers . . .'.[72] The existence of procedural safeguards, including judicial supervision, help to protect against arbitrariness, but it is submitted that in the health care context in the UK the procedures which exist are, in the main, ineffective.[73]

While the British courts have historically been reluctant to interfere in an assessment of patient 'best interests', in England and Wales, at least, the Official Solicitor has issued a Practice Note specifically to cover sterilisation cases.[74] The Note states that in virtually all cases an application must be made to the High Court for a declaration as to the best interests of the patient in undergoing sterilisation, and the court must, as a minimum, be satisfied as to (a) the likelihood of pregnancy, (b) the damage deriving from conception and/or menstruation, and (c) the relevance and appropriateness of any proposed medical and surgical techniques. Thus, although the determination of best interests in such cases still relies heavily on medical evidence, the element of arbitrariness in the process is, hopefully, minimised. No equivalent measure exists in Scotland, leaving its public and health authorities open to the challenge that interventions to sterilise patients are not 'in accordance with the law'. Most remarkably, it should be noted with some concern that there is no requirement for judicial involvement in such cases, and indeed *L, Petitioner* only came to court because the mother of the woman sought appointment as a tutor dative with the power to consent to medical intervention. Only at that stage was a curator *ad litem* appointed to argue the contrary case. The mother and the health care professionals were in perfect agreement as to the course of action that should be followed.

More recently still the Adults with Incapacity (Scotland) Act 2000 permits the medical practitioner primarily responsible for the treatment of an adult patient to certify that she is incapable in relation to a particular medical decision and 'to do what is reasonable . . . to safeguard or promote the physical or mental health of the patient.'[75] While the Act also provides for the appointment of proxy decision-makers who must be consulted before medical treatment is offered (where it is practicable to do so), it is submitted that this will be of limited practical value in terms of safeguarding the human rights of the patients themselves.

---

[71] See, *Open Door and Dublin Well Woman v Ireland*, above, n 21.

[72] Harris, O'Boyle and Warbrick, above, n 69, 341.

[73] In *Herczegfalvy v Austria* (1992) Series A, vol 244, at para 89, it was stated by the ECtHR that 'if a law confers a discretion on a public authority, it must indicate the scope of that discretion, although the degree of precision required will depend upon the particular subject matter.'

[74] *Practice Note (Official Solicitor: Declaratory Proceedings: Medical and Welfare Decisions for Adults Who Lack Capacity)* [2001] 2 FLR 158.

[75] Adults with Incapacity (Scotland) Act 2000, s 47.

Where proxies agree with the proposed intervention then this can go ahead, and it seems clear that sterilisation could easily be encompassed within the definition of 'treatment' designed 'to safeguard or promote the physical or mental health of the patient', certainly on the precedents that have gone before. More broadly, however, where a proxy disagrees with an intervention, the primary health carer can seek a second medical opinion which is sufficient to authorise the procedure in law. In such cases the proxy's only recourse is to go to court, but this is likely to be a lengthy and costly experience. And, while it is also the case that any 'other person having an interest' in the adult can go to court, this requires, of course, that such parties are aware of proposed interventions. A further crucial point to observe is that the 'best interests' test has been abandoned under the legislation—the Scottish Executive having taken the view that it was 'more protective than is appropriate for adults, as it would not give particular weight to the individual's own views.'[76] However, the Act does not offer a new test to replace it, requiring only that anything done for an adult under the Act should produce a 'benefit' for her—this being a highly subjective notion in itself.[77] Thus, the basis upon which decisions in respect of incapable adults are to be taken has been further obscured in Scotland, making it all the more difficult to determine whether the human rights of such persons are being duly respected.

Finally, it is worth noting that the case of the mental incapax is particularly compelling because such a person requires a voice in order to have their rights respected. Others must stand up so that they can be heard. Yet, the terms of the Human Rights Act 1998 are particularly saddening because they do not include provisions whereby actions can be brought before the UK courts on behalf of third parties.

(3) *Law Hospital NHS Trust v Lord Advocate*: right to life, freedom from inhuman and degrading treatment, and privacy

The decision in *Law Hospital* highlights the tendency of the British judiciary to pass the parcel of patient rights to the medical profession. That clinicians alone can determine the point at which a chronically ill patient's life should be ended can be objected to on a number of different grounds within the framework of human rights discourse and case law.

(a) Claiming a right to treatment: the 'continuous' consent

For the patient who has expressed a wish not to have her life terminated prematurely, or indeed, for the patient who has given no views on the matter, an

---

[76] *Adults with Incapacity (Scotland) Bill: Policy Memorandum: Explanatory Notes*, 8 Oct 1999, para 7.
[77] *Ibid*, para 8.

objection might be raised that the non-voluntary withdrawal of treatment violates Article 2. The success of such an argument depends on the extent to which Article 2 is seen as embodying an inalienable right, and on that point there is some dispute. The Commission has ruled, for example, that there is no positive duty to make passive euthanasia a crime.[78] Moreover, the ECtHR has held that a state's positive obligation to safeguard life is only 'to do all that could be *reasonably* expected of them to avoid a real and immediate risk to life of which they have or ought to have knowledge.'[79] An obvious element of health care provision that impacts on the reasonableness of what can be done is in the realm of resource allocation.

This matter was addressed in England in the case of *R v Cambridge Health Authority, ex parte B (a minor)*[80] in which a 10-year old girl suffering from non-Hodgkins lymphoma required a repeat course of chemotherapy costing in the region of £75,000. The health authority was of the opinion that no further intervention could be made to save the patient and refused to carry out the treatment. Continued intervention was judged to be *futile*. The child's father obtained independent medical advice which estimated the child's chances of survival with treatment at 10–20 per cent. The father sought judicial review of the health authority's decision.

At first instance Laws J took the unprecedented step of invoking the child's 'right to life' under the ECHR and required that the health authority show some substantial public interest to justify interfering with this right. Arguments based merely on resource implications were held to be insufficient. Since this was all that had been advanced, the decision was quashed and an order issued that it be re-taken. On the same day the Court of Appeal unanimously overturned this ruling. Their Lordships refrained from using the language of rights under the Convention, preferring simply to rule on the 'legality' of the decision. Moreover, they refused steadfastly to interfere in a decision that they considered to be one purely of resources. This seemingly harsh, yet pragmatic approach must be correct as far as it goes. In our less-than-ideal world of limited resources, it is not feasible to claim a right to life which requires treatment at all cost. And, there is no indication in the jurisprudence of the Commission or the ECtHR that any such interpretation of Article 2 would be upheld.[81] However, questions over the legitimacy of decisions as *between* treatments—that is, between conditions that are life-threatening and those that are not—may emerge as a fruitful area of debate, this being a matter of 'reasonableness' of state protection, and so a quasi-judicial review of human rights sensitivity on the

---

[78] *Widmar v Switzerland*, Appl No 20527/92 (1993), unreported.

[79] *Osman v United Kingdom* (2000) 29 EHRR 245 at 306.

[80] *R v Cambridge Health Authority, ex parte B (a minor)* (1995) 23 BMLR 1 (CA); 25 BMLR 5 (QBD).

[81] For similar attitudes from the South African courts concerning the problem of limited resources and their impact on human rights see *B v Minister of Correctional Services and Others* (1999) 50 BMLR 206 and *Soobramoney v Minister of Health, Kwa-Zulu-Natal* (1998), CCT 32/97 (Const Ct South Africa), (1999) 50 BMLR 224.

matter of allocation of scarce resources.[82] In this respect, we might witness a shift from the seemingly absolutist stance of the Court of Appeal in the case of *B*.

(b)   The humanity of allowing patients to starve in the name of best interests and human rights

The central role of *futility* in determining the limits of health care professionals' obligations to their patients was crucial to the legality of the decision in *Law Hospital* to withdraw artificial feeding and hydration from a patient in PVS. In like manner, the ECtHR has signalled that 'futile' interventions by a state do not form part of its obligations under the Convention.[83] Thus, futility is an important limiting factor on any rights that may be claimed under the ECHR or the Human Rights Act 1998. There are, however, innumerable shades of grey that surround the concept of *futility*, and it is rarely the absolute that it might appear at first sight.[84] Most often, futility is a relativist judgment arrived at by a process of weighing and balancing a number of potentially competing factors. Thus, for example, in the case of a patient in PVS much can be done to continue her life in a stable state for many years, so long as artificial feeding and hydration are provided. These patients are not in terminal decline; opportunistic infections can be treated with antibiotics; and basic care can address the problems of long-term institutionalisation. The decision to end the lives of such patients by the withdrawal of feeding and hydration in the name of futility is a dishonest assessment of both the decision and the desire behind it. Such assessments are quality of life judgments on the merits and demerits of permitting a vulnerable person to remain alive. As such, they are certainly not decisions that can be taken on purely medical grounds and in splendid isolation from other considerations, not least of which should be the basic human rights of the patients themselves. It should never be forgotten that the net effect of the current UK position is that these patients are left to starve to death. Such a state of affairs condemns patients to an end that is both degrading and de-humanising. How ironic, then, that at a time when human rights are needed most they are subjugated to professional assessments of 'futile treatment'. But we cannot divorce the *treatment* from the *patient*, and accordingly we cannot take decisions about the treatment without also taking decisions about the patient.

Yet, recent rulings on the legality of such action have indicated that the UK is not in breach of its obligations to honour the human rights of these patients regarding withdrawal decisions. In *NHS Trust v Mrs M; NHS Trust B v Mrs H*[85]

---

[82]   A R MacLean, 'The Human Rights Act 1998 and the Individual's Right to Treatment' (2000) 4 *MLI* 245.

[83]   *LCB v United Kingdom*, above, n 33.

[84]   See J K Mason and R A A McCall Smith, *Law and Medical Ethics*, 5th edn (Butterworths, Edinburgh, 1999), chs 15 and 16.

[85]   *NHS Trust A v Mrs M; NHS Trust B v Mrs H* [2001] 2 WLR 942.

declarators of legality were sought on the proposed withdrawal of feeding and hydration from two patients in PVS. In authorising this course of conduct the English High Court effectively endorsed the pre-existing position under *Bland* and *Law Hospital*, but went further in testing these precedents against possible human rights objections under the Human Rights Act 1998 (Articles 2, 3, and 8). Rather than considering the particularised reasoning of the President of the High Court (Dame Butler-Sloss) in respect of each of these provisions,[86] however, a few points of principle and policy should be noted.

The court clearly adopted a *good faith* approach to the issue, focusing on the fact that if a 'responsible body of medical opinion' had reached a conclusion as to futility, then there is little more to be said on the matter. This, however, makes professionalism and not principle the measure of patient protection. But, given that medical professionals are qualified only to comment on the medical futility of any proposed course of action, it is unclear why this should be determinative of the issue. It is true that the court retains for itself the ultimate role as arbiter of 'best interests', but as the Official Solicitor's Practice Note of 2001 makes clear,[87] an application to the High Court is little more than a confirmatory exercise in respect of the diagnosis of PVS from which a declarator of legality of withdrawal should follow.[88]

Second, in examining the content of the human rights laid before it, the court fixed on the principle of respect for personal autonomy and concluded that because the PVS patient could not consent to continued intervention, to continue to intervene against her 'best interests'—as determined by (medically qualified) others—would *violate* protection under Article 8. This, however, turns self-determination on its head. Indeed, why is this a relevant consideration in the context of someone who cannot meaningfully experience or exercise this state? It is precisely because the patient cannot do so that 'best interests' enters the equation. The error lies in the failure to appreciate that it is *respect* for the human being that is required, not only (or necessarily) respect for her 'right to choose'. The proper focus should be on respecting individual rights and interests as these are determined in a principled manner—not as they are determined by health care professionals. While policy may have driven the court to its particular interpretation, it does a great disservice to the broader obligation to uphold human rights.

In another respect too the court relied upon the incapacity of these patients to restrict their rights. It held that because PVS patients are insensate and cannot appreciate their state of being, it was not cruel and degrading to subject them to the vagaries of withdrawal of feeding and hydration, adopting the excessively narrow interpretation of Article 3 that a victim must be able to experience the

---

[86] For such an analysis, see A R MacLean, 'Crossing the Rubicon on the Human Rights Ferry' (2001) 64 *Mod L Rev* 775.

[87] *Practice Note*, above, n 74.

[88] *Ibid*, App 2.

inhuman treatment before a violation will occur.[89] This, however, is a distorted view of European jurisprudence which has held that a victim's own subjective reactions to treatment can impact on the question of whether violation has occurred (discussed further below).[90] In no way does it follow, however, that subjectivity is a pre-requisite to violation.

Finally, the equiparation of 'best interests' with futility as determined by the medical profession may mean that the precedent set in these cases is extended to other classes of patient in the future. For example, the British Medical Association has already issued guidance suggesting that an assessment of futility leading to the withdrawal of feeding and hydration may be appropriate for patients with dementia or those who have suffered serious stroke.[91] This is highly controversial,[92] and while no such ruling has so far been considered by the courts, the heavy and continuing emphasis placed on medical assessment rather than on a robust and principled approach to individualised human and patients rights may mean that an expansionist development of clinical discretion is inevitable. Moreover, this ruling leaves the human rights armoury significantly depleted should a challenge to such developments ultimately be required.

(c) Opting out: the right to refuse and the right to self-determination

By corollary, for the patient who has capacity and who wishes to determine the time of her own death, the continuation of treatment can be seen as an assault on her dignity and moral integrity. As such, this leads us to question whether Article 3 (inhuman and degrading treatment) could be invoked, alone or in combination with Article 8 (respect for private life). That such arguments might be made introduces, too, the interesting prospect of human rights arguments being advanced to justify, among other things, the legality of advance directives and the acceptability of assisted suicide.

What, then, has been the attitude of the Commission and the ECtHR to these matters in the health care context? In essence, we ask here, to what extent is the ultimate expression of self-determination protected under the Convention?

Two cases illustrate the general approach. First, we consider *Herczegfalvy v Austria*,[93] an ECtHR decision involving the detention, treatment and force feeding of a person of unsound mind. Inter alia, the applicant complained of abuses under Article 3 and Article 8. Under Article 3, which on its face admits of no exceptions, the ECtHR held that:

---

[89] Art 3 states: 'No one shall be subjected to torture or to inhuman or degrading treatment or punishment.'

[90] *Campbell and Cosans v United Kingdom* (1982) 4 EHRR 293, at para 28.

[91] British Medical Association, *Withholding and Withdrawing Life-prolonging Medical Treatment: Guidance for Decision-making*, 2nd edn (British Medical Journal Press, London, 2001).

[92] See Laurie and Mason, above, n 8.

[93] *Herczegfalvy v Austria*, above, n 73.

[I]t is for the medical authorities to decide, on the basis of the recognised rules of medical science, on the therapeutic methods to be used, if necessary by force, to preserve the physical and mental health of patients who are entirely incapable of deciding for themselves and for whom they are therefore responsible . . . [94]

It continued:

[T]he established principles of medicine are admittedly in principle decisive in such cases; as a general rule, a measure which is a therapeutic necessity cannot be regarded as inhuman or degrading. The court must nevertheless satisfy itself that the medical necessity has been convincingly shown.[95]

What is wholly absent from this ruling is a role for patient self-determination. It is assumed that those adjudged incompetent by the medical profession are incompetent in respect of all aspects of their lives. This is rarely the case.[96] Indeed, the circumstances of this case reveal that the patient was only adjudged partially incompetent when he entered hospital. No evidence is in fact put before the ECtHR that his condition had deteriorated. There is no provision here to entertain the possibility that a competent refusal could be given. Medical necessity is the key principle, the assumption being that the preservation of the physical and mental health should always be striven for. The decision barely pays lip-service to the self-determination interests of the individual. Yet, such interests must surely feature centrally in the assessment of what amounts to inhuman and degrading treatment. Indeed, in *Campbell and Cosans v United Kingdom* it was stated:

[T]he *Tyrer* case indicates certain criteria concerning the notion of 'degrading treatment'. . . it follows from the judgment that 'treatment' will not itself be 'degrading' unless the person has undergone—either in the eyes of others *or in his own eyes*— humiliation or debasement attaining a minimum level of severity.[97]

The second case of interest relates once again to force feeding but this time of a competent adult in prison.[98] On his arrest the applicant went on hunger strike and was force-fed on seven separate occasions. In holding that for both inhuman and degrading treatment a minimum level of suffering should be attained before a breach of Article 3 will be found, the Commission acknowledged that force feeding does involve degrading elements which, in certain circumstances, may be prohibited by Article 3. However, relying on Article 2 and the 'obliga-

---

[94] *Herczegfalvy v Austria*, above, n 73, para 82.

[95] *Ibid.*

[96] This was recognised by the English High Court in *Re C (mental patient: medical treatment)*, above, n 3, in which a 68-year-old schizophrenic inmate of Broadmoor was nonetheless held to be competent to refuse the amputation of his foot, even when medical opinion advised that non-intervention would result in death. The refusal was respected and the patient survived.

[97] *Campbell and Cosans v United Kingdom*, above, n 90, at para 28.

[98] *Appl No 10565/83 v Germany*, 7 EHRR 152. Admittedly this is not a medical law case as such, but it nevertheless has a direct bearing on the issue of self-determination. The English courts have made a similar cross-over between 'prisoner' and 'patient' in *Secretary of State for the Home Department v Robb* [1995] 1 All ER 677.

tion to secure to everyone the right to life', it held that a positive obligation was placed on the authorities to save lives when a person has been taken into their custody. The Commission was satisfied that the authorities acted in the applicant's best interests throughout when choosing:

> between either respect for [his] will not to accept nourishment . . . and thereby incur[ring] the risk that he might be subject to lasting injuries and even die, or to take action with a view to securing his survival although such action might infringe the applicant's human dignity.[99]

The matter seems to turn on the nature of the state's obligation, rather than on the content of the applicant's right. The state's custodial role undoubtedly played a part in this decision, lest it be seen in any way to be implicated in an interference with human life, whether or not any human right was being infringed. But this simply begs the question of what the *right* actually means for the individual concerned?

Seen from a rights perspective, the ruling is arguably a nonsense because it ignores completely the autonomy of the individual. The right to respect for life is surely *my* right to have *my* life respected should I wish it. If I refuse, and I am competent to do so, it is very difficult to see how one can justify intervention which, to all extents and purposes, is degrading to me precisely because of the fact that I resist it. It is particularly difficult to accept the justification offered: namely, acting to secure for me a right which I choose to forego.[100] Even considering this from the perspective of state obligations, we must ask, what is the nature of that obligation *with respect to* individual rights? Is it merely an obligation not to interfere, or should the state act positively to secure or bring about a certain state of affairs that further human rights? If it is the latter, this brings us back to the question of the content of those rights, and in the particular context of the right to life whether this includes a right to determine the time and manner of one's own demise.

The Commission has certainly been exposed to 'right to die' arguments. In *Application No. 25949/94* a Spanish national who suffered from tetraplegia argued that Article 2 encompasses a 'right to die' in that the 'right to life' reflects a person's right to control their lives, and that this includes a right to control one's own time of death. Unfortunately the action was declared inadmissible for failure to exhaust domestic remedies.[101] Also, in *R v UK*[102] the question at issue concerned prosecution of an individual for aiding and abetting suicide by

---

[99] *Appl No 10565/83 v Germany*, 7 EHRR 152, above n 98, at 154. Note that if the authorities had tried to justify the action on some other grounds, eg maintaining security and order, and there was some basis in law for this, that might have been different. They did not. They challenged an individual right with (supposedly) an individual right—dressed up as an obligation—and this is what is difficult to accept.

[100] In the UK prisoners can refuse food on the basis of the right to self-determination, see *Robb*, above, n 98. For commentary see [1995] *Med L Rev* 189.

[101] *Sampedro Camean v Spain*, Appl No 25949/94.

[102] Appl No 10083/82, 1983 DR 33.

issuing information on how to commit suicide. Although it dismissed the action as inadmissible, the Commission suggested that in other circumstances the right to privacy could arise in respect of aiding/abetting suicide. ·

These matters are of particular relevance at the time of writing, as the case of Dianne Pretty proceeds through the British courts. Mrs Pretty suffers from motor neurone disease and fears that she will experience a distressing death if she is prevented from gaining assistance from her husband to end her life when her condition worsens. Already her illness makes it impossible for her to take her own life by her own hand. She seeks to challenge the English law which out-laws assisted suicide, claiming that this is a breach of Articles 2, 3, 8, 9 and 14.

For such a development to occur domestically, and indeed for any human rights development to occur, a strong element of judicial willingness to grasp the nettle will be required. We face too the problem of the considerable margin of appreciation which is accorded to Contracting States in matters of this kind. All of the issues central to medical law are imbued with moral and ethical tension. As a consequence, there is considerable disparity of approach throughout the Contracting States, making the emergence of ECHR precedent highly improbable. Certainly, to see the emergence of an ECHR 'right to die', a strong consensus among states would be required, and this is clearly a long way off.[103] This having been said, nothing precludes the British courts from establishing precedents of their own.

In respect of the 'right to die', however, no such 'right' has been recognised by courts in jurisdictions with human rights traditions which are far more sophis-ticated and progressive than that in the United Kingdom. For example, in *Rodriquez v British Columbia (AG)*[104] the Canadian Supreme Court rejected an argument that the criminal law, by prohibiting assistance in suicide, violated the Canadian Charter of Rights and Freedoms, while the US Supreme Court ruled categorically in *State of Washington v Glucksberg et al*[105] and *Vacco et al v Quill et al*[106] that there is no constitutional 'right to die'. Nevertheless, as Blake has pointed out, the constitutional framework used to argue these cases 'facili-tated the characterisation of physician assisted suicide as a human rights issue.'[107] In the absence of an established domestic constitutional human rights framework, the UK is therefore unlikely to witness a rapid transformation of its own rights culture. This has entirely been borne out by the rulings delivered so far in the Pretty case.

On 18 October 2001 the Queen's Bench Division of the English High Court rejected all of Dianne Pretty's arguments.[108] The decision to choose how and

[103] In Europe, only the Netherlands and Belgium provide for any legal form of euthanasia, and in each case this is strictly controlled through the medical profession.

[104] *Rodriquez v British Columbia (AG)* 107 DLR (4th) 342 (SCC, 1993).

[105] *State of Washington v Glucksberg et al* 521 US 702 (1997), 117 S Ct 2258 (1997).

[106] *Vacco et al v Quill et al* 117 S Ct 2293 (1997).

[107] M Blake, 'Physician-assisted Suicide: A Criminal Offence or a Patient's Right?' (1997) 5 *Med L Rev* 294 at 296.

[108] *R (Pretty) v Director of Public Prosecutions and Other* [2001] EWHC Admin 788.

when to die was not accepted as an aspect of the right to life, and indeed, the 'right to life' and the 'right to self-determination' were presented as being in direct conflict. Moreover, the court held that even if the decision to take one's own life was encompassed under the right to respect for private and family life (Article 8(1)), any interference by the state to prohibit assisted suicide was amply justified under Article 8(2) as necessary in a democratic society. An appeal to the House of Lords is now expected.

Ultimately, the resolution of this case and others like it will turn on the willingness of the courts to adopt an openness towards an *ethos* of human rights. If they assume a narrow, legalistic interpretative approach to the individual rights contained in the ECHR and consider themselves constrained by existing case-law, then there is little prospect of change. Alternatively, there is always the option of taking a step back to consider the wider picture—that is, to assess the *values* more fundamental still than the particular rights articulated in the Convention and the Human Rights Act 1998, and which underpin these instruments. This calls for a holistic approach to giving effect to human rights. From such a moral ambience values such as respect for human dignity and self-determination emerge as guiding principles in the interpretation of individual rights. Accordingly, a less restrictive role for the judiciary is envisaged, and certainly one less shackled to traditional medical and societal mores. Yet, while it is perhaps too much to expect that major advances along these lines will first take place in an area as controversial as euthanasia, recent Scottish developments suggest, nonetheless, that such an attitudinal shift is generally unlikely to occur in the medico-legal sphere.

E.   A VIEW OF THINGS TO COME IN SCOTLAND?

In the final section of this chapter we examine this last proposition more closely. In June 2000 the Court of Session had the first opportunity to test its powers under the Scotland Act 1998 to challenge the legislative competence of the Scottish Parliament.[109] Under section 29(2)(d) of the 1998 legislation an Act of the Parliament is not law if 'it is incompatible with any of the Convention rights . . .' The Court of Session is empowered to review this matter in respect of any piece of legislation produced by the Parliament. The first Act to be passed by the Scottish legislature after its re-constitution on 1 July 1999 was the Mental Health (Public Safety and Appeals) (Scotland) Act 1999. The proposal was introduced on 31 August 1999 and treated as an emergency bill. The Act received the Royal Assent on 13 September 1999 and came into force immediately. Its terms were designed to prevent the release of mentally disordered offenders who had been detained under the mental health legislation[110] but who

---

[109] For general comment see C M G Himsworth and C R Munro, *The Scotland Act 1998* 2nd edn (W Green, Edinburgh, 2000).
[110] Mental Health (Scotland) Act 1984, as amended.

were now no longer considered to be treatable. Concerns had been raised by the House of Lords ruling in *R v Secretary of State for Scotland*[111] in which it was held that a non-treatable patient could not be lawfully detained under the provisions of the 1984 Act and must be released. This decision was shortly followed by that of *Ruddle v Secretary of State for Scotland*[112] in which the petitioner successfully obtained an absolute discharge in an appeal to the sheriff under section 63 of the 1984 Act on the ground that he was no longer treatable.[113]

The 1999 Act sought to change the position by making it a requirement before release of a 'restricted patient'[114] that the Scottish Ministers, and any sheriff to whom an appeal is lodged, are satisfied that the patient is not:

> suffering from a mental disorder the effect of which is such that it is necessary, in order to protect the public from serious harm, that the patient continue to be detained in a hospital, whether for medical treatment or not.[115]

This criterion must be considered first and foremost in the process of taking or reviewing a discharge decision. In particular, a sheriff must refuse an appeal if he is not satisfied that this 'serious harm test' is met.[116] No further consideration of the merits of the appeal need be undertaken.

In *A v The Scottish Ministers*[117] the validity of the 1999 Act was challenged by three restricted patients, alleging, inter alia, violations of their rights under Article 5 of the ECHR. Article 5(1) provides that:

> [e]veryone has the right to liberty and security of person. No one shall be deprived of his liberty save in the following cases and in accordance with a procedure prescribed by law: . . . (e) the lawful detention . . . of persons of unsound mind . . .

Moreover, Article 5(4) states that:

> [e]veryone who is deprived of his liberty by arrest or detention shall be entitled to take proceedings by which the lawfulness of his detention shall be decided speedily by a court and his release ordered if the detention is not lawful.

The applicants alleged that the new regime established by the 1999 Act amounted to one of preventive detention, and that they in particular were now subject to arbitrary deprivation of liberty because the reasons for their current detention were wholly unconnected with the original reasons for detention,

---

[111] *R v Secretary of State for Scotland* 1999 SC (HL) 17.

[112] *Ruddle v Secretary of State for Scotland* 1999 GWD 29–1395.

[113] Reid (concerning *R v Secretary of State for Scotland*), the subject of the original appeal to the House of Lords, was not released. While the court took the opportunity to lay down the general rule about treatability, the rule was held not to apply to Reid because his continued detention within a secure hospital environment helped him to control his behaviour and as a result was 'treatment' within the terms of the Act.

[114] Under s 63(1) of the 1984 Act 'restricted' patients are those who have come before the criminal courts at some stage prior to their incarceration.

[115] See ss 64 and 68 of the 1984 Act, as amended by the 1999 Act.

[116] *Ibid*, s 64 of the 1984 Act, as amended.

[117] Above, n 1.

being for the purposes of medical treatment. Moreover, they argued that there requires to be a link between the detention, its purpose and the place of detention, and that if preventive detention was what was envisaged then the most appropriate place was prison and not hospital. Finally, under Article 5(4) it was argued that the new law breached the requirement for a proper review of an appeal because a sheriff must dismiss an appeal once it is determined that the 'serious harm test' has been satisfied. In particular, he is precluded from reviewing whether the original grounds for detention are still met, namely the treatability of the patient.

The Inner House unanimously rejected all arguments by the applicants. It held that there had been no violations of Article 5, and drew heavily on existing ECHR jurisprudence as authority. In emphasising that the right to liberty is not absolute, the court cited *Soering v United Kingdom*[118] in which it was stated that

> . . . inherent in the whole of the Convention is a search for a fair balance between the demands of the general interest of the community and the requirements of the protection of the individual's fundamental rights.

It opined that the new regime struck a fair and just balance, and proceeded to demonstrate how the continued detention of the applicants was in conformity with the case law of the ECtHR. Thus, for example, the Inner House cited *Winterwerp v The Netherlands*[119] in which three requirements were laid down for the legality of detention in respect of persons of unsound mind. First, there must be a true mental disorder established by objective medical expertise. Second, the disorder must be of a kind or degree warranting compulsory confinement. Third, the detention only remains valid so long as the disorder persists. The court held that each of these criteria had been satisfied in the present case. Arising from this, however, are three further issues. Was the presence of mental disorder the only ground warranting detention of the applicants under Article 5? Can the grounds for detention be changed at any point and still make for a lawful detention? How is the adequacy of the medical evidence to be judged?

The court cited very recent Strasbourg authority to demonstrate that mental disorder is not the only basis on which detention can be justified and lawful. In *Litwa v Poland*[120] the ECtHR made it clear that those detained under Article 5(1)(e) can be so detained for the sole purpose of protecting the public, so long as it is necessary in the circumstances and other measures are insufficient to achieve the same end. In contrast, the Inner House could find no authority to support or refute the contention that it was unacceptable unilaterally for the state to change the grounds and nature of detention in respect of particular patients. And, in the absence of authority, it felt able simply to state that it was

---

[118] *Soering v United Kingdom* (1989) 11 EHRR 439 at para 89.
[119] *Winterwerp v The Netherlands* (1979) 2 EHRR 387.
[120] *Litwa v Poland*, (2001) 33 EHRR 53.

not a contravention of Article 5 to do so. There was no attempt at a principled analysis of the rights in issue or the arguments that might be made on the matter.

In respect of medical evidence, there was no discussion about how the adequacy of this is to be tested, although both Lord Philip and Lady Cosgrove noted that the medical community is far from agreed upon the susceptibility of certain types of patient to treatment, or indeed, on the diagnosis of many psychiatric conditions. Nonetheless, the court seemed satisfied that, when the time comes, the Scottish Ministers and the appeal courts will be able to find the requisite medical expertise. Moreover, the court opined that a medical environment was the most suitable to deal with those suffering from mental disorders, even if these were untreatable, and accordingly refused to hold that a transfer to prison would be more appropriate.

Finally, the court's conclusion that initial detention was lawful under Article 5(1)(e) on the fulfillment of the *Winterwerp* criteria was also the basis for its rejection of the argument under Article 5(4). As Lord Philip said:

> counsel submitted that what Art 5(4) required was a review of the conditions which, according to Art 5(1)(e) were essential to the lawful detention of a person on the ground of unsoundness of mind . . . I consider that the conditions which are essential to the lawful detention of the applicants in accordance with Art 5(1)(e) are the provisions introduced by the 1999 Act. So that 'lawfulness' has the same meaning in paragraph 4 as in paragraph (1)(e) of this Article.[121]

This entire judgment is coloured by the words of Lord Hope, quoted with approval by the Lord President in his speech:

> [I]n this area [the application of the Convention] difficult choices may have to be made by the executive or the legislature between the rights of the individual and the needs of society. In some circumstances it will be appropriate for the courts to recognise that there is an area of judgment within which the judiciary will defer, on democratic grounds, to the considered opinion of the elected body or person whose act or decision is said to be incompatible with the Convention.[122]

If *A* is a guide for the future—and the recent whole-hearted endorsement by the Privy Council suggests that it is[123]—then it would indicate that conservativism and not activism will be the order of the day among our judiciary in their approach to the task of giving effect to human rights in Scotland. As has been stated, the attitude of the judiciary towards this task is of crucial importance to its success, and that, of course, presupposes that there is only one view of 'success'. But, if we imagine for a moment that success will be measured by the extent to which the laws in Scotland and the rest of the United Kingdom offer

---

[121] Above, n 1, at 52D–E.
[122] Per Lord Hope of Craighead in *R v DPP, ex parte Kebilene* [1999] 3 WLR 972, quoted in *A*, above, n 1, at 19D–E.
[123] *A v The Scottish Ministers*, above, n 1.

strong and respectable protection for human rights, then we must ask how best can the judiciary achieve that goal. Does *A* offer us any guidance?

A sceptical view of the decision might see the case as one which negates consideration of the role of individual rights altogether, for it endorses a regime that does not require any balancing of interests to determine the optimal outcome. Public safety is the trump card. The Privy Council went so far as to present the case as a conflict between the rights of the detainee and those of the citizen to live in peace and security, holding overtly that the former had no precedence over the latter, and so, by implication, that the converse was indeed the case.[124] And, while both the Inner House and the Privy Council were able to find Strasbourg jurisprudence to substantiate their conclusions, the cynic might suggest that this is hardly surprising, given the vague and malleable nature of that jurisprudence. Authority can be found to support most propositions, or exceptions relied upon within the Articles themselves to accommodate them.

Perhaps, however, a more generous view finds 'balance' elsewhere. The 'serious harm test' requires just that—a risk of *serious* harm—and it must also be shown that continued detention is 'necessary' to safeguard public safety. Furthermore, the onus is on the Scottish Ministers to satisfy a sheriff of these facts, presumably by relying on relevant medical expertise. But are these *sufficient* safeguards for individual rights? A problem we currently face is in knowing what those individual rights actually are. The bare bones of the Articles give little in the way of guidance as to the content of most of the Convention rights, and as has been suggested above, the jurisprudence from Strasbourg is unhelpfully flexible. This brings us back, once again, to the domestic judiciary and its own attitude towards human rights. Is its role simply to test laws against established interpretations of these rights from Strasbourg, or is it to uphold and to further the body of human rights possessed by the citizens of this country? The attitude adopted will make all the difference to the nature and scope of the rights we may eventually be able to claim. In *A* there is little suggestion, for example, that their Lordships were seeking to carve out a jurisprudence on human rights for Scotland or the United Kingdom which places the individual at its core. This is not to suggest, however, that the court did not have in mind the collective interests of all individuals who constitute 'the public', but it is telling none the less that the 'public interest' is effectively allowed to trump the private interest to the extent of not even permitting a full hearing of all of the facts, when a *perceived* threat to the public interest is adjudged sufficiently 'serious'. And who will decide when that is so? In law, it is the Scottish Ministers and the sheriffs who will hear appeals from them. In practice, it is likely to be the profession of psychiatrists from whom the necessary medical evidence will be required, for only they are in a position to determine dangerousness. But even then this is a notoriously difficult and problematic concept to define and to assess. There is much scope, then, for dispute and conflicting views. And what will happen

---

[124] See, for example, per Lord Clyde, *ibid*, at 1346G–H.

when the Scottish Ministers or the sheriffs are faced with such conflicting views? Will they weigh everything in the balance, public interest and private interest together? Well, they cannot do so, for the law is clear that the 'dangerousness' question must be answered first. And so, when will that question be answered so as to prevent any further consideration of the issue of discharge? It is difficult not to imagine that political expediency will lead the decision-makers to err on the side of caution and place considerable store in *any* medical evidence suggestive of dangerousness. This might be defensible in the name of the public good, but it does nothing to foster a culture of respect for individual human rights.

F. CONCLUSION

What can we conclude from this? At present it would seem that the introduction of the Human Rights Act 1998 does not augur well for the advancement of medical law based on what has gone before in Strasbourg and the initial reactions of the domestic judiciary. In particular, the view of the role of self-determination in protecting human rights, such as it is, is at best unsophisticated and at worst disrespectful of interests that lie at the core of medical law. This is not to say, however, that much cannot be made of the potential of the human rights as incorporated into domestic law. As has been shown—particularly in the context of Article 8—there is scope for developing argument based on these fundamentals. One must hope that our courts avail themselves of the opportunities which incorporation of the ECHR brings to put more flesh on the bones of the young discipline of medical law. Ironically, medical lawyers spend much of their time calling for the courts to take responsibility away from the medical profession and to assume it themselves, yet in the context of the debate about incorporation of the ECHR many fear that the system which results will 'lead to a major shift in power from the Executive and Legislature to the Judiciary.'[125] It is suggested that in the context of medical law, domestic precedents and a lack of refinement in Strasbourg jurisprudence will mean that the likely approach of the courts will be to continue to give responsibility for the protection and development of patient rights to the medical profession. If such scepticism is not ill-founded the net result may be that the incorporation of the ECHR will be of little significance either for patient rights or the discipline of medical law generally.

An Afterword to this chapter appears at page 343 below.

---

[125] See Sir Nicholas Lyall, 'Whither Strasbourg? Why Britain Should Think Long and Hard Before Incorporating the European Convention on Human Rights' [1997] *EHRLR* 132 at 136.

13

The Protection of Property Rights

GEORGE L GRETTON*

A. INTRODUCTION

TO THE PRIVATE lawyer, the text of the European Convention for the Protection of Human Rights and Fundamental Freedoms (ECHR) comes as a shock. It is not legislation of any recognisable form, but rather a set of statements of certain liberal political ideas, of the sort one might expect to see in an election manifesto or in a letter to the editor. General principles claiming for themselves the status of law are unsettling enough, but one might at least hope that that they would have the virtues which general principles can have: a philosophical depth, an inner coherence of conception, an elegance of expression which seduces assent, a fertility in consequences, a rootedness in tradition, a rhetorical aspiration to a coming golden age. A text with such virtues might thaw the frozen heart. Alas, such virtues are not easy to find in the ECHR.

The ECHR forms a unity, and nothing is more common than to find that more than one article is involved in a given issue. Whilst it is Article 1 of the First Protocol that contains the core protection for property rights, and which will therefore be the main subject of this essay,[1] other Articles can be relevant, notably Article 6, providing procedural guarantees in the determination of rights, and Article 8, protecting family life and the home.

This chapter does not attempt a systematic exposition, let alone a complete one.[2] It aims in part at exposing some of the conceptual incoherence in which this aspect of the ECHR is bogged down, and in part at suggesting possible implications for Scots law. The essay deals with the ECHR, but it should be recalled that EU law also embodies similar fundamental principles.

---

* Lord President Reid Professor of Law, University of Edinburgh.

[1] And will be referred to simply as 'the Article'.

[2] There are many valuable texts, such as Robert Reed and James Murdoch *A Guide to Human Rights Law in Scotland* (2001), Kay Springham in Robert Reed (ed) *A Practical Guide to Human Rights Law in Scotland* (2001), and Richard Clayton and Hugh Tomlinson *The Law of Human Rights* (2000) ch 18.

B. THE TEXT OF ARTICLE 1 OF THE FIRST PROTOCOL

Much of the English-language literature on the ECHR treats it as an English-language text. There is seldom a hint that it might be authentic in any other language, let alone any suggestion that such versions might actually be worth looking at. The traditional blackletter lawyer will find that surprising. The traditionalist wants to scrutinise the legislative text, to interrogate it, and if that text is authentic in more than one language, that scrutiny needs to be done in more than one language. In the interpretation of EC instruments nothing is more common than to consult at least one other version.[3] Different authentic versions often differ substantially in meaning, partly because of human error and partly because whilst language may be neutral in the natural sciences, it is not neutral in law. Legal texts, like poetry, can border on the untranslatable.[4] The ECHR is in fact authentic in two languages, French and English. Here is the Article:

French	*English*
Toute personne physique ou morale a droit au respect de ses biens. Nul ne peut être privé de sa propriété que pour cause d'utilité publique et dans les conditions prévues par la loi et les principes généraux du droit international.	Every natural or legal person is entitled to the peaceful enjoyment of his possessions. No one shall be the public interest and subject to the conditions provided for by law and by the general principles of international law.
Les dispositions précédentes ne sortent pas atteinte au droit que possédent les états de mettre en vigueur les lois qu'ils jugent nécessaires pour régementer l'usage des biens conformément à l' intérêt général ou pour assurer le paiement des impôts ou d'autres contributions ou des amendes.	The preceding provisions shall not, however, in any way impair the right of a State to enforce such laws as it deems necessary to control the use of property in accordance with the general interest or to secure the payment of taxes or other contributions or penalties.

C. YOU CANNOT BE SERIOUS?

This text is about property. That central concept, around which everything turns, is expressed thrice:

---

[3] Actually, since EC legislation is authentic in eleven languages, no one can ever actually know the real meaning of any text. The only solution is the adoption of a single language, which should be (simplified) Latin.

[4] Take three ordinary words in German commercial law: *Gesellschaft*, *Kaufmann* and *Wertpapier*. Not one of them is translatable into English, except by a locution.

French	English
(1) Biens	(1) Possessions
(2) Propriété	(2) Possessions
(3) Biens	(3) Property

Poor as some translations of EU and international texts occasionally are, it is difficult to think of anything quite as spectacular as this. Neither text reflects the other, and each text is internally incoherent.[5] The suspicion that the drafting of the text was not regarded as a serious matter is difficult to suppress, and further examination rather supports than removes that suspicion. For example, possession is a concept which, far from coinciding with property, exists in contrast to it. This is common coin of European legal thought: as Ulpian said, and as lawyers have been saying ever since: *nihil commune habet proprietas cum possessione.*[6] Neither *biens* nor *propriété* means 'possessions.' 'Possession' in French is *possession*. In the French text the oscillation between *biens* and *propriété* is curious, and indeed unacceptable, but the tension is nothing like the downright opposition between property and possession.

These points are made to set the scene. The Strasburg[7] Court, in paying the precise wording of the article little attention, pays it all the attention it deserves.[8] But it was as unfortunate as it was predictable that the Human Rights Act 1998 enacted only the English version.[9]

D. LOGICAL STRUCTURE

The logical structure of the Article is as puzzling as its terminology. There are three sentences. In one of the leading cases, *Sporrong & Lönnroth v Sweden*,[10] it was said:[11]

> That Article comprises three distinct rules. The first rule, which is of a general nature, enounces the principle of peaceful enjoyment of property; it is set out in the first sentence of the first paragraph. The second rules covers deprivation of possessions and subjects it to certain conditions. The third rule recognises that the States are entitled, amongst other things, to control the use of property in accordance with the general

---

[5] See the appendix for other languages.

[6] Dig 41,2,12. ('Property and possession have nothing in common with each other.')

[7] The traditional English-language spelling—still reflected in ordinary pronunciation—was a good compromise between the French Strasbourg and the German Straßburg. English is not alone in having its own spelling: the city is Strasburg in Polish, Straatsburg in Dutch, Strasburgo in Italian, Estrasburgo in Spanish and Strasburk in Czech (not to mention Argentoratum in Latin). The term 'Strasburg Court' is used in this chapter in reference to the European Court of Human Rights.

[8] A rare example of close scrutiny is *Marckx v Belgium* (1979) 2 EHRR 330 at 372.

[9] The enactment of a foreign-language text would not have been without precedent: see the Carriage by Air Act 1961.

[10] *Sporrong & Lönnroth v Sweden* (1982) 5 EHRR 35. *Sporrong* was the case by which the Article came into its own.

[11] *Ibid*, para 61.

interest, by enforcing such laws as they deem necessary for the purpose; it is contained in the second paragraph.

This is quoted here because it is universally quoted, but whether it provides any enlightenment is doubtful.

The Article is divided into two paragraphs, with the first two sentences grouped into the first paragraph. There has been little discussion in the caselaw or commentaries of this paragraphing. Nowadays the first sentence is taken as the general principle and the second two sentences are giving detailed rules, but it appears that that is not how it was understood by the original drafters, who seem to have understood the first two sentences as laying down the general principle and the third as setting out the exceptions.

(1) 'Peaceful possession' and 'deprivation'

The Article's first sentence reads: 'Every natural or legal person is entitled to the peaceful enjoyment[12] of his possessions.' That sentence is unqualified: no exceptions are mentioned. The second sentence reads:

> No one shall be deprived of his possessions except in the public interest and subject to the conditions provided for by law and by the general principles of international law.

Nothing will be said here about what disturbance of 'peaceful possession' means in contrast with 'deprivation of possessions', except to say that presumably the latter is worse than the former. *Yet the former is prohibited absolutely while the latter is conditionally allowed.* A state must not disturb 'peaceful possession' but it is free to 'deprive' so long as it is 'in the public interest and subject to the conditions provided for by law and by the general principles of international law.' It is difficult to see how these two sentences are supposed to relate to each other. In the caselaw the first sentence is described as a general principle, with the details being given in the other two sentences of the Article. In other words, there is a tendency simply to ignore the first sentence for practical purposes. However, for convenience some interferences[13] which, though objectionable, are difficult to describe as either 'deprivations' or 'controls' have been branded as violating the first sentence, which thus has its uses.[14]

---

[12] 'Peaceful enjoyment' is, in the French text, 'respect'. Much could be said of this linguistic and conceptual mismatch.

[13] 'Interference' (French ingérence) is not a word found in the Article but has come to be used as the generic term.

[14] This was the approach in *Sporrong* itself.

(2) 'Deprivation' and 'control'

The second sentence says that:

> the preceding provisions shall not, however, in any way impair the right of a State to enforce such laws as it deems necessary to control the use of property in accordance with the general interest or to secure the payment of taxes or other contributions or penalties.

There is thus a contrast between 'deprivation', which the second sentence declares impermissible except under certain conditions, and 'control' which is generally permissible. (As are taxes and penalties and also, rather mysteriously, 'contributions'.) This deprivation/control distinction is fundamental to an understanding of the Article, and indeed is essential to any system of fundamental protection of property rights. As US Supreme Court Justice Oliver Wendell Holmes once said, 'government could hardly go on if to some extent values incident to property could not be diminished without paying for every such change in the general law'.[15] Thus a state cannot compulsorily purchase land without compensation, but is free to regulate the use of land through planning legislation without paying compensation. The deprivation/control distinction makes rough sense, but can be difficult to apply in practice. As David Anderson has observed, 'the [Strasburg] Court has bent over backwards to avoid classifying an interference with property as a deprivation'[16] as opposed to a control, though it should be noted that on occasion it has done the opposite.[17] It might be argued that the Court's approach tends to be result-orientated. It first asks itself whether the interference is of a sort which calls for compensation. If the answer is affirmative, it is likely to classify the interference as a deprivation. If not, it is likely to classify it as a control. It should be noted that 'deprivation' can be something less than actual expropriation. The Strasburg Reports have a number of horror stories of bungling state action (or inaction), which, while leaving ownership with the victim, has robbed that ownership of much of its value.[18]

---

[15] *Pennsylvania Coal v Mahon* 260 US 393 (1922).

[16] Anderson, 'Compensation for Interference with Property' [1999] *EHRLR* 543, 553.

[17] In *Sporrong & Lönnroth v Sweden* (1982) 5 EHRR 35, the Court held, by 10–9 majority, that where property had suffered from interminable planning blight the interference amounted to deprivation. In the USA the interpretation of the Fifth Amendment has also proved problematic in the same way. For a case parallel to *Sporrong*, in which regulatory interference so sterilised the value of land that it was held to amount to a 'taking', see the celebrated case of *Lucas v South Carolina* 505 US 1003 (1992).

[18] This writer's favourite is *Scollo v Italy* (1995) 22 EHRR 514 where an apartment owner, suffering from physical disability, wished to move into his own property, which was then tenanted. The tenancy duly came to an end in full compliance with Italian law, and the tenant was thus bound by law to remove. But *11 years later* the tenant was still there: every attempt by the owner to assert his rights had been baffled by the Italian legal system. It was held that there had been a 'deprivation.'

(3) 'Subject to the conditions provided for by law'

Deprivation is impermissible unless 'subject to the conditions provided for by law'. This is not easy to understand, and indeed may mean nothing. If the reference is to the 'law' of the ECHR it is superfluous. If the reference is to the 'law' of the state concerned, it borders on pointlessness, for what need is there to protect rights which are anyway protected by internal law?[19]

(4) 'The general principles of international law'

> No one shall be deprived of his possessions except in the public interest and subject to the conditions provided for by law and by the general principles of *international law*.

International law requires that a state which expropriates aliens must pay compensation, which must be—in the standard formula—prompt, adequate and effective. In *James v United Kingdom*[20] the Strasburg Court held that this part of the Article is meaningless since it confers no rights on *nationals* who have been expropriated. It protects only *aliens*, who are protected anyway. However, although this holding in *James* is well-known, in the *Gasus* case[21] the Court gave as one of its reasons[22] for refusing to protect the German company that that company, in agreeing to deliver goods to a Dutch company, *had implicitly agreed to accept Dutch law, including expropriative aspects of Dutch law*.[23] Thus we have the following result: the 'international law' clause in the Article does not protect those who are nationals (*James*) and it does not protect those who are not nationals (*Gasus*). It remains to add that the decision in *James* is of only limited significance, because the Strasburg Court takes the view that deprivation will in any case normally trigger a right to compensation: the distinction seems to relate to the *quantum* of compensation: the Convention probably sets lower minimum levels for the compensation of an expropriated national.

(5) 'In the public interest'

A deprivation is impermissible if it is not 'in the public interest.' This too seems to be virtually a dead letter. The Strasburg Court has never expressly held a

---

[19]   Though cf *Iatridis v Greece*, Appl 31107/96, judgment 25 March 1999.

[20]   *James v United Kingdom* (1986) 8 EHRR 123 ('Duke of Westminster' case).

[21]   *Gasus Dosier und Fördertechnik GmbH v Netherlands* (1995) 20 EHRR 403. See also commentary to n 46.

[22]   I do not wish to oversimplify this remarkable case, and ought to make it clear that a major reason behind the decision was the view that the action of the Dutch tax authorities was authorised under the third sentence of the Article, which is certainly a reasonably persuasive view.

[23]   Presumably, this argument would equally apply to, say, a German company which bought land in the Netherlands and then found itself expropriated.

deprivation to have been contrary to the public interest. A fortiori is it almost impossible to imagine a Scottish court holding UK or Scottish legislation to be contrary to the public interest. In one of the leading cases[24] the Strasburg Court has said:[25]

> The decision to enact laws expropriating property will commonly involve consideration of political social and economic issues on which opinions within a democratic society may reasonably differ widely. The Court, finding it natural that the margin of appreciation available to the legislature in implementing social and economic policies should be a wide one, will respect the legislature's judgement as to what is in the public interest unless that judgement be manifestly without reasonable foundation.

In another case it has said that

> a taking of property effected in pursuance of legitimate[26] social economic or other policies may be 'in the public interest' even if the community at large has no direct use or enjoyment of the property taken.[27]

(6) 'In the general interest'

By its third sentence the Article is disapplied to 'control', provided that the control is 'necessary . . . in accordance with the general interest'. Whether this is different from 'public interest' is unclear.[28] It is unlikely that any particular distinction was intended: we have here merely another example of sloppy drafting. The Strasburg Court has not attempted to distinguish the two concepts. A 'control' would breach the Article only if it were not 'necessary in the general interest' and thus the standard imposed is a laxer one than for 'deprivations'.

E. COMPENSATION

Compensation is central to any fundamental norm which protects property. Thus the Fifth Amendment of the US Constitution provides: '. . . nor shall private property be taken for public use without just compensation'. The ECHR Article says nothing about it. Whilst the ECHR does contain a general provision about the possibility of compensation for breach of Convention rights,[29] the

---

[24] *James v United Kingdom*, above, n 20.

[25] *Ibid*, para 46.

[26] The use of this word by the Court, not only here but elsewhere, is striking. That which is 'legitimate' does not infringe the ECHR. But when is something legitimate? It is legitimate if it does not offend against the Convention. One finds, of course, a similar cloudiness in the text of the ECHR, where we are often told that something is *unlawful unless authorised by law*.

[27] *James v United Kingdom*, above, n 20, at 142.

[28] In the French text 'public interest' is 'utilité publique' and 'general interest' is 'intérêt général'.

[29] Article 41, which authorises the Strasburg Court to order 'just satisfaction' (French satisfaction équitable).

question arises most obviously for property protection, and the silence is curious. Indeed, it is difficult to disagree with James Kingston[30] that a logical interpretation leads to the conclusion that 'compensation is mandatory only where the property is owned by aliens, and only where property is taken, rather than subjected to controls.'[31] The point is important and should be stressed. The second sentence of the Article permits 'deprivation' if it is in the public interest and if the principles of international law are observed. But since the Strasburg Court has held (albeit with puzzling logic) that the reference to international law applies only in favour of aliens, it follows that any deprivation is permissible against a national provided only that it is in the public interest. And it has already been observed that the Strasburg Court has never held any interference to have been against the 'public interest'. The same logic applies, even more strongly, to 'control' which will be a breach of the ECHR only if not in the 'general interest'.

Whether this result was intended, or, indeed, whether there ever was any coherent intention in the matter at all, is unclear. At all events, the Strasburg Court has in fact dumped the logic of the Article, and taken up the following position: (1) Where the interference is by way of 'deprivation', compensation is presumptively payable,[32] though not necessarily at full market value.[33] (2) Where the interference is by way of 'control' compensation is presumptively not payable, but nevertheless may in some cases be payable even though it is not doubted that the control was in the 'general interest.'

The decision as to whether compensation should be given is decided on a balancing basis. Thus the Strasburg Court has said that 'compensation terms are material to the assessment whether the contested measure respects the requisite fair balance and, notably, whether it imposes a disproportionate burden on the applicants.'[34] Again, it has said that

> the Court must determine whether a fair balance was struck between the demands of the general interest of the community and the requirements of the protection of the individual's fundamental rights.[35]

---

[30] In his excellent 'Rich people have rights too?' in Liz Heffernan (ed), *Human Rights: A European Perspective* (Round Hall, Dublin, 1994).

[31] *Ibid*, 291.

[32] 'The taking of property in the public interest without compensation is treated as justifiable only in exceptional circumstances.' (*Lithgow v United Kingdom* (1986) 8 EHRR 329.) 'The taking of property without payment of an amount reasonably related to its value will normally constitute a disproportionate interference, and a total lack of compensation can be considered justifiable only in exceptional circumstances.' (*Holy Monasteries v Greece* (1995) 20 EHRR 1.)

[33] 'Legitimate objectives of public interest . . . may call for less than reimbursement of the full market value.' *James v UK*, above, n 20, para 54. See also *Lithgow v United Kingdom*, above, n 32. But full compensation will sometimes be insisted on: see eg *Hentrich v France* (1994) 18 EHRR 440. Here Hentrich bought land, and the French Government immediately compulsorily acquired it from her for its purchase price plus 10% plus expenses: this was held in the circumstances to have been inadequate.

[34] *James v UK,* above, n 20.

[35] *Sporrong v Sweden,* above, n 10, 52.

But this approach is always subject to the fundamental principle that while 'deprivations' presumptively demand compensation, 'controls' presumptively do not. David Anderson has argued that 'it is not immediately obvious why a deprivation of property (however sensible) should give rise to a presumption of compensation, whereas a control on use (however capricious) should not.'[36] But here the writer finds himself in the unfamiliar position of defending the logic. The presumptions are surely reasonable. If a deprivation can be shown to be 'sensible' it may indeed be held *not* to trigger a compensation claim,[37] while, conversely, a capricious control *is* likely to trigger compensation. The presumptions are only presumptions, and, as such, will yield to the facts and circumstances of the individual case. An example is a Scottish case, *Booker Aquaculture v Scottish Ministers*, which is currently before the Court of Justice. Here EU law required the destruction of fish stocks where necessary to prevent the spread of disease, and the question is whether a right to compensation is implied, on the footing that EU law itself accepts the principles of the Convention. If the answer is negative, that is an example of a sensible deprivation.

F. WHAT IS 'PROPERTY'?

The question of what is protected by the ECHR has been the subject of numerous reported cases and much commentary, and it is unnecessary to say much here. As was mentioned above, the English text speaks of 'possessions' and 'property', words which might mean anything or (almost) nothing. The French term 'biens' means, according to *Petit Robert*, 'Chose matérielle susceptible d'appropriation, et tout droit faisant partie du patrimoine'. This is very wide. The Strasburg Court has refused to offer any definition. Condorelli has written that:

> la Commission et la Cour n'ont jamais identifié avec précision les frontières de ce fameux 'droit de propriété', c'est-à-dire qu'elles ont prudemment refusé de s'enfermer dans une définition rigide, qui risquerait de compromettre les possibilités d'élargir progressivement.[38]

---

[36] Anderson, above, n 16, 554.

[37] *Booker Aquaculture v Scottish Ministers*, C–20/00 and C–64/00, being an Article 234 reference from the Inner House: *Booker Aquaculture v Scottish Ministers* [1999] 1 CMLR 35; 2000 SC 9. The opinion of the Advocate General (20 September 2001) is that compensation is not required.

[38] Luigi Condorelli in Louis-Edmond Pettiti, Emmanuel Decaux and Pierre-Henri Imbert (eds) *La convention européenne des droits de l'homme* (Economica, Paris, 1999), 975. This imprecision and the possibility of endless enlargement, attract Condorelli; others may think differently.

In practice the Strasburg Court takes a broad view of 'property.'[39] Money claims,[40] leases,[41] and intellectual property rights[42] have all been held to be protected under the clause. Interestingly and importantly, public law rights have also been held protected. In other words, the Article ignores the dichotomy between public law and private law, and holds that some public law rights are property for the purposes of the Article. Examples include liquor licences[43] and social security benefits.[44] So it is quite clear that whatever 'property' may mean, it is not limited to its various shades of meaning within private law.

But the Strasburg decisions are free from the taint of consistency. For instance, although monetary claims have been held to be property, no protection against uncompensated expropriation was granted in *National & Provincial Building Society v United Kingdom*.[45] Or take the *Gasus* case.[46] Here a German company sold and delivered machinery to a Dutch company. Ownership was to pass when the price was paid.[47] Before paying, the buyer became insolvent and the Dutch tax authorities seized the machinery for unpaid taxes. Under Dutch law this seizure defeated the seller's rights, and the German company complained to Strasburg that its right of ownership had been violated. One of the grounds on which the complaint was rejected was that the German company did not really own the machinery: the company's right was merely that of a security for a debt, namely the price. Now, the question of whether retention of title is 'really' just a security right is one which is familiar to commercial lawyers round the world, and cannot be discussed here. But two remarks must be made. The first is that it is not easy to reconcile with either Dutch or German law, neither of which has adopted the American solution to the problem of declaring the seller's right to be merely a 'security interest.'[48] Secondly, and more importantly, the Court's approach indicates an extremely narrow understanding of property—ownership of a physical object, and nothing else. But then it is perhaps vain to expect any coherent view, for in the same case the Court found it necessary to say that the German company was not being deprived of its debt (at this stage recognised as 'property') since the Dutch company was still liable to pay. That suggests that the court felt that debts *are*

---

[39] As late as 1978 the UK was arguing that the Article protects nothing but the ownership of land: *Wiggins v UK* (1978) 13 DR 40. Is it not strange that the UK was prepared to ratify a text of whose meaning it knew nothing?

[40] *Stran Greek Refineries v Greece* (1994) 19 EHRR 293; *Pressos Campania Naviera v Belgium* (1995) 21 EHRR 301.

[41] *Mellacher v Austria* (1989) 12 EHRR 391.

[42] *Lenzing v UK* (1999) EHRLR 132.

[43] *Tre Traktorer v Sweden* (1989) 13 EHRR 483.

[44] *Gaygusuz v Austria* (1996) 23 EHRR 365; *Szrabjer v UK* [1998] EHRLR 230.

[45] *National & Provincial Building Society v United Kingdom* (1997) 25 EHRR 127. For an attempt to reconcile this decision with *Stran* and *Pressos* see S Grosz, J Beatson and P Duffy (eds) *Human Rights: The 1998 Act and the European Convention* (Sweet & Maxwell, London, 2000).

[46] *Gasus*, n 21.

[47] A standard clause in commercial sales contracts, which is recognised as effective (subject to varying qualifications) in most countries.

[48] See the Uniform Commercial Code Art 1–201(37) and Art 9.

protected by the ECHR, but securities for debts are *not*. It must be stressed just how odd this holding is. Suppose that a shipping company owes money to Lloyds Bank, secured by ship mortgage. The company becomes bankrupt and can pay nothing. Lloyds seeks to recover by enforcing the mortgage, but finds that legislation has made the mortgage invalid. Lloyds finds that instead of recovering the whole debt it recovers nothing. According to *Gasus*, Lloyds have nothing to complain about.

G. HORIZONTALITY

The ECHR was designed, in the aftermath of the Second World War, and with the abuses of fascism and communism in mind, to protect citizens from governments. Can it also have 'horizontal' effect, that is to say as between private parties? Strasburg does not accord it such effect.[49] But the Human Rights Act 1998 requires 'public authorities' to act in conformity with the ECHR, and it is arguable that the result is horizontality.[50] No doubt this issue, on which there has accumulated a substantial literature,[51] will be decided soon.[52] The issue has a special Scottish dimension, because legislation of the Scottish Parliament which is in breach of the Convention is void.[53] Thus suppose that it is held that the Abolition of Feudal Tenure etc (Scotland) Act 2000 breaches the Article. The consequence would not be that the expropriated superiors would have a claim for compensation. The consequence would be that they would be deemed not to have been expropriated in the first place.[54]

(1) Some traditional 'deprivations' in private law

Private law is full of situations where a person is 'deprived' of property. If Jack sells his house to Jill, he is deprived of it, but nobody would suggest that the ECHR had been breached. That is a case where the loss of property is

---

[49] See eg *X v United Kingdom* (1988) 10 EHRR 81, where a tenant complained that his lease had been lost by forfeiture (the English equivalent of irritancy). The Commission took the view that since this was a 'horizontal' question the Convention had no application. And cf *Bramelid v Sweden* (1986) 8 EHRR 116.

[50] The US courts have generally refused to go down this road, though they did in one celebrated case, where they were so keen to get a certain result that they cared little about how they did it: *Shelley v Kraemer* 334 US 1, 68 SCt 836 (1948).

[51] See T Raphael 'The problem of horizontal effect' [2000] *EHRLR* 493 discussing the question and citing the literature.

[52] It seems likely to this writer that some degree, at least, of horizontality will be accepted. In *J A Pye (Oxford) Ltd v Graham* (2001) 82 P&CR 302 the Court of Appeal seemed to take horizontality for granted, though on the facts it held that there had been no breach of Convention rights.

[53] Scotland Act 1998 s 29.

[54] However, under s 102 of the Scotland Act 1998 void legislation can sometimes have partial validity.

consensual and compensated. But there are also traditional categories where property rights pass (or perhaps are extinguished[55]) without compensation, or without consent. One is prescription. The Court of Appeal has held that title to land acquired by 'limitation' (acquisitive prescription) does not offend the Article, and this decision is surely right.[56] Again, sometimes Tom sells to Dick but it turns out that Harry was the owner. The basic rule in all European legal systems is *nemo plus juris ad alium transferre potest quam ipse haberet*, so that Harry will remain undivested owner. But all systems recognise certain exceptions, where Dick will be protected by his good faith. In such cases Harry is 'deprived', though of course he will have a financial claim against Tom. It seems most improbable that rules of this type could be held contrary to the ECHR. There is a public interest in protecting good faith purchasers, and the deprived owner is accorded compensation against the wrongful seller, albeit that such compensation is not always enforceable in practice. Or again, diligence does not, in itself, offend the ECHR, even if it involves intrusion into the home.[57] Nor does sequestration, even if the family home is affected.[58]

Or again, if Eve grants a security over her house to a bank, and she defaults on the loan, and the house is then sold, Eve has been deprived of her ownership, but this is not a breach of the ECHR.[59] Other examples could be suggested,[60] and one suspects that all such cases would be regarded as compliant with the ECHR, provided that they keep well within the boundaries of what has always been regarded as legitimate in the long story of European private law.[61] But it must always be borne in mind that the ECHR is construed according to the ever-shifting liberal consensus. That illegitimate children should not have the same inheritance rights as legitimate ones was once a universal principle, but illegitimacy became an idea unacceptable to the liberal consensus, and was accordingly held to violate the ECHR.[62]

---

[55] Property law distinguishes transfer from extinction.

[56] *J A Pye (Oxford) Ltd v Graham* (2001) 82 P&CR 302. I am grateful to Professor R R M Paisley for this reference.

[57] *K v Sweden* (1991) 71 DR 94. For discussion see Scottish Law Commission Report on Poinding and Warrant Sale (Scot Law Com No 177, 2000), para 2.47.

[58] This was, at least, the view taken in a (so far) unreported decision of Sheriff Principal Bruce Kerr in *Douglas Jackson (James Bell's Tr) v James Bell* (9 Nov 2000, Kilmarnock Sheriff Court). I am grateful to Professor R R M Paisley for this reference.

[59] *Wood v UK* (1997) 24 EHRR CD–69, in which it was held that neither Art 1 of the First Protocol nor Article 8 had been breached.

[60] For instance the right of a co-owner to insist on division or sale, based on the common European principle *nemo in communione detineri potest*, and embodying the common European *actio communi dividundo*. Leasehold irritancy without compensation is more problematic, and differing views are possible. The writer's view is that irritancy is probably Convention-proof. The Scottish Law Commission is reviewing the subject.

[61] It is apparent from the Strasburg caselaw that a legal rule which is widespread is less likely to be struck down than one which is peculiar to one or two systems.

[62] *Inze v Austria* (1987) 10 EHRR 394. This decision invoked not only Article 14 (non-discrimination) but also Article 1 of the First Protocol. The logic is obscure.

Finally, it must be recalled that all such private law issues are subject to the ECHR only to the extent that it takes horizontal effect.

(2) Some untraditional interferences and deprivations

It is evident the possibilities of challenges based on the Article are limited only by the limits of ingenuity and of the willingness to litigate, which is to say, hardly limited at all. There are some particularly obvious possibilities on the horizon, such as the right to roam, the community right to buy, feudal abolition and land registration. The first two have, at the time of writing, not yet been enacted. A few words will be devoted to the second two.

(a) Feudal abolition

The Abolition of Feudal Tenure etc (Scotland) Act 2000, when it comes fully into force, will extinguish all superiorities. There will be full compensation for the loss of the right to feuduty.[63] Barony titles, which often have substantial values,[64] will survive, though as non-feudal rights. The other main value attaching to superiorities is the right to enforce certain real burdens, and to collect money for waiving them. The Abolition of Feudal Tenure etc (Scotland) Act 2000 allows some such burdens to survive by being 're-allotted' to other land owned by the (ex-)superior. The Act also has certain other provisions whereby some real burdens will survive, and there is also a compensation mechanism in relation to 'development value' burdens. The overall picture is that the Abolition of Feudal Tenure etc (Scotland) Act 2000 tries to respect the legitimate interests of superiors as far as is consistent with getting rid of the whole system. Whether that will be sufficient to comply with the Article is a matter of much current speculation. The awkward fact remains that all superiorities will be extinguished, and most of them without compensation. Will this be regarded as one of those 'exceptional' cases where uncompensated deprivation is permissible? This writer's prediction is: yes. The deprivation involved is slight,[65] and the public interest is strong. Moreover, feudal abolition has to be looked at in the round: taken together with the Land Tenure Reform (Scotland) Act 1974 superiors are receiving full compensation for loss of feuduty. (It may also be remarked that the extinction of superiorities includes the ultimate Crown superiority, so that the class of those divested includes the state itself.) It is noteworthy that in a recent decision the Lands Tribunal, in discharging a real burden,

---

[63] In fact, of course, few feuduties are still exigible anyway.

[64] A typical price would be £50,000. Of course, most superiorities are not baronies.

[65] And much less significant in monetary terms than the consequences of the leasehold enfranchisement legislation which was approved by the Strasburg Court in *James v United Kingdom,* above, n 20.

rejected the superior's claim that the discharge would trigger a ECHR-based claim for compensation.[66]

(b) Land registration

The Registration Act 1617 created a property register, known as the Sasine Register. If Jack owns land and wishes to transfer ownership to Jill (because of sale, donation or whatever), he delivers to her the appropriate deed, and she registers it in the Sasine Register. Registration is compulsory in this sense, that if she does not register she will not become owner, but will only have personal rights against Jack. If you don't register you don't become owner. The converse is not true, however: it is not always the case that if you do register you do become the owner. If Jack had sold 50 hectares to Jill and it later turned out that a small boundary strip actually belonged to the neighbour, Alice, then Alice would remain owner. In other words, the Sasine Register adhered to the familiar principle of Roman law: *nemo plus juris ad alium transferre potest quam ipse haberet.*

The Land Registration (Scotland) Act 1979 introduced a new property register, the Land Register, based on different principles. The new register is gradually replacing the old one. The new register keeps the principle that if you don't register you don't become owner. But it goes further. To a large extent (not wholly) it abandons the *nemo plus* principle. In other words, if you do register you do become the owner. In the example, Jill would become the owner of everything, including the boundary strip. Alice would be expropriated. Of course, because of this possibility the staff of the Keeper of the Registers carefully check all applications, and there are rules about rectification of the register and also about compensation for those who suffer from mistakes by the Keeper.[67]

Two articles fall to be considered. One is, of course, Article 1 of the First Protocol of the ECHR. Alice has been deprived of her property. However, it is likely that there is no breach of the Article. It can be argued that the overall system, as a package, is in the 'public interest' and in addition Alice will either be able to recover ownership by rectification of the Register, or, if she cannot (and there are certain hurdles which make rectification difficult and sometimes impossible) then she would be entitled to full compensation from the Keeper. Of course, monetary compensation is not always adequate, and it seems to the writer just possible—not likely but perhaps possible—that the deprivation

---

[66] *Strathclyde Joint Police Board v Elderslie Estates*, at the time of writing reported only at 2001 GWD 27–1101. Curiously, it seems that the Tribunal took the view that its decision would amount to a 'deprivation'. Given that it wished to refuse compensation, one might have expected it to classify the decision as a 'control' case. In the writer's view, that would have been an own goal, since the superiors were not being deprived of their superiority: they were merely being refused permission to use it in a certain manner, this refusal being in the public interest.

[67] In the eyes of the law all registration is done by the Keeper.

would be regarded as so arbitrary as to amount to a breach of the Article.[68] It must not be forgotten that the issue of horizontality does not arise here, for the deprivation is at the hand of a state official, the Keeper. Jill is the beneficiary of the deprivation, but it is the state which expropriates Alice.[69]

It is a truism that the different parts of the ECHR do not lead separate lives. They interact. The Article must be read with Article 6:

> In the determination of his civil rights and obligations or of any criminal charge against him, everyone is entitled to a fair and public hearing within a reasonable time by an independent and impartial tribunal established by law . . .

Does land registration comply, bearing in mind that the protection of property rights is one of the vital aspects of Article 6? And here one must have some doubt. It is true that Alice has the right to go to court for a review of the decision taken by the Keeper. And it is true that, in the aftermath of *County Properties*,[70] it is clear that, in considering whether an administrative process is ECHR-compliant, one must look at the whole system, not just its first stage. The analogy is that the Reporter corresponds to the Keeper. But there are major differences too. To quote from *County Properties*:[71]

> We would add that, while the Reporter may not be, on his own, an 'independent and impartial tribunal' for the purposes of Art 6(1), it is important to bear in mind that he is bound to conduct the inquiry in accordance with statutory rules designed to give all parties to the inquiry fair notice of matters upon which they may wish to be heard, and a full opportunity to present to the Reporter any relevant evidence or submissions. Moreover, the written report to be prepared by the Reporter will require to contain findings in fact, a summary of the evidence upon which such findings in fact are based, details of the Reporter's assessment of those findings in fact and of the planning issues involved and reasons for the Reporter's recommendation to the Scottish Ministers.

This quotation shows how wide a gulf yawns between the Keeper and a Reporter. This is, of course, not the Keeper's fault. The Land Registration (Scotland) Act 1979 simply does not give him this sort of role. Now, it might be thought that the exigencies of the situation are such that, even with the best will in the world, the Keeper could not have acted differently. After all, the story was cock-up rather than conspiracy: nobody at Register House realised, we will suppose, that Alice was being expropriated. But it is worse than that. The Land Registration (Scotland) Act 1979 envisages the Keeper sometimes making deliberate expropriative decisions without any sort of hearing and sometimes without even informing the victim of what is happening. It is not easy to give

---

[68] The writer knows of no Strasburg case in point, but cf *Hentrich v France* (1994) 18 EHRR 440.

[69] To non-conveyancers it should be explained that this sort of thing is, though obviously uncommon, something that does happen.

[70] *County Properties v Scottish Ministers* 2001 SLT 1125, reversing the Outer House decision reported at 2000 SLT 965.

[71] *Ibid,* para 19.

examples without descending into the depths of conveyancing law and practice. Two short and under-explained examples must suffice:

(i) Jack has occupied the boundary strip for many years without objection. It is unlikely that there will be any objection in the future. The Keeper decides to register Jill, albeit with an exclusion of indemnity. This expropriates Alice. The Keeper is not obliged to inform Alice of what is happening. Indeed, s/he is actually *forbidden* to do so.[72]

(ii) Adam conveys land to Eve, including a boundary strip which the Keeper agrees that Adam owns. The Keeper registers Eve as owner of the whole. Some months later Deirdre argues that Adam had previously promised to convey that strip to her, Deirdre, that Eve knew this (and so was not in good faith) and demanding that the Keeper rectify the Register by deleting Eve's name (for this strip only) and substituting Deirdre's.[73] The Keeper is able to do this if s/he takes the view that the registration in favour of Eve was due to her 'fraud or carelessness'[74] and s/he is able to take this decision without any sort of procedure whereby Eve can be given a fair hearing, or, indeed, any hearing at all.

Of course, someone divested by the Keeper's act has recourse the courts. But this is not by way of appeal. The Keeper's decision takes immediate, and not suspended, effect. Alice and Eve are not owners fighting to keep ownership. They are ex-owners, seeking to acquire ownership from the person who has, by the Keeper's decision, replaced them. The expropriation *has already happened*. Even if they are successful in court, their reacquisition of ownership is not retrospective.[75]

In the USA, registration of title of this type, once attempted, is almost dead in practice, except in a few localities in a few states. The reasons for its failure are complex, but the constitutional position has played a part. In 1895 Illinois enacted a system of registration of title. The Illinois Supreme Court promptly struck the law down, on the ground that it involved an unconstitutional delegation of the judicial power, for the Registrar was acting as a judge in land causes.[76] This decision had a powerful effect in the USA. The legislative response was to ensure that the registration system meets at least the minimum standards of a judicial determination of rights. This includes a requirement that due process be observed, at any rate on first registrations, in relation to possible competing claimants.[77]

---

[72] Land Registration (Scotland) Rules 1980 Rule 21(2).

[73] Cf *Higgins v North Lanarkshire Council* 2000 GWD 31–1236.

[74] Land Registration (Scotland) Act 1979.

[75] *Stevenson-Hamilton's Exrs v McStay* 1999 SLT 1175; *Keeper of the Registers of Scotland v M R S Hamilton Ltd* 2000 SC 271.

[76] *The People v Chase* 165 Ill 527; 46 NE 454 (1896).

[77] For some discussion of this point see *The People v Simon* 176 Ill 165, 52 NE 910 (1898), in which the replacement Illinois legislation was upheld.

This brief di███████████ffice. Perhaps the system introduced in 1979 complies with th████████████rhaps it does not. It is important to appreciate that this type of████████████n is *not* part of the common European legal heritage. The wri████████████no country on the continent where the land registration departm████████████ unilateral act, and without the affected party being given an opportunity to be heard, transfer the ownership of land from one person to another.[78]

<h2>H. EVOLUTION AND LIBERALISM</h2>

Five stages can be distinguished in the development of property protection under the ECHR. In the first stage protection simply did not exist: it was omitted from the original text. The second stage began with the addition of protection in the First Protocol in 1952.[79] This second stage lasted a quarter of a century, during which the Article existed more in theory than practice, for in this period not a single case reached the Strasburg Court. The third stage began in 1976, when the Court heard its first case.[80] The fourth stage lasted from 1976 to 1982, with the great *Sporrong* case. The fourth stage was from 1982 to 1999: the Article had fairly and squarely arrived, but the Strasburg Court was still somewhat conservative in its approach. The fifth phase began in 1999: of all the cases in which the Court has held in favour of the applicant, in relation to the Article, half have happened since 1999. In other words, the pace has quickened. These stages correspond to changes in the European liberal consensus. In the middle of the twentieth century, property was not sacred, except to a minority of conservative thinkers. This was a time when nationalisation of industry was widespread, and many advocated land nationalisation. For landlords and shareholders there was little sympathy. Hence the original omission of property protection, and when it was introduced the text was deliberately weak.[81] The European liberal consensus has changed: property protection is a rising star.

---

[78] For instance, in Germany the Grundbuchamt would refuse to register Jack in respect of the boundary strip. If, by error, it did so, the effect would be that the register would indeed be inaccurate but Alice would still be the owner. If Beatrice were to buy in good faith at this stage, Beatrice would indeed become the owner, and so Alice's right would be extinguished, but that is simply part of the widespread, and presumably unobjectionable, principle that good faith acquirers should, at least in some types of case, be protected.

[79] For the history of the origins of the Article, see A W B Simpson, *Human Rights and the End of Empire* (Oxford University Press, Oxford, 2001).

[80] *Handyside v UK* (1976) 1 EHRR 737.

[81] This explains the otherwise puzzling silence about compensation.

The ECHR is authentic only in French and En̶ ̶ ̶ ̶ ̶ ̶ versions in the official languages of other subscribing states. ̶ ̶ ̶ ̶ ̶ ̶ ̶mples:

Usage number	French	Italian	Portu̶			Spanish
1	Biens	Beni	Bens			Bienes
2	Propriété	Proprieta	Prop		a	Propriedad
3	Biens	Beni	Bens			Bienes

The versions for the other four Romance l̶ ̶ ̶ ̶ ̶ ̶ntly translated from the French. But now look at:

Usage number	Danish	Dutch	E̶			Swedish
1	Ejendom	Eigendom	̶		m	Egendom
2	Ejendom	Eigendom	̶		̶um	Egendom
3	Ejendom	Eigendom	̶		gentum	· Egendom

It appears that there exists a Germanic form, which departs radically from both the French and the English texts, and which has the merit of cohering with the approach of the European Court of Human Rights, which is to disregard the inconsistent terminology of the authentic versions.[82] It remains to observe that while official translators have disagreed as to whether or not to follow the French text, they are unanimous in regarding the English one as hopeless.[83]

POSTSCRIPT

In this essay I failed to foresee the issue on which the first big case on Article 1 Protocol 1 was decided in the Scottish courts: diligence on the dependence. *Karl Construction Ltd v Palisade Properties plc*[84] held that the existing system, whereby inhibition on the dependence can be granted without cause shown, is contrary to the Article. The decision was a bombshell for civil court practice. Whilst Lord Drummond Young was careful to say that his decision did not necessarily extend to arrestment on the dependence, it has been so extended in a Sheriff Court case,[85] and surely rightly so. Whether *Karl* itself was right may be debated.[86] To the present writer, at least, it was a welcome decision, for the existing rules were oppressive.

---

[82] Although Estonian is not a Germanic language, Estonian legal culture is Germanic.

[83] At least, so far as I have checked. The Convention has official versions in a very large number of languages.

[84] 2002 SLT 312. It is understood that the decision has not been reclaimed.

[85] *Fab-Tek Engineering Ltd v Carillion Construction Ltd*, Dunfermline Sheriff Court, 22 March 2002, not yet reported.

[86] For criticism see David Logan and Scott Blair 'Inhibitions on the Dependence: An Alternative View' 2002 SLT (News) 119.

14

The Human Rights Act and the Criminal Law: An Overview of the Early Case-Law

CONOR A GEARTY*

A. INTRODUCTION

I N THE AUTUMN of 2000, the legal profession was girding itself for a radical transformation. 2 October of that year was supposed to mark the moment at which the 'terrible beauty' of the Human Rights Act 1998 would take a firm grip of our legal culture. We already had Lord Hope's assurance that, as a result of the measure, 'the entire legal system' would be subjected to a 'fundamental process of review and where necessary reform by the judiciary'.[1] The impact was expected to be especially dramatic in the criminal field. All practitioners were required to be trained in the Act and experts pointed to experience in other jurisdictions such as in New Zealand and Canada, where equivalent measures had had a profound effect. Many expected nothing short of a transformation of our law. The Scottish experience of human rights in the post-devolution, pre-implementation phase, dealt with elsewhere in this volume,[2] was to hand, inspirational to some, horrifying to others.

Reality—or rather the short-term reality that is all that has surfaced after (at the time of writing) just ten months or so of the Act's full operation throughout the United Kingdom—has proved to be something of a surprise. To start with, the courts have not been inundated with human rights cases. Nor are proceedings that would have taken place anyway now all being repackaged as 'human rights' cases. A statistical update from the Lord Chancellor's Department covering the very early months showed that in the Court of Appeal Criminal Division, the number of cases received actually fell from 2643 between 2 October 1999 and 31 January 2000 to 2491 between 2 October 2000 and 31 January 2001.[3] Of these

---

* Professor of Human Rights Law, King's College London and Member, Matrix Chambers.

[1] *R v DPP, ex parte Kebilene* [1999] 3 WLR 972 at 988.

[2] See chapter by Ferguson and Mackarel in this volume.

[3] Data obtained from the website of the Lord Chancellor's Department, posted at http://www.lcd.gov.uk/.

cases, no more than 277 contained human rights points. In the Crown Court, in the three months after implementation, there were 168 occasions on which Human Rights Act 1998 issues were raised: this was less than half of one per cent of the cases heard by the Crown Court. After an initial flurry of argument, human rights points before magistrates' courts also fell in the first months of the Act's operation. These statistics should perhaps be treated with caution. They relate only to the first three to four months of the legislation's operation in England and Wales: the trends spotted here may have been reversed during the first six months of 2001: we do not yet know. The data concentrate on the quantitative rather than the qualitative. Nevertheless it is hardly the deluge that was expected.

It is perfectly true that the Human Rights Act 1998 has not leapt on the English common law or the English criminal process like a street-wise mugger, in one fell swoop robbing these ancient souls of all their conceptual baggage.[4] Nor did the old common law ways return to their jurisprudential home on 2 October 2000 to find the place ransacked, with treasured heirlooms rooted in statute and venerable tradition lying broken on the floor and trendy new, European artefacts puffing themselves out on the mantelpiece. The effect of the Human Rights Act 1998 has been much more subtle than this, and the power of the established legal culture into which it has been inserted has proved itself altogether too entrenched to surrender to the foreign intruder without a fight. What we have seen since 2 October 2000—right across UK law—has been a fascinating battle, with the pre-existing common law and statute-based system of law seeking to receive the Human Rights Act 1998 on its own terms, desiring not to be subjugated by the measure but rather to make it fit in with the prevailing legal climate.

At times it has seemed as though the operating assumption has been that the Human Rights Act 1998 must be interpreted 'as far as possible' to be compatible with pre-existing law, rather than the other way round.[5]

Viewed overall, therefore, the effect of the Act has been rather conservative. The judges have not been inclined to permit the Human Rights Act 1998 to destabilise pre-existing frameworks of law, whether of statutory or of common law origin. There is an important qualification that needs immediately to be made to this statement. As cases have begun to wind their way into the senior appellate courts, a further, even more conservative, dimension to the reception of the Human Rights Act 1998 into domestic law has begun to reveal itself. In three leading cases, the senior judiciary have shown themselves willing to use the Human Rights Act 1998 as a battering ram with which to burst apart legislative provisions that they have regarded as unprincipled, alien growths on the familiar terrain of their own common law.[6] In these cases the European Convention

---

[4] For Scotland see Ferguson and Mackarel, above, n 2.
[5] See Human Rights Act 1998, s 3(1).
[6] *R v Offen* [2001] 2 All ER 154; *R v A* [2001] 3 All ER 1; *R v Lambert* [2001] 3 All ER 577.

for the Protection of Human Rights and Fundamental Freedoms (ECHR) has been the means by which 'normal' common law services have been enabled to be resumed with statutory attacks on common law principle which would previously have been unquestioned now being successfully and conclusively undermined. A subsidiary battle for adjudicative supremacy has also being taking place, between the Scottish and the London-based courts, with the latter holding most of the best appellate cards and being frequently inclined to play them. All of these struggles have been played out more or less exclusively in the criminal law sphere, and it may well be that they provide the best indicators of the future, as far as this extraordinary legislative measure is concerned.

B. THE SUBSTANTIVE CRIMINAL LAW

Before turning to the main topic of this section of the chapter, we should note briefly what might be thought to have been obvious, namely that the rights set out in the ECHR are not available to organs of the State and this is regardless of whether or not they can characterise themselves as 'victims' of some law of which those organs disapprove. The issue came up in a recent decision of the House of Lords, in *R v Weir*.[7] In that case, counsel for the DPP argued that the denial to his client of an extension of time in which to apply to the House of Lords for leave to appeal violated his right of access to a court under Article 6(1) of the ECHR. As Lord Bingham remarked, however, 'it would stand the convention on its head to interpret it as strengthening the rights of prosecutors against private citizens.'[8] While this is undoubtedly true there may yet be mileage in such arguments in different legal contexts. Suppose for example that the BBC wished to resist proceedings under the Official Secrets Act 1989 by relying on Article 10 of the ECHR: would the Corporation's status as a public authority under section 6 of the Act deprive it of the right to rely on the Convention? This can hardly be the case. Does the same apply to a local authority which seeks to invoke the Convention in some squabble with the government over property rights? As we can see therefore, *Weir* settles part, but only part, of this complex issue.

Turning now to the substantive law, an accurate first impression would be that not very much has happened. This is not surprising, as the opportunities to challenge established law in some of the key areas are few and far between. The ECHR does not set out to reform the criminal law: any changes that might occur are incidental to the procedural rights guaranteed in the document. There have been suggestions that differences in the ages of consent in the criminal law and the substance of the law on self-defence may be open to challenge.[9] An

[7] *R v Weir* [2001] 2 All ER 216.
[8] *Ibid*, at para 17.
[9] A Ashworth, 'The Human Rights Act and the Substantive Criminal Law: A Non-Minimalist View' [2000] *CLR* 564.

important decision of the European Court of Human Rights (ECtHR) may be regarded as having an indirect effect on the substantive criminal law. In *ADT v United Kingdom*,[10] police officers had carried out searches at the home of the applicant, a practising homosexual, and had seized various items, including photographs and videos. On the basis of this evidence, the applicant had been charged with gross indecency under section 13 of the Sexual Offences Act 1956 (with the decriminalisation of sexual acts between consenting male adults in private not applying when there are more than two men). He was duly convicted. On these facts the ECtHR was unanimous that the applicant's right to respect for privacy had been infringed. The activity for which he had been prosecuted had been wholly private. A very restricted number of friends had been involved. The circumstances were such that it was most unlikely that others would have become aware of what was going on. There had been no intention to circulate the video. No doubt in the post- Human Rights Act 1998 era, and mindful of this decision, the police will be very reluctant before initiating similar prosecutions in future. So perhaps in a way the substance of the criminal law has been changed, albeit in a covert way and as a result of the discretionary non-deployment of the law rather than through any more formal move.[11]

One example of an explicit formulation of the criminal law in a Convention-oriented way has however arisen in Jersey, in *AG v Prior*.[12] In that case, the Bailiff Sir Philip Bailache ruled that the lack of correlation between mental illness as it is objectively defined and the category of persons deemed insane under the M'Naghten rules made the latter an inappropriate set of criteria to use to determine who was legally insane in Jersey. Remarkably the issue had never previously arisen and the Bailiff allowed himself to be persuaded that the imminent application of the ECHR into local Jersey law (as a result of the Human Rights (Jersey) Law 2000) made that document, and the Strasbourg case law under it, of direct relevance to the decision he had to make. As is well-known, the case law on the right to liberty in Article 5 of the ECHR stresses the need for objective medical evidence before persons can be incarcerated or otherwise detained on account of alleged psychiatric or other mental illness.[13] As is also well known—perhaps notorious is a better word—the M'Naghten rules have been so inflexibly deployed by the courts that certain types of ordinary physical ailments fall within their ambit (eg epilepsy). Professor Mackay and I have remarked in our article that 'this is an extremely important ruling', being the first case in which the M'Naghten rules have been tested by reference to the Strasbourg case law.[14] It is not improbable that it will inspire similar challenges in England and Wales. If so, we could see a very dramatic change in the substance of our criminal law as a result of a Convention-based challenge.

---

[10]   *ADT v United Kingdom* (2000) 31 EHRR 803.
[11]   See further 'Gay Sex Group Offered £15,000 Compensation', *The Guardian* 27 July 2001.
[12]   *AG v Prior* 2001 JLR 146. See the note by R Mackay and C A Gearty in [2001] *CLR* 560.
[13]   See in particular *Winterwerp v Netherlands* (1979) 2 EHRR 387.
[14]   See Mackay and Gearty, above, n 12, 563.

C. THE IMPACT OF THE HUMAN RIGHTS ACT ON CRIMINAL PROCEDURE

It was always expected that the greatest impact of the Human Rights Act 1998 on the criminal law was going to be in the procedural arena. This is certainly where most of the main challenges have arisen. As noted above, the ECHR does not set out to deliver any changes to the substance of the criminal law as such. Instead it extends certain basic procedural safeguards to persons suspected of offences or facing criminal charges (in Articles 5 and 6 of the Convention). Substantive changes are incidental to the policing of these process-based rights. As is well known, the gateway to the procedural safeguards available in Article 6 is the concept of a 'criminal charge'. The case-law in Strasbourg shows that the term is autonomous and takes its meaning, not from how some process is described in domestic law alone, but rather from the kind of process it is in terms of, among other matters, the sort of punishment to which it can lead. In recent years, Parliament has embarked on many initiatives in which the civil process has been deployed in fields, and with consequences, that might have been considered to have been more appropriately described as criminal. One might have thought that the implementation of the Human Rights Act 1998 would have lead to a robust re-characterisation of these offences to accord with their penal thrust. The courts have, however, been extremely reluctant to impose the concept of a 'criminal charge' so as to allow entry into such processes of the full panoply of Article 6 protection.[15] The courts have been sensitive to the political importance that has been attached to such legislative initiatives and have chosen not to view them as wholesale attacks on common law principles of criminal culpability. This has been one of the main ways in which the Human Rights Act 1998 has failed to live up to the (perhaps over ambitious) expectations that some criminal practitioners and others had for it.[16]

[15] See in particular *B v Chief Constable of the Avon and Somerset Constabulary* [2001] 1 All ER 562 [sex offender orders under s 2 of the Crime and Disorder Act 1998]; *R (McCann) v Manchester Crown Court* [2001] EWCA Civ 281 (1 March 2001) and *R v Marylebone Magistrates Court ex parte Clingham* [2001] EWHC Admin 1 (11 Jan 2001) [anti-social behaviour order under s 1 of the Crime and Disorder Act 1998]; *Greenfield v Secretary of State for the Home Department* [2001] EWHC Admin 129 (22 Feb 2001) [disciplinary proceedings against a prisoner]; *McIntosh v HM Advocate* 2001 SC (PC) 89 [confiscation orders]; *Goldsmith v Commissioner of Custom and Excise*, Woolf LCJ and Poole J, 25 April 2001, reported in *The Times*, 12 June 2001 [proceedings for condemnation of goods forfeited by Customs and Excise authorities not criminal proceedings to which the presumption of innocence was required to be applied]; *R (Fleurose) v Securities and Futures Authority*, Morison J, 26 June 2001, reported in *The Times* 15 May 2001 [decisions of the disciplinary and appeal tribunals of this authority do not amount to the determination of a criminal charge for the purposes of Art 6]. Cf *Gough and others v Chief Constable of Derbyshire; R (Miller) v Leeds Magistrates Court; Lilley v DPP* Queen's Bench Division 13 July 2001 [football banning orders not a penalty so no violation of Art 7 involved in their retrospective application].

[16] But cf (from the VAT world) *Han and Yau v Customs and Excise Commissioners* (2001) 151 NLJ 1033; *Goldsmith v Commissioner of Custom and Excise*, 25 April 2001, reported in *The Times*, 12 June 2001; and (from tax law) *King v Walden (Inspector of Taxes)* Jacob J, 18 May 2001, reported in *The Times* 12 June 2001.

Three other areas have been to the fore, relating to the privilege (or right) against self-incrimination, the exclusion of unlawfully or wrongfully obtained evidence, and the operation of the burden of proof. We shall consider each of these in turn. As regards the first of these, the Strasbourg case law on 'the right to silence' is certainly extensive, with the ECtHR often taking a very strong line on the matter. True, in the course of the past year there have been cases on self-incrimination which have failed to get off the ground or to succeed completely before the ECtHR.[17] From the British perspective, however, the outstandingly important decisions of recent times have been *Condron v United Kingdom*[18] and *IZL, GMR and AKP v United Kingdom*.[19] Also highly relevant has been a case originating from Ireland, *Heaney, McGuinness and Quinn v Ireland*.[20] Viewed as a whole, these three decisions have not been lacking in robustness from a criminal process perspective.

The *IZL, GMR and AKP* decision may be viewed for present purposes as a sequel to the well-known *Saunders* case which first alerted so many practitioners to the potential of Article 6 in the commercial sphere.[21] In *Condron*, the Strasbourg court found a violation of Article 6(1) in the decision of a trial judge to leave to the jury the opportunity to draw adverse inferences from the silence the applicants had chosen to adopt when they had been interviewed by the police. Significantly the case involved the highly controversial legislative changes on the right to silence that were introduced by the Conservative government in 1994, in section 34 of the Criminal Justice and Public Order Act. The 'starting point'[22] for the Court's analysis was the set of principles set out in the well-known decision on the right to silence from Northern Ireland, *John Murray v United Kingdom*.[23] Like *Murray*, the *Heaney, McGuinness and Quinn* decisions also emerged out of the conflict in Ireland and produced a remarkable, unanimous decision that the power in Ireland's counter terrorism law (in the Offences Against the State Act 1939, s 52) to demand answers to certain questions was effectively incompatible with the guarantees set out in Article 6 of the Convention. Interestingly the impugned section had previously survived challenge in the Irish Supreme Court.[24]

The local 'right to silence' story since 2 October 2000 has been rather different. The domestic cases on this important dimension to the Human Rights Act

---

[17]   See *L (A Child) v United Kingdom* [2000] 2 FCR 145 [disclosure of expert report in course of criminal trial did not infringe privilege against self-incrimination]; *Serves v France* 4 May 2000 [reports drafted in disciplinary proceedings used in subsequent criminal proceedings: application in respect of alleged breach of Art 6(1) found to be inadmissible]; and *Staines v United Kingdom* 16 May 2000 [statements made under legal compulsion but not damaging could be admitted; application to the effect that this breached Art 6 held to be inadmissible].

[18]   *Condron v United Kingdom* (2000) 31 EHRR 1.

[19]   *IZL, GMR and AKP v United Kingdom* 19 Sept 2000.

[20]   *Heaney, McGuinness and Quinn v Ireland* 21 Dec 2000.

[21]   *Saunders v United Kingdom* (1997) 23 EHRR 313.

[22]   *Condron v United Kingdom*, above, n 13, at para 55.

[23]   *John Murray v United Kingdom* (1996) 22 EHRR 29.

[24]   *Heaney and McGuiness v Ireland and the Attorney General* [1996] 1 IR 580.

1998 have drawn a great deal of attention largely on account of the remarkable facts in the most important of them. *Brown v Stott*[25] began life in Scotland before the general implementation date and therefore wound its way up to the Privy Council as early as November 2000, with the decision of the Board being released on 5 December 2000, just two months after general implementation of the Act. It will be remembered that this was the case in which a women's admission that she had been the driver of a car underpinned her subsequent prosecution on a drink-related charge. At first instance the High Court of Justiciary held that the use in subsequent criminal proceedings of admission-based evidence procured under compulsory statutory powers (as existed in this case) infringed the accused's right to a fair trial under Article 6(1) of the ECHR. The facts of the case were somewhat atypical but the decision appeared to have implications for a whole range of law enforcement activities such as, in particular, the deployment of speed cameras. It seemed as though any statutory power requiring a person to answer any question could only be deployed where it was clear that any answers that might be given, however revealing or incriminating, would not be used to that person's disadvantage in any subsequent criminal proceedings.

In the event, the Privy Council unanimously overturned the Scottish decision. In so doing, their Lordships did not however rely on the fact that Parliament remained sovereign under the Human Rights Act 1998 and that it had been Parliament that had explicitly and clearly authorised such questioning—with the clear view that the answers given would have to be capable of underpinning subsequent prosecutions if the provision were to have any efficacy. It is respectfully suggested that this would have been the right way to have approached the case.[26] Instead their Lordships found that the use of compulsorily obtained answers did not itself violate Article 6 of the ECHR, so no question of a breach of the Convention arose. Their Lordships ruled that the privilege against self-incrimination that was implicit in the right to a fair trial in Article 6(1) was not absolute in the way that the right to a fair trial was. It was subject to exceptions, and divining what these were required the courts to balance the value of the right against the public interest in permitting exceptions to it in particular cases. The case before them fell within one of the exceptions.

The *Brown* decision has been controversial, with some lawyers feeling that the Convention right to a fair trial has been badly eroded, and others arguing that the Privy Council misread the relevant Strasbourg case law.[27] It is the first example of the London-based Privy Council taking a different view of the Convention from that which had prevailed in the Scottish courts. We may in due course have a definitive adjudication on these points from the ECtHR. In the meantime *Brown* has been followed in England and Wales. In *DPP v Wilson*[28] it

---

[25] *Brown v Stott* 2001 SC (PC) 43; [2001] 2 All ER 97.
[26] See Human Rights Act 1998, ss 3(2) and 6(2).
[27] Note however that an intervention in the case from JUSTICE was broadly supportive of the reasoning eventually adopted in the case.
[28] *DPP v Wilson* [2001] EWHC Admin 198.

was held to apply 'with equal force' to an admission obtained under compulsion under section 172(2)(b) of the Road Traffic Act 1988 as it did to section 172(2)(a).[29] In *Attorney General's Reference (No 7 of 2000)*,[30] the Court of Appeal (Criminal Division) has held that the use by the Crown in the prosecution of a bankrupt for an offence under the Insolvency Act of documents which were delivered up to the Official Receiver under compulsion but which did not contain statements made under compulsion was acceptable under Article 6(1).

We turn now to the second of our three procedural areas, covering the exclusion of unlawfully obtained evidence. This was an area in which much action was expected, but in the event what has occurred has been less than revolutionary. There would seem to be some difference of judicial view as to whether the infringement of Article 6 of the ECHR is sufficient to render a trial unsafe for the purposes of appeal.[31] An analogous question is whether a court is bound to exclude evidence which has been obtained in breach of a defendant's Convention rights. The ECtHR has never been as determined on the latter point as might have been expected.[32] Therefore it was not entirely surprising that in *R v P and others*,[33] the House of Lords should have held, firstly, that the issue of evidence obtained in breach of the Convention should properly be dealt with by reference to the well-known test of admissibility in section 78 of the Police and Criminal Evidence Act 1984 and, secondly (following inevitably from this first point), that there was no principle of law that required the exclusion of such evidence merely because a 'human rights' violation had been involved. This was because the Article 6(1) requirement for a 'fair' trial was not necessarily breached by the inclusion of such material.[34] On the related question of whether the ECHR now provides a defence to entrapment by the police which has hitherto not existed in English law, the Human Rights Act 1998 case law has been similarly disappointing for defendants. In *R v Shannon*,[35] decided just before implementation, the Court of Appeal held, citing the well-known Strasbourg decision of *Texeira di Castro v Portugal*,[36] that the Convention does not rule out entrapment as such.[37]

---

[29] *DPP v Wilson* [2001] EWHC Admin 198, paras 17 and 28 *per* Sullivan J.

[30] *Attorney General's Reference (No 7 of 2000)* [2001] EWCA Crim 888.

[31] See *R v Davis and others (No 2)*, CA 17 July 2000 and more recently *R v Williams* [2001] EWCA Crim 932 (14 March 2001); *R v Kansal* Court of Appeal Criminal Division 24 May 2001. Cf *R v Togher* [2001] 3 All ER 417. The issue is briefly discussed in *Lambert*, above, n 6, by Lord Clyde (para 159) and Lord Hutton (paras 199–203).

[32] See *Schenk v Switzerland* (1988) 13 EHRR 242 and, more recently, *Khan v United Kingdom* 12 May 2000.

[33] *R v P and others* [2001] 2 All ER 58.

[34] See further *R v Bailey, Brewin and Ganji* [2001] EWCA Crim 733.

[35] *R v Shannon* [2001] 1 WLR 51.

[36] *Texeira di Castro v Portugal* (1999) 28 EHRR 101.

[37] See further *Nottingham City Council v Amin* [2000] 1 WLR 1017; *Attorney General's Reference (No 3 of 2000)* Court of Appeal Criminal Division 17 May 2001.

Our final area of review in this section takes us to the case-law on the burden of proof. The famous *Kebilene* litigation[38] had already indicated, well before implementation, that this was likely to be a key area. Also the clear words of Article 6(2), that 'Everyone charged with a criminal offence shall be presumed innocent until proved guilty according to law', seemed very promising from a defendant's point of view. Initially, the impact of the Act in this field was less than seismic. The Court of Appeal decision in *R v Lambert, Ali and Jordan*[39] gave an indication of how things were likely to go as early as the summer of 2000, with its emphasis that Article 6(2) had to be construed broadly, involving as it did the need to find a fair balance between the general interest and the individual. True in *CPS v K,* it was held by the House of Lords that a defendant should be acquitted if an honest belief that the complainant was over the relevant statutory age could be established, but this reworking of the law was achieved without reliance upon the Convention.[40] In contrast, in *Parker v DPP*[41] the irrebuttable presumption under the Road Traffic Act 1988, section 15(2), that the proportion of alcohol in an accused's breath, blood or urine at the time of an alleged offence was not less than the proportion in the specimen provided was held not to be in breach of Article 6(2).

In *R v Benjafield, Leal, Rezvi and Milford,*[42] the making of a drug confiscation order (under the Drug Trafficking Act 1994 and the Criminal Justice Act 1988 as amended by the Proceeds of Crime Act 1995) was held to be compatible with the ECHR. The Court of Appeal (Lord Woolf LCJ, Judge LJ and Collins J) held that Article 6 (2) did in effect apply to the making of such orders, not directly (because no charge with a criminal offence was explicitly in issue) but rather indirectly through Article 6(1)'s overarching requirement for fair proceedings. However Article 6(2) did:

> not prohibit rules which transfer[red] the burden to the accused to establish a defence, providing the overall burden of proof remain[ed] on the prosecution, nor [did] it necessarily prohibit presumptions of law or fact provided that these [were] within reasonable limits.[43]

Deploying this 'broad and flexible approach,'[44] the court found the transfer of the burden in the cases before them to be unobjectionable: the public interest in acting against serious criminals was very high and there were many safeguards for accused persons built into the legislation. However, in *HM Advocate and HM Advocate General for Scotland v McIntosh,*[45] the defendant was even more comprehensively defeated, with the Board finding that Article 6(2) had no

[38] *Kebilene,* above, n 1.
[39] *R v Lambert, Ali and Jordan* [2001] 1 All ER 1014.
[40] *CPS v K* [2001] UKHL 41 (24 July 2001).
[41] *Parker v DPP* Queen's Bench Division, 7 Dec 2000.
[42] *R v Benjafield, Leal, Rezvi and Milford* [2001] 2 All ER 609.
[43] *Ibid,* para 75, citing *Salabiaku v France* (1988) 13 EHRR 379.
[44] *Ibid,* para 77.
[45] *HM Advocate v McIntosh* 2001 SLT 304; [2001] 2 All ER 638.

application whatsoever to such orders, but that, even if it had applied, there would have been no breach of its terms in the case before them. This is a second example of a decision of the Privy Council overturning an interpretation of the ECHR offered by the Scottish courts.[46] The result of *Benjafield* and *McIntosh* is that the confiscation order process, previously so controversial, has been greatly strengthened and legitimised by the realisation that its draconian procedures, far from flouting human rights standards, are (from a Convention perspective at least) in full compliance with them. In a very recent decision, the ECtHR has lent its support to the Privy Council's analysis of this area of the law.[47]

Notwithstanding these decisions on the very particular issue of drug confiscation orders, the issue of the transfer of the burden of proof remains a controversial one, with it being difficult to generalise as between different statutory frameworks.[48] This is clear from the most important decision on burdens of proof since implementation of the Human Rights Act 1998, the decision of the House of Lords on appeal from the Court of Appeal in *R v Lambert*.[49] Here we have our first example of what was mentioned briefly in the introduction to this chapter, the co-option of the ECHR as an ally in the common law's long-standing opposition to the way in which Parliament has interfered with some of its most cherished principles. The defendant was caught in possession of a duffle bag containing cocaine and charged with possession of a Class A controlled drug with intent to supply in breach of section 5(3) of the Misuse of Drugs Act 1971. In a routine application of settled law, the prosecution at his trial was required to prove the possession by him of the bag after which—if he desired to rely on an escape route also set out in the Act[50]—the burden was cast upon him as defendant to prove, on the balance of probabilities, that he had not known that the bag contained the controlled drug. This was a task that he singularly failed to discharge.

On appeal to the House of Lords, none of their Lordships regarded the case as other than entirely clear regardless of where the burden of proof was found to lie in the individual circumstances before them. Nor did they extend the reach of the fair trial guarantees set out in Article 6 of the ECHR back in time to cover the conduct by judges of trials that had taken place before the Human Rights Act 1998 came into effect.[51] But what their Lordships were prepared to use the case to achieve was a restructuring of the burden of proof in relation to the

---

[46] In *McIntosh v HM Advocate* 2000 SLT 1280; 2000 SCCR 1017. For a recent further example of the overturning of a Scottish ruling in the Privy Council, see *Millar v Dickson* 2001 SLT 988, a set of decisions which has widespread implications for criminal justice north of the Border: see 'Scots ruling opens way for re-trials' *The Guardian* 27 July 2001.

[47] *Phillips v United Kingdom*, 5 July 2001.

[48] Cf the approach of the Court of Appeal Civil Division in *R (H) v Mental Health Review Tribunal, North and East London Region and another*, 28 March 2001.

[49] *R v Lambert* [2001] 3 All ER 577.

[50] Misuse of Drugs Act 1971, s 28(3).

[51] *Lambert,* above, n 49, per Lord Slynn at para 14; Lord Hope at para 107; Lord Clyde at paras 139–140; Lord Hutton at para 176; cf the different views of Lord Steyn on this point at paras 27–31.

offence before them. The effect of the decision is that defendants charged with this offence—and one assumes similarly composed offences—need now only raise evidence in relation to their lack of knowledge of what is in their possession after which it 'will be for the prosecution to show beyond reasonable doubt that the defence is not made out by the evidence.'[52] The way this radical surgery was performed on a settled and long standing piece of primary legislation was by way of the Human Rights Act 1998, and in particular the requirement in section 3 of that Act that statutory provisions be read so far as 'possible' in a way that is consistent with Convention rights. The Strasbourg case-law did not prohibit the reversal of the burden of proof but it required such switches to be 'confined within reasonable limits which take into account the importance of what is at stake and maintain the rights of the defence.'[53] Since Article 6(2) is

> not absolute and unqualified, the test to be applied is whether the modification or limitation of that right pursues a legitimate aim and whether it satisfies the principle of proportionality.[54]

Freed both from the strict words of the Convention and from the rigours of the pre-existing UK case law, four of their Lordships felt able to conclude that the placing of the legal burden on the defendant in a case such as the one before them was in all the circumstances inappropriate.[55] Those circumstances included the academic criticism that had been levelled at the way in which the burden of proof had been altered by Parliament in many cases,[56] the guidance on the issue offered by comparative case law and the judgments of the Privy Council,[57] and the fact that Parliament had already modified the burden of proof in statutes passed in very recent times after the Human Rights Act 1998 implications of a burden of proof question analogous to that before the House had been drawn to its attention.[58] Underlying the approach of the majority was a distaste for the way in which successive parliaments had interfered with the common law's traditional approach to the proof of guilt in criminal cases. As Lord Steyn remarked, it 'is a fact that the legislature has frequently and in an arbitrary and indiscriminate manner made inroads on the basic presumption of

---

[52] *Ibid*, para 94 per Lord Hope. See further Lord Slynn at para 17; Lord Steyn at para 41; and Lord Clyde at para 157. Lord Hutton dissented on this point: see paras 192 and 197–98.

[53] *Salabiaku v France* (1988) 13 EHRR 379, 388 quoted by Lord Hope in *Lambert*, above, n 49, para 87.

[54] *Lambert*, above, n 49, para 88 per Lord Hope, citing *Ashingdane v United Kingdom* (1985) 7 EHRR 528. To similar effect are Lord Slynn at para 17; Lord Steyn at para 34; and Lord Clyde at paras 150–52.

[55] Particularly A Ashworth and M Blake, 'The Presumption of Innocence in English Criminal Law' [1996] *CLR* 306.

[56] *Lambert*, above, n 49, Lord Slynn at para 17; Lord Steyn at paras 37–41; Lord Hope at paras 82–94; Lord Clyde at paras 153–56.

[57] On which see particularly *ibid*, Lord Steyn at para 40; Lord Hope at paras 85–86 and 90; and Lord Clyde at para 147.

[58] *Ibid*, Lord Hope at paras 92–3, referring to the decision is *Kebilene*, above, n 1 and the subsequent provisions on the point in the Terrorism Act 2000 and the Regulation of Investigatory Powers Act 2000.

innocence.'[59] Now the judges had the chance, via section 3 of the Human Rights Act 1998, to restore the law to the position from which the majority of their Lordships clearly felt it should never have been allowed to drift. The beauty of section 3(1) from the judicial point of view was that it allowed the courts perfectly legitimately to twist the words of a statute so as to make it Convention-compatible. Freed from the anxiety that would undoubtedly have attended striking down a major piece of anti-drugs legislation, this is what the majority of their Lordships in *Lambert* duly did.[60]

D. CONCLUSION

A similar case to *Lambert*, and emerging from an equally controversial field, is the decision of the House of Lords in *R v A*.[61] The issue before the Appellate Committee in that case was the compatibility with Article 6(1) of the Convention of a 'rape shield' law which had been very recently enacted by Parliament and the effect of which was greatly to restrict the questions that could be put to complainants in cross-examination.[62] These statutory restrictions applied to questions about alleged sexual activity by the complainant not only conducted with third parties but also with the defendant in the case of which such cross-examination would have been a part. This was too much for their Lordships who unanimously transformed the section (once again using their section 3 Human Rights Act 1998 powers) so as to allow questions on alleged prior sexual experience between an accused and a complainant where, with

> due regard always being paid to the importance of seeking to protect the complainant from indignity and from humiliating questions . . . the evidence (and questioning in relation to it) [was] nevertheless so relevant to the issue of consent that to exclude it would endanger the fairness of the trial under Article 6 of the Convention.[63]

The common law courts have long regarded with suspicion attempts by the legislative branch to fix in advance the way in which evidence in a criminal trial can be deployed, with the issue having been particularly controversial in the field of sexual offences.[64] It is nevertheless surely not impossible to view the statutory provision under scrutiny in *A* as reflecting a deliberate choice by the legislature

---

[59]   *Lambert*, at para 32. See also Lord Hope at paras 76 and 82.

[60]   See *ibid*, Lord Slynn at para 17; Lord Steyn at para 42; Lord Hope at para 84; and Lord Clyde at para 157–58.

[61]   *R v A*, above, n 6.

[62]   Youth Justice and Criminal Evidence Act 1999, s 41.

[63]   *R v A*, above, n 6, Lord Steyn at para 46, whose formulation was explicitly supported by Lord Slynn at para 15, Lord Hope at para 110, Lord Clyde at para 141, and Lord Hutton para 163. Cf *JM v United Kingdom*, Appl No 41518/98, 28 Sept 2000 (allegation that cross-examination of a complainant in a rape case by the accused violated her Art 3 rights: case settled following introduction of legislation to deal with the matter).

[64]   See *DPP v Morgan* [1976] AC 182, followed by Sexual Offences (Amendment) Act 1976.

that in a situation which is bound to be unfair to one side, the burden of unfairness should henceforth be placed upon the defendant. Now, under the guise of section 3(1) of the Human Rights Act 1998 and emboldened by the traditional concerns of the common law of criminal procedure and of evidence, the House of Lords has placed that burden of unfairness back on the complainant.[65] The case is similar in some respects to an early example of this new brand of common law assertiveness that appears to have been ushered in by the Human Rights Act 1998, *R v Offen*.[66] This was the well-known decision of Lord Woolf CJ, Steel and Richards JJ sharply diluting the effect of section 2 of the Crime (Sentences) Act 1997 (now s 109 of the Powers of Criminal Courts (Sentencing) Act 2000), a provision which purported to impose automatic life sentences on persons previously convicted of a serious offence. As in *Lambert* and *A*, the court felt able to redesign the statute under cover of section 3(1), building upon an intense judicial dislike of the provision, a 'get-out' clause in the form of a provision for 'exceptional circumstances,' and a short line of pre-existing authority on which it could work. In *Offen*, as in *A* and *Lambert*, there was a clash of cultures between the judiciary and Parliament, with the Human Rights Act 1998 enabling the former to see off the latter earlier and more effectively than might otherwise have been the case.

It is now appropriate briefly to suggest some conclusions that might be drawn from the foregoing analysis of the case law. First, it is clear that there has been plenty of activity in the courts even though as noted above the number of human rights cases might have been less than expected, expressed as a percentage of the total throughput of the courts in the criminal sphere. Secondly, such activity should not however be mistaken for reform. The litigation has not generated a large amount of change. The end results of cases has, with a very few important exceptions, remained largely the same. A third general observation which flows from the scrutiny of the case law conducted here is how willing the courts have been, anxious even, to get away from the notion of absolute rights and to reduce most of their decisions to a question of balancing the rights of the individual against the interests of the community. Such a quasi-utilitarian calculus is to be found in many of the ECHR's articles that have not been discussed here (eg Articles 8–11) and, despite its not explicitly appearing in Article 6(1) and (2), the courts have effectively implied such a balancing dimension into the words of those two provisions. There have of course been indicators from the Strasbourg court that such an approach is not inappropriate, but the UK courts—particularly the English courts—have taken it very far indeed.

The most remarkable feature of the case law since 2 October 2000 has been the way in which the pre-existing legal culture has sought to embrace the Human Rights Act 1998 and to incorporate it within the framework of laws and practice that is already in place. This is most evident in the way in which the

---

[65] See K Cook, 'Sexual History Evidence: The Defendant Fights Back' (2001) 151 *NLJ* 1133, subtitled '*R v A* may be the first nail in the coffin of legislation designed to reduce sexual history questioning'.

[66] *R v Offen* [2001] 2 All ER 154.

question of evidence obtained in breach of human rights has been effortlessly accommodated within section 78. But it is (somewhat paradoxically) clear too in the way in which decisions have been able most effectively to challenge pre-existing arrangements, on such matters as the burden of proof and the deployment of evidence in criminal trials, where those arrangements have themselves been imposed by Parliament in opposition to deeply-entrenched common law assumptions about what is fair and just. In this respect the Human Rights Act 1998 has had a profoundly conservative effect on the law, being the means through which embattled, even dormant, common law principles have been able to secure for themselves an unexpected renaissance. In sharp contrast to such an approach, where the prevailing legal position has been one with which the judiciary have been in broad agreement, as on the civil/criminal distinction for example, human rights challenges have not progressed very far. The courts have shown themselves willing to defer to the will of Parliament where no important issue of common law principle has been in issue. Very occasionally an alertness to the political importance of a question has been able to trump common law assumptions about the judicial function, as in the decision in February 2001 that the Home Secretary's fixing of the tariff for mandatory life prisoners involves no breach of Article 6.[67] There are powerful dicta on the need to respect parliament from both Lord Woolf and Lord Bingham, in *Benjafield* and *McIntosh* respectively. Of course it does go the other way: the courageous ruling of Lord Woolf in *Thompson and Venables v News Group Newspapers Ltd*[68] is testimony to this. But the overall effect of the first nine months of full-scale litigation in the criminal field has been of a judiciary with a reluctance to wade too deeply into political waters, unless the area under scrutiny is one in which the common law has a strongly preferred position which has been overlooked or attacked by Parliament.

It is right to end on a note of caution. It is very early days for the Human Rights Act 1998. The judicial reticence that was the main characterisation of the opening months of UK-wide human rights litigation may already be falling away as the Act beds down and the judges develop a fresh confidence about their role and how far they can push their powers under the Act. *Offen, Lambert* and *A* may be pointers in that direction. In Ireland it took 30 years and a new generation of judges before a succession of rulings on criminal process rooted in the 1937 Constitution began to emerge. It is hardly likely to take so long here. The 'pro-life' groups are limbering up to restrict the protective ambit of the abortion legislation. The punitive sanctions imposed by the new Terrorism Act are very likely to be challenged. Other matters will no doubt throw themselves to the fore through the exigencies of litigation. The Act may not yet dominate the criminal law but there is no reason to doubt that its influence—at least within the cultural, legal and political contexts identified in this article—will continue to grow.

---

[67] R *(Anderson and Taylor) v Secretary of State for the Home Department* [2001] All ER (D) 280.
[68] *Thompson and Venables v News Group Newspapers Ltd* [2000] 4 All ER 737.

15

The European Convention on Human Rights and Scots Criminal Law

PAMELA R FERGUSON* and MARK M MACKAREL**

A. INTRODUCTION

WHILST THE Human Rights Act 1998 gave the European Convention for the Protection of Human Rights and Fundamental Freedoms (ECHR) 'further effect' in the United Kingdom from 2 October 2000,[1] some aspects of Scots law and indeed the Scottish Parliament had already been subject to the standards of the ECHR through the provisions of the Scotland Act 1998. In this chapter, we consider the status of the ECHR in Scots law and review the emerging case law that has involved the consideration of Convention rights. For reasons which will be explained, the immediate effect of the elevated status of the ECHR in Scots law was primarily on aspects of Scots criminal law and procedure.

The Scotland Act 1998 created a devolved Parliament for Scotland and set out the structure and duties of the Scottish Executive, as well as the powers and restrictions on the Parliament and its officers and institutions.[2] Issues of law concerning the application of the ECHR through that Act are termed 'devolution issues'. The Parliament formally assumed its powers on 1 July 1999 but other parts of the Scotland Act 1998, including those provisions concerning the application of the ECHR to the Scottish Executive and to prosecutions, came into force on 6 May and 20 May 1999 respectively.[3] In broad terms, the Scotland Act 1998 provides that the Scottish Parliament and Scottish Executive cannot legislate or act in a manner that is incompatible with the ECHR.[4] This position made the ECHR applicable to aspects of Scots law in advance of the entry into force of the Human Rights Act 1998.

* Professor of Scots law, University of Dundee.
** Lecturer in Law, University of Dundee.

[1] See The Human Rights Act 1998 (Commencement No 2) Order 2000 (SI 2000 No 1851).
[2] See generally: A C Page, C Reid and A Ross, *A Guide to the Scotland Act 1998* (Butterworths, Edinburgh, 1999); C M G Himsworth and C R Munro, *The Scotland Act 1998* 2nd edn (W Green, Edinburgh, 2000).
[3] Scotland Act (Commencement) Order 1998. SI 1998/3178.
[4] Or with European Community law.

B. THE PRIOR POSITION

Prior to the Scotland Act 1998 the ECHR had no status in legislation. The position of the Scottish courts towards its relevance to legal argument was more restrictive than the stance adopted by the English courts.[5] While the English judiciary had held that the ECHR could be used as an aid to statutory construction under restricted circumstances, the Scottish approach was epitomised by Lord Ross's statement in *Kaur* v *Lord Advocate*:[6]

> So far as Scotland is concerned, I am of opinion that the court is not entitled to have regard to the Convention either as an aid to construction or otherwise. . . . [A] Convention is irrelevant in legal proceedings unless and until its provisions have been in incorporated or given effect in legislation. To suggest otherwise is to confer upon a Convention concluded by the Executive an effect which only an Act of the legislature can achieve.[7]

This view was reiterated in judgments such as *Moore* v *Secretary of State for Scotland*,[8] where a reference to the ECHR in the submission by the pursuer's counsel was described by the court as 'an illegitimate attempt to get round the difficulties in domestic law.'[9] The court endorsed Lord Ross's comments in *Kaur*, stating that 'the Convention plays no part in our municipal law so long as it has not been introduced by legislation.'[10]

It has been suggested that the rejection of the ECHR by the Scottish Courts during this time

> . . . may well have been encouraged by a determination to uphold the separateness and distinctiveness of the Scottish legal system through the over-strict application of constitutional doctrine.[11]

An additional explanation may be that the Scottish judiciary considered that the rights provided by the ECHR were already safeguarded by domestic Scots law. Scots criminal law in particular has been fiercely defended as containing extensive safeguards for the accused.[12] This is illustrated by cases such as *Montes and Others* v *HM Advocate*,[13] in which the court considered the fairness of police interrogation of foreign witnesses. Lord Weir found that that the concept of a

---

[5] See *Salomen* [1966] 3 All ER 871, and *R* v *Secretary of State for the Home Department, ex parte Brind* [1991] 1 AC 696.

[6] *Surjit Kaur* v *Lord Advocate* 1980 SC 319.

[7] *Ibid*, at 329.

[8] *Moore* v *Secretary of State for Scotland* 1985 SLT 38.

[9] *Ibid*, at 41.

[10] *Ibid*.

[11] J Murdoch, 'Scotland and the European Convention' in B Dickson (ed), *Human Rights and the European Convention* (Sweet & Maxwell, London, 1997).

[12] See, for example, C Gane and C Stoddart, *Criminal Procedure in Scotland, Cases and Materials* 2nd edn (W Green, Edinburgh, 1994).

[13] *Montes and Others* v *HM Advocate* 1990 SCCR 645.

fair trial was well protected under Scots law; even if the court had been able to consider the provisions of the ECHR and its jurisprudence, there was no need to do so.[14]

The approach to the ECHR embodied in *Kaur* was altered by two judgments in 1996. In both *T, Petitioner*[15] and *Anderson v HM Advocate*,[16] Lord Hope, then Lord Justice General, held that the Convention could be referred to in Scottish courts in the same limited circumstances as in England:

> In my opinion, the courts in Scotland, should apply the same presumption as [in England], namely that, when legislation is found to be ambiguous . . . , Parliament is to be presumed to have legislated in conformity with the Convention, not in conflict with it.[17]

This position was subsequently approved and reiterated in *Mcleod, Petitioner*.[18]

C. THE SCOTLAND ACT 1998

The Scotland Act 1998 gives effect to rights under the ECHR in two main ways. First, the Scottish parliament has no power to legislate contrary to Convention rights. Secondly, the Scottish Executive has no power to make subordinate legislation or take executive action outside of their devolved competence, hence any acts of the Scottish Executive must be compatible with Convention rights.

(1) The Scottish Parliament

The terms under which the Scottish Parliament must comply with the ECHR are unequivocal. Section 29 of the Scotland Act 1998 specifically provides that it is outwith the legislative competence of the Parliament to enact any legislation that is incompatible with the ECHR.[19] The section also prevents the Scottish Parliament amending the Human Rights Act 1998, in that it is a 'protected provision' under section 4 of that Act.[20] Further, section 101 provides that legislation stemming from the Scottish Parliament must 'be read as narrowly as is

---

[14] More recently, in the case of *HM Advocate v Wilson, Cairns and Others* (unreported, 15 June 2001: available at http://www.scotcourts.gov.uk.) which concerned the confidentiality of communications between an accused and an expert witness instructed by the defence, Lord Reed stated: 'Reference to the European Convention of Human Rights appears to me to add nothing of substance . . . to our domestic law.' His Lordship held that the Convention did not confer any right on the defence to prevent the Crown from adducing as a witness at trial an expert who had carried out an investigation for the defence.

[15] *T, Petitioner* 1997 SLT 724; 1996 SCLR 897.

[16] *Anderson v HM Advocate* 1996 SLT 158.

[17] Above, n 15, 733–734; 910–911. See now s 3 of the Human Rights Act 1998.

[18] *McLeod v HM Advocate (No2)* 1998 JC 67; 1998 SLT 233.

[19] Scotland Act 1998, s 29(2)(d).

[20] *Ibid*, s 29(2)(c).

required for it to be within competence.'[21] Therefore the courts must, where possible, give legislation of the Scottish Parliament a meaning that is compatible with the ECHR. Where that legislation cannot be given a compatible meaning, it will be outside the competence of the Scottish Parliament and will be struck down.

Bills presented to the Scottish Parliament are also subject to scrutiny prior to their enactment. Under section 31 of the Scotland Act 1998, the member of the Scottish Executive overseeing the Bill must state that the Bill is within the legislative competence of the Parliament, and therefore compatible with Convention rights. Provision is also made under section 33 for the Advocate-General for Scotland,[22] or the Lord Advocate,[23] to refer a Bill to the Privy Council during a four-week period following the measure's passage through the Scottish Parliament. Section 35 provides that when the Secretary of State has reasonable grounds for believing that a Bill would contravene the UK's international obligations, the Secretary of State may make an order that forbids the Presiding Officer from submitting the Bill for Royal Assent.[24] Finally, section 100 allows the Lord Advocate, Advocate General and other law officers, and anyone who could be regarded as a 'victim' for the purposes of Article 34 of the ECHR or section 7 of the Human Rights Act 1998, to seek judicial review of the legislation. The Scottish Parliament will also be subject to section 6 of the Human Rights Act 1998 in that it is regarded as a 'public authority' for the purposes of that Act. This in contrast to the Westminster Parliament, which is expressly excluded from the ambit of the Act.

(2) The Scottish Executive

Sections 52–54 of the Scotland Act 1998 transfer functions within 'devolved competence' to the Scottish Executive. This comprises the First Minister, the other Scottish Ministers appointed by the First Minister, the Lord Advocate and the Solicitor General for Scotland.[25] The inclusion of the Lord Advocate as a member of the Scottish Executive had a particular significance on cases involving challenges using the ECHR in the period immediately following the Scotland Act 1998 entering into force. Section 57(2) of the Scotland Act 1998 states that no member of the Scottish Executive 'has power to . . . do any . . . act, so far as [it] is incompatible with any of the Convention rights . . .' As will be seen later in the chapter, this restriction on the actions of the Lord Advocate has given rise

---

[21] Scotland Act 1998, s 101(2).
[22] *Ibid*, s 87 establishes the Advocate-General for Scotland who is the Scottish Law Officer to the Westminster Parliament and advises the Government on matters of Scots law.
[23] The Lord Advocate is the head of the prosecution service in Scotland.
[24] Scotland Act 1998 s 126(10) defines these as excluding the ECHR.
[25] *Ibid*, s 44.

to most of the cases concerning ECHR matters coming before the court during the initial period of the Scotland Act 1998 being in force.

An exception to the requirement that the Lord Advocate must act in a manner that is compatible with the ECHR is set out in section 57(3) of the Scotland Act 1998. This provides that section 57(2) does not apply to the Lord Advocate while acting in the capacity as the head of the prosecution service in Scotland where, as a result of primary legislation, the Lord Advocate could not have acted any differently. This subsection adds to the various provisions throughout both the Human Rights Act 1998 and the Scotland Act 1998 to ensure that the Westminster Parliament and United Kingdom legislation remain supreme.

(3) Raising a 'devolution issue' before the Scottish Courts

Schedule 6 of the Scotland Act 1998 sets out the circumstances under which a devolution issue may arise and the procedures that are to be followed. A 'devolution issue' includes matters as to whether legislation enacted by the Scottish Parliament is compatible with the ECHR, whether a function of Scottish Ministers is within their legal competence, and whether an act or omission of the Scottish Executive is compatible with the ECHR.[26]

A devolution issue may originate either in proceedings specifically brought to challenge the competence of legislation or an act of the Scottish Executive, or indeed may arise in the course of other proceedings. In criminal proceedings, a court generally has discretion whether to decide the issue itself or to refer the matter to the High Court of Justiciary sitting as an appeal court.[27] Cases referred to the High Court may be further appealed to the Judicial Committee of the Privy Council.[28] If a devolution issue comes before a court comprising two or more judges of the High Court, the matter can either be decided by that court or be referred to the Privy Council.[29]

Schedule 6 also provides for further rules specifying the manner and time in which a devolution issue must be raised. The procedures in criminal cases are contained in the Act of Adjournal (Devolution Issues Rules) 1999.[30] This is subordinate legislation made by the Lord Commissioners of Justiciary and the rules seek to ensure, where possible, that devolution issues are considered prior to trial. Where a criminal case is to be heard on indictment,[31] the Act of Adjournal

---

[26] Consideration of a devolution issue may arise in proceedings throughout the United Kingdom, and provision for this is made under Schedule 6. This chapter focuses on Scottish proceedings, only.

[27] Scotland Act 1998, Sch 6, para 7. The High Court of Justiciary is the supreme court in Scots criminal matters.

[28] *Ibid*, Sch 6, para 13.

[29] *Ibid*, paras 10 and 11.

[30] SI 1999 No 1346 (hereafter referred to as Act of Adjournal). This added a new chapter (chapter 40) to the Act of Adjournal (Criminal Procedure Rules) 1996. Similar Rules for civil matters are contained in the Act of Sederunt (Devolution Issue Rules) 1999, SI 1999 No 1345.

[31] That is, solemn procedure (before a jury).

requires the party raising the devolution issue to give notice within seven days of being served with the indictment.[32] This notice is to be given to the court, the other parties and to the Advocate General.[33] The aim of deciding any devolution issue prior to the proceedings themselves is a sound one, given the delay that would ensue should such points be raised during trial. This position also avoids the problems caused where an incorrect determination of a devolution issue leads to an acquittal.[34] The Advocate General may refer any devolution issue to the High Court for its opinion, but this does not affect the outcome of either conviction or appeal.[35]

Whilst it seems sensible for devolution issues to be resolved prior to trial, this may not always be possible. For example, the admission of evidence into criminal proceedings may raise ECHR issues that were unforeseeable. This has caused the courts some difficulties. The requirement to give notice of a devolution issue within seven days from service of the indictment was challenged by the accused in the case of *HM Advocate v Dickson*.[36] The requisite notice required under the Rules had not been given, and when the Crown attempted to rely on this lack of notice, the defence countered by arguing that the Act of Adjournal was ultra vires. The trial judge took the view that this issue was of such importance that it ought to be considered by a bench of three judges.

The Act of Adjournal was enacted by the Lords Commissioners of Justiciary on 4 May 1999 and it was argued that the authority to promulgate such an Act was derived from provisions which did not themselves come into force until 6 May 1999.[37] The court held that the Act of Adjournal was not ultra vires. Its authority derived from the Criminal Procedure (Scotland) Act 1995,[38] whose paragraphs were to be read as conferring separate and alternative justifications for the making of Acts of Adjournal. In respect of the date of enactment, the provisions of the Scotland Act 1998 had been 'enacted' prior to 6 May, though not then in force.

Defence counsel also argued that in requiring written notice of a devolution issue within seven days from service of the indictment, the Act of Adjournal 'narrowed' the rights enshrined in the ECHR, in particular, the requirement in Article 6(3)(b) that persons are to be given 'adequate time' for the preparation of their defence. The Act of Adjournal also required an accused to provide written details of the 'facts and circumstances and contentions of law on the basis of

---

[32] Act of Adjournal (Devolution Issues Rules) 1999, Rule 40.6.

[33] *Ibid*, Rule 40.2(1).

[34] Under Scots law, an acquittal under solemn procedure cannot be appealed, only a reference made on the point of law: Criminal Procedure (Scotland) Act 1995, ss 106(1) and 123.

[35] Criminal Procedure (Scotland) Act 1998, s 288A inserted by the Scotland Act 1998. The procedure in civil matters under the Act of Sederunt follows a broadly similar strategy, with notice of the devolution issue to be notified in the pleadings. See the Act of Sederunt, above, n 30, Rule 25A.4.

[36] *HM Advocate v Dickson* 2000 JC 93; 1999 SCCR 859. See the five bench decision at 2001 SCCR 397.

[37] See Schedule 6 and s 98 of the Scotland Act 1998, and the Scotland Act 1998 (Commencement) Order (SI 1998 No 3178).

[38] Criminal Procedure (Scotland) Act 1995, s 305.

which it is alleged that a devolution issue arises.' This was challenged in *Dickson* on the basis that it imposed hurdles on an accused for which there was no equivalent on the part of the prosecution, hence was 'biased in favour of the State'. The court did not accept that the requirements of the Act of Adjournal restricted an accused's rights under the ECHR.

The defence sought to exclude evidence of an interview between the accused and customs officials. Counsel for the accused argued that it was impossible for the terms of the Act of Adjournal to be complied with in respect of the seven-day notice period, since the admissibility of the evidence only became an issue when the Crown attempted to introduce it, during the course of the trial. However, the Court held that since the Crown must supply a list of its productions with an indictment,[39] the accused's solicitors could have readily ascertained that the transcript of the interview was to be led as evidence as part of the prosecution case. It was further noted that Rule 40.5(1) of the Act of Adjournal provides that a court may allow a devolution issue to be raised at a later stage of the proceeding, on cause shown. The court remitted the case to the trial judge, who subsequently held that the devolution issue could have been raised within the time limits of Rule 40.2, or at least prior to the trial.

It was established in the case of *HM Advocate v Montgomery and Coulter*[40] that an accused may amend the minutes of notice under Rule 40. The case concerned pre-trial publicity; the media had reported certain pre-trial comments made by a High Court judge, and the responses to these comments from the Lord Advocate. The two accused argued that the failure of the Crown to take action to prevent these comments being reported amounted to a breach of Article 6 of the ECHR, since this discussion in the press could prejudice their right to a fair trial.[41] In a later 'addition to the Minute' the accused introduced a further argument, and the Crown argued that this addition to the Minute was incompetent since it had not conformed to the time limits required by the Act of Adjournal.

The Court held that where a devolution issue also amounted to a preliminary plea (in this case, a plea of oppression)[42] then it should be dealt with by means of a preliminary diet. Such diets are dealt with under section 72 of the Criminal Procedure (Scotland) Act 1995. This allows the court to consider 'any other . . . notice . . . which has been intimated to the court and to the other parties at least 24 hours before that [preliminary] diet.'[43] It followed from this that the additional Minute could be competent. According to the Lord Justice General, the task of the court was to 'meld' the procedures in the relevant sections of the

---

[39] As required by Criminal Procedure (Scotland) Act 1995, s 66(5).

[40] *HM Advocate v Montgomery and Coulter* 1999 SCCR 959.

[41] Note that the court stressed that at issue were questions as to the correct procedure to be followed in such a case—the merits of the accused's submissions were not discussed. See now *Montgomery and Coulter v HM Advocate* 2000 JC 111; 2001 PC 1, discussed below.

[42] See nn 90–91.

[43] Criminal Procedure (Scotland) Act 1995, s 72(3).

Criminal Procedure (Scotland) Act 1995 with those in the Act of Adjournal.[44] Under the latter, a devolution issue could be raised later if cause were shown for the failure to raise the issue at an earlier stage. In the words of the Lord Justice General:

> In deciding whether an accused person has shown . . . cause, the court should have regard to all the circumstances; the mere fact that those circumstances disclose some failure on the part of the accused person or his representatives will not necessarily mean that he has not shown cause for allowing the issue to be raised late.
>
> Part of the cause for allowing an issue to be raised late may be its *prima facie* significance, particularly for the course of proceedings as a whole.

The presiding judge was accordingly entitled to conclude that cause had been shown, and the Crown appeal was refused.

Despite the decision in *Dickson*, in a number of subsequent cases the court has held that the time for an accused to challenge the admissibility of evidence as being in breach of Article 6 of the ECHR is when that evidence is tendered by the Crown—see the cases of *Campbell, Robb, McKenna*, and in particular *Brown v Stott*, discussed below.

D. AN 'ACT' OF THE LORD ADVOCATE

Since section 57(2) of the Scotland Act 1998 prohibits the Lord Advocate from doing any act that is incompatible with the ECHR, the question of what amounts to an 'act' has arisen in a number of cases.[45] In *HM Advocate v Little*[46] the court held that the raising of an indictment could, in the particular circumstances of the case, be an 'act of the Lord Advocate' for the purposes of section 57(2).[47] In *HM Advocate v Campbell*[48] it was argued that the holding of an identification parade by the police was an act by the Lord Advocate since the parade

---

[44] The Lord Justice-General is the most senior judge in Scotland in the High Court of Justiciary, which deals with criminal matters. He assumes the title of Lord President while sitting in the Court of Session, in civil matters.

[45] In *HM Advocate v Scottish Media Newspapers* 2000 SLT 331; 1999 SCCR 599 the LJG, Lord Rodger, observed: 'The Lord Advocate is a member of the Scottish Executive . . . and, as such, by virtue of section 57, he has no power to do any act so far as it would be incompatible with any of the Convention rights to be incorporated next year by the Human Rights Act 1998. Until the Human Rights Act comes into force, s 57(2) of the Scotland Act is to have effect as it will have effect after that time (s 129(2)). It follows that, subject to s 57(3), which does not apply in this case, the Lord Advocate cannot move the court to grant any remedy which would be incompatible with the European Convention on Human Rights.' This view was significant in the interim period prior to the Human Rights Act 1998 coming into force. The Lord Advocate (and the prosecution service which the Lord Advocate heads) could have attempted to avoid the restraints of s 57(2) by claming that the issuing of search or arrest warrants was not an act of the Executive, but of the courts.

[46] *HM Advocate v Little* 1999 SLT 1145; 1999 SCCR 625. See also text to n 67 below.

[47] *Little* was followed in the case of *HM Advocate v McCann*, 19 July 1999, unreported. While the sheriff accepted that the bringing of an indictment could give rise to a devolution issue, he found that no devolution issue arose in the circumstance of the case.

[48] *HM Advocate v Campbell* 1999 SCCR 980. See also commentary to n 103.

took place on the instruction of the procurator fiscal. However the Court held that no act occurred within the section until the Crown attempted to lead evidence of the conduct and results of the parade. *Little* was distinguished; the Crown had conceded in *Little* that the decision to prosecute a particular case could itself be regarded as an 'act' of the Lord Advocate, but this was in the special circumstances of that case. The relevant act in *Little* was the decision to prosecute the charges such a long period of time after the accused had first been charged.[49] The correct time for the accused in the present case to challenge the identity parade was when the Crown sought to adduce its findings as evidence.

That the tendering of evidence was to be regarded as an act of the Lord Advocate for the purposes of section 57(2) of the Scotland Act 1998 was made clear in the case of *HM Advocate v Robb*.[50] Lord Penrose held that:

> . . . acts and omissions of the Lord Advocate in prosecuting crime, and acts and omissions in his capacity as head of the criminal prosecuting system, and acts and omissions in the investigation of deaths would all have been within the scope of subsection (2).

A similar decision was reached in *Paton v Ritchie*,[51] in which the accused sought a ruling in advance of the trial as to the admissibility of confession evidence. Here it was accepted that an attempt to lead such evidence would be an act of the Lord Advocate, but again the Court emphasised that in Scots law issues concerning the admissibility of evidence are to be resolved by the trial judge as they arise in the course of a trial. The Court accordingly held that it would be premature and inappropriate for it to rule on the issue of admissibility at a pre-trial hearing.

The timing of raising such issues was also considered in *McKenna v HM Advocate*.[52] The accused was charged with murder. The Crown gave notice to the accused of its intention to lead evidence of statements given by a witness to the police. While such statements would generally be inadmissible in Scots law as hearsay, the witness had since died, and legislation provides that such statements can be led in evidence in these circumstances.[53] The accused argued, inter alia, that the serving of the notice was a breach of Article 6 of the ECHR, since the use of such evidence would infringe his right to a fair trial.[54] Even after having served such a notice, the Crown may opt to close its case without having led the evidence in question, hence the court held that the mere fact that a notice had been served could not in itself infringe the right to a fair trial. According to Lord Penrose, there would have to be extreme circumstances before an accused

---

[49] See further text to n 67, below.

[50] *HM Advocate v Robb* 2000 JC 127; 1999 SCCR 971. *Robb* was approved in *Montgomery and Coulter v HM Advocate* 2000 JC 111; 2001 PC 1. See also commentary to n 101.

[51] *Paton v Ritchie* 2000 JC 271; 2000 SLT 239; 2000 SCCR 151.

[52] *McKenna v HM Advocate* 2000 SLT 508; 2000 SCCR 159.

[53] Criminal Procedure (Scotland) Act 1995, s 259(5).

[54] The court emphasised that the protection provided by the ECHR was similar to that afforded under national law by a plea of oppression—see *Hamilton v Byrne* 1997 SCCR 547 at 549.

person could argue prior to the trial itself that the introduction of such evidence would be so prejudicial as to infringe the prospects of a fair trial. It was accepted by his Lordship that evidence which had been obtained by irregular means might fall in to the category of allowing a court to determine in advance that its admission would amount to a miscarriage of justice.[55] However, as a more general rule, the issue of whether particular evidence should not be admitted lest it imperil the prospects of a fair trial ought to be resolved during the trial, and the fairness of the trial judged as a whole.

The question of what amounted to an act of the Lord Advocate also arose in the case of *Starrs v Ruxton*,[56] in which the accused argued that summary prosecution before a temporary sheriff was a breach of the ECHR.[57] The Solicitor General for Scotland, representing the Lord Advocate at the appeal, advised the court that the Lord Advocate expected procurators fiscal to be bound by the ECHR, and would not take the point that something which was done by a procurator fiscal was not equivalent to his act as Lord Advocate and as a member of the Scottish Executive. The court therefore accepted that the decision of the procurator fiscal in continuing the prosecution in the present case constituted an act of the Lord Advocate.[58]

When the case of *Montgomery and Coulter v HM Advocate* (referred to above) reached the Privy Council,[59] the three English judges hearing the case cast doubt on whether an accused person could claim that his or her right to a fair trial was at risk by the decision of the Lord Advocate to initiate criminal proceedings.[60] They reasoned that such claims should be directed at the trial court, rather than the prosecutor. Lords Hope and Clyde robustly defended the stance taken hitherto by the High Court of Justiciary in concluding that a decision to prosecute could in itself raise issues of Convention rights, and this stance has now been accepted by the Privy Council in *Brown v Stott*.[61]

Many of the cases described above involved assertions that an act of the Lord Advocate had prejudiced the accused's rights to trial 'within a reasonable time', 'by an independent and impartial tribunal' or to 'a fair and public hearing'. These rights are contained in Article 6(1) of the ECHR. Aspects of the 'fair trial' requirement are fleshed out in Article 6(3) of the ECHR, and have given rise to cases relating to specification of charges, oppression and the right to legal representation. Article 6(2) of the ECHR provides for a presumption of innocence,

---

[55] An example of this could be the use of evidence recovered from a search which was based on a defective search warrant.

[56] *Starrs v Ruxton* 2000 SLT 42; 2000 JC 208.

[57] See discussion to nn 77–78 below.

[58] The initial prosecution had commenced on 5 May 1999, but the Lord Advocate did not become a member of the Executive until 20 May 1999 hence it was the date on which the adjourned trial was due to commence (8 July 1999) that was crucial.

[59] See now *Montgomery and Coulter v HM Advocate* 2000 JC 111; 2001 PC 1; [2001] 2 WLR 779.

[60] The English judges were Lords Hoffmann, Slynn and Nicholls.

[61] *Brown v Stott* 2001 SC (PC) 43; [2001] 2 All ER 97.

and Scots criminal law has also been tested against this requirement of the ECHR. The relevant cases are considered, below.

E. TRIAL WITHIN A REASONABLE TIME

In *Smith v Lord Advocate*[62] Lord Prosser stated:

> In considering the words 'within a reasonable time', it is important to consider the total time involved. It will often be possible to criticise some period of delay within that overall time. But it is the reasonableness of the total time which is in issue . . .[63]

Pre-trial delay was also pled in the case of *McNab v HM Advocate*.[64] The accused had pleaded guilty to attempted murder in May 1997. Her victim died in December that year, and on 3 June 1998 the accused was informed that she was to be indicted for murder. The murder indictment was served on 13 May 1999, for trial on 21 June 1999. She took a plea in bar of trial, arguing that the period from 3 June 1998 to 13 May 1999 constituted an unreasonable delay. During that period the accused was not on remand awaiting trial, but was in the course of serving a 12-year sentence for the attempted murder. It was accordingly conceded by her counsel that she had not suffered any prejudice as a result of the delay.

The Lord Justice Clerk, Lord Cullen, emphasised the distinction between a plea in bar of trial based on 'oppression', and one based on a breach of Article 6(1) of the ECHR. In respect of oppression, the delay must be shown to have gravely prejudiced the accused's prospects of receiving a fair trial.[65] The Court of Appeal held that the delay here was not unreasonable, since the court could take into account the demands of other, more pressing cases, such as those involving child witnesses or where the accused was on remand. The Court did, however, accept that under the ECHR an accused need not show that he or she had suffered, or was likely to suffer, prejudice as a result of a delay in order for that delay to be considered 'unreasonable.'[66]

As noted above, the case of *HM Advocate v Little*[67] also concerned the right to trial within a reasonable time. The accused faced seven charges of a sexual nature, ranging from shameless indecency to rape and sodomy. The accused had first been charged by the police in respect of some of these matters on 4 January 1988, but the indictment containing these and other charges was not served until

---

[62] *Smith v Lord Advocate* 2000 SCCR 926.

[63] *Ibid*, at 930. This was approved in *PF Linlithgow v Watson and Burrows* (Appeal Nos 2324/00 and 2326/00, available at http://www.scotcourts.gov.uk) See also *Hendry v HM Advocate* 2001 SCCR 59 in which a period of 18 months from charge to trial was not considered to be unreasonable, despite including a 5-month period during which the police failed to execute a petition warrant.

[64] *McNab v HM Advocate* 2000 JC 80; 2000 SLT 99; 1999 SCCR 930.

[65] *McFadyen v Annan* 1992 JC 53.

[66] Reference was made to *Eckle v Federal Republic of Germany* (1982) 5 EHRR 1.

[67] Above, n 46.

4 February 1999—a period of 11 years and one month. Lord Kingarth accepted that the right to trial within a reasonable time was separate from the right to a fair trial, hence the accused could allege that his trial had been unreasonably delayed without requiring to show that this delay would affect his ability to receive a fair trial. Given the delay, the Crown required to provide a relevant and adequate explanation. It was unable to do so. The court applied the case of *Dougan v UK*[68] in which the time period from charge to service of the indictment had been 12 years and 11 months, and sustained the plea in bar, even though no prejudice had been sustained by the accused. This was also in accordance with *Dougan*, in which the applicant had also been unable to show that he had been prejudiced by the length of proceedings.[69]

The Crown had argued that the court required to balance the accused's right to a speedy trial against the public interest in the prosecution of serious offences; and in particular to consider the needs of the alleged victims of such crimes. The court was not persuaded by these arguments, and pointed out that while some of the ECHR's Articles specifically provided for a limitation of a person's rights, Article 6 contained no such provision.[70] In bringing an indictment so long after the date on which the accused was first charged, the Lord Advocate had acted in a way that was incompatible with Article 6 of the ECHR.

That his trial had not commenced within a reasonable time was also contended by the accused in *McLean v HM Advocate*.[71] He argued that the social work department had been aware for a considerable time of the incident to which the first charge related, hence whether his trial was held within a reasonable time should be calculated by reference to the date of knowledge of that department, despite the fact that the police and prosecution remained unaware of the circumstances until a much later date. In rejecting this argument, the court stressed that in calculating whether the pre-trial period has been reasonable, it is the time between being charged and being tried on that charge which is crucial. Reference was made to *Eckle v Federal Republic of Germany*[72] in which it was said that the time period 'begins to run as soon as a person is "charged" '.[73] The commencement of activities by criminal justice authorities was the crucial starting point, and the appeal was therefore refused.[74]

---

[68] *Dougan v UK* 1997 SCCR 56.

[69] See also *Crummock (Scotland) Ltd v HM Advocate* 2000 JC 408; 2000 SLT 677; 2000 SCCR 453.

[70] See also *Montgomery and Coulter v HM Advocate* 2000 JC 111; 2001 PC 1, in which Lord Hope stated: 'Article 6, unlike Articles 8 to 11 of the Convention, is not subject to any words of limitation. It does not require nor indeed does it permit a balance to be struck between the rights which it sets out and other considerations such as the public interest.' (*Ibid,* at 40–41). Articles 8 to 11 allow for the rights contained therein to be restricted in the interests of, inter alia, 'national security', 'public safety', or 'the prevention of disorder or crime'.

[71] *McLean v HM Advocate* 2000 JC 140; 2000 SCCR 112.

[72] *Eckle v Federal Republic of Germany* Series A, No 51; (1982) 5 EHRR 1.

[73] Series A, No 51; (1982) 5 EHRR 1 at para 73.

[74] Note that in *Dyer v Watson and Brown* 2001 SCCR 430, it was held that although the Convention right was concerned with the period from the accused being charged, prior lapses of time, and the reasons for delay during these periods, could also be considered.

In *Valentine, Wells and Others v HM Advocate*[75] periods ranging from 18 months to 23 months had elapsed between charge and commencement of the trial, in respect of the four accused. The then Lord Justice General, Lord Rodger, held that these delays were not unreasonable:

> Part at least of the *raison d'être* of the venerable system of public prosecution in Scotland is indeed that independent, legally qualified, prosecutors should examine police reports and should identify, discuss and resolve concerns about the case before deciding whether to embark upon serious proceedings, such as those against the appellants . . . These procedures take time. But it is time which is, generally, well spent in the interests of justice and in the interests of securing a fair trial. Attempts by the courts to second-guess the procurator fiscal and to say that he or she had been unduly cautious, had pursued an unnecessarily detailed line of enquiry or had exaggerated the difficulties of some course of action, could only have a chilling effect on the work of conscientious procurators fiscal. It would be wrong to apply the Convention in such a way as to bring that about.[76]

F. AN INDEPENDENT AND IMPARTIAL TRIBUNAL

As noted above, in *Starrs v Ruxton*[77] the two accused appeared on summary complaint before a temporary sheriff, and argued that a person holding such a post did not amount to 'an independent and impartial tribunal', as required by Article 6(1) of the ECHR.[78] This contention was not directed solely at the individual temporary sheriff who was hearing this particular case, but was recognised to be a point of more general importance. It was argued that in prosecuting accused persons before such courts, the Lord Advocate was doing an act inconsistent with the ECHR.

The Solicitor General explained the operation of the appointing methods to the Court, and stated that while the power of appointment lay with the Secretary of State, in practice the Lord Advocate played a major role, compiling a list of suitable applicants to be interviewed for the post of temporary sheriff, and thereafter a list of provisional candidates. He also made the final selection for appointment, albeit in consultation with the Lord President. The practice had developed whereby persons who wished ultimately to become permanent sheriffs were appointed initially as temporary ones. Moreover, while statute

---

[75] *Valentine, Wells and Others v HM Advocate* 2001 SCCR 727.

[76] In contrast, in *HM Advocate v DP* 2001 SCCR 210, a delay of 23 months was regarded as unreasonable where the two accused were 13 year old children who had been charged with rape.

[77] Above, n 56. See also the case of *Ruxton v Johnstone and Gunn*, 11 Nov 1999, (unreported) in which the issue was the same as in *Starrs v Ruxton*, but here a temporary sheriff had adjourned the trial and a permanent sheriff had decided the issue. This was not competent since the permanent sheriff was not the trial judge.

[78] The Secretary of State was empowered to appoint temporary sheriffs by the Sheriff Courts (Scotland) Act 1971, s 11(2).

specified that the appointment of a temporary sheriff was to subsist until recalled by the Secretary of State,[79] in practice the Lord Advocate made one-year appointments. Unlike permanent sheriffs, who receive a salary, temporary sheriffs were paid on an *ad hoc* basis.

Could temporary sheriffs constitute an 'independent and impartial' tribunal, given that the Lord Advocate, a member of the Executive, and a party in criminal cases, had such a role in 'hiring and firing' them? Reference was made to the case of *Findlay v United Kingdom*[80] in which the European Court of Human Rights stated:

> In order to establish whether a tribunal can be considered as 'independent', regard must be had *inter alia* to the manner of appointment of its members and their term of office, the existence of guarantees against outside pressures and the question whether the body presents an appearance of independence.

'Impartiality' meant that:

> . . . the tribunal must be subjectively free of personal prejudice or bias.
> . . . it must also be impartial from an objective viewpoint, that is, it must offer sufficient guarantees to exclude any legitimate doubt in this respect.[81]

The High Court concluded that while there was nothing irregular in the fact that temporary sheriffs were appointed by a member of the Executive, such an appointment 'is consistent with independence only if it is supported by adequate guarantees that the appointed judge enjoys security of tenure.' The one-year term of appointment suggested 'a reservation of control over the tenure' which 'reinforced the impression that the tenure . . . is at the discretion of the Lord Advocate. It does not, at least *prima facie*, square with the appearance of independence.' There was also force in the argument that temporary sheriffs who were keen to be given permanent posts 'might be influenced in their decision-making to avoid unpopularity with the Lord Advocate'. In holding that the prosecution of crimes before a temporary sheriff was a breach of Article 6 of the ECHR, the court in *Starrs v Ruxton* was at pains to point out that it was the *appearance* of independence and impartiality that was at issue. Lord Reed stated:

> . . . I wish to make it plain that I am not suggesting that any temporary sheriff has ever allowed his judicial conduct to be influenced by any consideration of how he might best advance his prospects of obtaining the renewal of his office, or his promotion to a permanent appointment. Nor am I suggesting that any official or Minister has ever sought to interfere with the judicial conduct of a temporary sheriff or would ever be

---

[79] Sheriff Courts (Scotland) Act 1971, s 11(4).
[80] *Findlay v United Kingdom* (1997) 24 EHRR 221 at para 73.
[81] *Ibid*, at para 73. Reference was also made to s 11(d) of the Canadian Charter of Rights and Freedoms, which provides: 'Any person charged with an offence has the right . . . to be presumed innocent until proven guilty according to law in a fair and public hearing by an independent and impartial tribunal.'

likely to do so. There is however no objective guarantee that something of that kind could never happen; and that is why these appeals must succeed.[82]

Following *Starrs v Ruxton*, it was claimed, in the case of *Millar v Dickson*,[83] that:

> the Lord Advocate (and thus the respondent procurators fiscal who conducted the prosecutions) acted incompatibly with the convention right of the accused under Article 6(1) by prosecuting them before temporary sheriffs who were not an independent and impartial tribunal; that such proceedings were accordingly *ultra vires* and null; and that the convictions and sentences [of the appellants] should accordingly be quashed.[84]

These cases had been prosecuted before temporary sheriffs between 20 May 1999 (the date on which section 57 of the Scotland Act 1998 took force) and 11 November 1999 (the date on which the High Court gave its judgment in *Starrs v Ruxton*). In light of the decision in *Starrs v Ruxton*, the Privy Council allowed the appeals. It follows that all prosecutions heard by temporary sheriffs after 20 May are invalid, unless the accused had waived his or her right under Article 6.[85] It is possible that the Crown may wish to seek retrial in some serious cases. The impact of this decision becomes apparent when one considers that persons who, for example, were disqualified from driving following conviction for road traffic offences, and who consequently lost their jobs, may seek compensation because their cases were heard before a temporary sheriff.

In the case of *Clark v Kelly*[86] the accused contended that the District Court in Kirkcaldy was not an independent and impartial tribunal. This was based on the fact that the clerk of the District Court acts as a legal assessor and assists a lay Justice of the Peace in respect of the law. It was argued that District Court clerks did not have the requisite security of tenure to be considered 'independent and impartial' as established in *Starrs*. It was further contended that when a clerk retires with a JP at the close of a case, this deprives the accused of a public hearing. The High Court held that the clerk of the district court was not a member of the court, and that the practice of communication between Justice and clerk outwith open court did not breach Article 6(1) of the ECHR. The court did, however, hold that any matter which could be the object of a relevant submission by one of the parties should be declared in open court. This could include the situation where the legal advice given by the clerk was possibly controversial, or where the clerk advised the justice that a party's submission or a case cited was in fact erroneous.

---

[82] *Starrs v Ruxton*, above, n 56, at 74. See now the Bail, Judicial Appointments etc. (Scotland) Act 2000 in respect of other judicial offices.

[83] The case was cojoined with others appealing the same point of law: *Millar v Dickson* 2000 JC 648; 2001 SLT 988.

[84] *Ibid*, 2001 SLT 988, at 990.

[85] *Ibid*. The mere fact that the accused had not raised the issue at trial was not to be regarded as equivalent to a waiver of this right.

[86] *Clark v Kelly* 2000 SCCR 821.

G.   SPECIFICATION OF CHARGES

Article 6(3)(a) of the ECHR provides an accused with the right 'to be informed . . . in detail, of the nature and cause of the accusations against him.' In *McLean v HM Advocate*[87] the accused had been indicted for trial on two charges of attempted murder. The first charge libelled that the incident in question had occurred 'between 1 November 1994 and 27 November 1994'. The accused argued that the lack of specification of the actual date of the alleged offence meant that the charge was not sufficiently precise to fulfil the requirements of this Article.[88] This argument was rejected by the presiding judge, and his decision was upheld by the High Court on appeal. The court regarded the suggestion that an actual date required to be libelled as 'too extreme a proposition' and it was stressed that the degree of detail that was necessary in any particular charge was dependent on the nature of the crime and the circumstances of the case.[89]

H.   OPPRESSION

As already noted, the accused in the case of *Montgomery and Coulter v HM Advocate*[90] argued that pre-trial publicity had prejudiced their right to a fair trial.[91] The Judicial Committee of the Privy Council held that the test for this under Article 6 of the ECHR was similar to that of oppression at Common Law, but that the public interest in crimes being detected and in offenders being punished could not be balanced against the right under Article 6. According to Lord Hope:

> The right of an accused to a fair trial by an independent and impartial tribunal is unqualified. It is not to be subordinated to the public interest in the detection and suppression of crime. In this respect it might be said that the Convention right is superior to the common law right.
>   . . . An assessment of the weight to be given to the public interest does not come into the exercise.[92]

Oppression as a plea in bar of trial was also pleaded in *Buchanan v McLean*.[93] Article 6(3)(c) of the ECHR provides that everyone has a right to:

---

[87]   Above, n 71.

[88]   The argument was based on the case of *Brozicek v Italy* (1989) 12 EHRR 371 in which the European Court of Human Rights referred to the fact that the charge against Brozicek had 'sufficiently listed the offences . . . , stated the place *and date* thereof' (at para 42, emphasis added).

[89]   It should be noted that the Crown had an implied latitude of three months from any date specified—see Sch 3, para 4(1) of the 1995 Act.

[90]   2001 SLT 37; 2000 SCCR 1044.

[91]   Pre-trial publicity was held by the European Court of Human Rights to be a breach of Article 6(2) in *Allenet de Ribemont v France* (1995) 20 EHRR 557.

[92]   Above, n 90, 1106.

[93]   *Buchanan v McLean* 2000 SLT 928; 2000 SCCR 682; 2001 SCCR 980.

defend himself in person or through legal assistance of his own choosing or, if he has not sufficient means to pay for legal assistance, to be given it free where the interests of justice so require.

The accused argued that the limits to Legal Aid rates set by the Criminal Legal Aid (Fixed Payments) (Scotland) Regulations 1999[94] were too low to provide for adequate legal representation, and that the Lord Advocate was acting contrary to the Convention in proceeding with a prosecution in such circumstances. However the High Court pointed out that the accused's solicitors had undertaken to represent him on the basis of the allowances provided for by the Regulations, hence that it had not been demonstrated that the accused would not be effectively defended by a lawyer.[95] This decision was upheld by the Privy Council.[96]

I. LEGAL REPRESENTATION PRIOR TO THE TRIAL

Reference has already been made to *Paton v Ritchie*.[97] The accused was detained by police and had confessed to a crime during an interview with them, at a time when his solicitor was not present. Section 14 of the Criminal Procedure (Scotland) Act 1995 allows the police to detain a suspect for questioning for up to six hours, and gives the suspect the right to have his or her solicitor informed. It does not give the suspect a right to have access to a solicitor prior to being interviewed by the police. The accused contended that Article 6(3)(c) of the ECHR now required accused persons to be told that they could have their solicitors present during interviews, if they so wished.[98] The court held that Article 6(3) of the ECHR did not create a right for an accused to have access to legal advice before or during police questioning. *Murray v United Kingdom*[99] was distinguished; in that case, the law of Northern Ireland allowed a trial judge to draw adverse inferences from the silence of an unrepresented accused during police questioning. This was not the case in Scots law.[100] The appeal was therefore refused and remitted to the sheriff to proceeds as accords.

In *HM Advocate v Robb*[101] the accused was a 15-year-old boy who had been interviewed by the police without his solicitor being present. The boy's mother and a social worker were present, but the police had refused the accused's request for a solicitor. According to Lord Penrose, whether the lack of a

---

[94] SI 1999 No 491, Reg 4 and Sch 1.
[95] See also *Gayne v Vannett* 1999 SLT 1292.
[96] Above, n 93, 2001 SCCR 475, 2001 SLT 780.
[97] Above, n 51.
[98] This may also be said to be required by the presumption of innocence, contained in Article 6(2)—see below.
[99] *Murray v United Kingdom* (1996) 22 EHRR 29.
[100] See *Robertson v Maxwell* 1951 JC 11.
[101] Above, n 50.

solicitor rendered the circumstances of an accused's confession unfair, hence inadmissible, was a matter for the trial judge:

> The evidence of prior statements by the accused may be excluded by the trial judge as inadmissible, and therefore never come before the jury. If it does, the jury will be directed that the evidence can be taken into account only if they accept that the statements were made, accurately recorded and spoken to in evidence, and that they were fairly obtained.[102]

The court confirmed that the ECHR does not provide a right to a solicitor during police questioning.

In *HM Advocate v Campbell*[103] it was argued that failure to delay an identification parade until the accused's solicitor could attend was a breach of Article 6(3)(b) and (c) of the ECHR. This provides that an accused is to have 'adequate time and facilities to prepare his defence', and the right 'to defend himself in person or through legal assistance'. In respect of the merits of the case, the court stressed that Article 6 contains no specific provision requiring the presence of an accused's solicitor at an identification parade. It further emphasised that in determining whether an accused has had a fair trial, the European Court of Human Rights considers the entirety of the trial proceedings.

As well as the Article 6 of the ECHR requirement of trial within a reasonable time, Article 5(3) also entitles an accused 'to trial within a reasonable time or to release pending trial.' Prior to the case of *Burn, Petitioner*[104] it was the practice of the Crown to oppose bail when the accused first appeared on petition on the ground that further enquiries were being conducted into the case, and that this necessitated the accused being remanded in custody. It was common practice for the nature of these enquiries not to be specified.[105] The accused was then committed for further examination. The Court held in *Burn* that:

> . . . the Crown must provide sufficient general information relating to the particular case to allow the sheriff to consider the merits of their motion that the accused should be committed to prison and detained there for further examination.[106]

In particular, where the Crown oppose bail due to a perceived risk that the accused will interfere with witnesses, or hinder a search of premises, they ought to explain the basis for such concerns.[107]

---

[102] 2000 JC 127, at 131; 1999 SCCR 971, at 977.

[103] Above, n 48.

[104] *Burn, Petitioner* 2000 JC 403; 2000 SCCR 384.

[105] See *Boyle v HM Advocate* 1995 SLT 162, per Lord McCluskey.

[106] Above, n 104, at 406. *Boyle v HM Advocate*, was overruled. See now the Bail, Judicial Appointments etc (Scotland) Act 2000.

[107] A similar decision was reached in the English law case of *R v DPP ex parte Lee* [1999] 2 All ER 237.

J. THE PRESUMPTION OF INNOCENCE

The case of *HM Advocate v McIntosh*[108] concerned confiscation orders made under the Proceeds of Crime (Scotland) Act 1995. The respondent had successfully argued before the High Court that assumptions about the origins of property that the Act permitted the court to make in quantifying the confiscation order offended the presumption of innocence, contained in Article 6(2) of the ECHR.[109] This decision would have had a significant impact on legislative measures taken throughout the United Kingdom concerned with confiscating the assets of crime. Upholding the Crown appeal, the Judicial Committee of the Privy Council found that the confiscation measures under the Proceeds of Crime (Scotland) Act 1995 were a financial penalty for an offence for which the respondent had already been convicted, and compared the assumptions involved in quantifying the confiscation order to the civil process of tracing. According to Lord Bingham, the measures under the Proceeds of Crime (Scotland) Act 1995:

> ... serve the legitimate aim in the public interest of combating [drug trafficking]. They do so in a way in a way that is proportionate. ... In my opinion a fair balance is struck between the legitimate aim and the rights of the accused.[110]

K. SELF-INCRIMINATION

The privilege against self-incrimination flows from the presumption of innocence. The Privy Council again reversed a decision of the High Court of Justiciary in the case of *Brown v Stott*.[111] The Court considered the obligation imposed under road traffic legislation on the keeper of a vehicle to give information to the police as to who was driving the vehicle at a particular time.[112] The Judicial Committee held that this requirement did not infringe Article 6 of the ECHR. The Court emphasised that a person could not be convicted on the basis of an answer to that question alone, and that the measure was part of a proportionate response to the public interest in maintaining road safety. Lord Bingham stated:

> All who own or drive motor cars know that by doing so they subject themselves to a regulatory règime ... imposed ... because the possession and use of cars ... are recognised to have the potential to cause grave injury ... If ... one asks whether [the

[108] *HM Advocate v McIntosh* 2001 SLT 304; 2001 SCCR 191; [2001] 3 WLR 107; [2001] 2 All ER 638.
[109] *McIntosh v HM Advocate* 2000 SLT 1280; 2000 SCCR 1017. A contrary decision was reached by the English Court of Appeal- see *The Times*, 28 Dec 2000.
[110] Above, n 108, 2001 SCCR 191, at 208.
[111] *Brown v Stott* 2001 SC (PC) 43; [2001] 2 WLR 817; [2001] 2 All ER 97, overruling *Brown v Stott* 2000 SLT 379; 2000 SCCR 314.
[112] Road Traffic Act 1988, s 172(2).

relevant section] represents a disproportionate legislative response to the problem of maintaining road safety, whether the balance between the interests of the community at large and the interests of the individual is struck in a manner unduly prejudicial to the individual, whether (in short) the leading of this evidence would infringe a basic human right of the respondent, I would feel bound to give a negative answer.[113]

Similarly, Lord Steyn stated:

The fundamental rights of individuals are of supreme importance but those rights are not unlimited: we live in communities of individuals who also have rights.[114]

This is a pragmatic decision, but is somewhat surprising given the contrary jurisprudence from the European Court of Human Rights.[115]

L. THE HUMAN RIGHTS ACT COMING 'ON STREAM'

The provisions of the Scotland Act 1998 that brought the ECHR to bear on aspects of Scots criminal law and procedure were an intermediate stage to the full application of the Human Rights Act 1998. The Scotland Act 1998 makes the ECHR relevant to the workings of the Scottish Parliament and its Executive. As we have seen, this has resulted in most of the 'devolution issues' being raised thus far being tied to 'acts' of the Lord Advocate in his capacity as head of the Scottish prosecution process. The Human Rights Act 1998 sees the application of the ECHR being widened to 'public authorities', however that phrase is defined by the courts, and its being given 'further effect' through its enhanced status as a relevant source of law.[116]

The manner in which the Scotland Act 1998 and the Human Rights Act 1998 provide for the interpretation of legislation as compatible with the ECHR is subtly different. Section 3 of the Human Rights Act 1998 requires that primary and subordinate legislation be read and given effect in a manner compatible with the ECHR. Should primary legislation be considered to be incompatible with the ECHR, the court may make a declaration of incompatibility to that effect.[117] Subordinate legislation that is incompatible may be set aside. Acts of the Scottish Parliament are subordinate legislation. As we have described, an Act of the Scottish Parliament is only within its competence if it is compatible with the ECHR, otherwise the legislation is ultra vires.

[113] Above, n 111, 2001 SCCR 62, at 81–82.
[114] Above, n 111.
[115] See, for example, the case of *Saunders v United Kingdom* (1997) 23 EHRR 313, which was distinguished by the Privy Council.
[116] Human Rights Act 1998, s 2.
[117] Human Rights Act 1998, s 4.

M. CONCLUSIONS

Scots lawyers revealed themselves to be in varying states of readiness for the ECHR issues that arose under the Scotland Act 1998 and Human Rights Act 1998. A number of legal institutions such as the Crown Office and Procurator Fiscal Service implemented training programmes for their staff, and it is clear from the emerging case law that criminal defence lawyers quickly acclimatised themselves to raising Convention arguments. Since the Scotland Act 1998 has been in force, the manner in which it has made the ECHR applicable to criminal prosecutions through its application to acts of the Lord Advocate has already been wide, and shows no sign of abating. The large number of cases that have considered a ECHR point in relation to Scots criminal law and procedure does not necessarily point to a general malaise or unfairness in Scots law. Rather, the provisions of the Scotland Act 1998, and now the Human Rights Act 1998, provide the basis by which criminal law can be tested against ECHR standards without going through the Appeal system and then to Strasbourg as was required prior to the 1998 legislation. Thus, it is only now that fundamental aspects of law and procedure can be tested against the ECHR by domestic courts. There can be no doubt that decisions such as those in *Starrs v Ruxton* and *Brown v Stott* have proved to be part of the growing pains in Scotland's emerging human rights jurisprudence.[118] However, testing Scots criminal law against the standards of the ECHR can only serve to further the long term fairness and integrity of the proud tradition of criminal law in Scotland.

---

[118] See also *Hoekstra and others v Lord Advocate (No 3)* 2000 SCCR 367. This case saw a previous hearing set aside on the basis that Lord McCluskey could not be seen to be impartial; newspapers had reported Lord McCluskey's criticism of the Convention and its role in domestic law. He had declared that the Convention provided a 'field day for crackpots, a pain in the neck for judges and legislators and a goldmine for lawyers.'

16

Writing Wrongs: Third-party Intervention Post-incorporation

ANDREA LOUX*

INTRODUCTION

COUNTRIES THAT ENJOY a rights culture have a legal infrastructure that supports and promotes human rights litigation in the courts. An essential element of that infrastructure is pressure groups and their 'cause lawyers'. 'Cause lawyers' are lawyers who engage in litigation in order to alter 'some aspect of the social, economic and political status quo'.[1] Through both direct representation and intervention in ongoing cases, cause lawyers ensure that the voice of their constituency is heard when courts are taking significant human rights decisions. Cause lawyers participate in the judicial process to testify to changing social conditions and to articulate, and persuade others, of their vision of justice. In turn, their participation in human rights litigation gives legitimacy to otherwise unaccountable courts when they are taking decisions of significant political, social and moral value.

This paper argues that the participation of pressure groups and their lawyers in human rights litigation as interveners is an essential element of 'bringing rights home' to Scotland. It begins with an examination of pressure group participation in direct action cases and the problems that can arise in the relationship between complainer and pressure group. It then discusses third-party intervention in Scotland and the intervention of JUSTICE in *Brown v Stott*.[2] After highlighting the need for third-party intervention in qualified rights cases, the chapter concludes with an exploration of pressure group third-party intervention and the potential impact of interventions on the UK's emerging rights culture.

---

* Ms Loux is a lecturer in law at the University of Edinburgh. This chapter is a work in progress and comments are welcome. In memory of Letitia Campbell.
   [1] A Sarat, *Cause Lawyering: Political Commitments and Professional Responsibilities* (Oxford University Press, Oxford 1998) at 4.
   [2] 2001 SLT 59.

CAUSE LAWYERING IN 'DIRECT ACTION' CASES

Cause lawyers who wish to participate in human rights litigation must do so either as interveners or through direct representation of clients who are victims or potential victims of human rights violations. Under the terms of the Act only an actual victim or potential victim has *locus standi* or title and interest to challenge a human rights violation.[3] The adoption of the 'victim' test from the European Convention on Human Rights and Fundamental Freedoms (the 'ECHR') was the focus of much dissent during the passage of the Act.[4] In England groups such as Greenpeace and the World Development Movement had been granted standing to bring judicial review actions in their own name.[5] The Human Rights Act, therefore, was a regressive step in the development of standing rights of NGOs. In Scotland, where title and interest is more limited,[6] the Human Rights Act provisions were less controversial.

So long as a 'willing victim' can be located, pressure groups can participate in human rights litigation by backing direct action cases. So-called 'straw' pursuers lend their circumstance and most importantly their name to pressure groups so that test cases can be litigated. Whilst in form the control over the litigation belongs to the pursuer, in reality it lies with the pressure group, or perhaps more accurately, the pressure group's lawyers.

Direct action cases exact a toll, however, on both the pursuer and on the pressure group. Test cases are brought as part of a pressure group's overall political strategy. Pressure groups in the UK conduct test-case litigation as much to gain publicity and to lobby Government and back-benchers for legislative change, as to achieve genuine progressive legal precedent.[7] Given the continued emphasis on parliamentary democracy in the Human Rights Act, it is uncertain whether litigation will usurp legislation as the primary route to achieving progressive change. Thus a group's litigation strategy must fit within its general political strategy.

Effective use of the media is an essential part of any pressure group's tactics. Indeed complainers are selected by pressure groups not only with an eye for their legal status and factual circumstances, but also for their articulateness, appearance, and other characteristics that make a complainer media friendly.[8]

---

[3] Human Rights Act 1998, s 7(1).

[4] See J Manioh and D Nicol, 'The Human Rights Act, Representative Standing and the Victim Culture', [1998] 6 *EHRR* 730.

[5] *R v Inspectorate of Pollution, ex p Greenpeace Ltd (No 2)* [1994] All ER 329 *R v Foreign Secretary, ex p World Development Movement* [1995] 1 All ER 611.

[6] Lord Hope of Craighead, 'Mike Tyson Comes to Glasgow—A Question of Standing' [2001] *PL* 294–307.

[7] Interview with Angela Mason, Executive Director Stonewall, 9 October 1998.

[8] In order to find the complainers for the case *Sutherland v UK*, for example, Stonewall advertised for underage men who were willing to pursue a case and then selected the best candidates from those who applied. *Ibid.* Media considerations are also taken into account when Stonewall and

The 'sword of truth' wielded by the country's media, however, is always double-edged for both the pressure group and the complainer. Complainers know that they must be prepared for significant invasions of their personal privacy; complainers and their families are regularly door-stepped by tabloids and journalists even go through the litigants' bins, searching for 'dirt' of the head-line grabbing variety.[9] Where a complainer does come forward, the individual and family may need significant support from the pressure group and the community it serves.[10]

The irony of using the media to advance a political strategy based on a test case, is that the celebrity a pressure group so carefully nurtures can undermine its power to control the litigation. Once a complainer becomes a celebrity in his or her own right, the power relationship between a pressure group and the complainer reverses. Where once a sole individual sought the expert advice and support of the pressure group, the celebrity complainer quickly develops his or her own constituency that can support the complainer in any dispute that may arise between the complainer and the pressure group over the conduct of the legal case or the political campaign.[11] Such a loss of control could be fatal to a pressure group's political strategy.

The emotional costs to the pursuer and the supporting pressure group, coupled with the loss of control that litigation necessarily involves, makes direct action cases less appealing to pressure groups. Even without counting the significant financial outlay that such cases involve (even when legally aided), it is understandable why pressure groups desired a Human Rights Act that would give them sufficient title and interest to sue as representative of a group rather than the power behind an individual complainer.

Despite repeated parliamentary debate on the standing provisions, the 'victim' test was adopted. The Lord Chancellor, however, did not anticipate foreclosing the participation of pressure groups in human rights litigation. In his view, pressure groups could be heard as interveners. Responding to amendments of the 'victim' test for *locus standi* he stated that the victim test:

> in no way precludes a third party from making submissions about the implication of convention rights in written briefs if a written brief is invited or accepted by the court, as I believe will happen. As regards oral interventions by a third party, I dare say that the courts will be equally hospitable to oral interventions provided that they are brief.[12]

The Lord Chancellor was referring to the increasingly common participation of third-party interveners in the English courts and at the House of Lords. Lord

---

RankOutsiders decide to back a pre-existing case. *Ibid*; Interview with Duncan Lustig-Prean, of RankOutsiders, 2 September 1998.

[9] Interview with Duncan Lustig-Prean.
[10] Interview with Angela Mason.
[11] *Ibid*.
[12] HL Deb Vol 583, col 834 (24 November 1997).

Mackay of Drumadoon intervened to remind the Lord Chancellor of the absence of such a procedure in the Scottish courts:

> As a Scots lawyer I intervene with a certain diffidence in this private conversation between my English colleagues. If it be the case, as I believe it is, that the Scottish courts would not entertain third party interveners in civil proceedings in the same way as the English courts might do, is there not a risk that by leaving the matter to the courts to work out the practice, there may develop a different practice in Scotland from that in England when dealing with the same United Kingdom Bill? If it is the objective of the Bill to bring rights home, is it not correct that they should be brought home in one jurisdiction as in another? It may be that that is a matter on which the noble and learned Lord the Lord Chancellor wishes to reflect at further length. I do not understand that the Scottish courts would welcome either written or oral submissions from third party interveners as their English brethren do.[13]

THIRD-PARTY INTERVENTIONS IN SCOTLAND

Third-party interveners present information or argument to the Court that is necessary or helpful to the Court in reaching its decision that will not, or cannot, without a great deal of difficulty, be presented by the parties to the litigation. Some interveners will provide expert factual data that is not generally or easily available to the litigants.[14] *Amicus curiae* interveners provide legal argument based upon their knowledge of international law or comparative jurisdictions.[15] Finally there are 'perspective' interveners—persons other than parties who will be affected by a decision and from whom the court may, in the interests of justice, wish to hear.[16] The third-party intervener will often, though not inevitably, be allied with one party or another as to the result in a case. Their role in the litigation, however, is to contribute evidence and argument that is different from that presented by the parties or other interveners in the litigation.

Third party intervention was an unknown practice in the Scottish courts and the potential for its adoption caused a significant amount of disquiet in the legal community once the Lord President announced that rules permitting third-party intervention would be issued.[17] On Human Rights Day (2 October 2000), an Act

---

[13]   HL Deb Vol 583, col 834 (24 November 1997).

[14]   R Charteris, 'Intervention—in the Public Interest?, 2000 *SLT* (News) 87.

[15]   See, eg, intervention of JUSTICE in *R v Secretary of State for the Home Department, ex parte V & T, The Times* (13 June 1997) (HL).

[16]   See, eg, intervention of Liberty, Justice for Women and Southall Black Sisters in *R v Smith*. For a further exploration of *amicus* and perspective interventions see A Loux, 'Hearing a "Different Voice": Third-Party Intervention in Criminal Appeals', in M Freeman (ed), *Current Legal Problems 2000* (Oxford University Press, Oxford, 2000).

[17]   For a summary of such concerns, see Charteris, above, n 14, 89–90. Ms. Charteris was the assistant to the Lord President during the period when the rules on public interest intervention were being drafted.

of Sederunt came into force that permits third parties to intervene on issues of the public interest in judicial review proceedings.[18] Those wishing to intervene in judicial review proceedings are to file a 'Minute of Intervention' that sets out their name and description, the issue on which they wish to intervene and the reasons why the potential intervener believes that the issue is one of public interest. The court will grant leave to intervene where it is persuaded that the issue raises a matter of public interest, that the propositions of the intervener will be relevant to the proceedings and where the intervention 'will not unduly delay or otherwise prejudice the rights of the parties'. The rules make provision for the award of expenses to the parties where the intervention causes additional expense and is in the interest of justice. Once leave is granted, other than in exceptional circumstances, interventions are to be submitted to the court in writing and be no longer that 5,000 words, including appendices.

The fear that the Scottish courts would be flooded with NGO's seeking to lobby judges was unfounded. In fact, no public interest intervention has to date occurred at the Court of Session . Despite the apparent disinterest in Scotland in intervening in human rights litigation, Scots law has seen its first intervention. The Act of Sederunt proved to be too little, too late. The public interest intervener rules were too little because third-party intervention is limited to judicial review actions in the Court of Session.[19] They were too late because the provisions of the Human Rights Act came into effect in Scotland via the provisions of the Scotland Act in July, 1999. The first third-party intervention in Scotland was filed by an English NGO at the Privy Council in an appeal from the decision of the High Court of Justiciary in *Brown v Stott* issued 4 February, 2000.

Brown v Stott tested the compatibility of the terms of the Road Traffic Act 1998 (RTA) with Article 6 of the ECHR. Margaret Anderson Brown was charged with theft of a bottle of gin after the police were called to the Asda Superstore in Dunfermline at 3:00 am on 3 June 1999. Smelling alcohol on Brown's breath and clothes, the officers enquired how she had travelled to the store. She said that she had arrived by car and pointed out her Ford Fiesta in the superstore car park to the police when she was being taken to the station. At the station the keys to her car were found in Brown's handbag, and pursuant to the officer's powers under section 172 (2) (a) of the RTA she was required to state that she had been driving the car at 2:30 am when she travelled to the superstore. Section 172 (2) states that where the driver of a car is alleged to be guilty of an offence the keeper of the car must provide information as to the identity of the driver when asked to so by the police.

At her trial for theft and driving after consuming an excess of alcohol, Brown's agent lodged a minute indicating an intention to raise a devolution issue. Under the terms of the Scotland Act section 57 (2), the Lord Advocate as

---

[18] SSI 2000, No. 317, 'Act of Sederunt (Rules of the Court of Session Amendment No 5)(Public Interest Intervention in Judicial Review) 2000.

[19] *Lord Advocate's Reference No 1 of 2001* 2002 SLT 466, 484 (per Lord McCluskey). For a discussion of the need for third-party intervention in the criminal courts, see Loux, above, n 16.

a member of the Scottish Executive has no power to act in a way incompatible with the ECHR unless he or she is acting to give effect to a provision of primary legislation 'that cannot be read or given effect in a way which is compatible with Convention rights'.[20] It was argued that the procurator fiscal could not use Brown's compelled statement that she was driving the car because to do so violated her right to a fair trial under Article 6(1) of the Convention. The sheriff refused to hold that the minute raised a devolution issue and Brown appealed to the Court of Session.

The Court of Session held that the use of the compelled statement did indeed violate Brown's Article 6 right to a fair trial. The court also held that the RTA was silent as to the use of the information gathered pursuant to its terms. This meant that the Act could be 'read down' so as to give effect to its terms without violating the Convention. It would still be a offence for the keeper of a car not to identify the driver of the vehicle, but the procurator fiscal could not use the reply 'to incriminate the keeper at any subsequent trial'.[21] To do so would violate the keeper's Article 6 rights and therefore be beyond the powers of the Lord Advocate under the Scotland Act.

On appeal at the Privy Council, the British human rights organisation JUSTICE intervened as an *amicus curiae* intervener to make representations regarding the nature of Article 6 of the ECHR and the privilege against self-incrimination. In its intervention JUSTICE argued that Article 6 rights are not absolute, but rather that the general public interest is relevant to its interpretation. In their view,

> there is a clear and obvious interest in the prosecution of RTA offences. This public interest can justify a more restrictive interpretation of the right against self-incrimination in the context of RTA prosecutions than would be permitted in relation to other offences, so long as any such interpretation leaves intact the twin pillars of the rights against self-incrimination: protection from improper compulsion and unfair use of compulsorily obtained evidence.[22]

JUSTICE's membership is composed of lawyers and the organisation is the British Section of the International Commission of Jurists. Many were surprised that JUSTICE chose to intervene on the side of the government in a human rights case arising out of a criminal prosecution. The Executive chose to intervene because of the group's interest in Article 6 and the central importance of what was in their view the correct interpretation of that article. JUSTICE was also concerned that the decision in *Brown*, if permitted to stand, might bring the Human Rights Act into disrepute.[23] The decision, which interpreted an Act of Parliament that applied equally in England, had sent shockwaves through the

---

[20] Scotland Act 1998, s 57 (2)–(3).
[21] *Brown v Stott*, 2000 SLT 396.
[22] Third Party Intervention on Behalf of JUSTICE, at 9–10.
[23] Interview with Roisin Pillay, 26 February 2001.

English legal establishment. It highlighted the potential dramatic impact of the Human Rights Act once it came into force in England.

The Privy Council overturned the decision of the Court of Session in *Brown* on the ground that the constituent rights of Article 6, including the right against self-incrimination, are not absolute. Lord Bingham of Cornhill expressly acknowledged the help of JUSTICE's written intervention.[24] Lord Hope of Craighead did not expressly acknowledge the help of the interveners, but did rely upon Keir Starmer's text, *European Human Rights Law*.[25] Mr Starmer was an author of the intervention.

In Scotland, some are angry that an English NGO intervened in a Scottish case to overturn a decision of the Court of Session and frustrated that no intervener appeared at the Privy Council to support the Respondent. As Lord Hope of Craighead said, 'it is not the function of the court to invite interested parties to intervene. It is up to interested parties to take the initiative.' It has been suggested that Liberty, a legal NGO with a direct interest in Article 6 and direct Scottish links was the obvious group to take that initiative.[26] It is of course uncertain, given the controversy surrounding the decision in *Brown*, and indeed the scope of Article 6, whether the presence of an intervener at the High Court of Justiciary or Liberty at the Privy Council would have influenced the decision of either court. The decision in *Brown* nevertheless highlights the potential influence of *amicus curiae* interventions.

PERSPECTIVE INTERVENTION AND QUALIFIED RIGHTS CASES

It is not merely as an *amicus*, however, that third parties have a role in human rights litigation. Under the provisions of the Human Rights Act third parties have a significant role to play in assisting judges as 'perspective interveners'. Unlike an *amicus* intervener, who represents the public interest more generally, a perspective intervener represents the interests of her constituency. Perspective intervention is particularly useful to both the court and the constituency of cause lawyers when the court is required to apply the doctrine of proportionality. Articles 8–11 of the ECHR contain qualified rights, the interference with which by a public authority can be justified with reference to a variety of societal interests. Perspective interveners can help the court assess the relative weight of the individual and societal interests at stake.[27]

Qualified rights cases involve some of the most controversial aspects of human rights litigation. Such cases also have the greatest potential for development by

---

[24] *Brown v Stott*, 2001 SLT 59 at 63.

[25] *Ibid*, at 79.

[26] Lord Hope of Craighead, 'Law Reform: Strategies to Legislation' (Address delivered 16 March 2001).

[27] Public Law Project, *Third Party Interventions in Judicial Review* (Public Law Project, London, 2001), at 2.

the domestic judiciary because they can fall within the 'margin of appreciation' given to the UK by the European Court of Human Rights. The margin of appreciation is a doctrine by which the European Court of Human Rights leaves the resolution of particular legal questions to the domestic authorities of a state because there is no uniform 'European' position on the issue or the issue is of a type most appropriately decided on a domestic basis. In recent years the UK's position on such questions as the rights of transsexuals and the regulation of obscene and blasphemous speech has been held to fall within the 'margin of appreciation'.[28] If the courts, and in particular the superior courts, independently judge the actions of public authorities against the guarantees of the Convention in areas where the European Court of Human Rights has refused to intervene, there is significant potential for judges to define (some would say impose) distinct national human rights values in their judgements.

Take for example the facts of *Wingrove v UK*.[29] In *Wingrove*, the European Court of Human Rights held that the refusal of a BBFC certificate for the film 'Visions of Ecstasy' on the grounds that it was blasphemous was a permissible restriction on speech under Article 10(2) because it is 'necessary in a democratic society . . . for the protection of the . . . rights of others'. The Court granted the UK a significant margin of appreciation:

> because there is no common European position on the prohibition of blasphemous speech and because a wider margin of appreciation is generally available to the Contracting States when regulating freedom of expression in relation to matters liable to offend intimate personal convictions within the sphere of morals or, especially, religion. Moreover, as in the field of morals, and perhaps to an even greater degree, there is no uniform European conception of the requirements of 'the protection of the rights of others' in relation to attacks on their religious convictions. What is likely to cause substantial offence to persons of a particular religious persuasion will vary significantly from time to time and from place to place, especially in an era characterised by an ever growing array of faiths and denominations. By reason of their direct and continuous contact with the vital forces of their countries, State authorities are in principle in a better position than the international judge to give an opinion on the exact content of these requirements with regard to the rights of others as well as on the 'necessity' of a 'restriction' intended to protect from such material those whose deepest feelings and convictions would be seriously offended.[30]

Under the Human Rights Act, a producer in the position of Mr. Wingrove could challenge the decision of the BBFC on the grounds that their decision violates Article 10 of the ECHR and in the current context of the United Kingdom is not 'necessary to protect others'. If such a case were to arise, the court would be invited to abolish the common law offences of blasphemy and blasphemous libel since the basis of the BBFC's decision in *Wingrove* was its mandate 'to

---

[28] *Sheffield and Horsham v UK* (1999) 27 EHRR 163; *Handyside v UK* (1976) EHRR 737; *Wingrove v UK* (1997) 24 EHRR 1.
[29] (1997) 24 EHRR 1.
[30] *Ibid*, at 30–31.

avoid issuing [a] classification certificate . . . in respect of [a] . . . work infringing the criminal law'.[31]

Whether a court would take up the opportunity to abolish the common law offence of blasphemy in light of Convention guarantees and current societal norms remains to be seen. Certainly such a step would be a legitimate exercise of the court's authority. Blasphemy is a common law offence and the Act requires courts as public authorities to ensure that the common law is consistent with Convention guarantees. The European Court of Human Rights grants a large margin of appreciation in this area and thus leaves the question of the appropriateness of criminalising blasphemy to the 'domestic authorities'. If such a case as that in *Wingrove* were to arise, the court would be required to re-evaluate and perhaps reorient the common law of blasphemy in light of the guarantees of Article 10.

The court in such a case would have to evaluate the offence of blasphemy and its consistency with the Convention's guarantees in light of current societal conditions because the Convention is a 'living document'.[32] Considerations might include circumstances such as the increased level of tolerance for 'unpopular' speech of all kinds in the UK,[33] the place of Christianity in current UK society, and the appropriateness of a common law criminal offence that solely punishes offences against Christianity.[34] The case would raise questions regarding the ability or desire of the parties to present the panoply of factual data and legal argument that the court would wish to have when taking such a significant decision of public policy.

One solution to this dilemma would be for the court to request that an *amicus curiae* be appointed to inform the court of data and argument absent from the parties' submissions. There are, however, significant difficulties with relying on an appointed *amicus* in human rights litigation. In Scotland, the appointment of an *amicus* is at the discretion of the Lord Advocate's department; the court cannot appoint an *amicus* 'at its own hand'.[35] Even where an *amicus* has been appointed, an *amicus* is unlikely to have as ready access to data and legal materials argument as pressure groups or other interested experts in the field, thus making her investigations a costly exercise.[36] Finally, whilst a successful

---

[31] *Ibid*, at 17.

[32] *Tyrer v UK* (1978) 2 EHRR 1.

[33] This is significant in light of the fact that the most recent prosecution for blasphemy, that of Gay News in 1979, was a private prosecution and that the blasphemy law had not been used before that case since 1922. In Scotland, it is suggested that blasphemy would not be prosecuted by the Crown as such and could not be the subject of a private prosecution, although blasphemous material could be prosecuted as obscenity or breach of the peace. G Maher, 'Blasphemy in Scots Law', 1977 *SLT* (News) 257 at 260.

[34] The common law of blasphemy only applies to Christianity. *R v Chief Metropolitan Stipendiary Magistrate, ex parte Choudhury* [1991] 1 All ER 306 at 318.

[35] *T, Petitioner*, 1997 SLT 724.

[36] Interview with Philip Havers, QC, 9 June 1999. Mr Havers is a member of JUSTICE's working party on interventions and acted for the Royal College of Nursing in *R v North and East Devon Health Authority, ex parte Coughlan* [2001] QB 213. He has also acted as an appointed *amicus curiae*.

amicus within the limits of time and money can ensure that the court makes an informed decision, an independent *amicus* does little to bolster the legitimacy of the court when it is forced to step into the policy-making arena.

In addition to the evidence and argument provided by the parties, the court in a blasphemy case could allow written submissions from representatives of those groups who believe themselves to be affected by the law of blasphemy.[37] Such participation is sensible in light of the Article 10(2) exception relied upon by the BBFC—the control of freedom of expression 'for the protection of others'. If a law is to be either upheld or abolished which purports to protect members of society, a legitimate decision can only be made by a court that has heard from those 'others', as well as from those whose fundamental freedoms are curtailed in the name of such 'protection' or who are not protected from such harm.

The participation of such interveners would not only provide the court with the information and argument necessary to make an informed decision, it would grant legitimacy to the public policy decision of an otherwise unaccountable court. Courts that are empowered to decide cases involving fundamental human rights exercise significant powers to define the nature not only of those legal rights, but of society itself. The determination of whether the power of the state can be used to protect the sensibilities of Christians, thereby elevating the Christian religion above all others, for example, is one of vital importance in the context of multi-cultural Britain. When a court takes such a decision it is essential that the judgement be viewed not only as informed but also as constitutionally legitimate.

It is often said that a system of human rights is antithetical to majoritarian democracy (or at least operates as a check on such a majority's tendency to tyranny). The protection of minorities and minority interests, however, cannot be achieved by insulated autocrats operating within a closed system of legal discourse. The legitimacy of the legal process in the context of constitutional human rights litigation depends on an ongoing societal 'dialogue'. For a dialogue to take place, courts must agree not only to hear, but to listen, to those voices shut out of the majoritarian political process. The courts' doors must be 'opened . . . [so that] the courtroom can properly be seen as part of the democratic process', even as it acts to protect fundamental rights from the vicissitudes of that process.[38]

CAUSE LAWYERING AND THIRD-PARTY INTERVENTION

Third-party intervention in Scotland as a procedural tool has a number of advantages for cause lawyers over direct action cases. Interventions are limited

---

[37] The European Court of Human Rights heard from three interveners in *Wingrove*: Rights International, Interights and Article 19. The Court relied on the interveners' submissions for evidence that blasphemy laws are still in force throughout Europe. See (1997) 24 EHRR 1 at 30.

[38] D Feldman, 'Public Interest Litigation and Constitutional Theory in Comparative Perspective', (1992) 55 *MLR* 44, at 56.

to presenting evidence and argument on public interest issues as set out in the minute of intervention. Interveners are independent of the parties and are not responsible for presenting the whole of any one party's case. As a third-party intervener a pressure group has no control over the strategy of the parties, save where the intervener and a party choose to act in concert; on the other hand they are not bound by a party's strategy either. For example in the case *R v Kahn*[39] the defendant was convicted of a Class A drug offence based upon evidence gathered by a bugging device placed by the police. On appeal, the pressure group Liberty intervened to bring to the attention of the Court the relevant case-law of the European Court of Human Rights. Ultimately they argued that whilst they agreed with the defendant on the question of Article 8 right to privacy, the Article 6 case-law did not require the evidence against the defendant to be excluded. As an intervener, a pressure group can be heard by the court on a matter of law, principle or politics without necessarily having regard to the legal position of the complainer.

As discussed above, in some instances pressure groups must struggle for control of cases that they have backed in the first instance. Given the choice, pressure groups in particular cases might wish to intervene rather than involve themselves with the care, attention, and division of responsibility for decision-making with a particular complainer. Intervention would also permit pressure groups to make representations to the court when an action has been filed by a 'rogue complainer', a litigant who files a case in ignorance of, or in contradiction to, a group's established litigation strategy.[40]

Intervention, so long as the Court of Session does not 'in the interests of justice' award expenses to the parties, is also far less costly for a pressure group than direct action cases. Interventions in Scotland are to be submitted in writing. Written submissions are preferred both by interveners and the judiciary because they are inexpensive to produce and less time consuming for the court to 'hear'. Written submissions can be easily and cheaply prepared either by in- house staff of a pressure group or *pro bono* by interested practising lawyers or academics.

Legal academics with their in-depth knowledge of legal issues, the law of other jurisdictions, and theoretical insights can make significant contributions to human rights litigation through written interventions. In the US and Canada academics have been a mainstay of rights litigation. In Scotland, the rules of the Faculty of Advocates make limited and peripatetic appearances before Court of Session almost impossible, save for distinguished members who do so by special permission. Intervention by written brief allows academics to represent pressure group clients before the courts.

The relative cost of intervention enables pressure groups to participate more widely in litigation than is possible through direct action. Direct action test

---

[39] [1994] 4 All ER 426.
[40] See W Rubenstein, 'Divided We Litigate: Addressing Disputes Among Group Members and Lawyers in Civil Rights Campaigns' (1997) 106 *Yale LJ* 1623.

cases will no doubt continue to form a part of pressure group strategy, but where that is not possible or desirable, groups will not be foreclosed from the litigation process. Scotland, unlike its southerly neighbour, has not had a strong tradition of cause lawyering. The Human Rights Act coupled with new rules permitting interventions presents an opportunity to create one.

Cause lawyering through interventions would aid in the development of a national rights culture. In the US, the *amicus* or intervener Supreme Court Briefs are widely available in law school libraries and now are regularly posted on the Internet. The creation of a rights culture in Scotland is as much about education as pressure group organisation because of the relative novelty of the recognition of human rights in Scots law. Intervener briefs would be quickly circulated and their arguments refined if the practice of intervention were to become commonplace.

If academics choose to write interventions, the worlds of legal scholarship and legal practice would be brought closer together. Politically committed academic lawyers could push forward the human rights agenda both within the academy and in the courts. In the US, a significant amount of pro bono activity surrounds rights litigation by all sorts of lawyers. This is because law school has whetted the appetite of even merger and acquisitions lawyers for constitutional litigation. Interventions would encourage a rights culture to flourish in the training ground of Scotland's lawyers and judges.

The important role that interveners play in creating and sustaining a rights culture would ensure that the impact of the introduction of the practice of written interventions would not be limited to the narrow realm of judicial decision-making. As for its effect on the judicial process, written interventions could foster the democratic dialogue demanded by the constitutional change wrought by the Human Rights Act. The practice of written interventions ensures a democracy of ideas in a context where some litigants, both individuals and pressure groups, are better funded than others. Litigation is an expensive business. The best resourced arguments are not always the best. The receipt of written submissions would mean that a broader canvass of opinion is possible than that available in oral argument. Intervener memorials could ensure that 'minority' voices within Scotland and the United Kingdom are heard when the crucial initial decisions on novel human rights questions are being decided.[41]

The constitutional project of the Labour party has democratised not only the process of legislation through the creation of a Scottish Parliament, but potentially the process of adjudication via the incorporation of the ECHR. Court procedure in the United Kingdom has been based on the maxim that 'judges are not legislators'. Under the Human Rights Act that is no longer the case despite the

[41] For a critical view of pressure group participation in litigation, *see* C Harlow, 'Public Law and Popular Justice', (2002) *MLR* 1–18. Professor Harlow acknowledges that the courts have taken on new constitutional functions that may demand new procedures and has herself advocated wider rights of participation where there is a 'democratic deficit' coupled with judicial constitution-making. *Ibid*. 2, 16–17.

fact that the ultimate sovereignty of Parliament has been maintained. Courtrooms cannot and should not become parliaments; one purpose of the Convention is to protect human rights from the vicissitudes of parliamentary majoritarian democracy. The courts, nevertheless, must respond to the challenges to the legitimacy of judicial decision-making raised by their new role under the Human Rights Act. Interventions in human rights cases would reinforce the traditional function of the court as an informed adjudicator and legitimate its new role as human rights legislator. In the process, interveners could contribute to the broader political project of 'bringing rights home'.

Afterword to Chapter 12

Dianne Pretty died, unassisted, on 11 May 2002. Only 13 days previously she had lost another battle before the European Court of Human Rights to uphold her claim to control the time and manner of her own death. In a display of unprecedented judicial alacrity, Mrs Pretty's case was heard—and dismissed—by the House of Lords[1] and then the European Court[2] in a matter of months. To many, this expeditious treatment of her cause may be the only show of respect that her choice to die received.

It is apposite to comment briefly on the ECtHR decision, since this embodies the clearest indication of how human rights arguments may fair in the realm of the so-called 'right to die'. In sum, there is no such right. Of all the Articles invoked in the Pretty case those with most chance of success were Articles 2 and 8, and for this reason we shall concentrate on how the Court sought to dismiss them.

Article 2 cannot be read, we are told, to include a 'right to die' for its underlying ethos is to protect life, and that alone is the source of any positive obligation on the state. We are further informed that '[Article 2] is unconcerned with issues to do with quality of living or what a person chooses to do with his or her life'.[3] It therefore does not admit any right to self-determination. Such a feature of our human rights, if it is to be found at all, is located in the domain of Article 8(1)—and this is entirely in keeping with the expansionist nature of this right as has been discussed in this chapter. The European Court found, for example, that 'the notion of personal autonomy is an important principle underlying the interpretation of [Article 8's] guarantees'.[4] Moreover, the Court was willing to accept that state imposed fetters on a choice to die constituted an interference with the right to respect for private life. To this extent, the ECtHR was more sympathetic than the House of Lords had been towards the idea that human rights discourse should be a holistic enterprise. However, and as was predicted, significant developments in human rights jurisprudence are fragile beasts when they seek recognition in areas as controversial as euthanasia. In the final analysis, the ECtHR invoked the margin of appreciation and had little trouble accepting the United Kingdom's arguments that Article 8(2) applied to Mrs Pretty's case since the prohibition on assisted suicide could be justified as 'necessary in a democratic society'. Why was it *necessary*? Because the state is duty bound to protect the general class of vulnerable citizens who might suffer were the law

---

[1] *R (on the application of Pretty) v DPP* [2001] UKHL 61.
[2] *Pretty v United Kingdom*, Application 2346/02, 29 April 2002.
[3] *Ibid*, para 39. Compare *LCB v United Kingdom* (1999) 27 EHRR 212 discussed in the body of this chapter.
[4] *Ibid*, para 61.

otherwise, and it was no answer to say that Dianne Pretty was not herself vulnerable because her case would doubtless set a precedent that would be open to a clear risk of abuse.

This decision, and that of the House of Lords before it, are as unsurprising as they are uninspiring. There is little of scholarly interest to say about them because they simply confirm what human rights are not in the hands of a timid judiciary in a deeply-divided pluralistic society. This having been said, the reader should not take from this that the author would necessarily have it otherwise. It is simply to emphasise that in such an area human rights provide very blunt tools to make much of an impact. This chapter was originally written in 1998 when crystal ball gazing was at its peak and wide sweeping reforms in all areas, including medical law, were anticipated. The tone then was one of scepticism, and this seems entirely to have been borne out by practice. The Big Questions in medical law concerning life and death will not be addressed through the interpretation of the Human Rights Act or the European Convention on Human Rights. Were this chapter to be written anew today it would look very different, and its focus would be at the margins of medical law—such as the realm of judicial review—where most changes are now taking place. This, of course, is not to suggest that this is a marginal area of the discipline, but the point remains that we are simply tinkering at the edges.

Appendix to Chapter 9

CANADIAN CHARTER OF RIGHTS AND FREEDOMS

Section 1—GUARANTEE OF RIGHTS AND FREEDOMS

The Canadian Charter of Rights and Freedoms guarantees the rights and freedoms set out in it subject only to such reasonable limits prescribed by law as can be demonstrably justified in a free and democratic society.

Section 2—FUNDAMENTAL FREEDOMS

Everyone has the following fundamental freedoms:

a) freedom of conscience and religion;
b) freedom of thought, belief, opinion and expression, including freedom of the press and other media of communication;
c) freedom of peaceful assembly; and
d) freedom of association.

Section 6—MOBILITY RIGHTS

(2) Every citizen of Canada and every person who has the status of a permanent resident of Canada has the right

a) to move to and take up residence in any province; and
b) to pursue the gaining of a livelihood in any province.

(3) The rights specified in subsection (2) are subject to

a) any laws or practices of general application in force in a province other than those that discriminate among persons primarily on the basis of province of present or previous residence.

Section 7—LEGAL RIGHTS

Everyone has the right to life, liberty and security of the person and the right not to be deprived thereof except in accordance with the principles of fundamental justice.

Section 15—EQUALITY RIGHTS

(1) Every individual is equal before and under the law and has the right to the equal protection and equal benefit of the law without discrimination and, in particular, without discrimination based on race, national or ethnic origin, colour, religion, sex, age or mental or physical disability.

(2) Subsection (1) does not preclude any law, program or activity that has as its object the amelioration of conditions of disadvantaged individuals or groups including those that are disadvantaged because of race, national or ethnic origin, colour, religion, sex, age or mental or physical disability.

Section 24—ENFORCEMENT RIGHTS

(1) Anyone whose rights or freedoms, as guaranteed by this Charter, have been infringed or denied may apply to a court of competent jurisdiction to obtain such remedy as the court considers appropriate and just in the circumstances.

Section 28—RIGHTS GUARANTEED EQUALLY TO BOTH SEXES

Notwithstanding anything in this Charter, the rights and freedoms referred to in it are guaranteed equally to male and female persons.

Section 32—APPLICATION OF CHARTER

(1) This Charter applies

  (a) to the Parliament and government of Canada in respect of all matters within the authority of Parliament including all matters relating to the Yukon Territory and Northwest Territories; and

  (b) to the legislature and government of each province in respect of all matters within the authority of the legislature of each province.

(2) Notwithstanding subsection (1), section 15 shall not have effect until three years after this section comes into force.

Index